FAIRY TAIL

16

Hiro Mashima

Translated and adapted by William Flanagan
Lettered by AndWorld Design

KC
KODANSHA COMICS

Fairy Tail volume 16 is a work of fiction. Names, characters, places, and incidents are the products of the author's imagination or are used fictitiously. Any resemblance to actual events, locales, or persons, living or dead, is entirely coincidental.

A Kodansha Comics Trade Paperback Original

Published in the United States by Kodansha Comics, an imprint of Kodansha USA Publishing, LLC, New York.

Publication rights for this English edition arranged through Kodansha Ltd., Tokyo.

First published in Japan in 2009 by Kodansha Ltd., Tokyo.

ISBN 978-1-935-42935-7

Printed in the United States of America.

www.kodanshacomics.com

9 8 7 6 5 4 3 2 1

Translator/Adapter: William Flanagan
Lettering: AndWorld Design

Contents

Honorifics Explained

Throughout the Kodansha Comics books, you will find Japanese honorifics left intact in the translations. For those not familiar with how the Japanese use honorifics and, more important, how they differ from American honorifics, we present this brief ov w.

Politeness has always been a critical facet of Japanese culture. Ever since the feudal era, when Japan was a highly stratified society, use of honorifics—which can be defined as polite speech that indicates relationship or status—has played an essential role in the Japanese language. When addressing someone in Japanese, an honorific usually takes the form of a suffix attached to one's name (example: "Asuna-san"), is used as a title at the end of one's name, or appears in place of the name itself (example: "Negi-sensei," or simply "Sensei!").

Honorifics can be expressions of respect or endearment. In the context of manga and anime, honorifics give insight into the nature of the relationship between characters. Many English translations leave out these important honorifics and therefore distort the feel of the original Japanese. Because Japanese honorifics contain nuances that English honorifics lack, it is our policy at Kodansha Comics not to translate them. Here, instead, is a guide to some of the honorifics you may encounter in Kodansha Comics books.

-**san**: This is the most common honorific and is equivalent to Mr., Miss, Ms., or Mrs. It is the all-purpose honorific and can be used in any situation where politeness is required.

-**sama**: This is one level higher than "-san" and is used to confer great respect.

-**dono**: This comes from the word "tono," which means "lord." It is an even higher level than "-sama" and confers utmost respect.

-kun: This suffix is used at the end of boys' names to express familiarity or endearment. It is also sometimes used by men among friends, or when addressing someone younger or of a lower station.

-chan: This is used to express endearment, mostly toward girls. It is also used for little boys, pets, and even among lovers. It gives a sense of childish cuteness.

Bozu: This is an informal way to refer to a boy, similar to the English terms "kid" and "squirt."

Sempai/
Senpai: This title suggests that the addressee is one's senior in a group or organization. It is most often used in a school setting, where underclassmen refer to their upperclassmen as "sempai." It can also be used in the workplace, such as when a newer employee addresses an employee who has seniority in the company.

Kohai: This is the opposite of "sempai" and is used toward underclassmen in school or newcomers in the workplace. It connotes that the addressee is of a lower station.

Sensei: Literally meaning "one who has come before," this title is used for teachers, doctors, or masters of any profession or art.

-[blank]: This is usually forgotten in these lists, but it is perhaps the most significant difference between Japanese and English. The lack of honorific means that the speaker has permission to address the person in a very intimate way. Usually, only family, spouses, or very close friends have this kind of permission. Known as yo-bisute, it can be gratifying when someone who has earned the intimacy starts to call one by one's name without an honorific. But when that intimacy hasn't been earned, it can be very insulting.

FAIRY TAIL

16

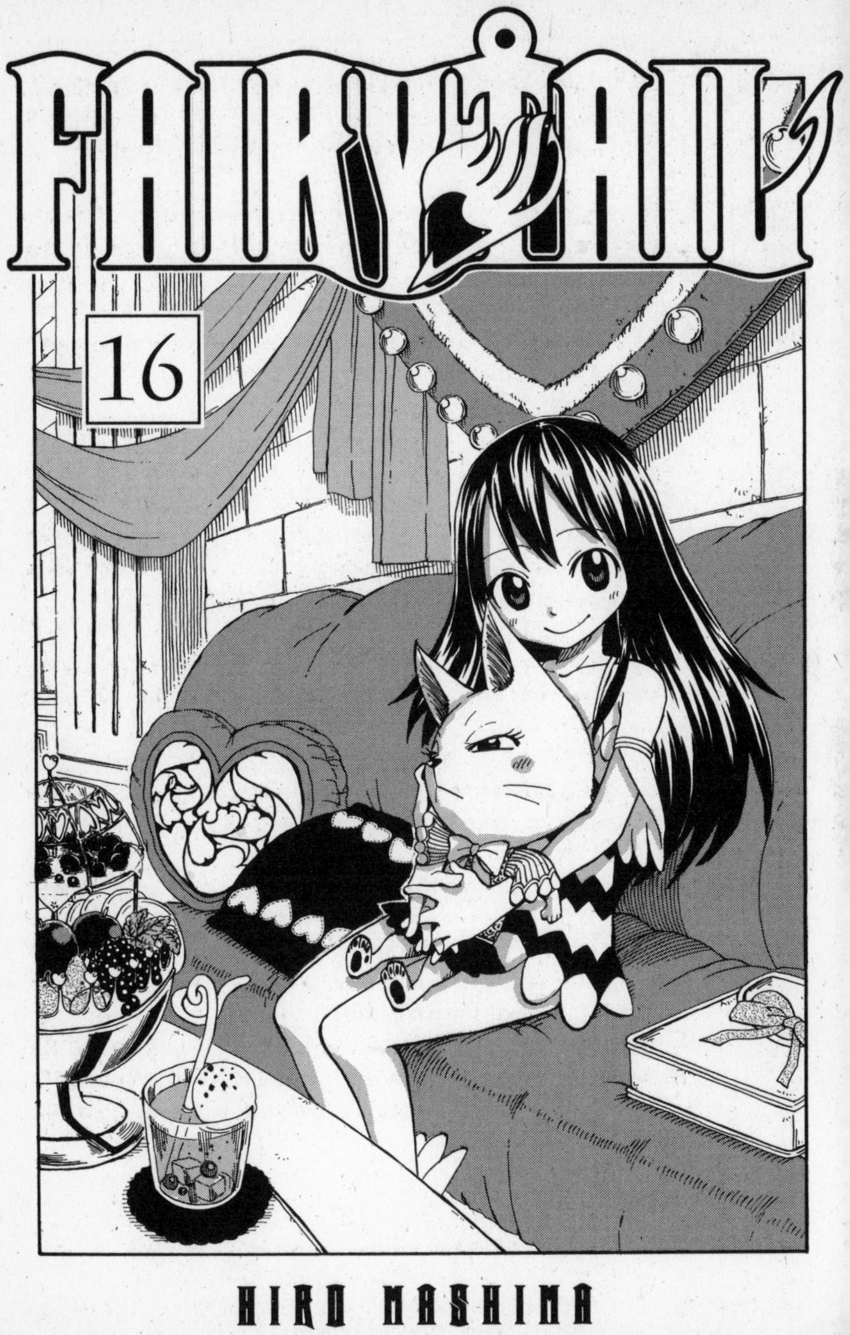

HIRO MASHIMA

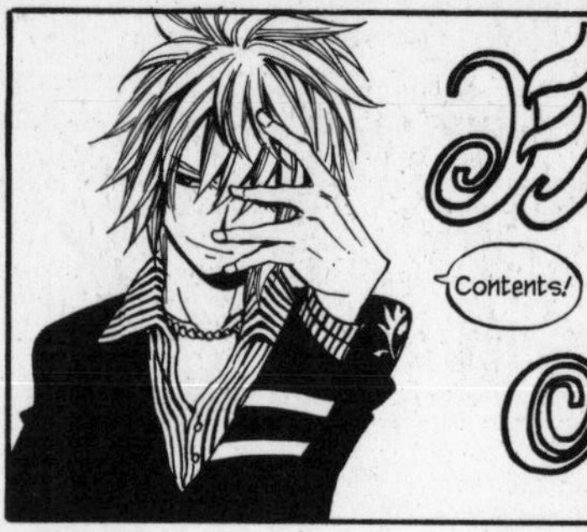
Contents!

FAIRY TAIL 16 CONTENTS

Published in serial form by Weekly Shônen Magazine 2009 Volumes 16 - 24.

FAIRY TAIL

Chapter 127, Sacrifice for Justice

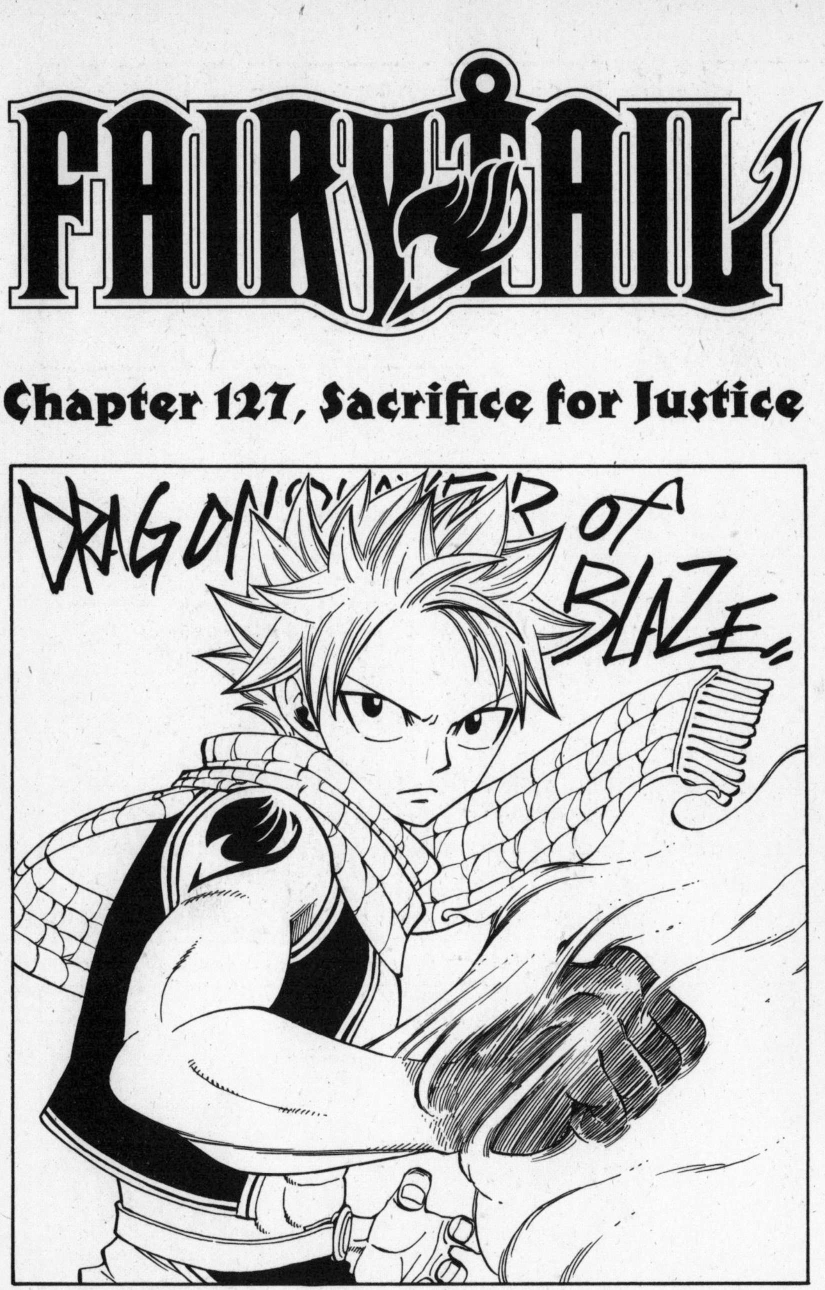
DRAGON
of
BLAZE...

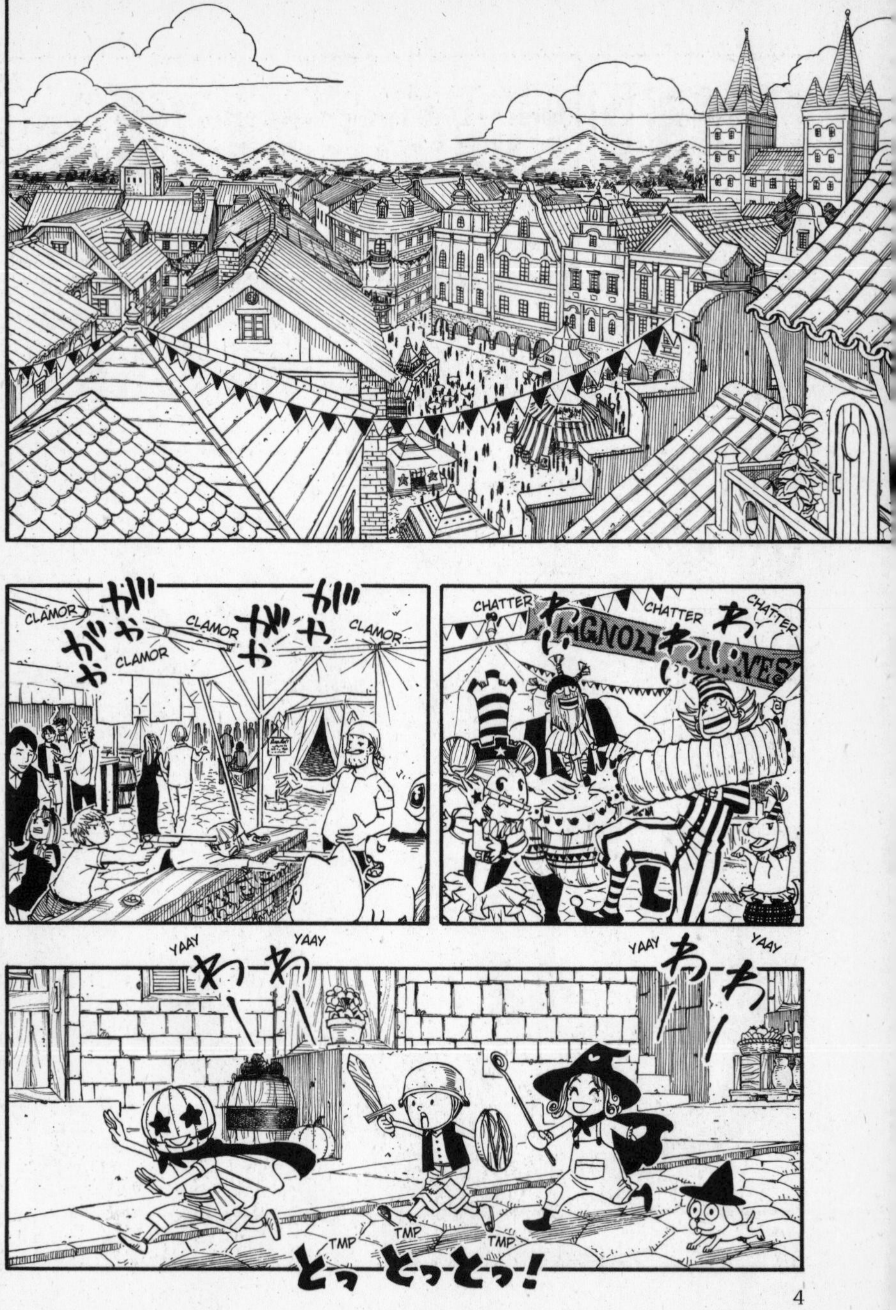
CHATTER
CHATTER
CHATTER
わいわい
CLAMOR
CLAMOR
CLAMOR
CLAMOR
がやがや
がやがや
YAAY
YAAY
わーわー
YAAY
YAAY
わーわー
TMP
TMP
TMP
とっとっとっ!

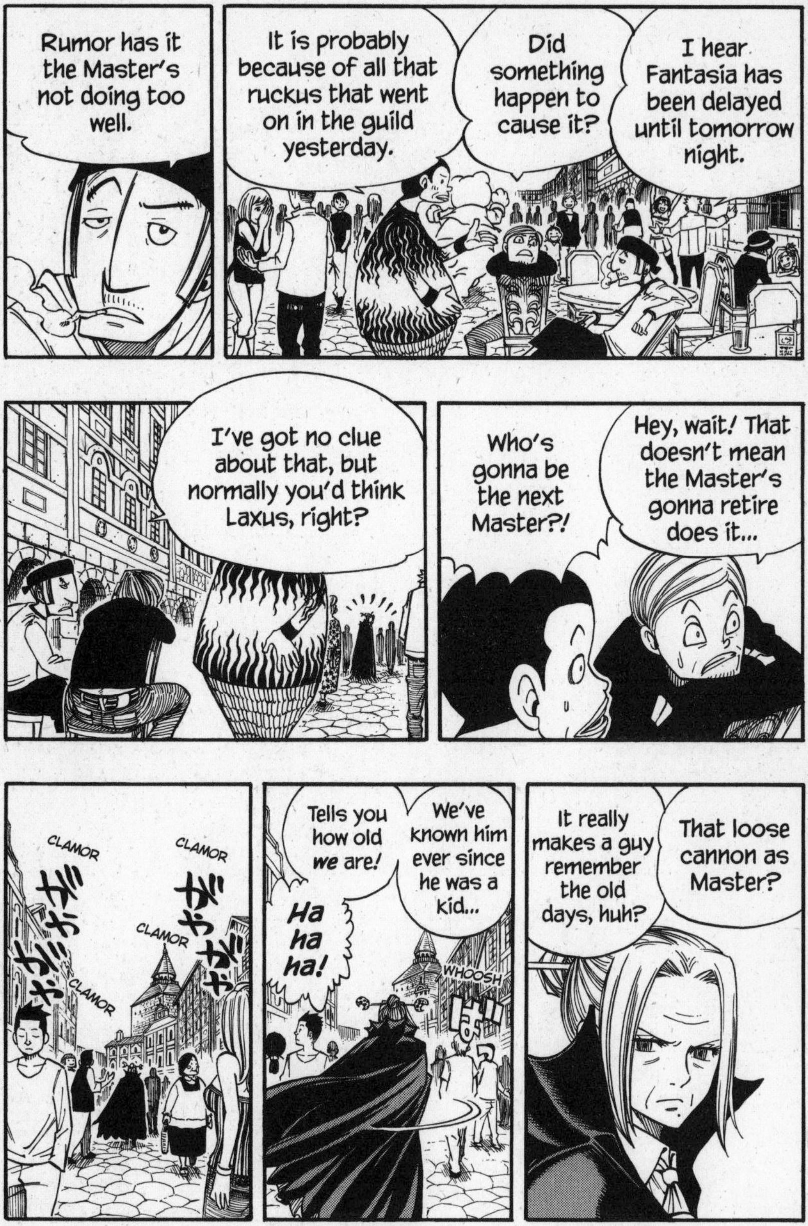
I hear Fantasia has been delayed until tomorrow night.
Did something happen to cause it?
It is probably because of all that ruckus that went on in the guild yesterday.
Rumor has it the Master's not doing too well.
Hey, wait! That doesn't mean the Master's gonna retire does it...
Who's gonna be the next Master?!
I've got no clue about that, but normally you'd think Laxus, right?
That loose cannon as Master?
It really makes a guy remember the old days, huh?
We've known him ever since he was a kid...
Tells you how old *we* are!
Ha ha ha!
WHOOSH
CLAMOR
CLAMOR
CLAMOR
CLAMOR

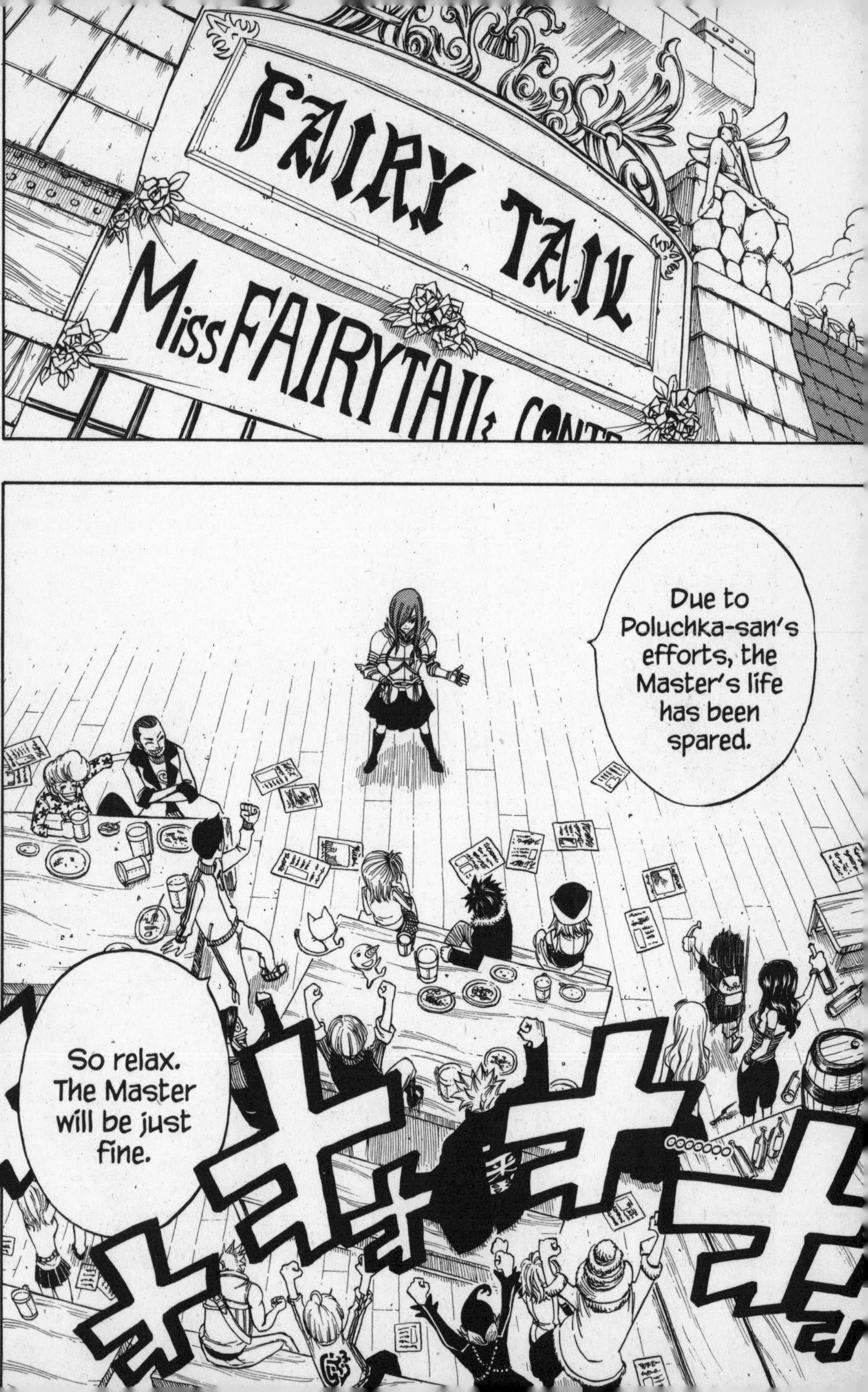
FAIRY TAIL
Miss FAIRYTAIL
Due to Poluchka-san's efforts, the Master's life has been spared.
So relax. The Master will be just fine.

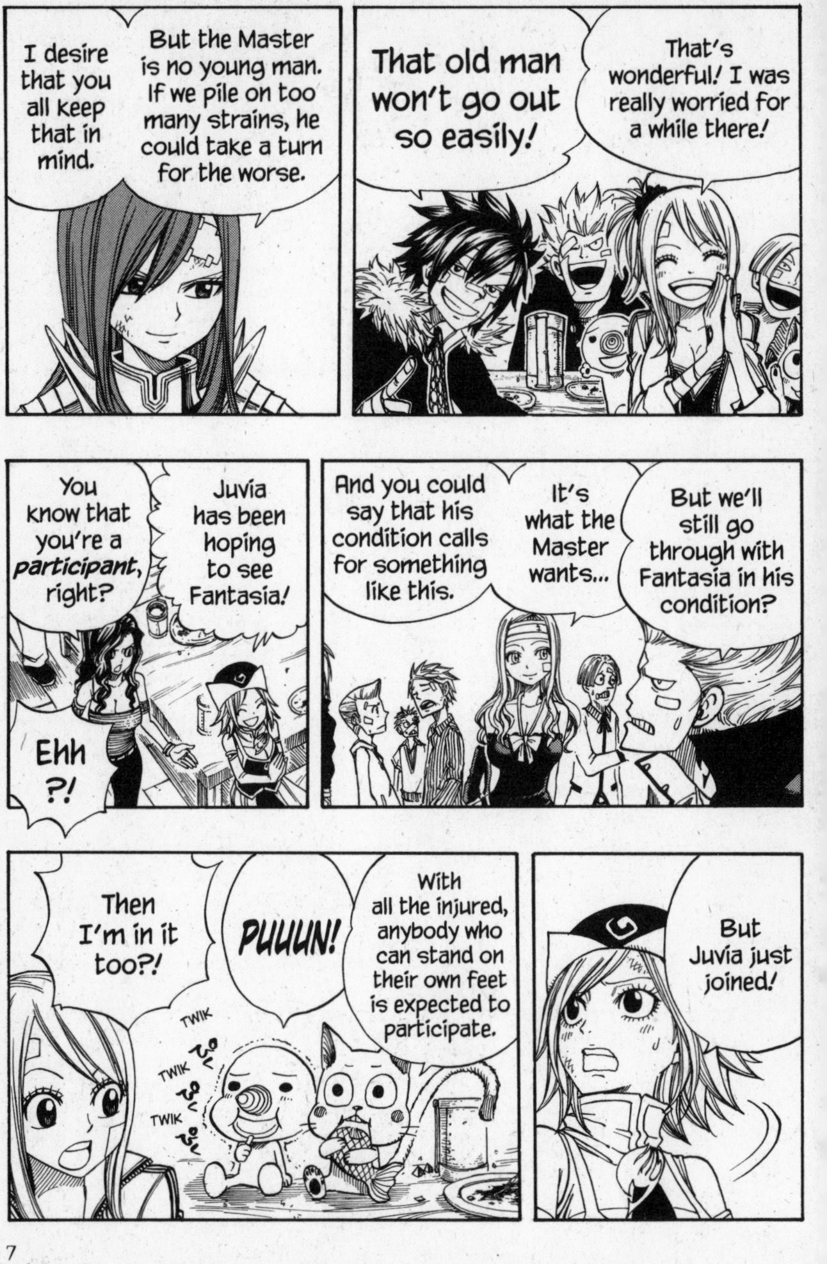
That's wonderful! I was really worried for a while there!
That old man won't go out so easily!
But the Master is no young man. If we pile on too many strains, he could take a turn for the worse.
I desire that you all keep that in mind.
But we'll still go through with Fantasia in his condition?
It's what the Master wants...
And you could say that his condition calls for something like this.
Juvia has been hoping to see Fantasia!
You know that you're a *participant*, right?
Ehh ?!
But Juvia just joined!
With all the injured, anybody who can stand on their own feet is expected to participate.
PUUUN!
TWIK
TWIK
TWIK
Then I'm in it too?!

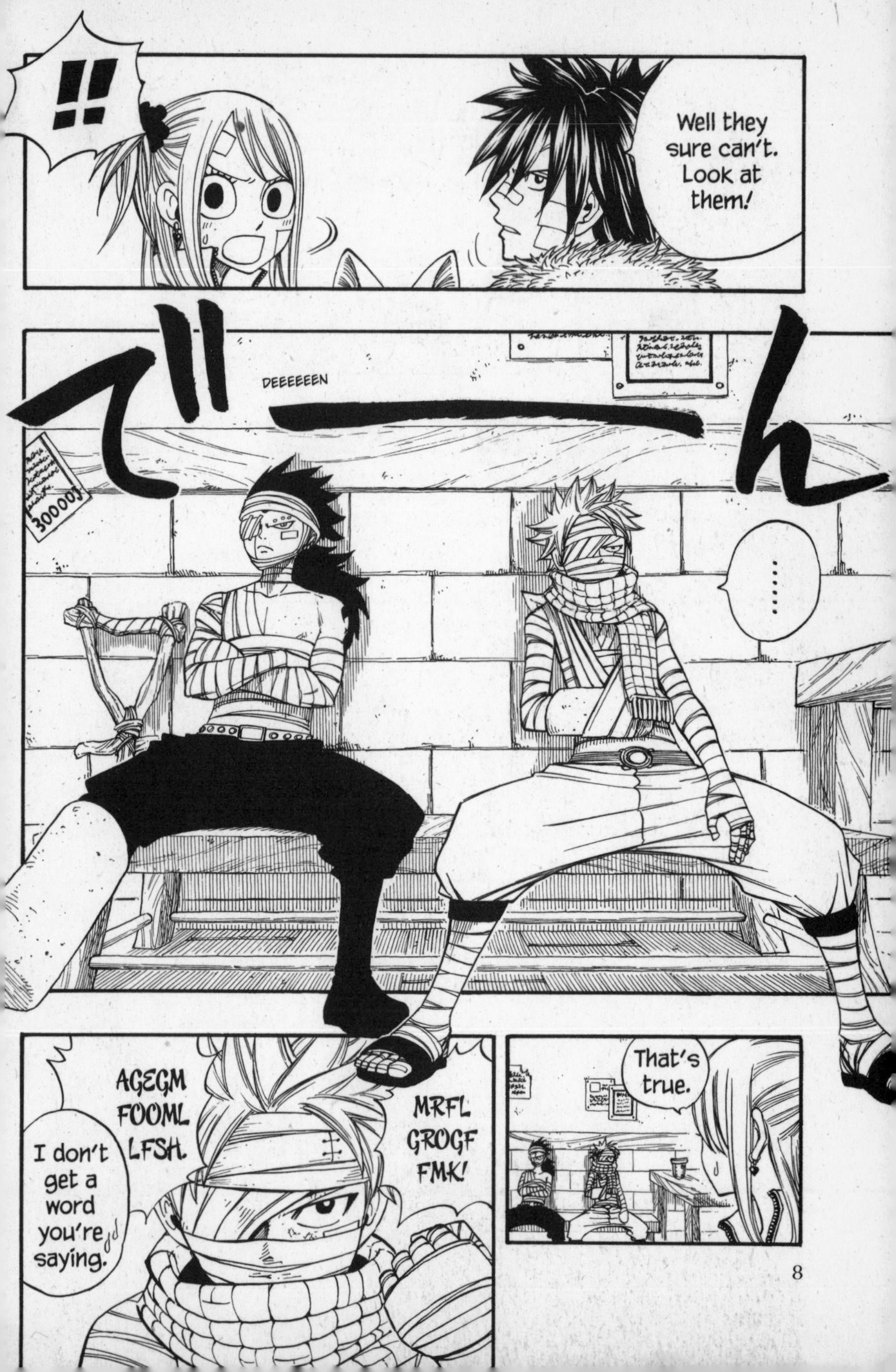
Well they sure can't. Look at them!
!!
でーん
DEEEEEEN
......
That's true.
MRFL GROGF FMK!
AGEGM FOOML LFSH.
I don't get a word you're saying.

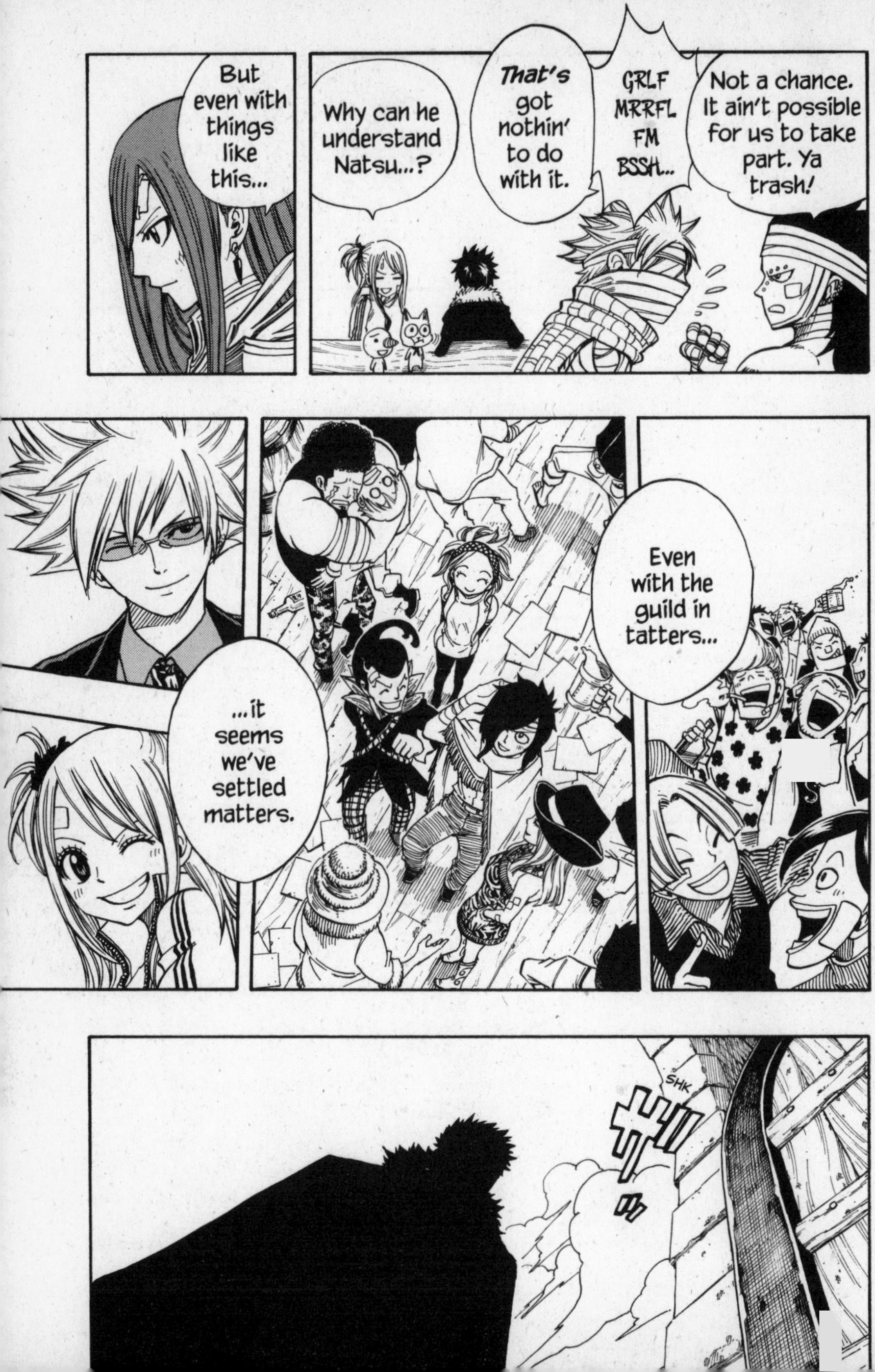

Not a chance. It ain't possible for us to take part. Ya trash!
GRLF MRRFL FM BSSH...
That's got nothin' to do with it.
Why can he understand Natsu...?
But even with things like this...
Even with the guild in tatters...
...it seems we've settled matters.
SHK

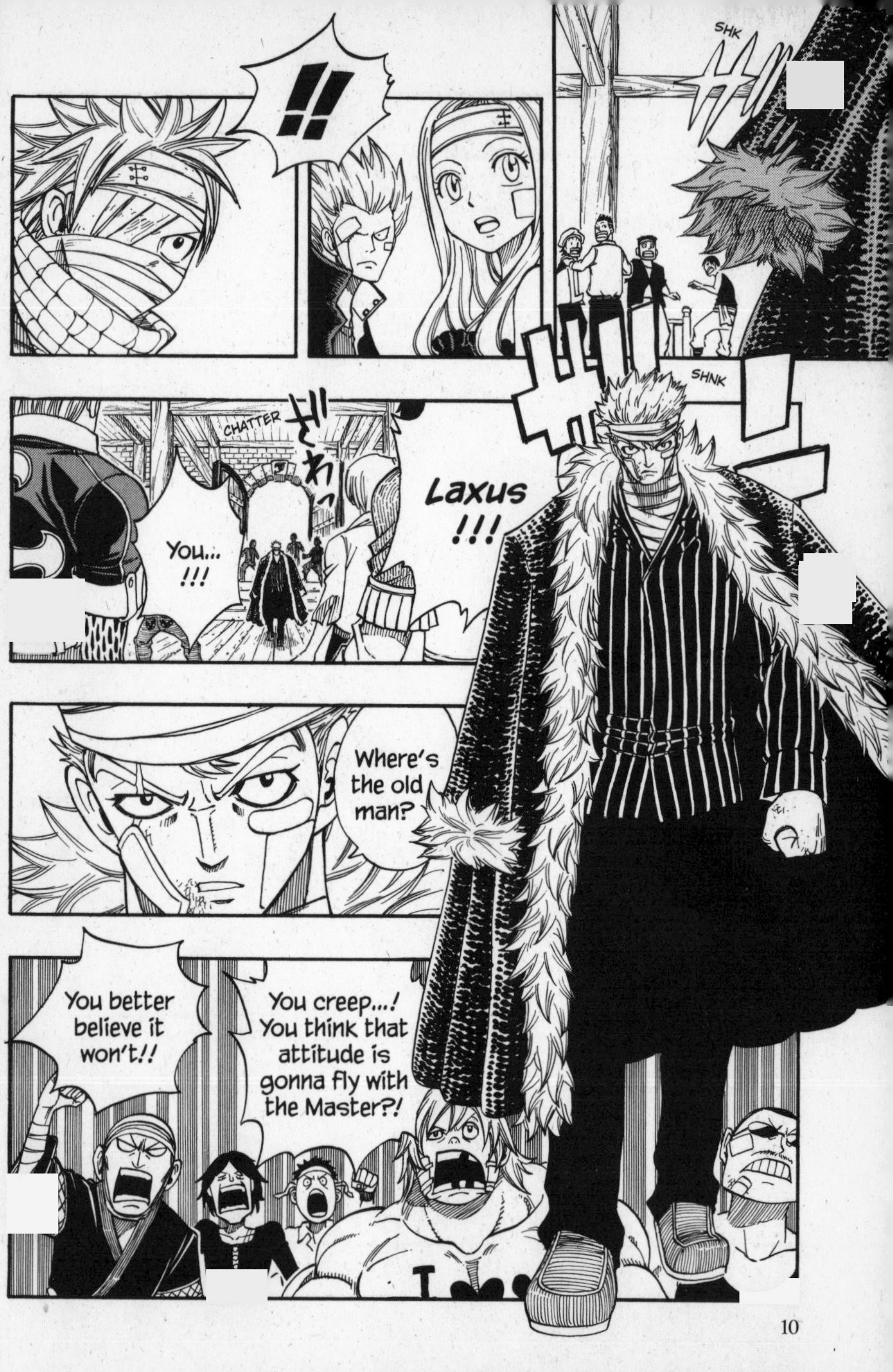
SHK
!!
SHNK
CHATTER
Laxus !!!
You... !!!
Where's the old man?
You creep...! You think that attitude is gonna fly with the Master?!
You better believe it won't!!

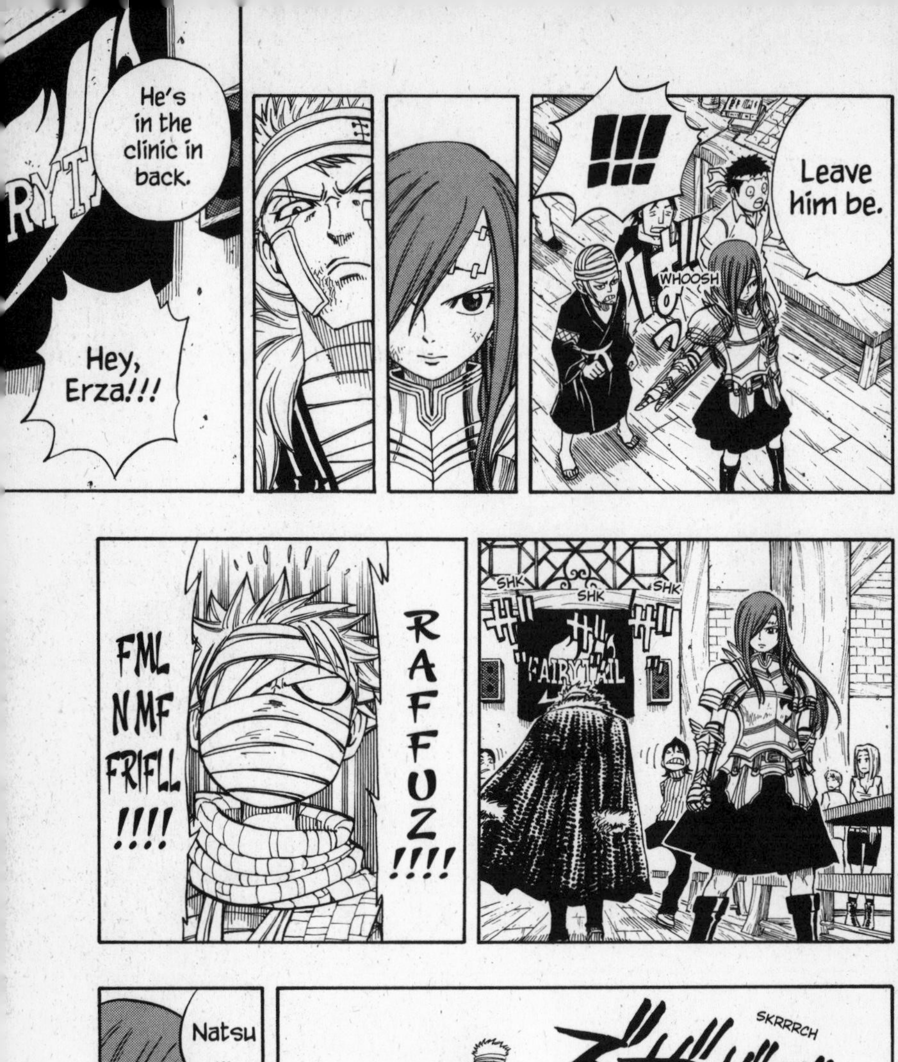
!!!
Leave him be.
WHOOSH
He's in the clinic in back.
Hey, Erza!!!
SHK
SHK
SHK
FAIRYTAIL
RAFFUZ!!!!
FML NMF FRIFLL!!!!
SKRRRCH
Natsu ...

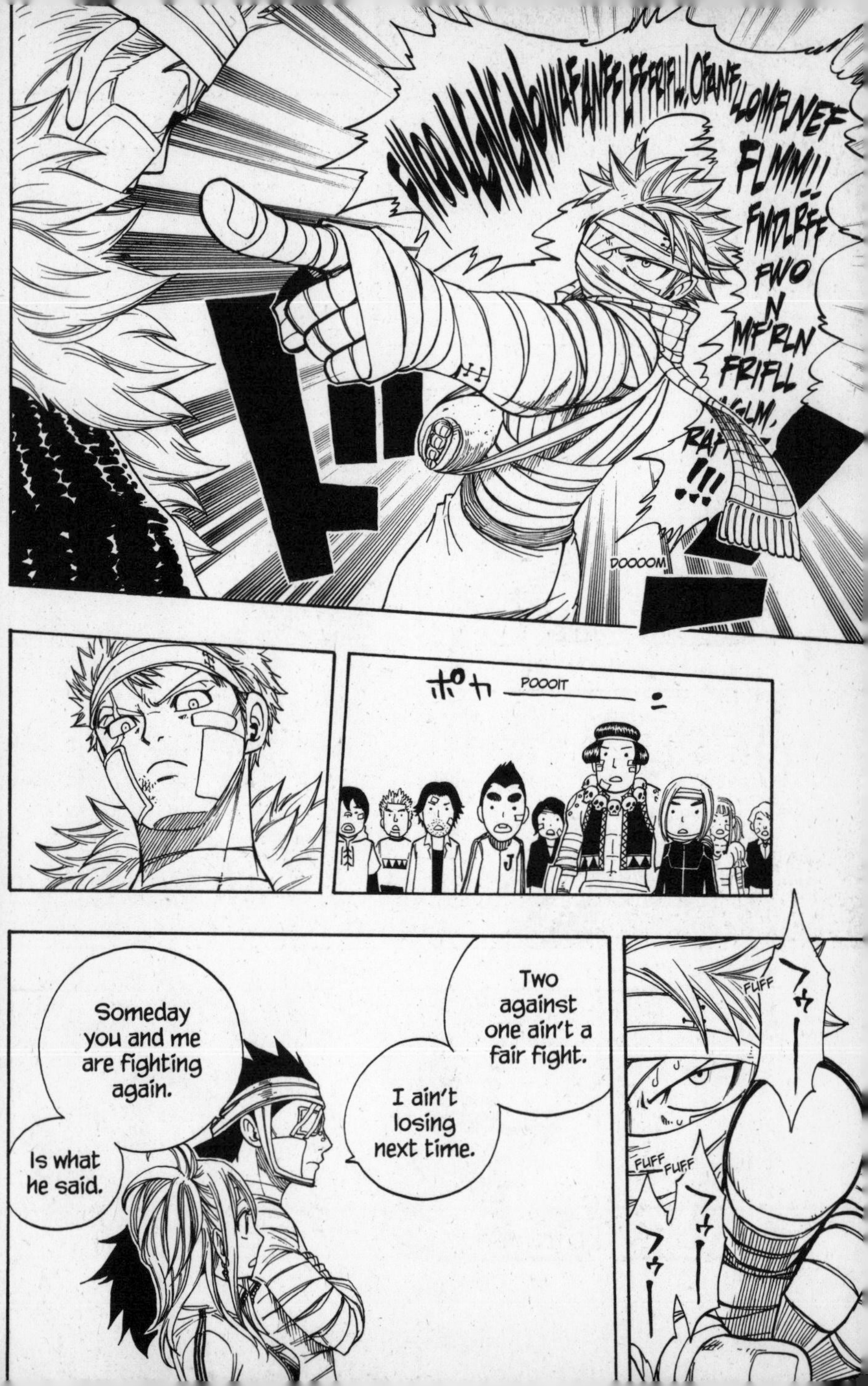

DOOOOM
POOOIT
FUFF
FUFF FUFF
Two against one ain't a fair fight.
Someday you and me are fighting again.
I ain't losing next time.
Is what he said.

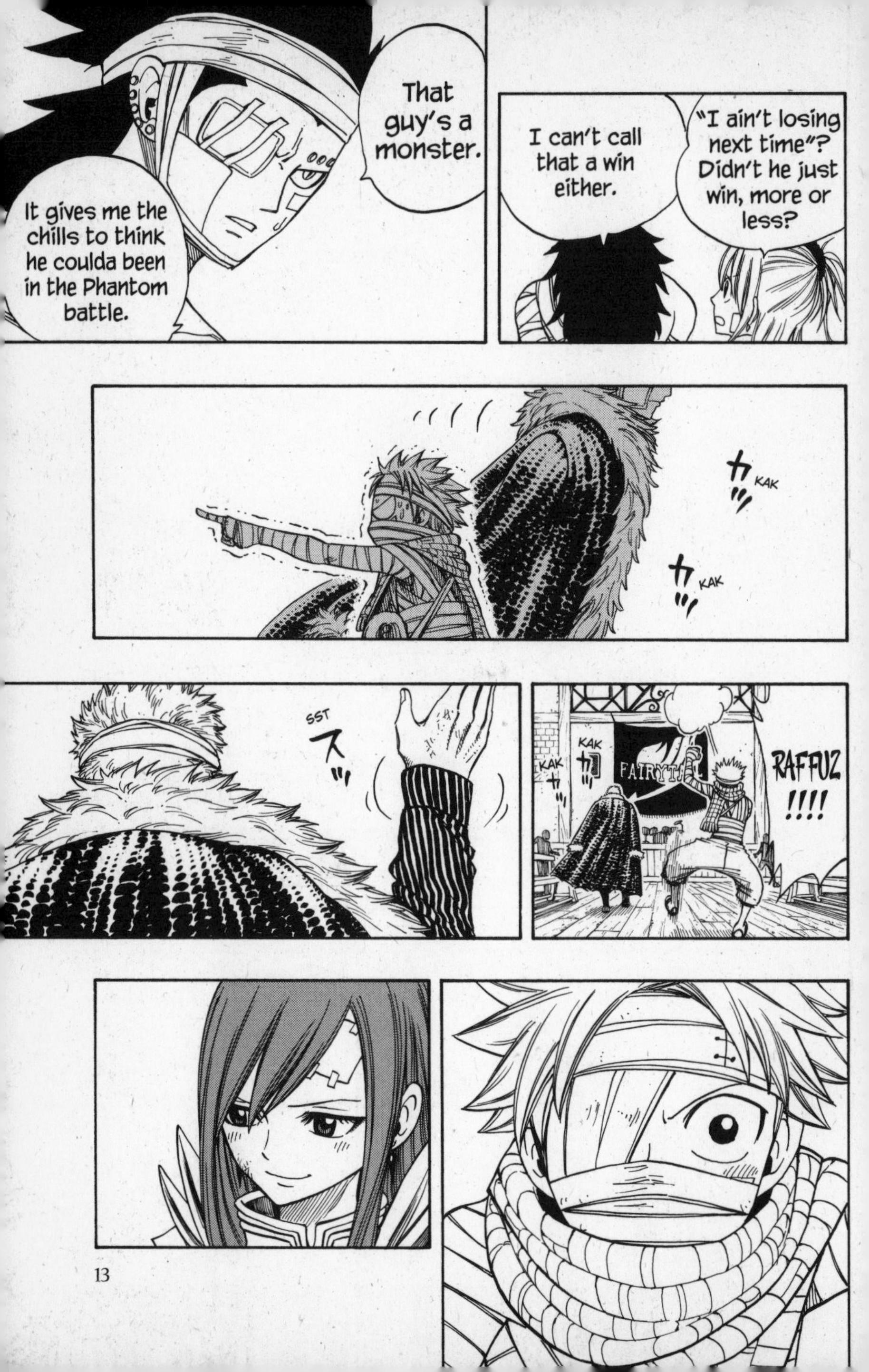
"I ain't losing next time"? Didn't he just win, more or less?
I can't call that a win either.
That guy's a monster.
It gives me the chills to think he coulda been in the Phantom battle.
KAK
KAK
RAFFUZ !!!!
KAK
KAK
SST

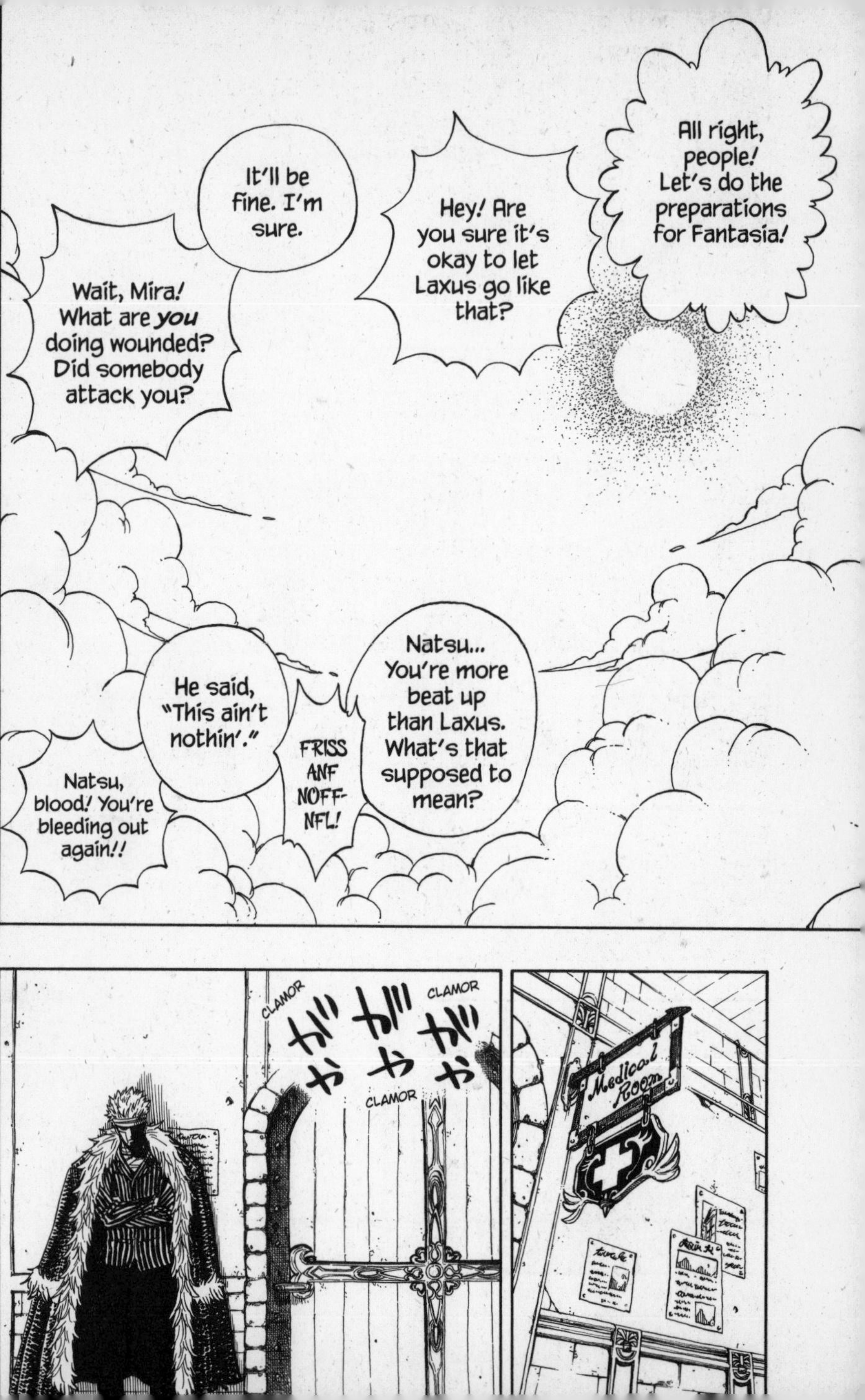

All right, people! Let's do the preparations for Fantasia!
Hey! Are you sure it's okay to let Laxus go like that?
It'll be fine. I'm sure.
Wait, Mira! What are *you* doing wounded? Did somebody attack you?
Natsu... You're more beat up than Laxus. What's that supposed to mean?
FRISS ANF NOFF-NFL!
He said, "This ain't nothin'."
Natsu, blood! You're bleeding out again!!
Medical Room
CLAMOR
CLAMOR
CLAMOR

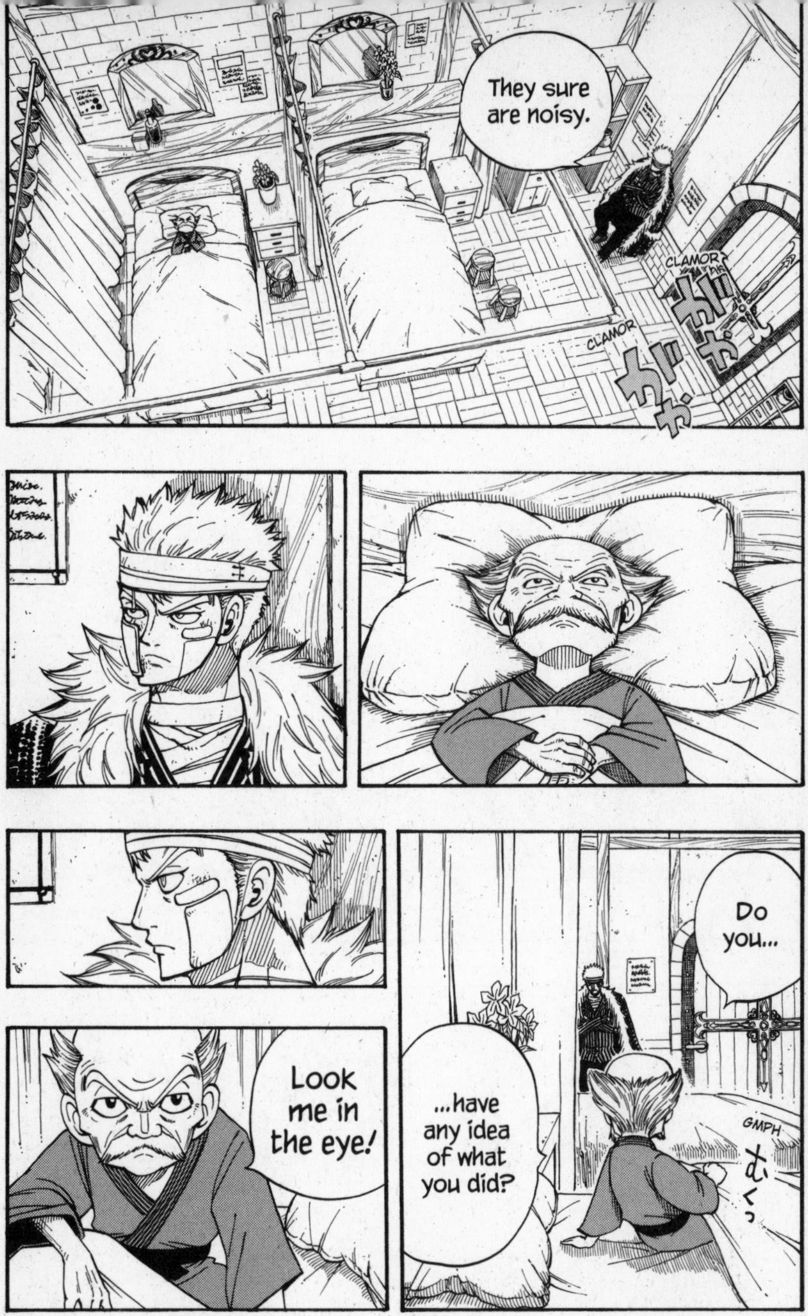
They sure are noisy.
CLAMOR
CLAMOR
Do you...
...have any idea of what you did?
GMPH
Look me in the eye!

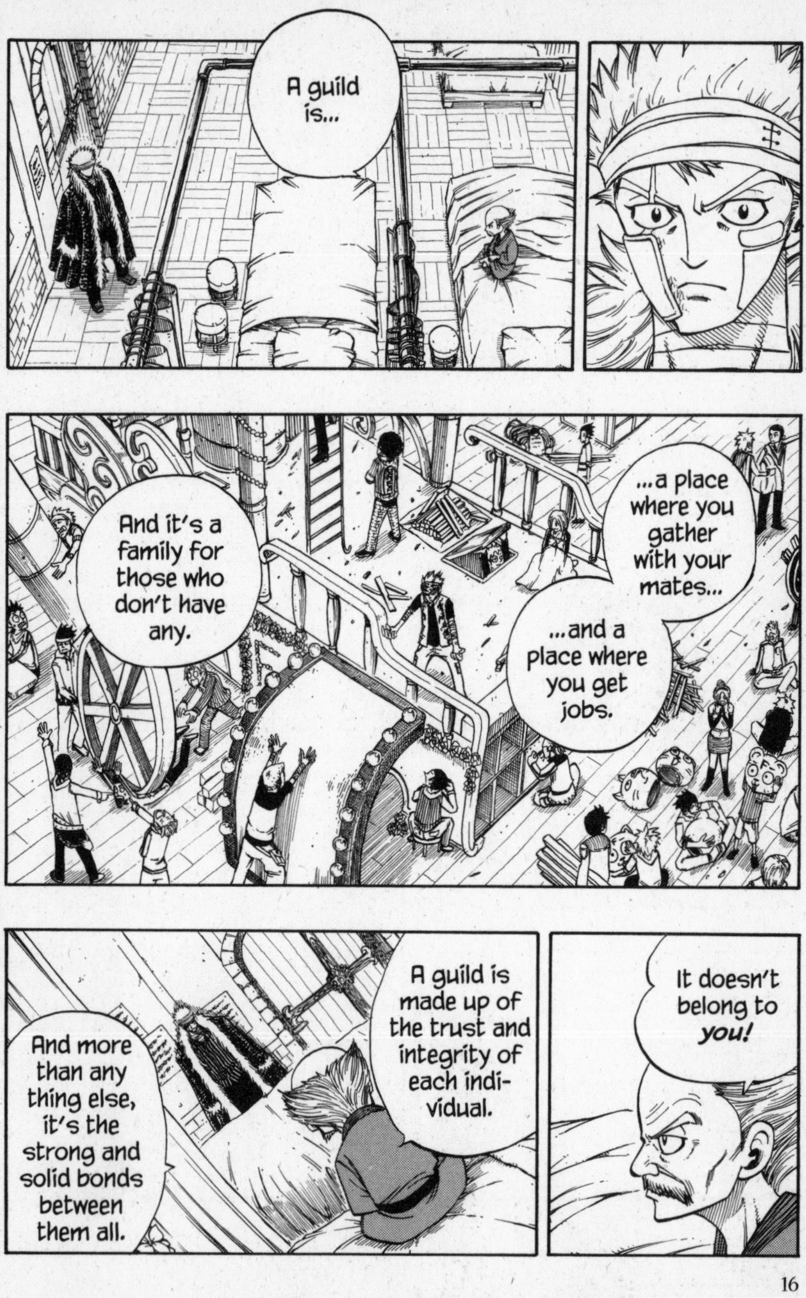
A guild is...
...a place where you gather with your mates...
...and a place where you get jobs.
And it's a family for those who don't have any.
It doesn't belong to *you!*
A guild is made up of the trust and integrity of each indi-vidual.
And more than any thing else, it's the strong and solid bonds between them all.

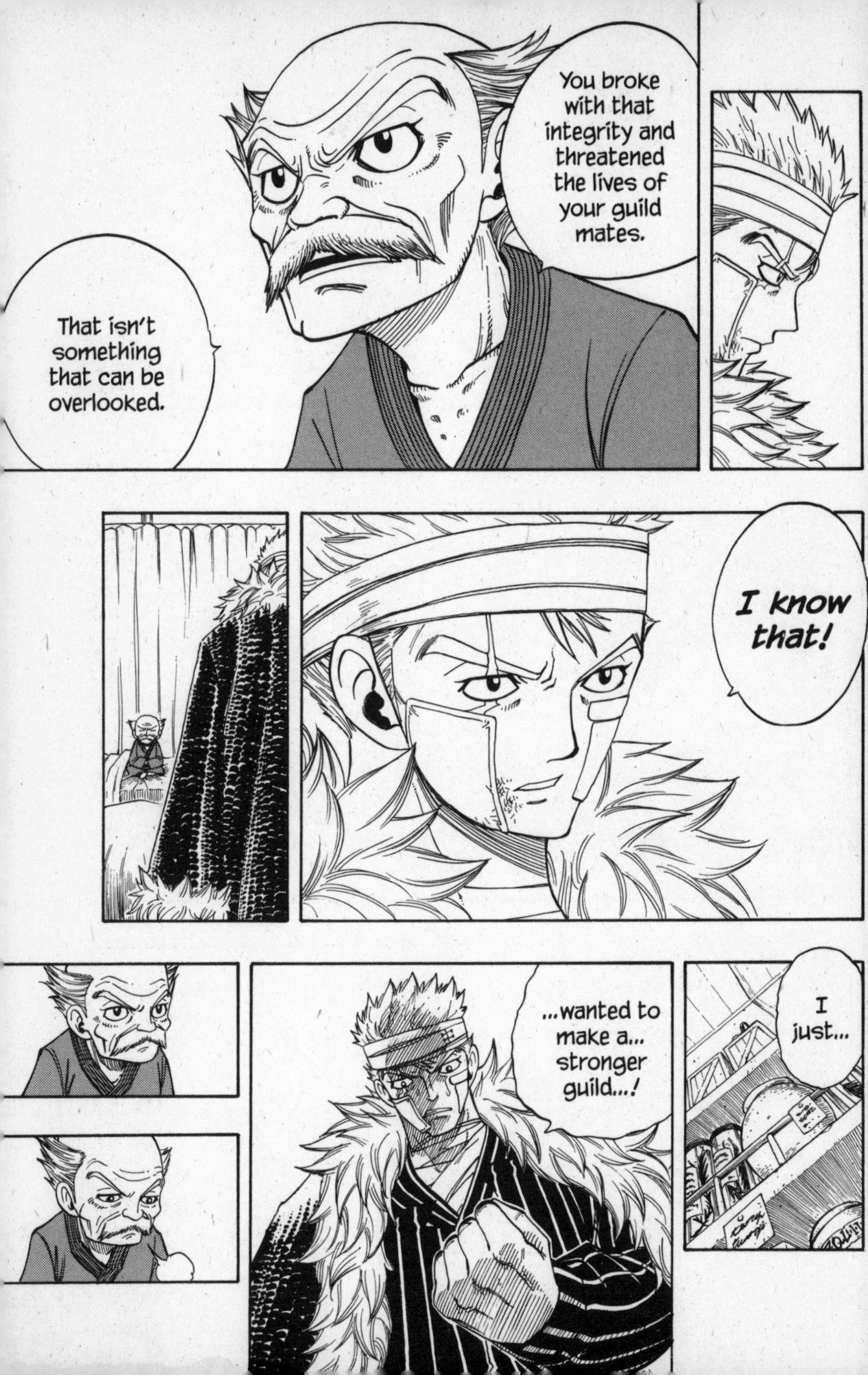
You broke with that integrity and threatened the lives of your guild mates.
That isn't something that can be overlooked.
I know that!
I just...
...wanted to make a... stronger guild...!

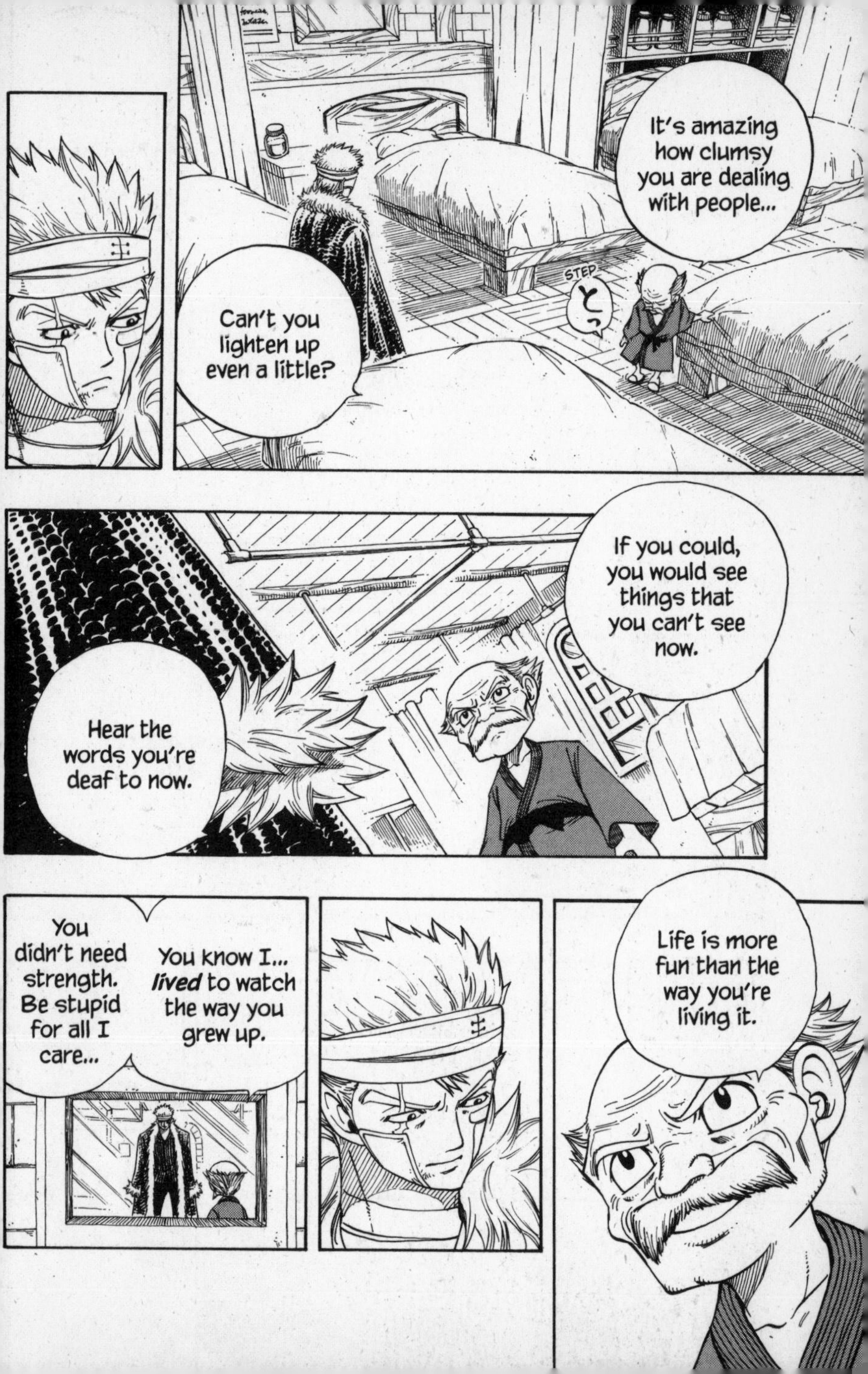
It's amazing how clumsy you are dealing with people...
STEP
Can't you lighten up even a little?
If you could, you would see things that you can't see now.
Hear the words you're deaf to now.
Life is more fun than the way you're living it.
You know I... *lived* to watch the way you grew up.
You didn't need strength. Be stupid for all I care...

But as long as you were full of energy ...

...that was all I was hoping for.

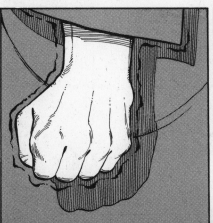

Laxus!

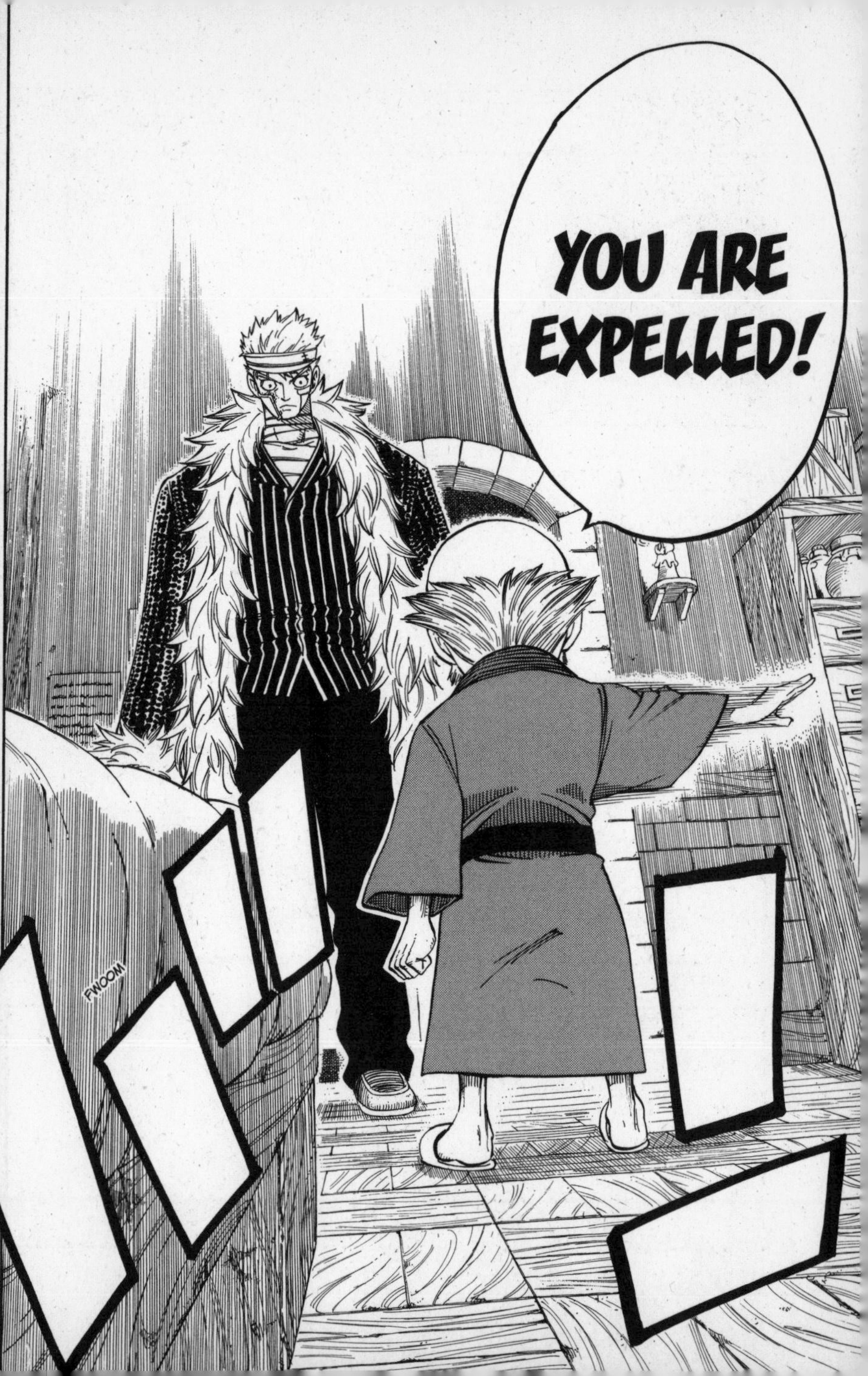
YOU ARE EXPELLED!
FWOOM

Yeah...

Thanks for puttin' me up.

Gramps ...

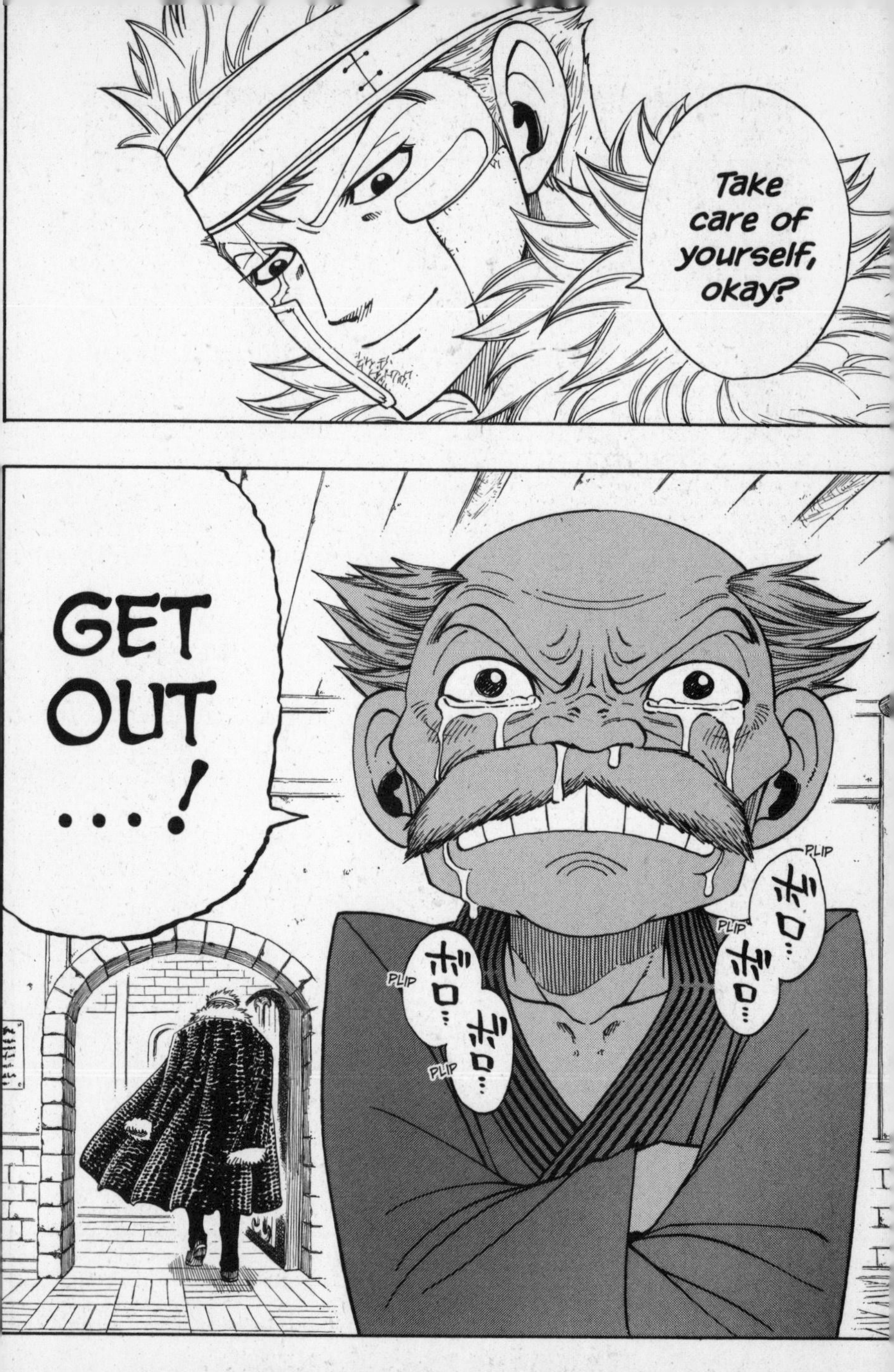
Take care of yourself, okay?
GET OUT ...!
PLIP
ボロ…
PLIP
ボロ…
PLIP
ボロ…
PLIP
ボロ…

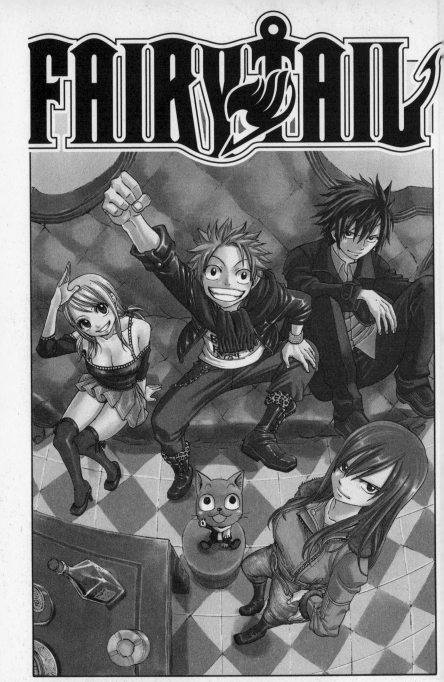

FAIRY TAIL

Chapter 128, Fantasia

ポカ POOOOOIT _____ :

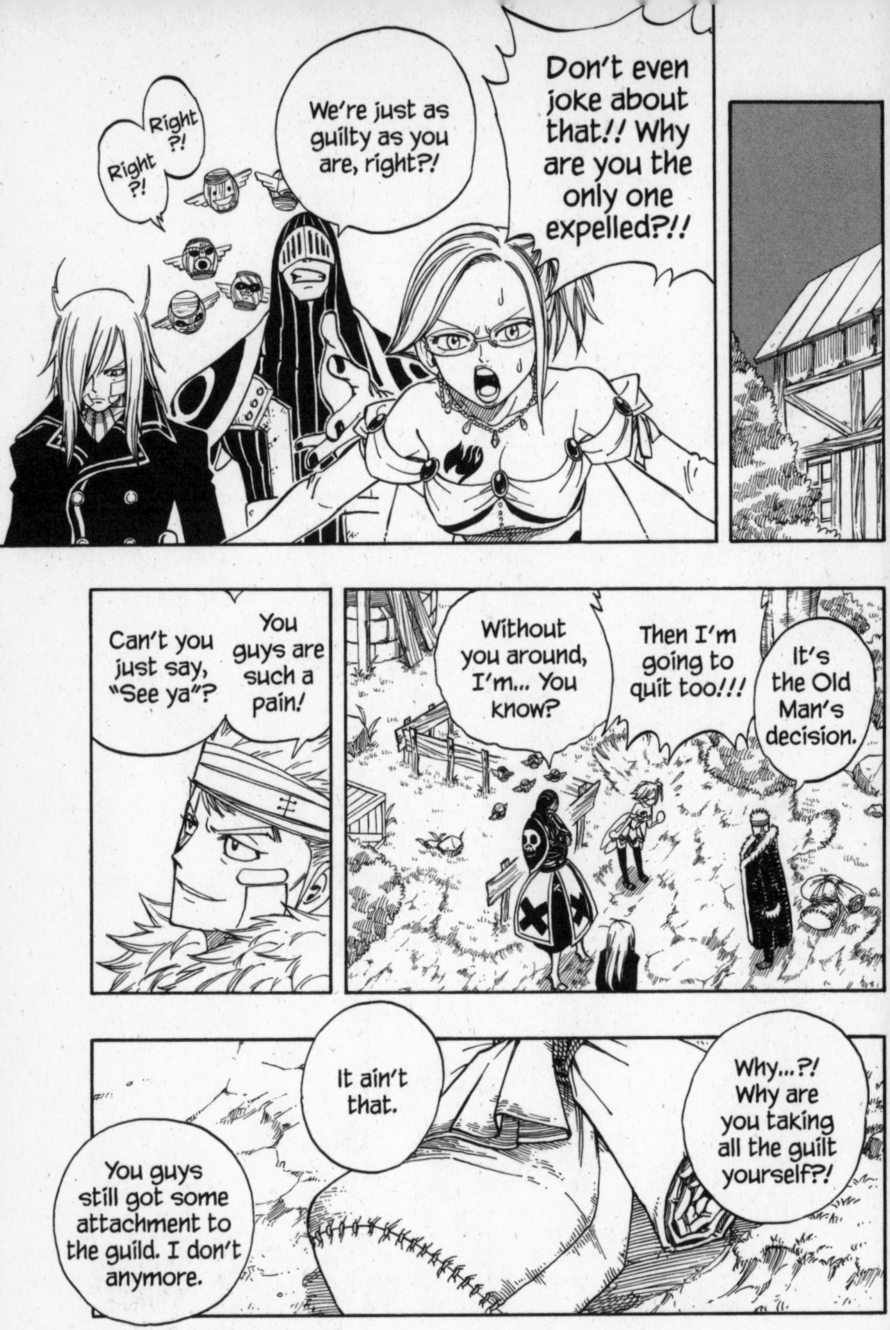
Don't even joke about that!! Why are you the only one expelled?!!
We're just as guilty as you are, right?!
Right?!
Right?!
It's the Old Man's decision.
Then I'm going to quit too!!!
Without you around, I'm... You know?
You guys are such a pain!
Can't you just say, "See ya"?
Why...?! Why are you taking all the guilt yourself?!
It ain't that.
You guys still got some attachment to the guild. I don't anymore.

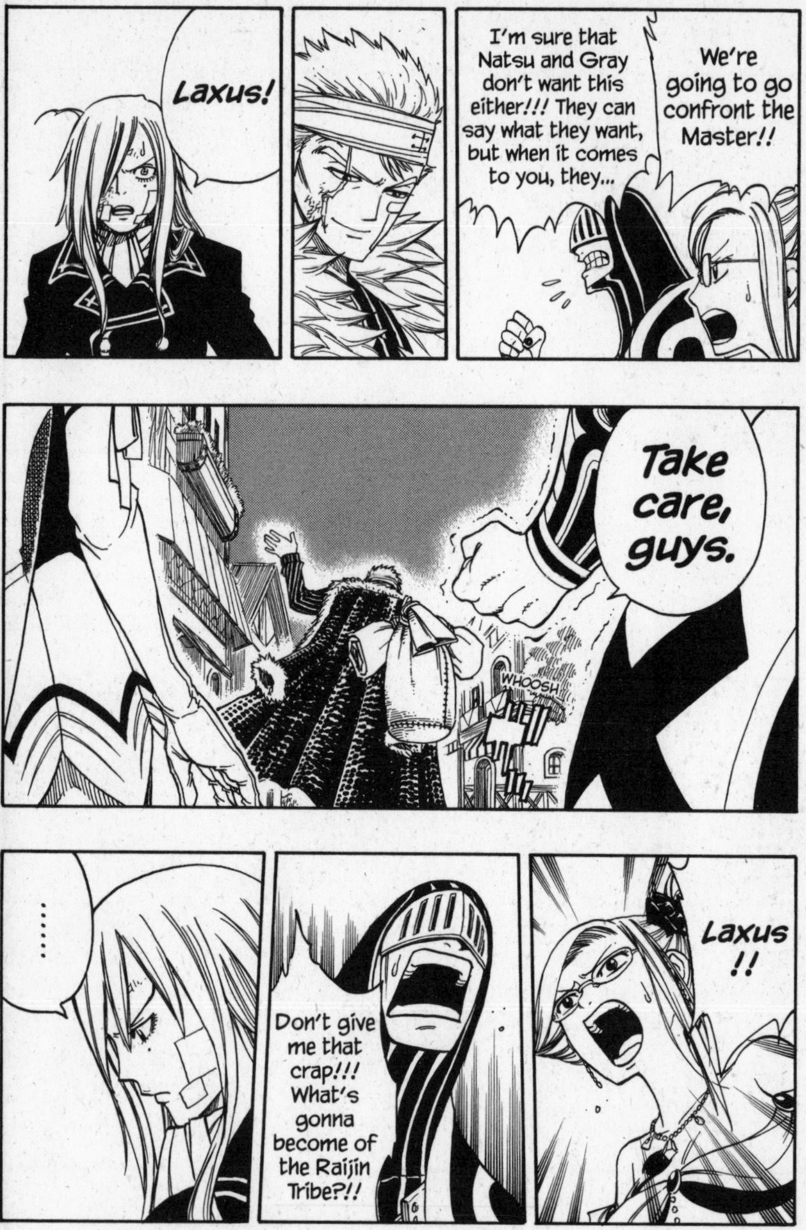
We're going to go confront the Master!!
I'm sure that Natsu and Gray don't want this either!!! They can say what they want, but when it comes to you, they...
Laxus!
Take care, guys.
WHOOSH
Laxus !!
Don't give me that crap!!! What's gonna become of the Raijin Tribe?!!
......

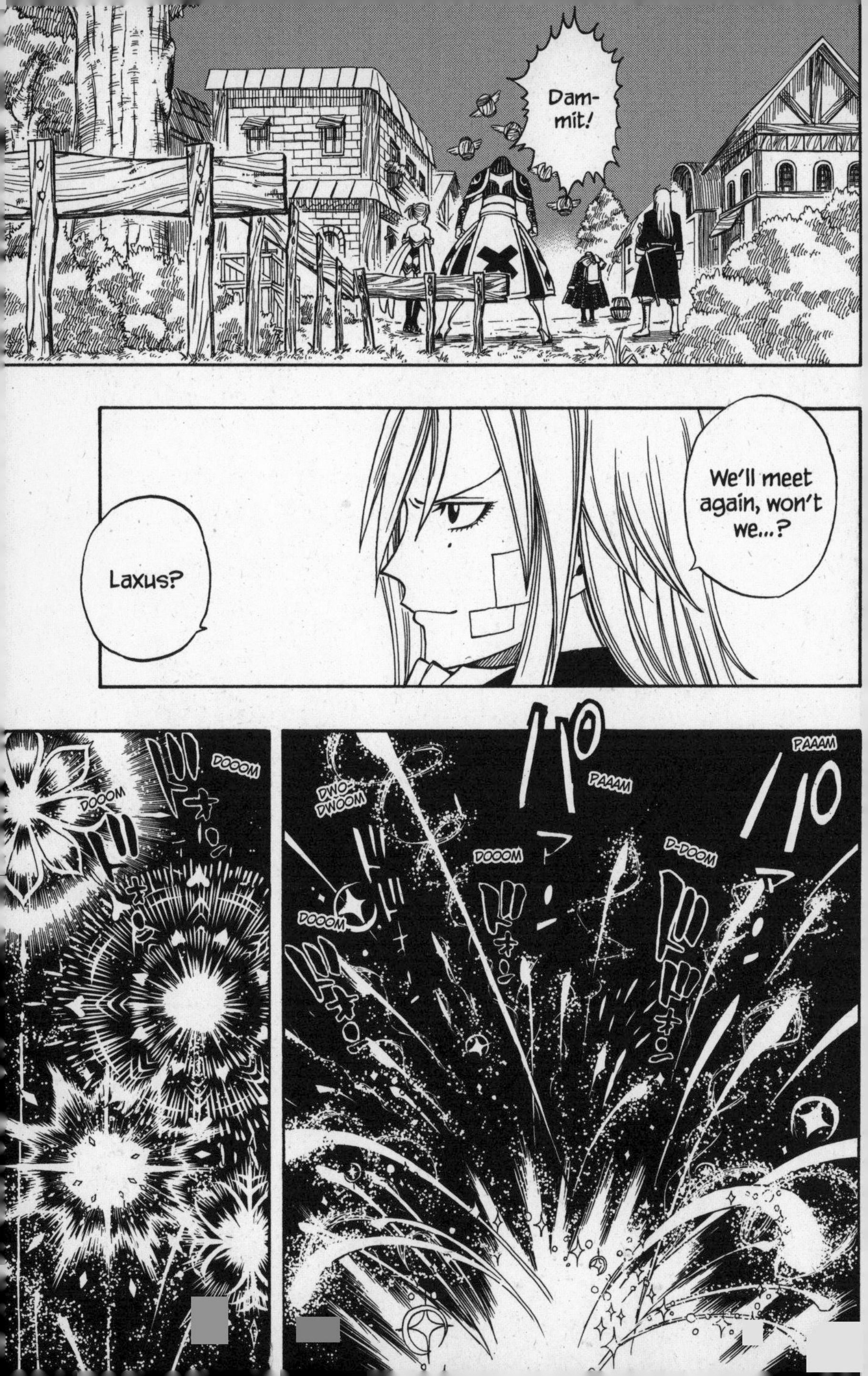
Dam-
mit!
We'll meet again, won't we...?
Laxus?
PAAAM
PAAAM
D-DOOM
DWO-DWOOM
DOOOM
DOOOM
DOOOM
DOOOM

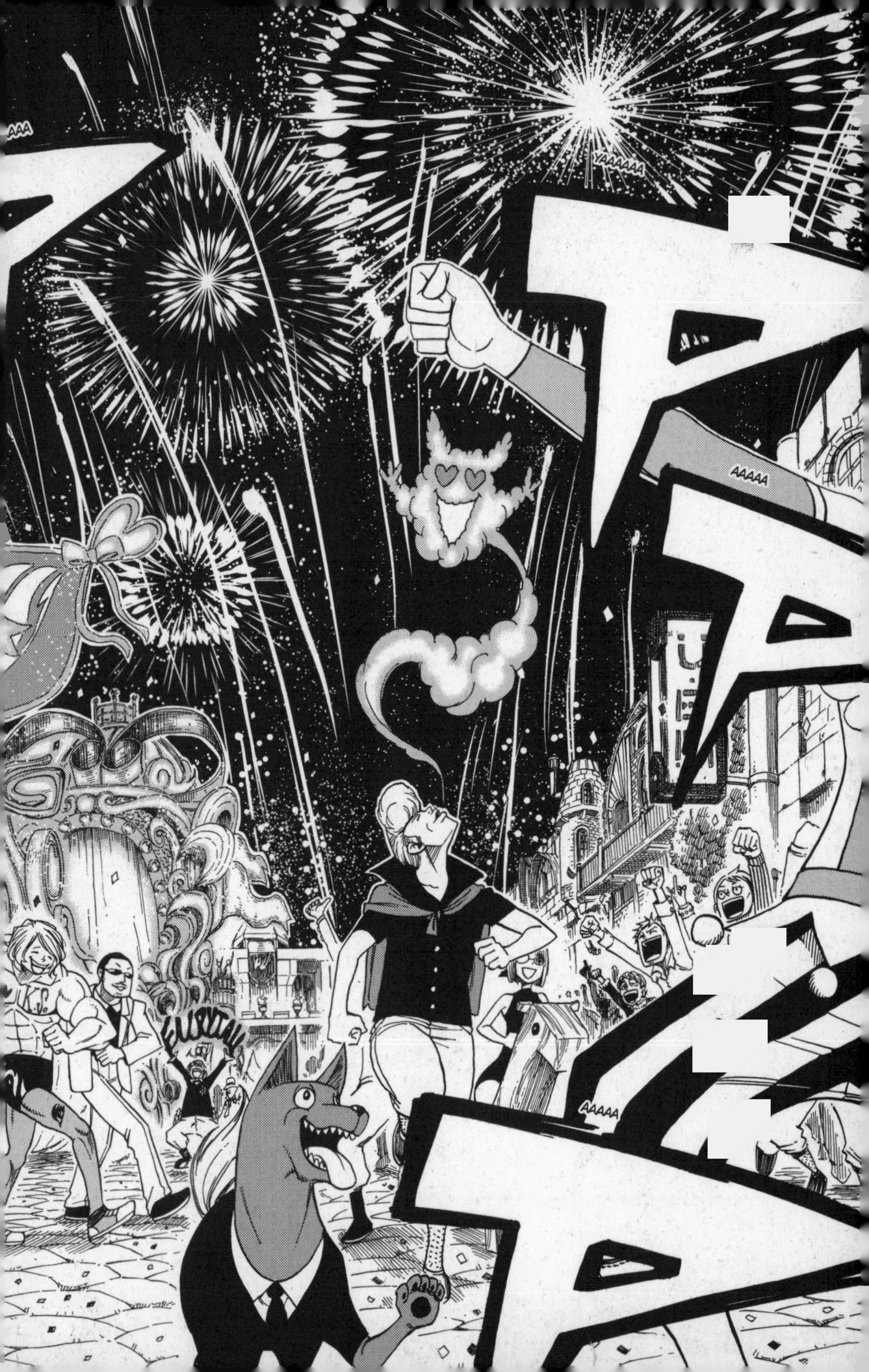
YAAAAAA
AAA
AAAAA
AAAAA

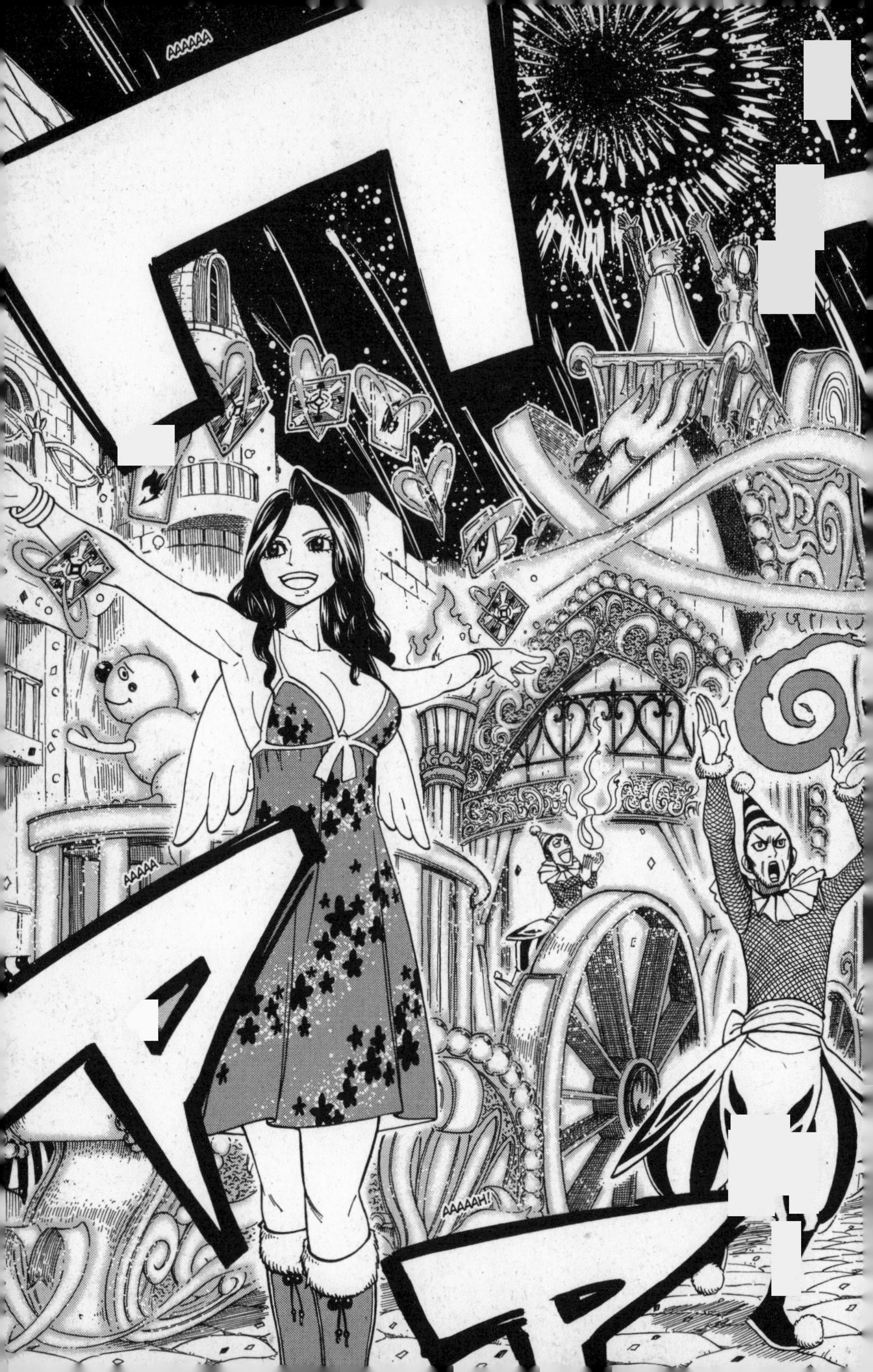
AAAAAA
AAAAA
AAAAAH!

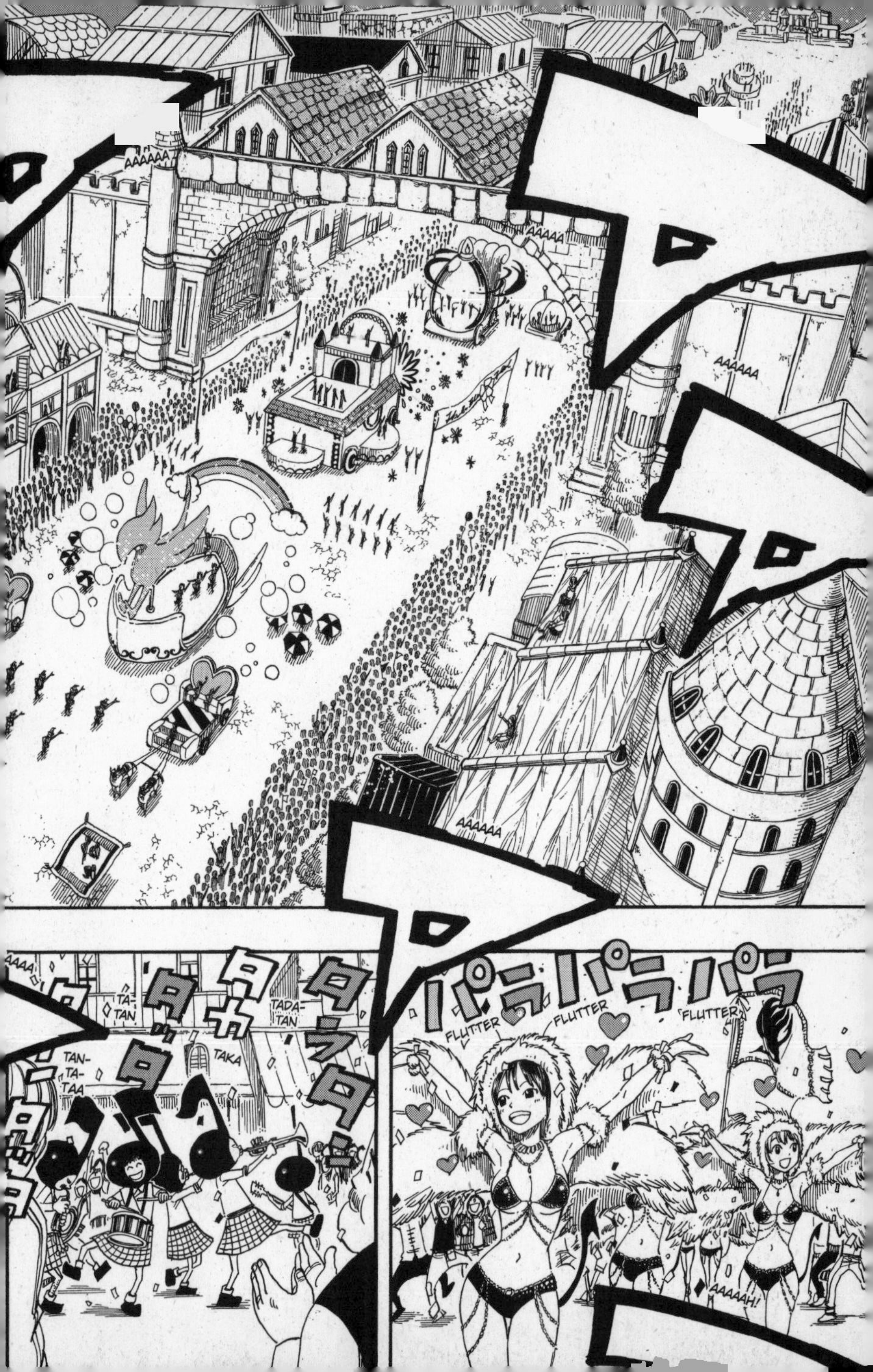
AAAAA
AAAAAA
AAAAAA
AAAAAA
パラパラパラ
FLUTTER
FLUTTER
FLUTTER
AAAAAH!
AAAA
TADA-TAN
TA-TAN
TAKA
TAN-TA-TAA

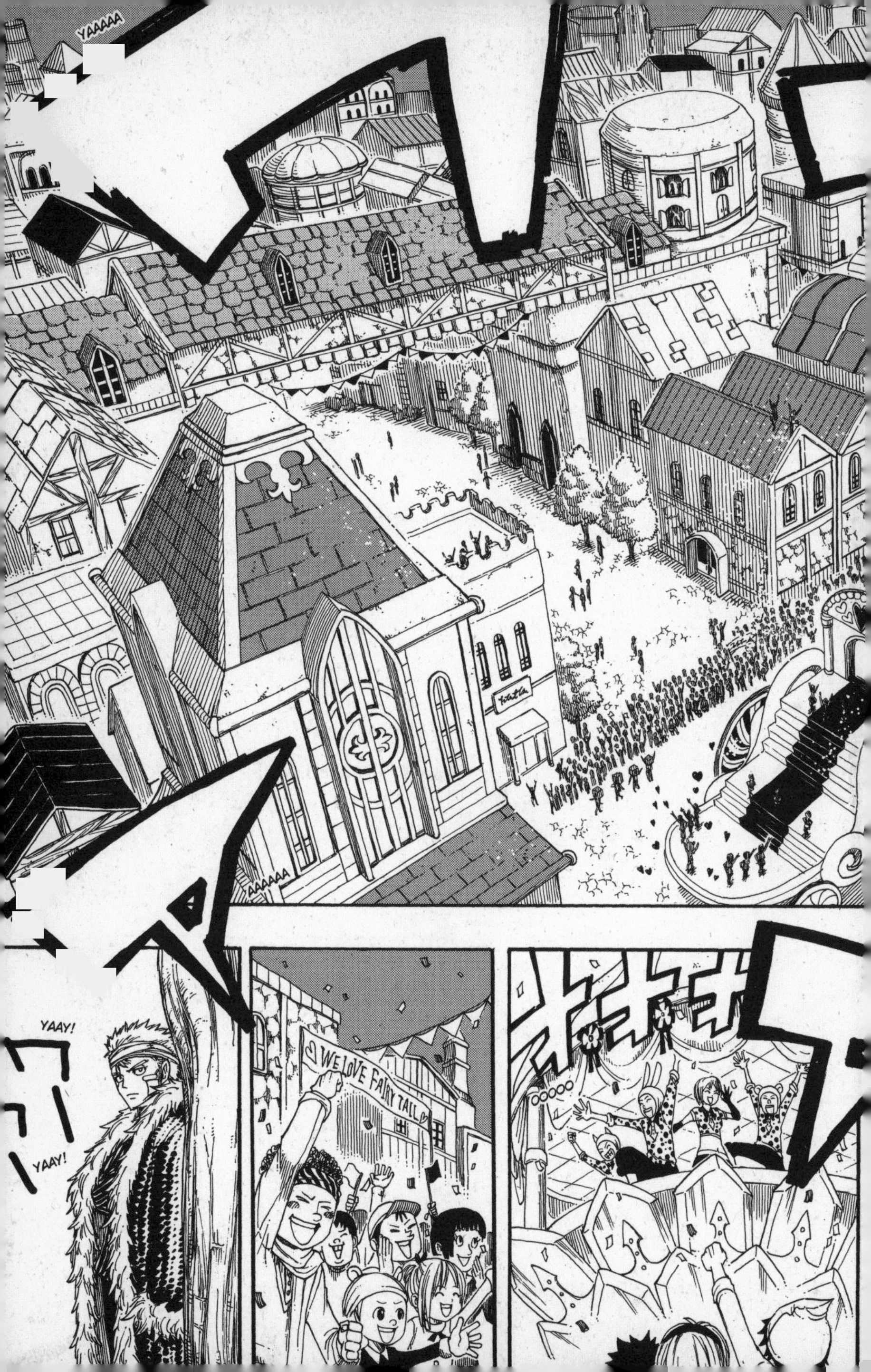
YAAAAA
AAAAAA
WE LOVE FAIRY TAIL
YAAY!
YAAY!

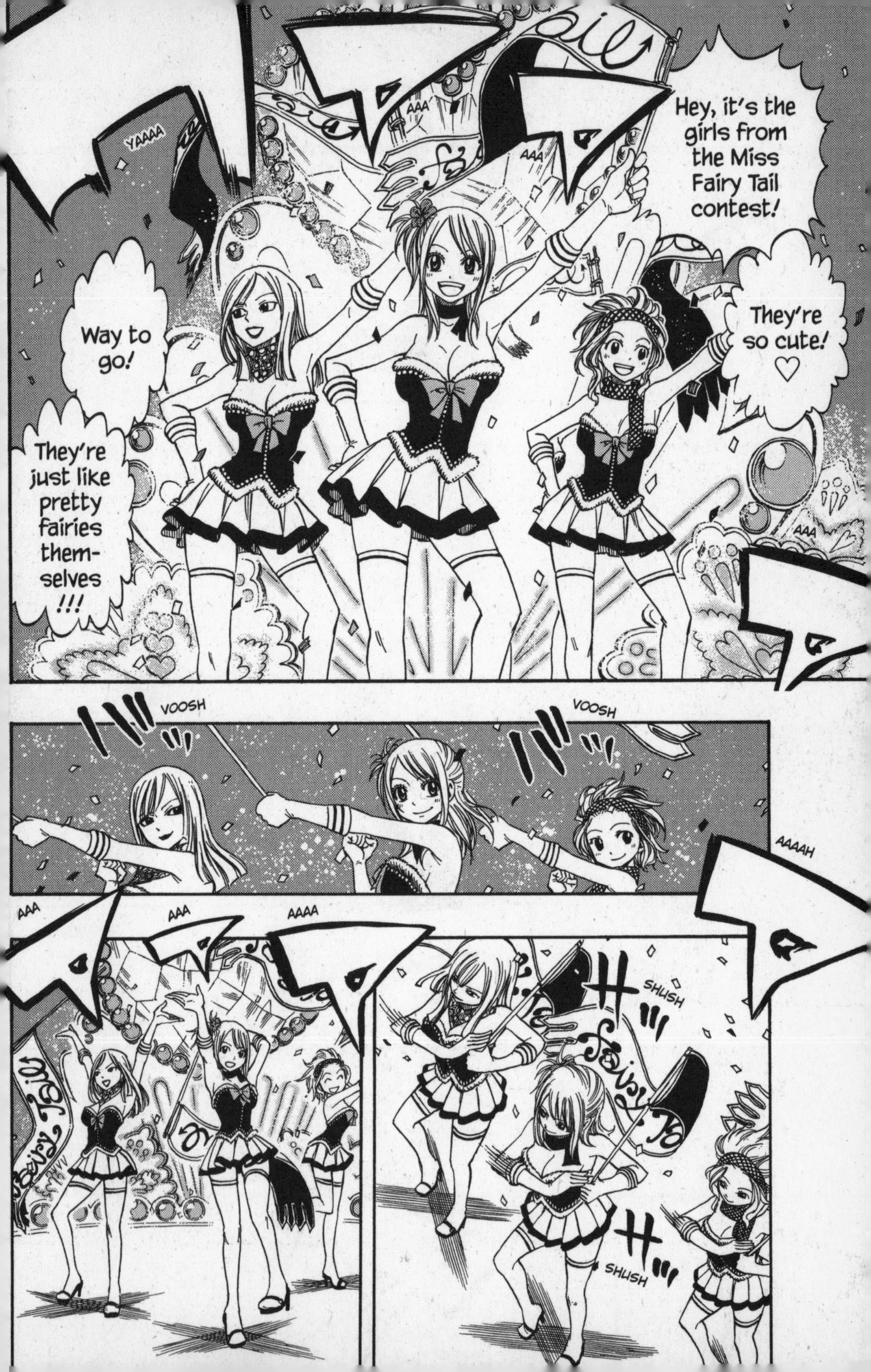
AAA
Hey, it's the girls from the Miss Fairy Tail contest!
They're so cute! ♡
AAA
YAAAA
Way to go!
They're just like pretty fairies themselves!!!
AAA
VOOSH
VOOSH
AAAAH
SHUSH
SHUSH
AAAA
AAA
AAA

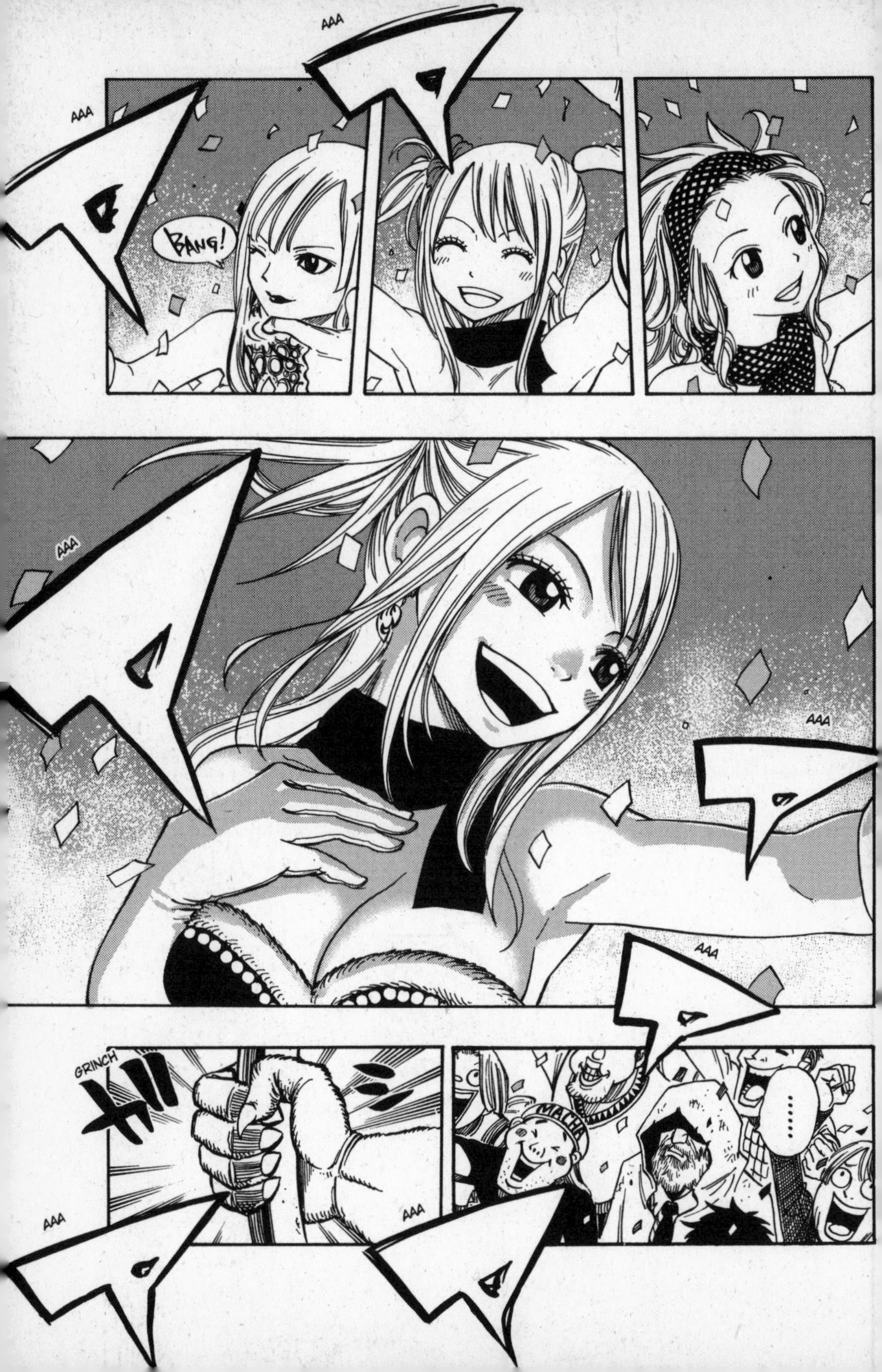AAA
AAA
BANG!
AAA
AAA
AAA
MACHA
AAA
GRINCH
AAA

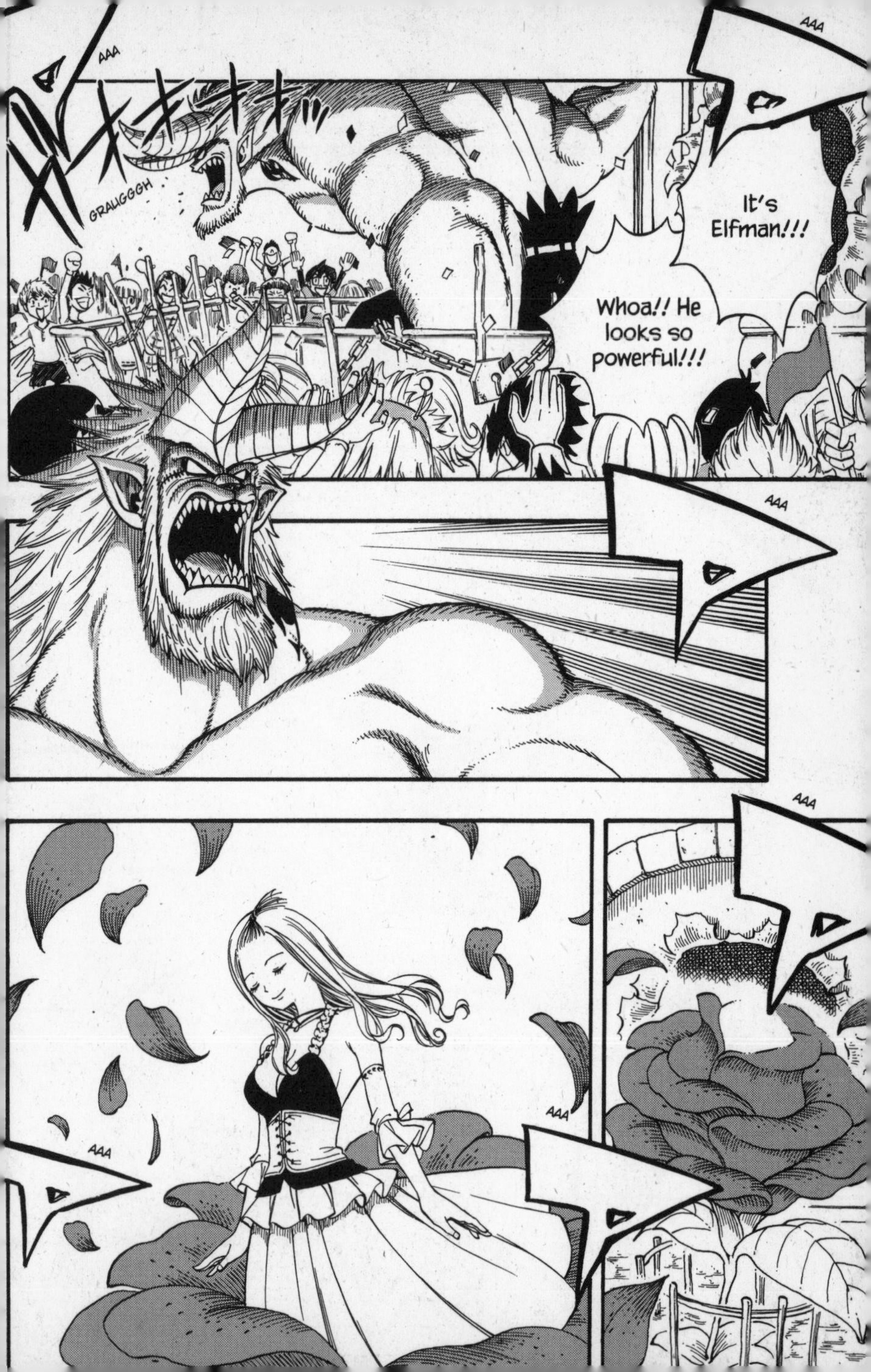
AAA
It's Elfman!!!
Whoa!! He looks so powerful!!!
AAA
GRAUGGGH
AAA
AAA
AAA
AAA

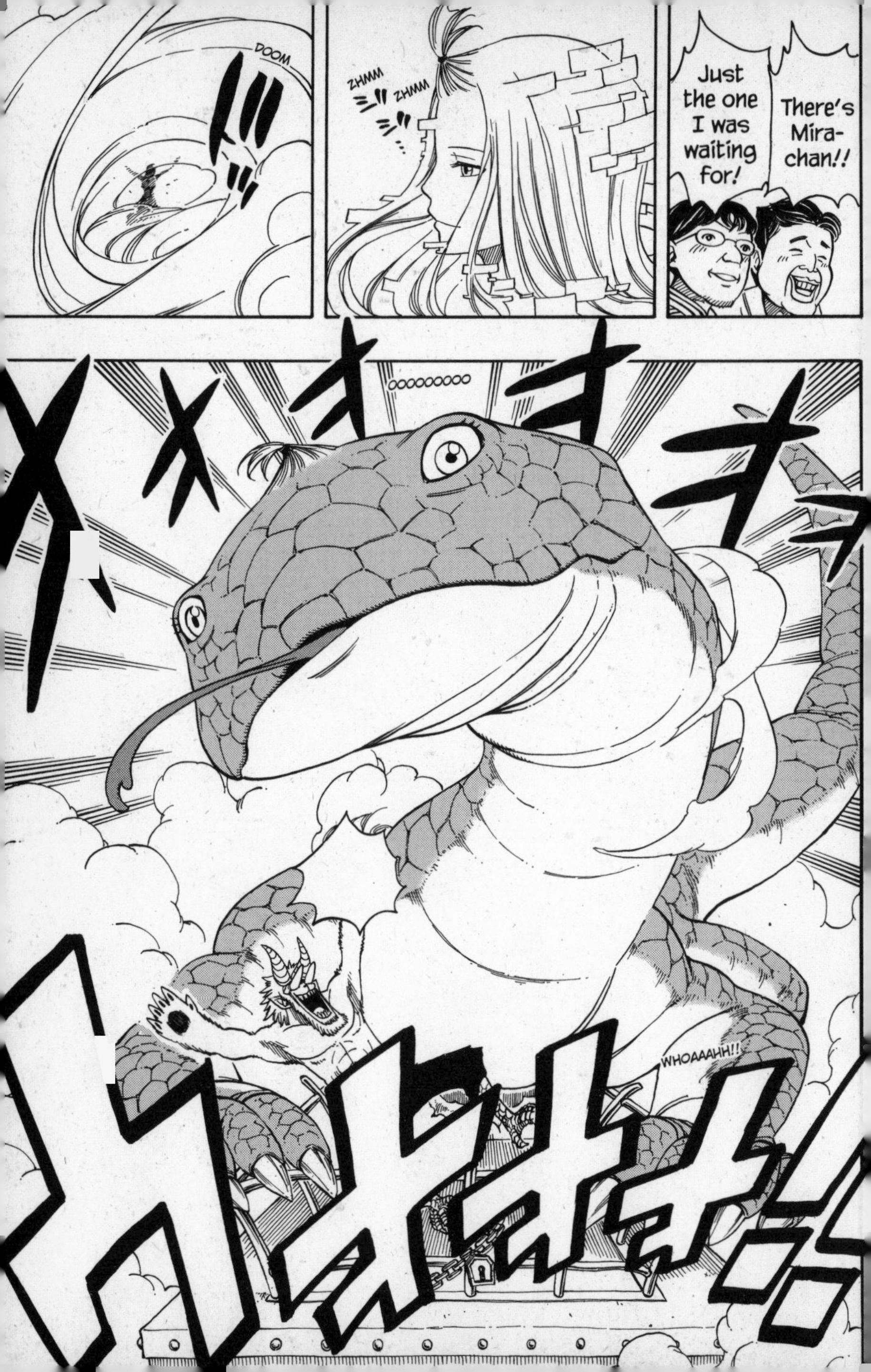
There's Mira-chan!!
Just the one I was waiting for!
ZHMM
ZHMM
DOOM
OOOOOOOOO
WHOAAAHH!!

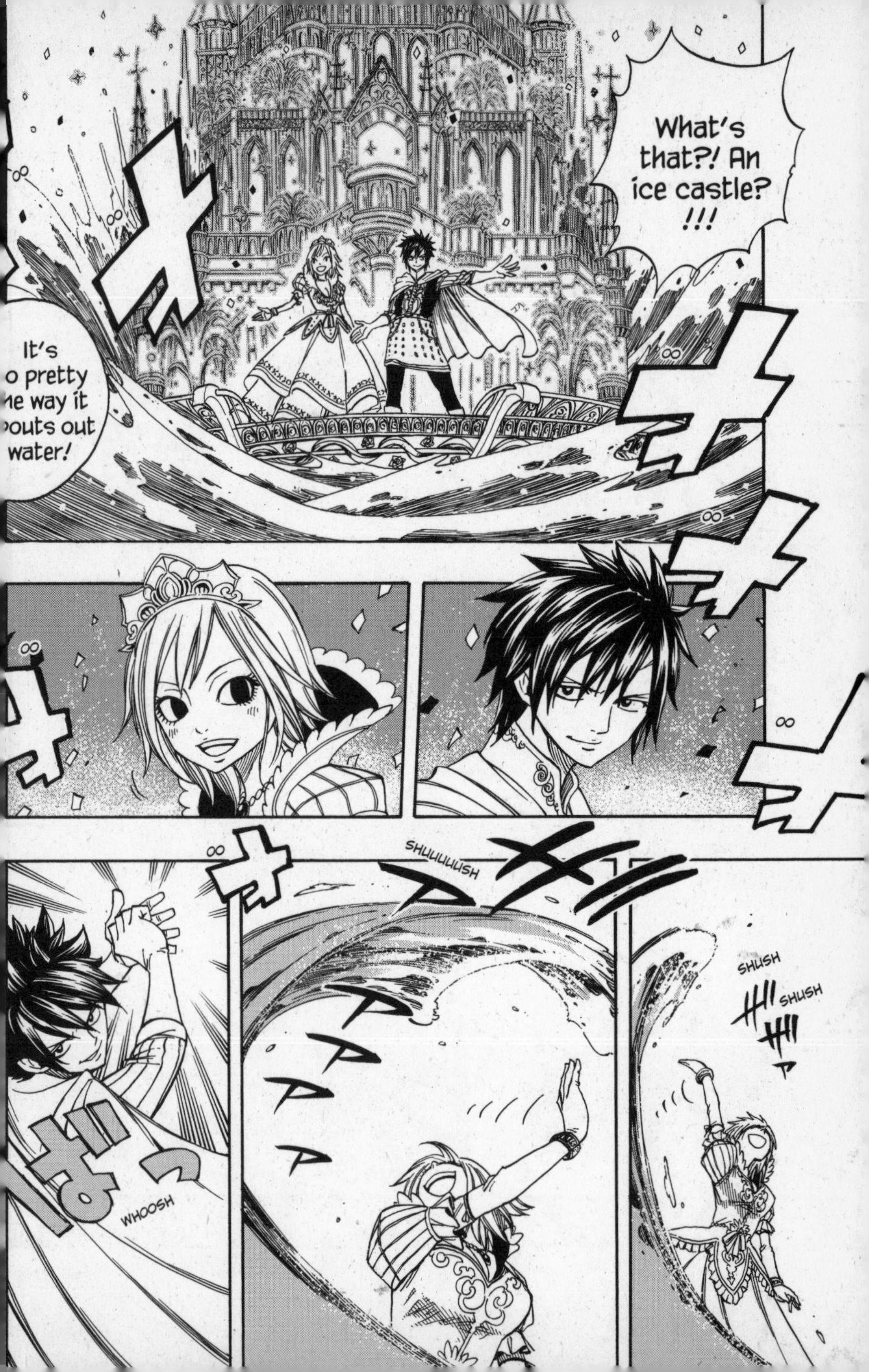
What's that?! An ice castle? !!!
It's o pretty ne way it pouts out water!
SHUSH
SHUSH
SHUUUUUSH
WHOOSH

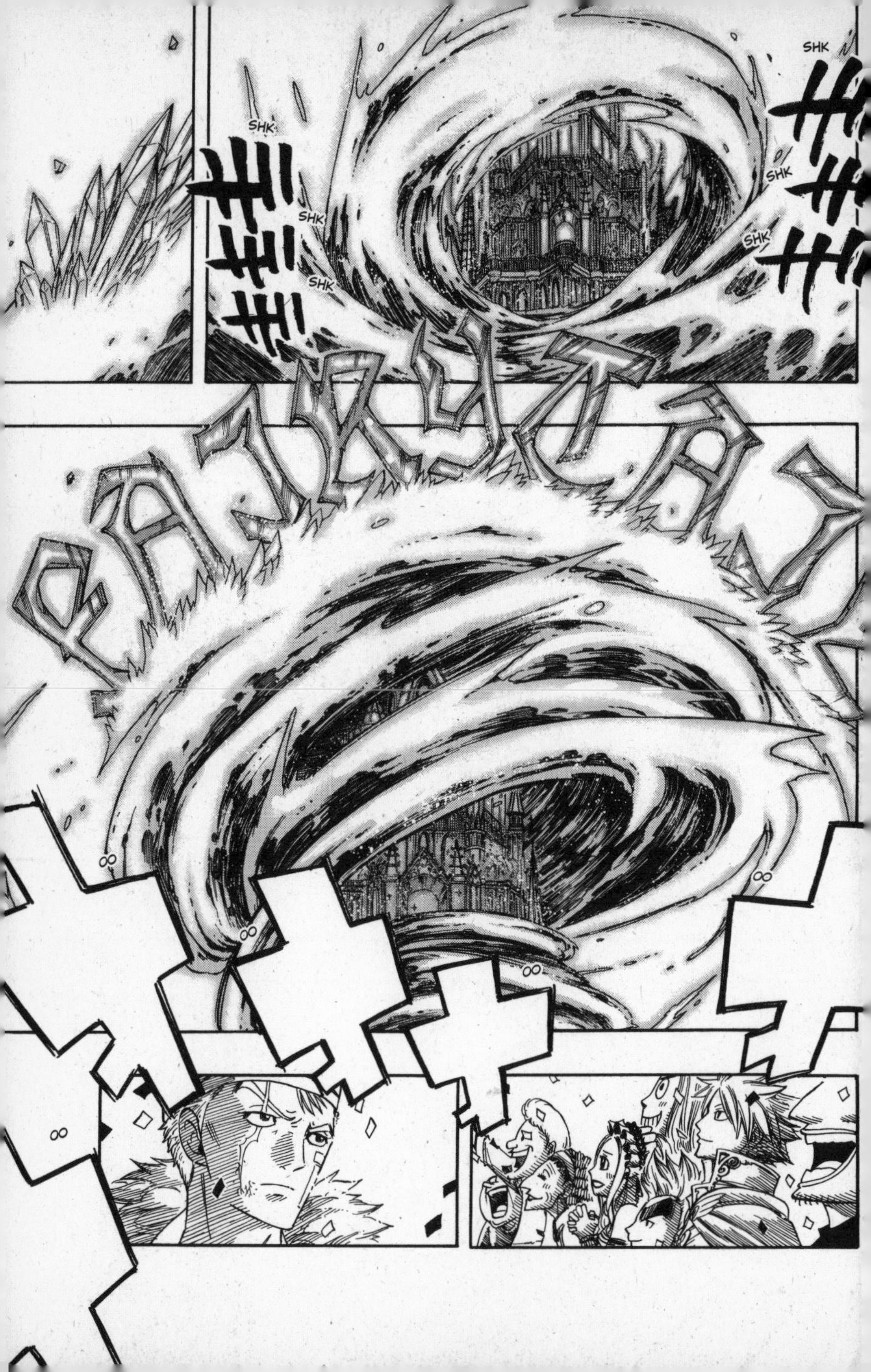
SHK
SHK
SHK
SHK
SHK
SHK

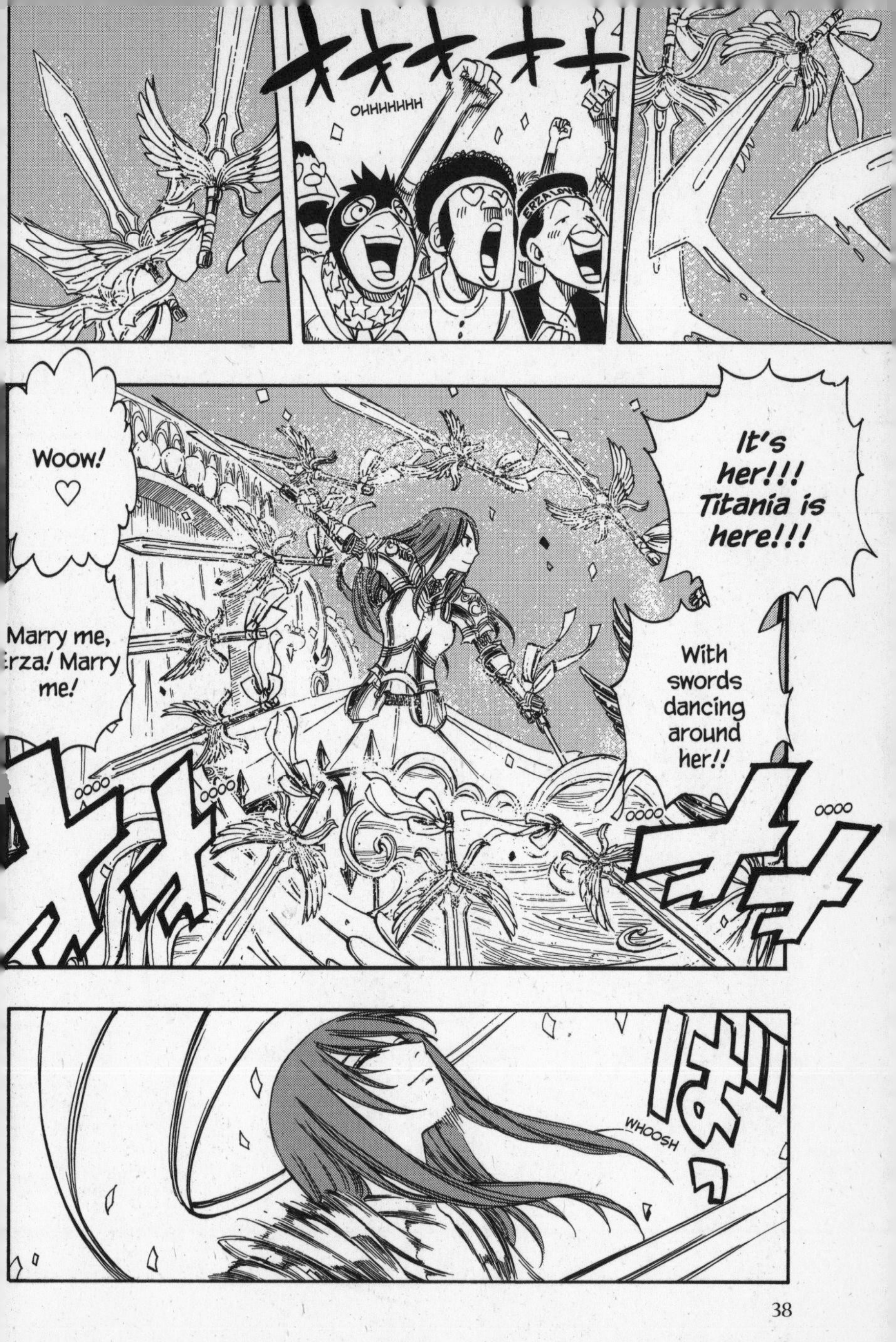
OHHHHHHH
It's her!!! Titania is here!!!
With swords dancing around her!!
oooo
oooo
Woow! ♡
Marry me, Erza! Marry me!
oooo
oooo
WHOOSH

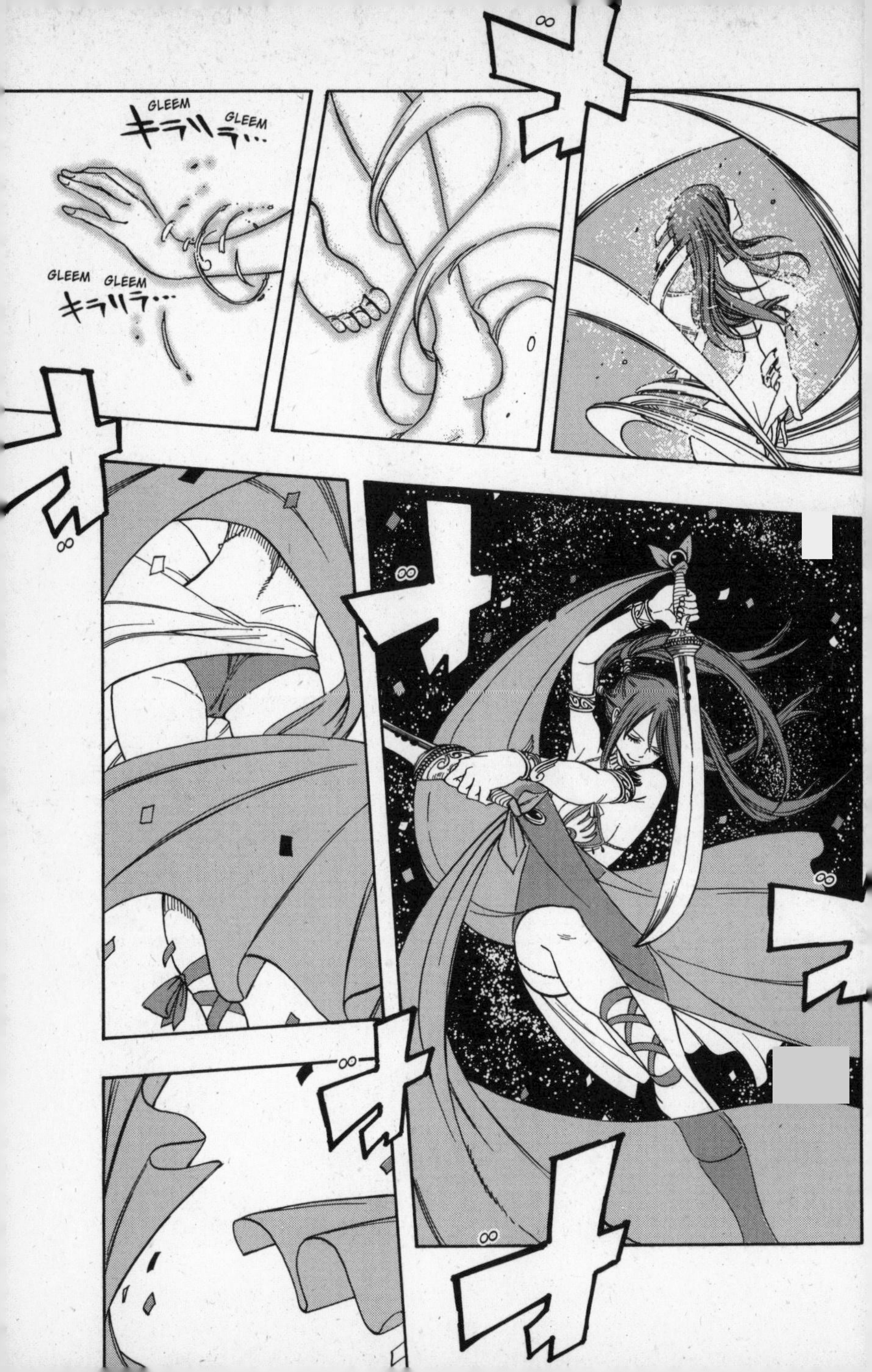
GLEEM GLEEM
キラリラ…
GLEEM GLEEM
キラリラ…

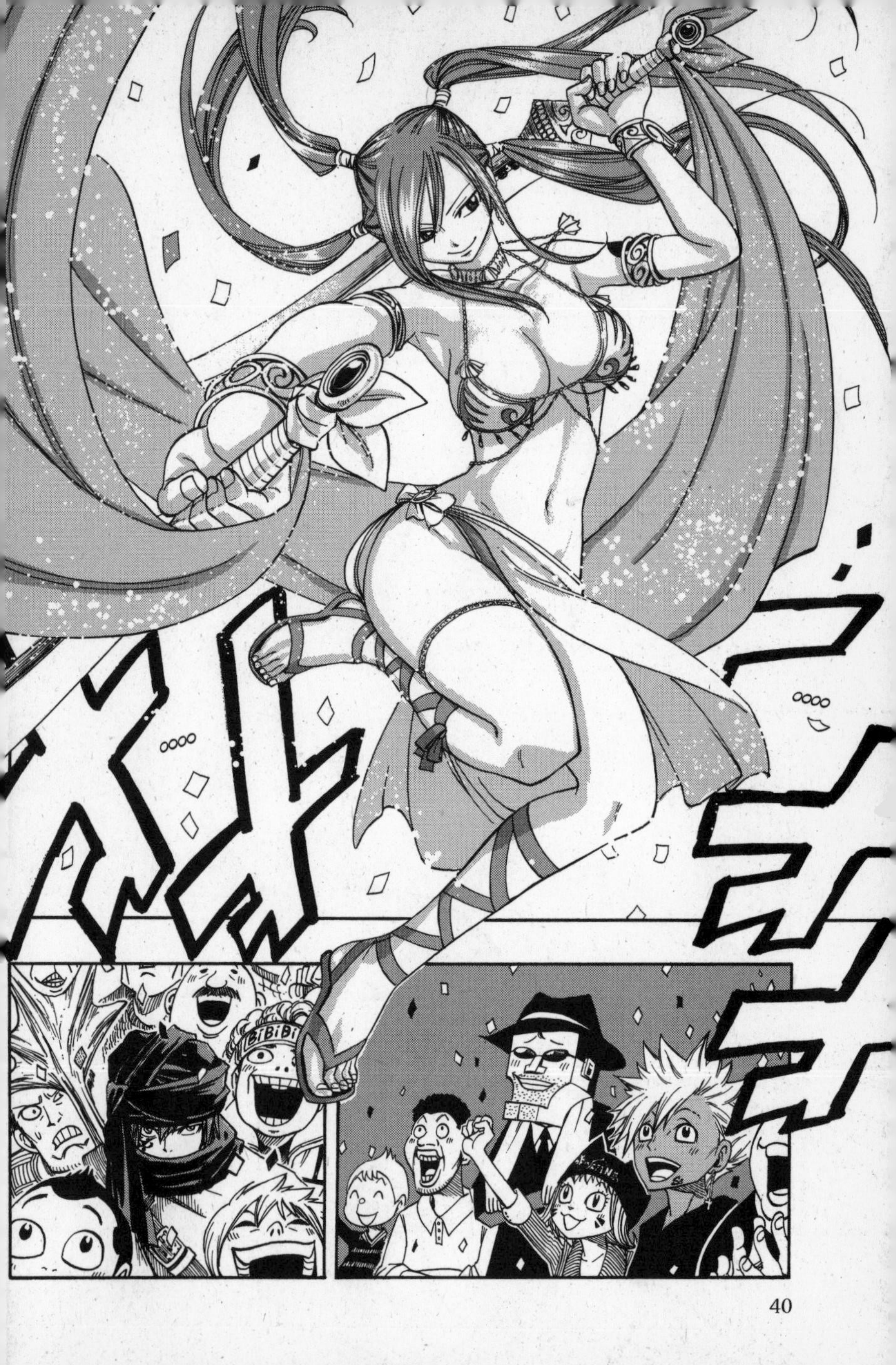
oooo
oooo
BiBiBi

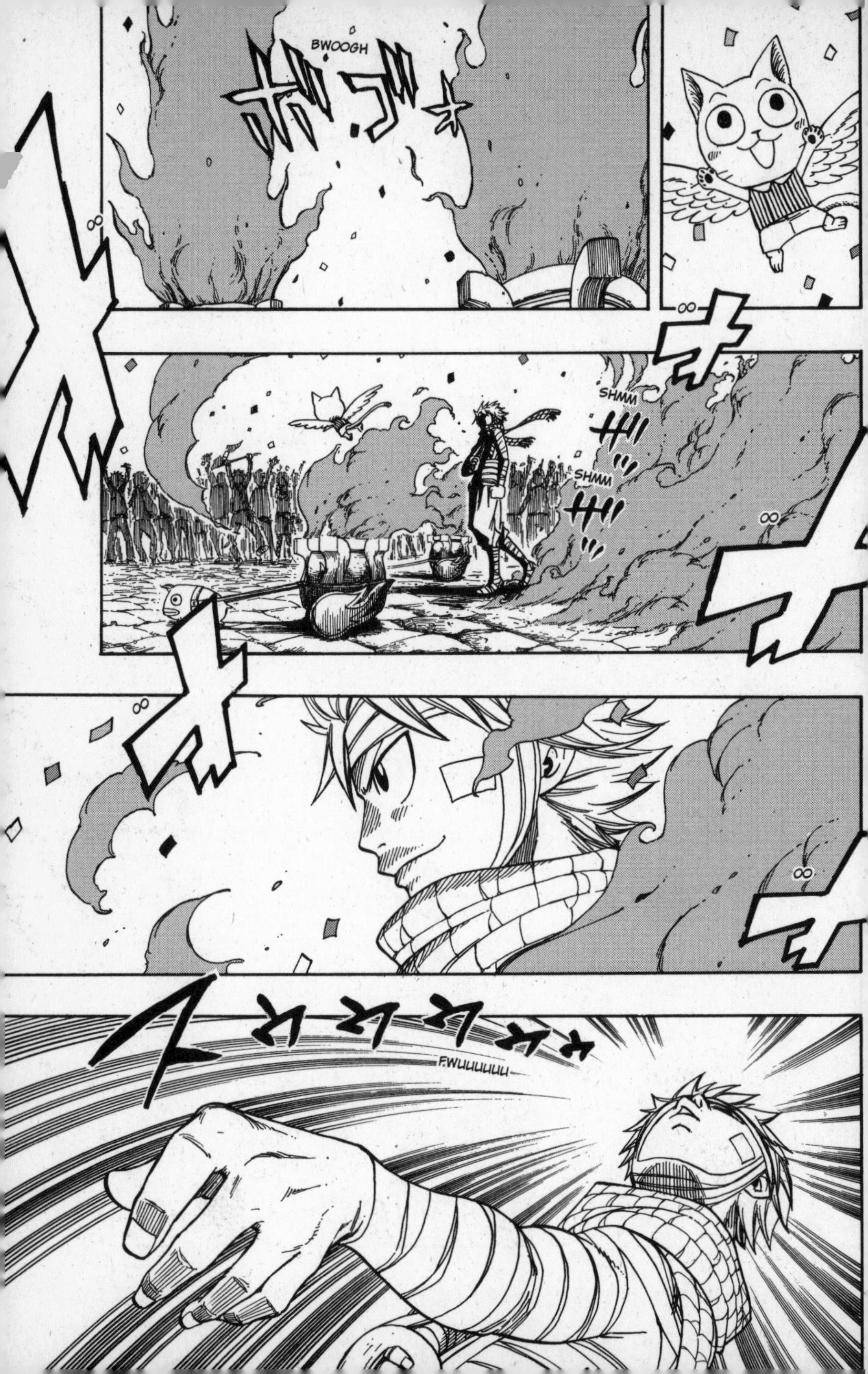
BWOOGH
SHMM
SHMM
FWUUUUUUU

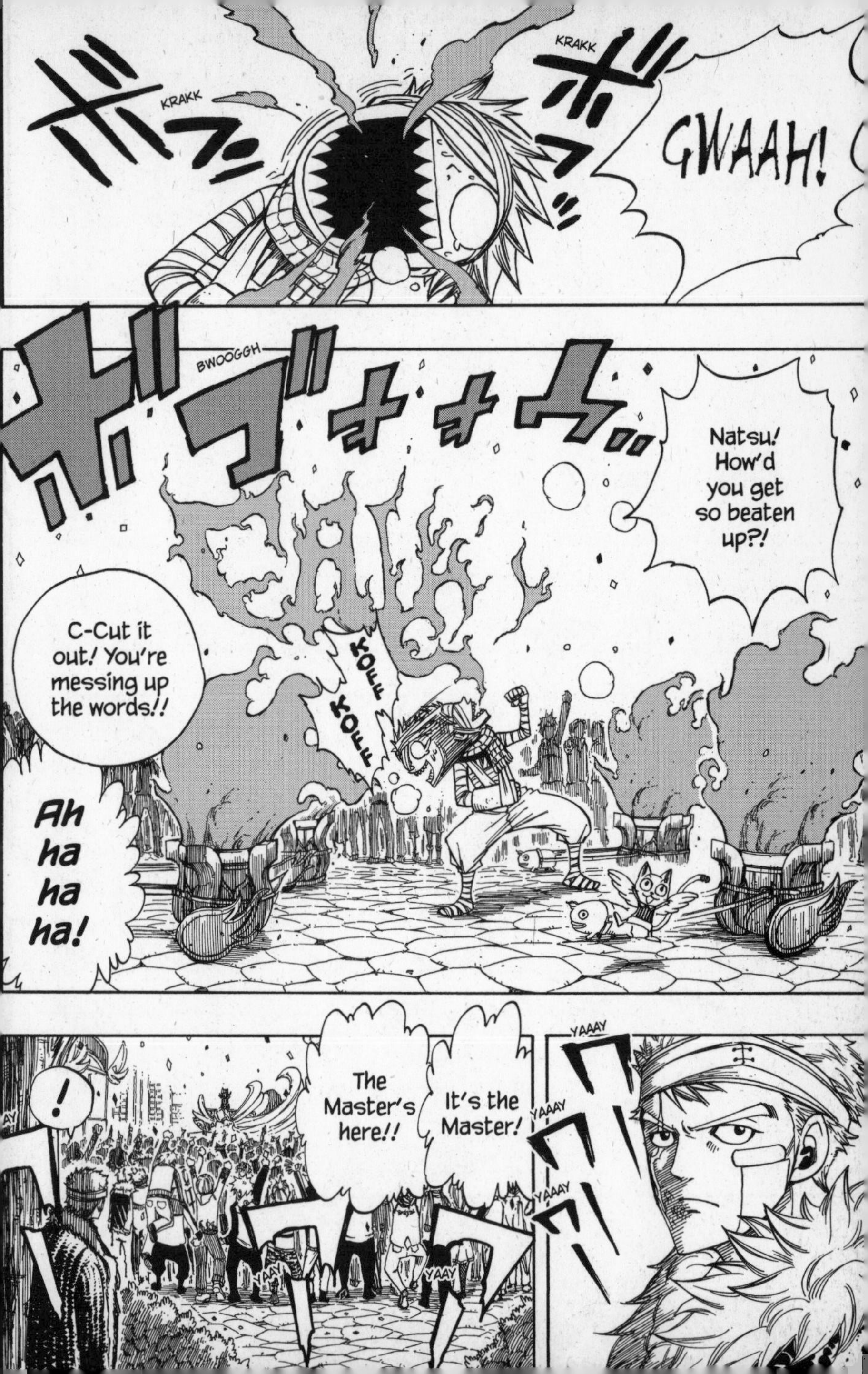
KRAKK
KRAKK
GWAAH!
BWOOGGH
Natsu! How'd you get so beaten up?!
KOFF KOFF
C-Cut it out! You're messing up the words!!
Ah ha ha ha!
YAAAY
YAAAY
YAAAY
It's the Master!
The Master's here!!
!
YAAY
YAAY

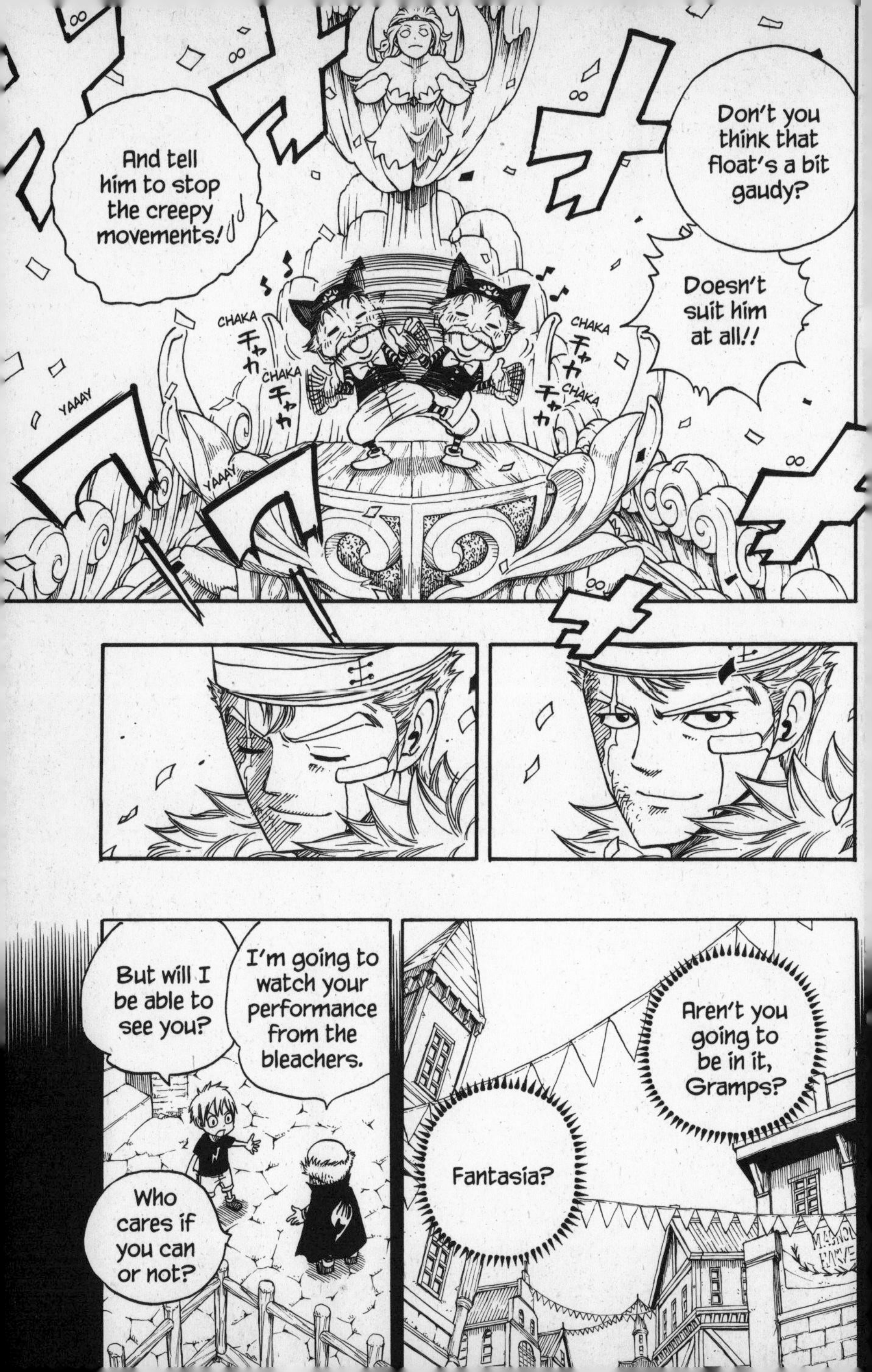
Don't you think that float's a bit gaudy?
Doesn't suit him at all!!
And tell him to stop the creepy movements!
CHAKA チャカ
CHAKA チャカ
CHAKA チャカ
CHAKA チャカ
YAAAY
YAAAY
Aren't you going to be in it, Gramps?
Fantasia?
I'm going to watch your performance from the bleachers.
But will I be able to see you?
Who cares if you can or not?

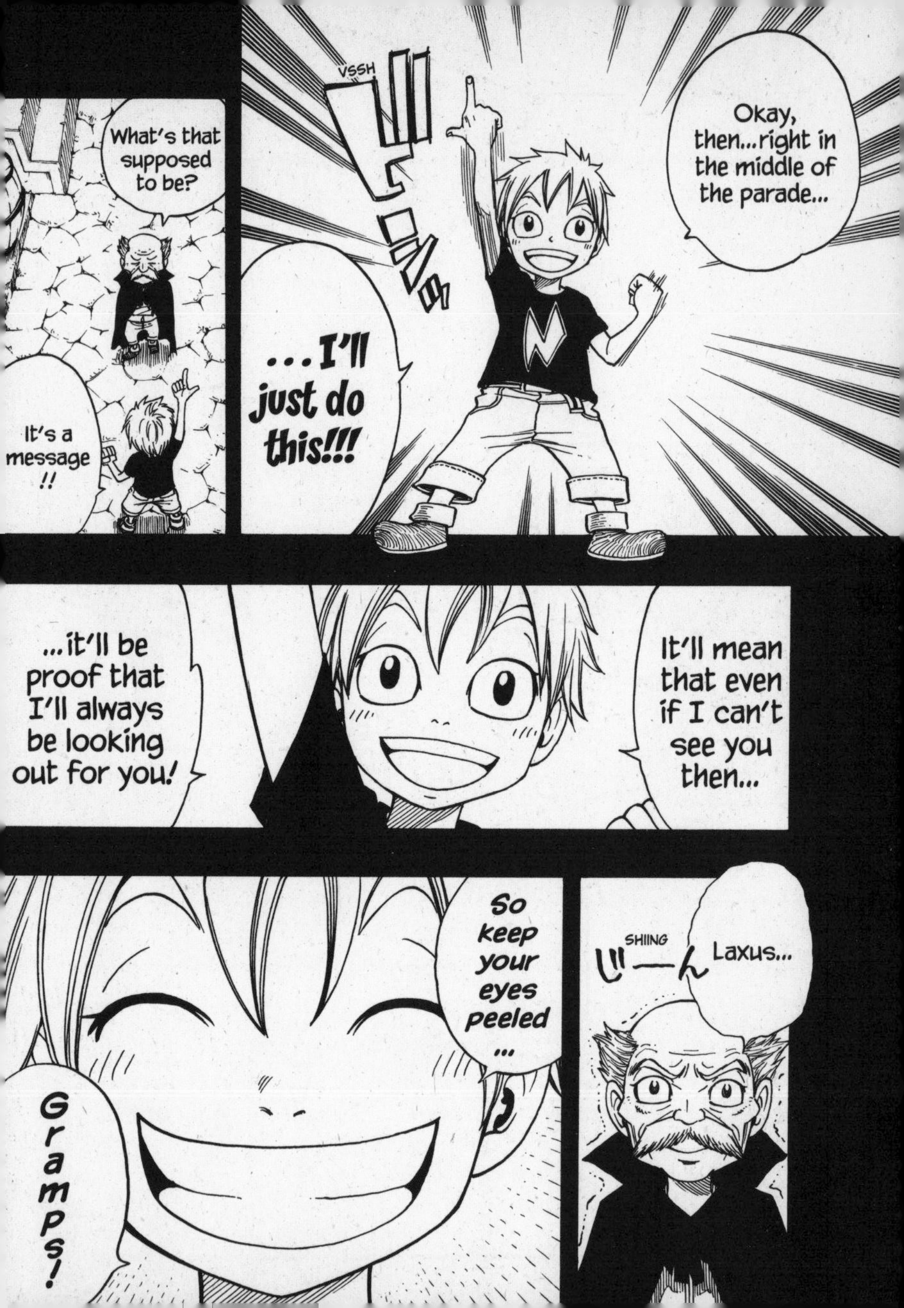
Okay, then...right in the middle of the parade...
VSSH
...I'll just do this!!!
What's that supposed to be?
It's a message!!
It'll mean that even if I can't see you then...
...it'll be proof that I'll always be looking out for you!
SHIING
Laxus...
So keep your eyes peeled...
Gramps!

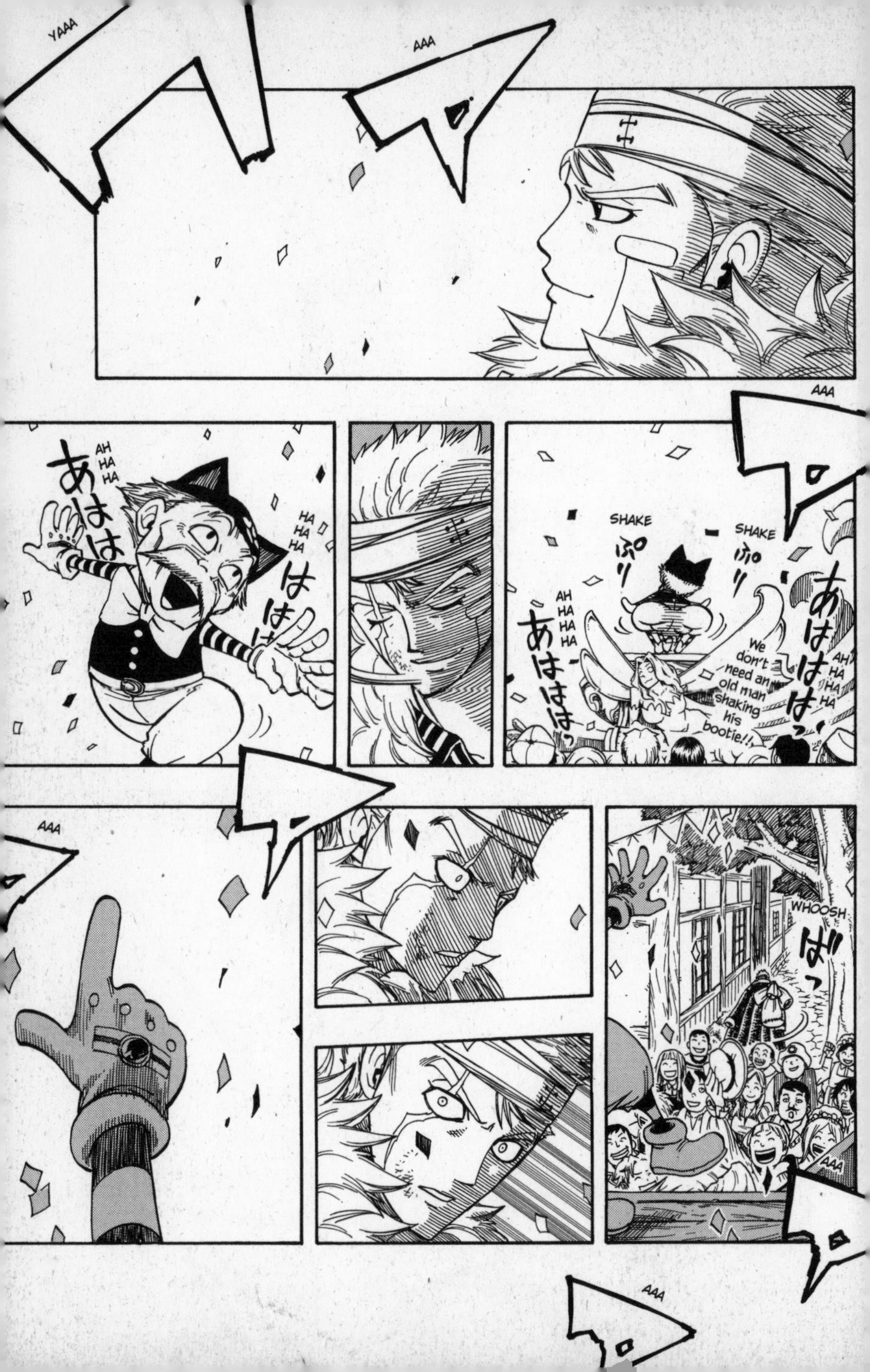
YAAA
AAA
AAA
SHAKE
ぷり
SHAKE
ぷり
AH HA HA HA HA
あははは
AH HA HA HA
あははははっ
We don't need an old man shaking his bootie!!
AH HA HA
あはは
HA HA HA
ははは
WHOOSH
ばっ
AAA
AAA
AAA

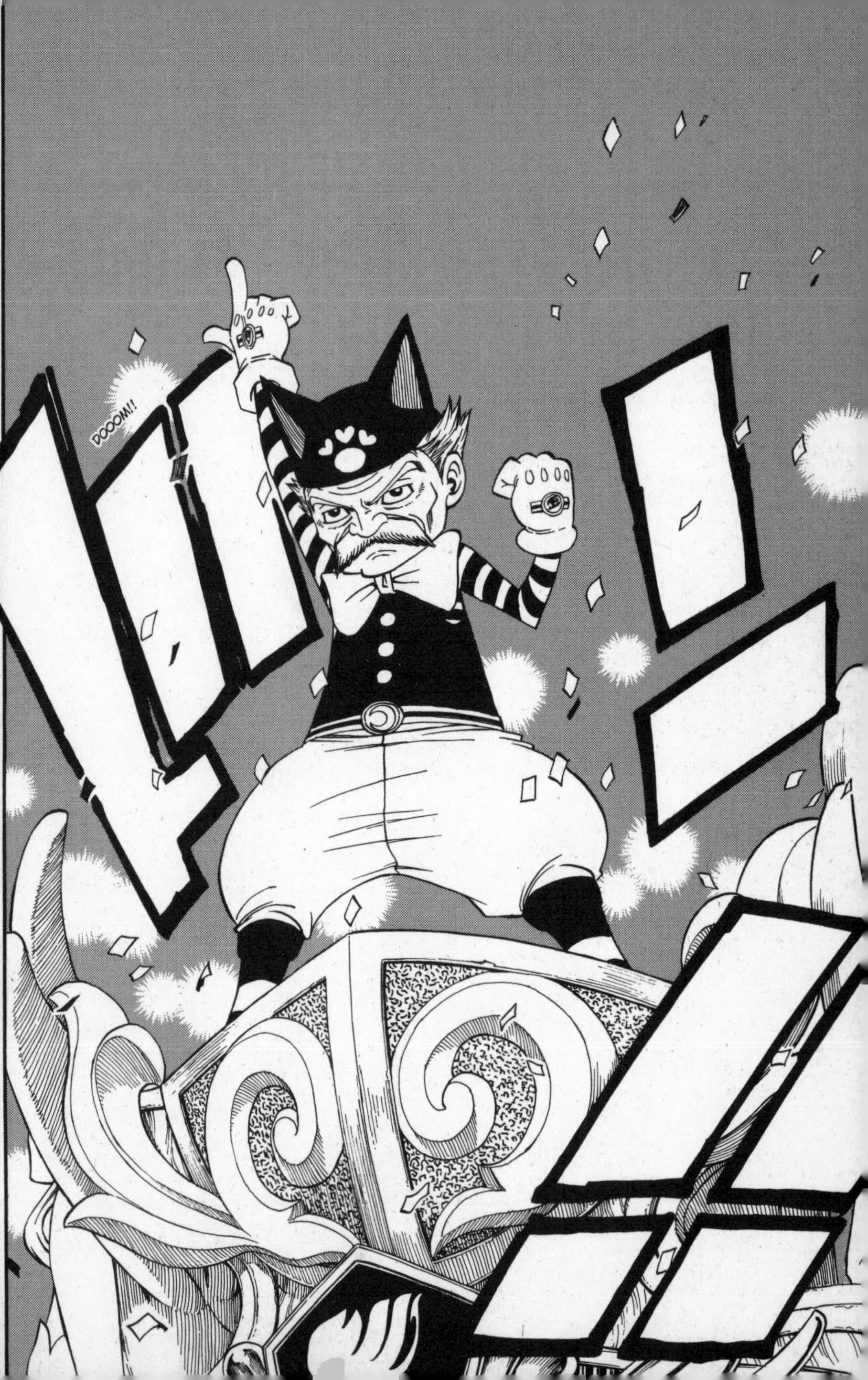
DOOOM!!

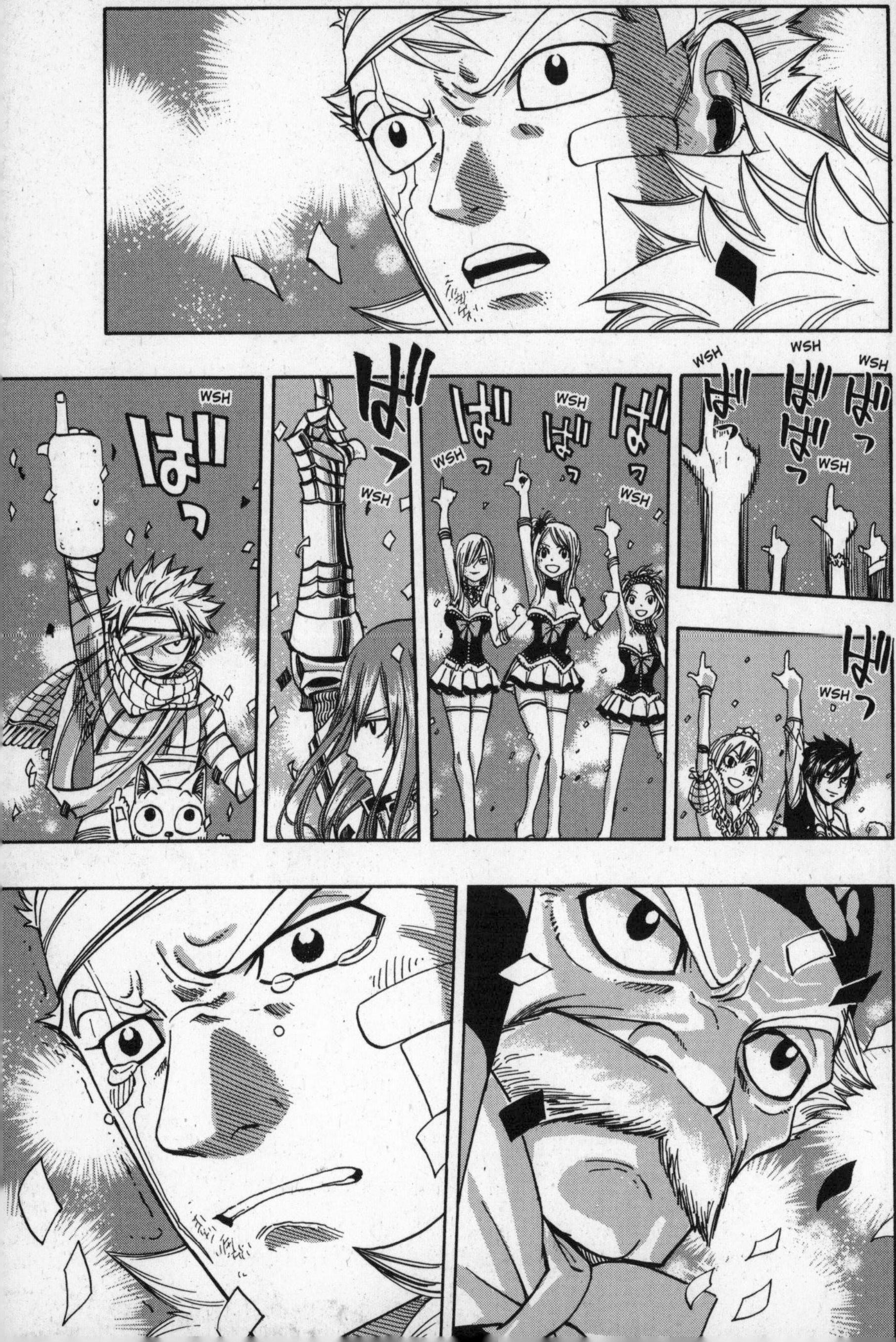
WSH
ばっ
WSH
ばっ
WSH
ばっ
WSH
ばっ
WSH
ばっ
WSH
ばっ
WSH
ばっ
WSH
ばっ
WSH
ばっ
WSH
ばっ
WSH

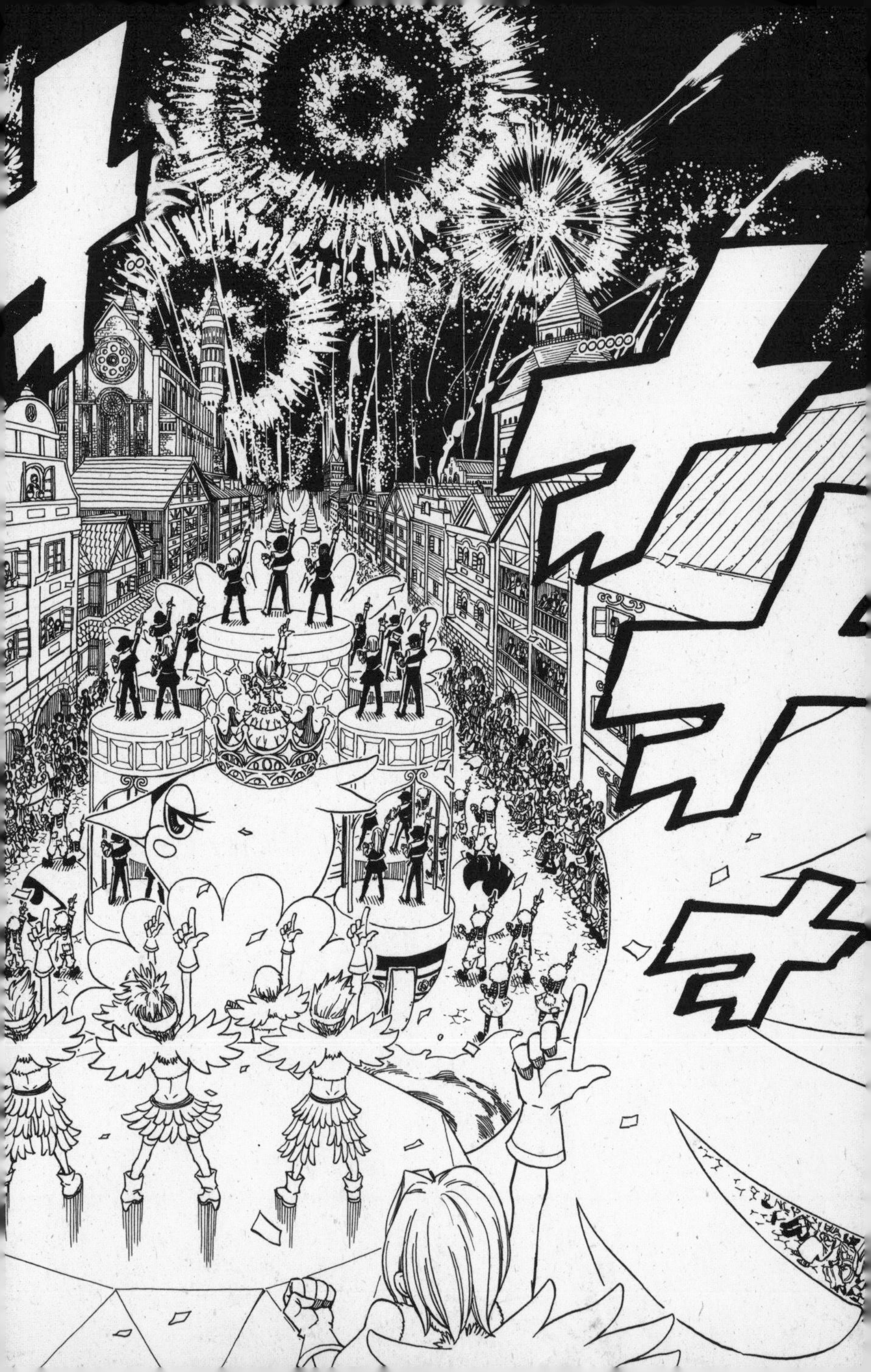

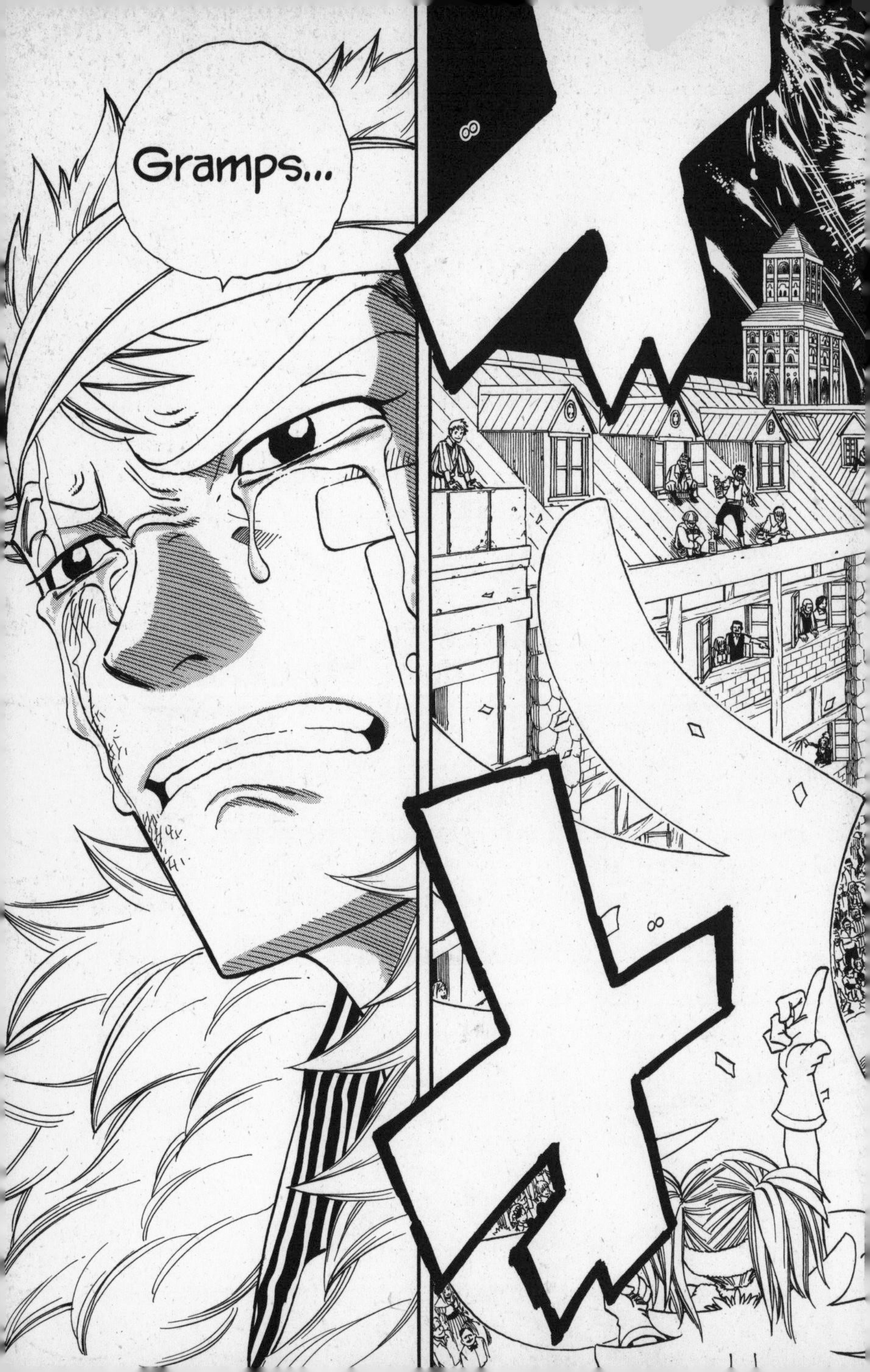
Gramps...

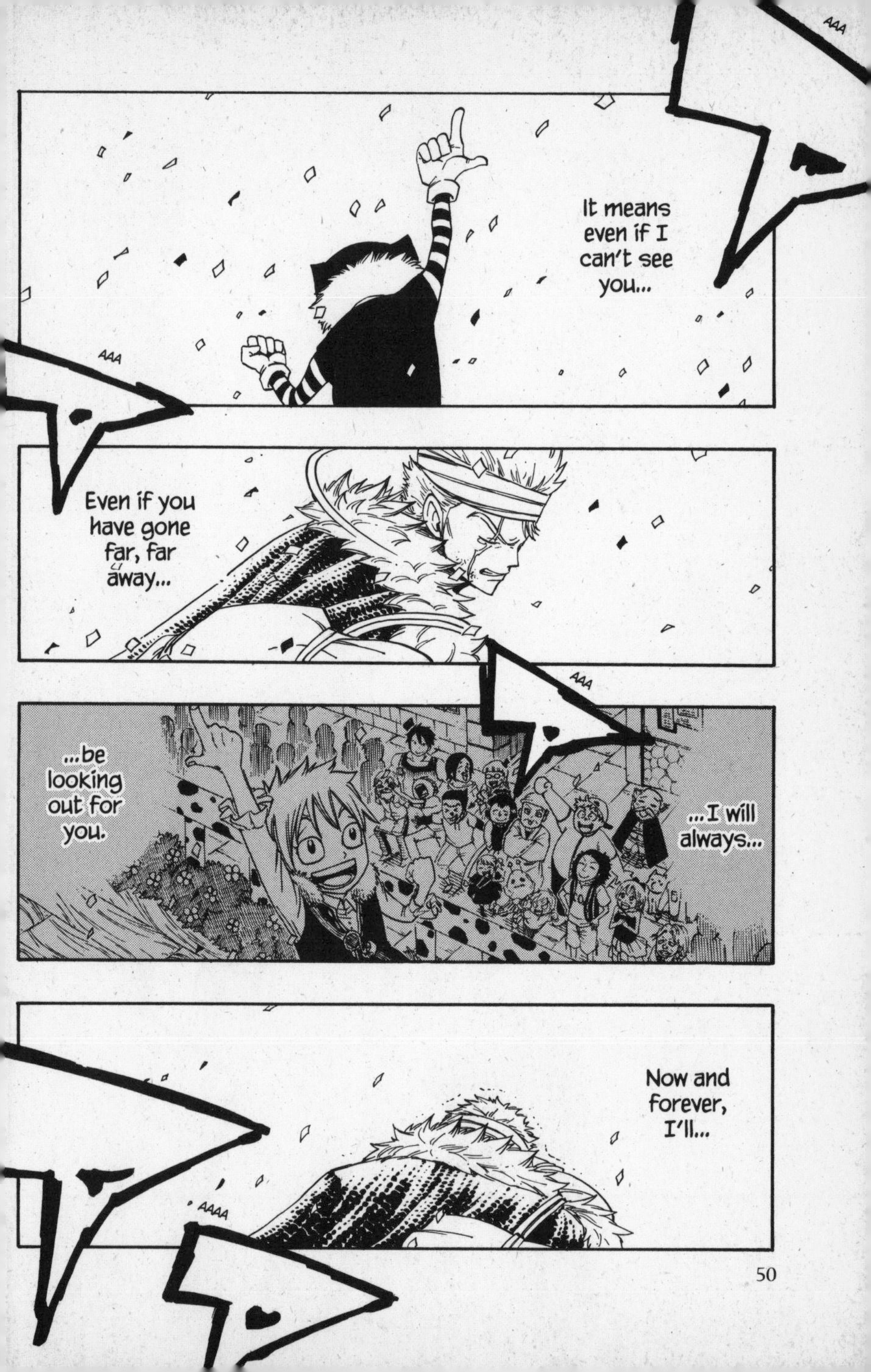
AAA
It means even if I can't see you...
AAA
Even if you have gone far, far away...
AAA
...I will always...
...be looking out for you.
Now and forever, I'll...
AAAA

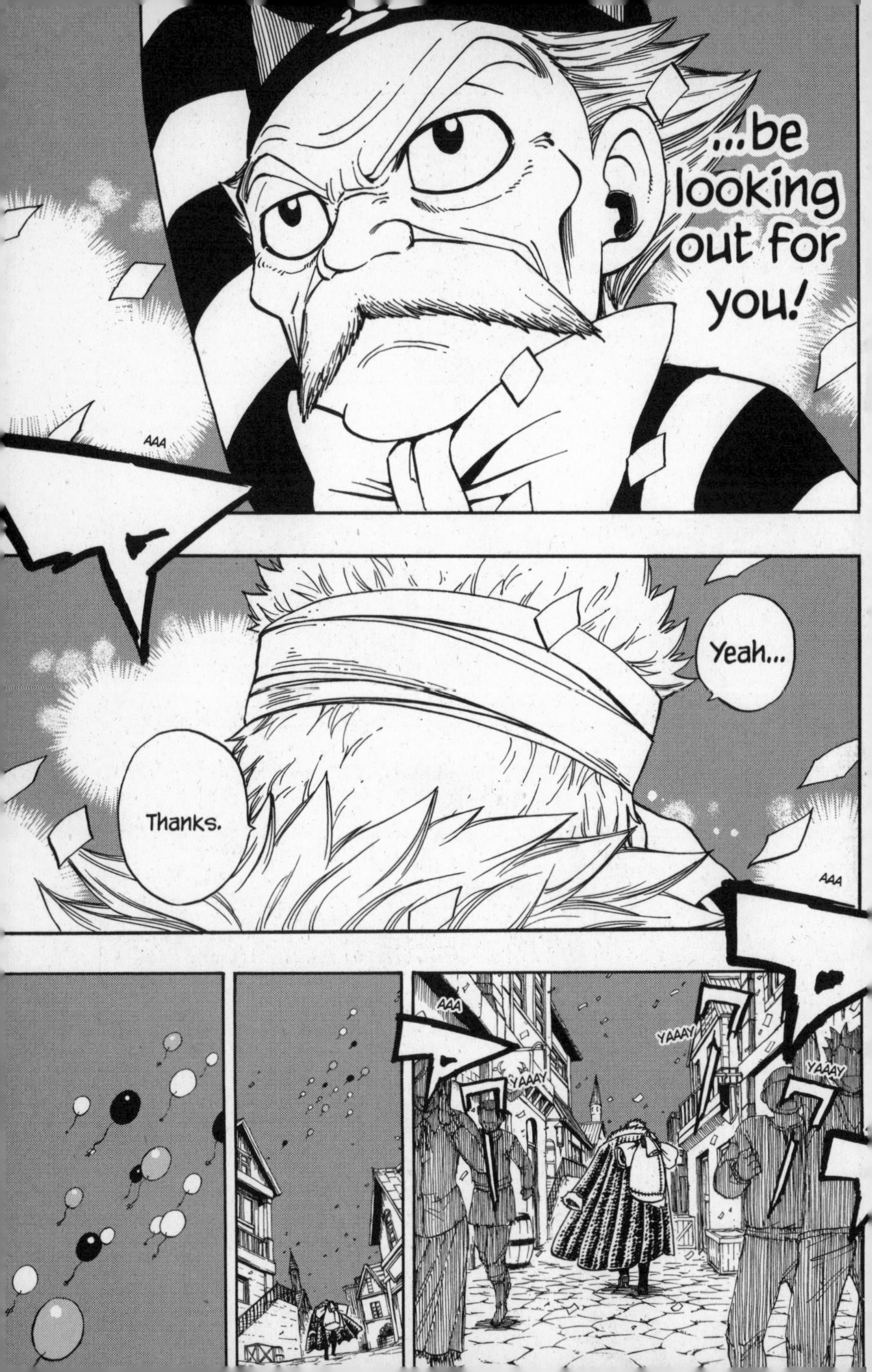
...be looking out for you!
AAA
Yeah...
Thanks.
AAA
YAAAY
YAAAY
AAA
YAAAY

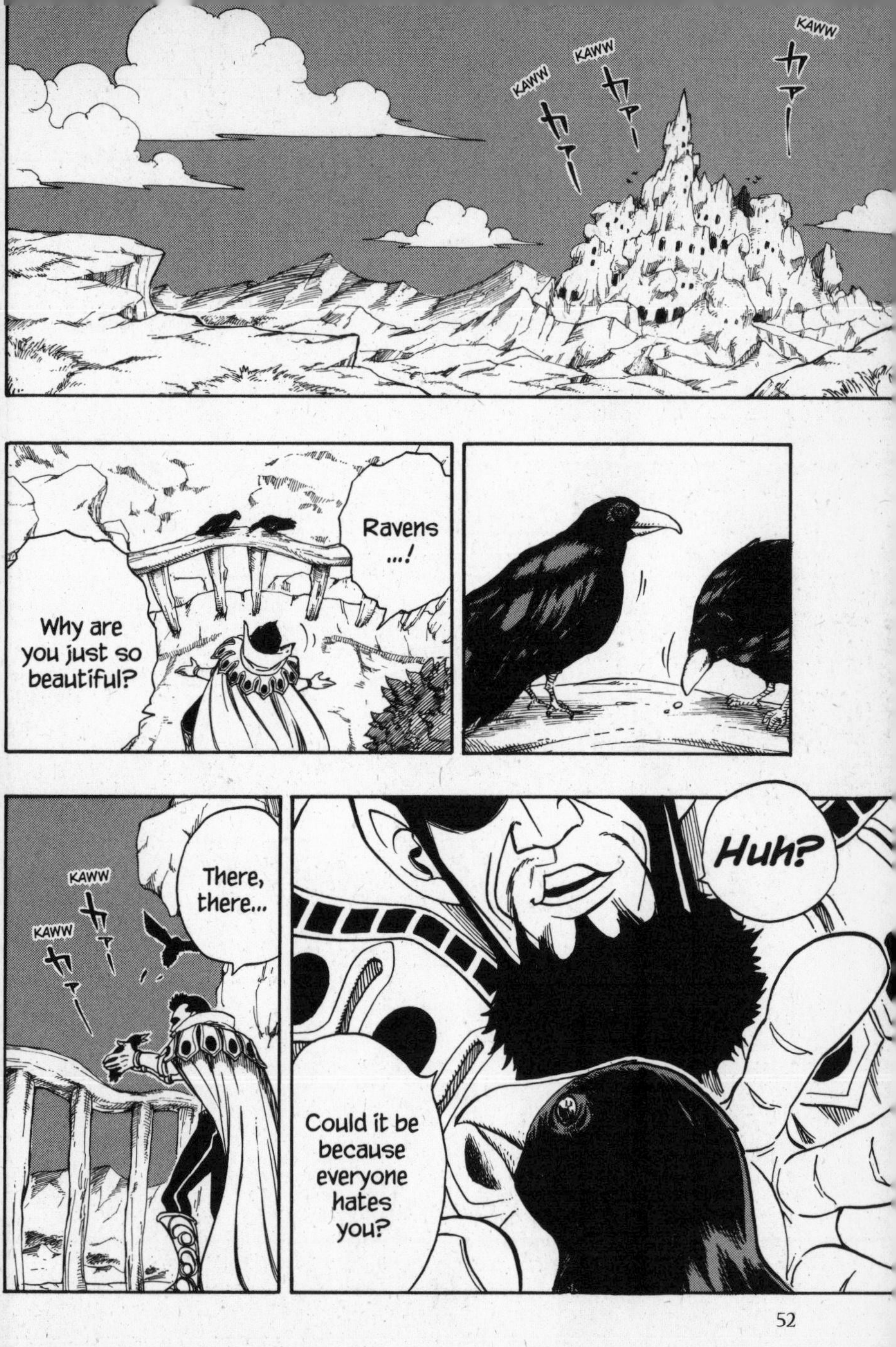
KAWW
KAWW
KAWW
Ravens ...!
Why are you just so beautiful?
Huh?
Could it be because everyone hates you?
There, there...
KAWW
KAWW

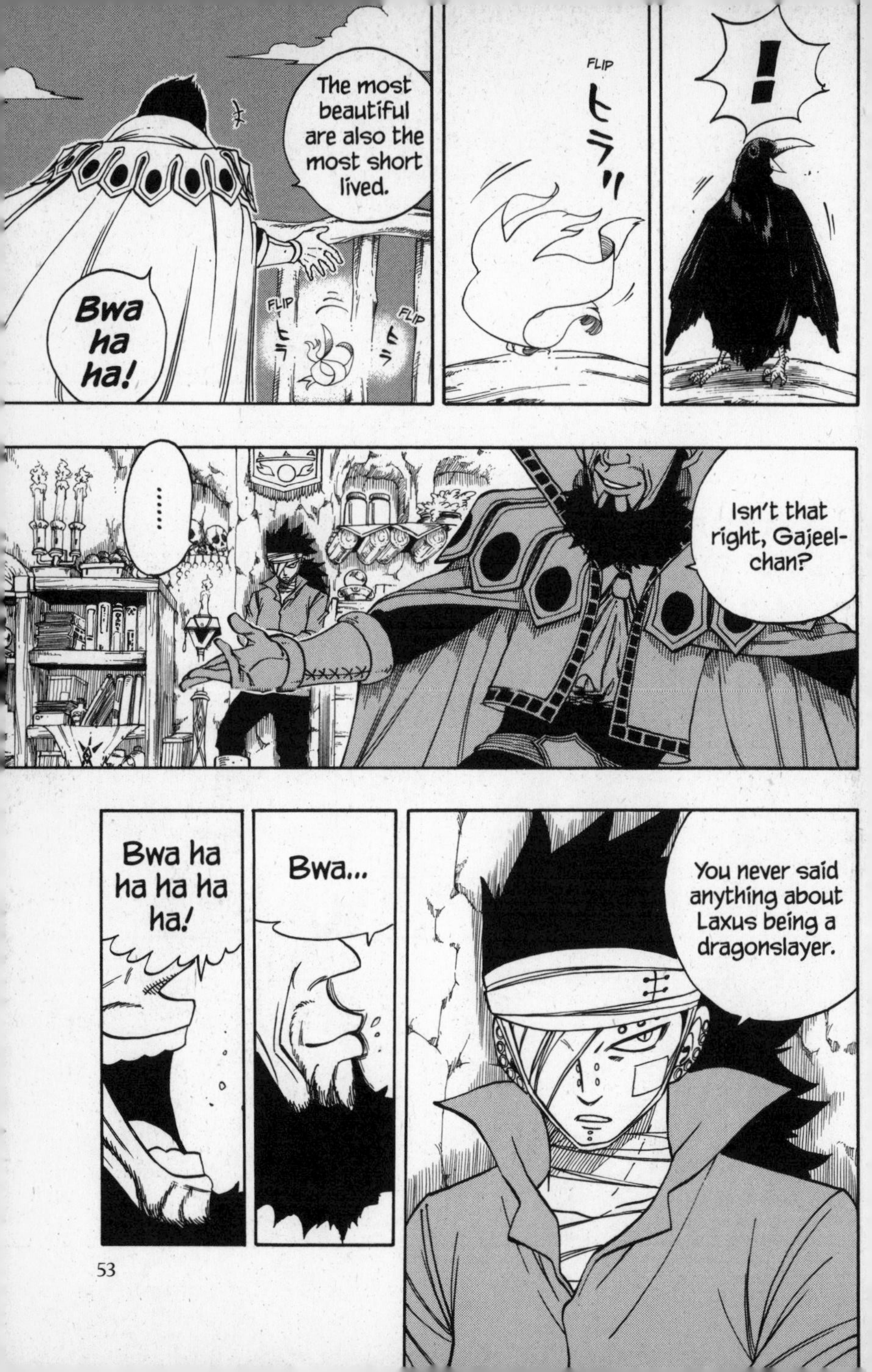
!
FLIP
ヒラッ
The most beautiful are also the most short lived.
Bwa ha ha!
FLIP
ヒラ
FLIP
ヒラ
Isn't that right, Gajeel-chan?
......
You never said anything about Laxus being a dragonslayer.
Bwa...
Bwa ha ha ha ha ha!

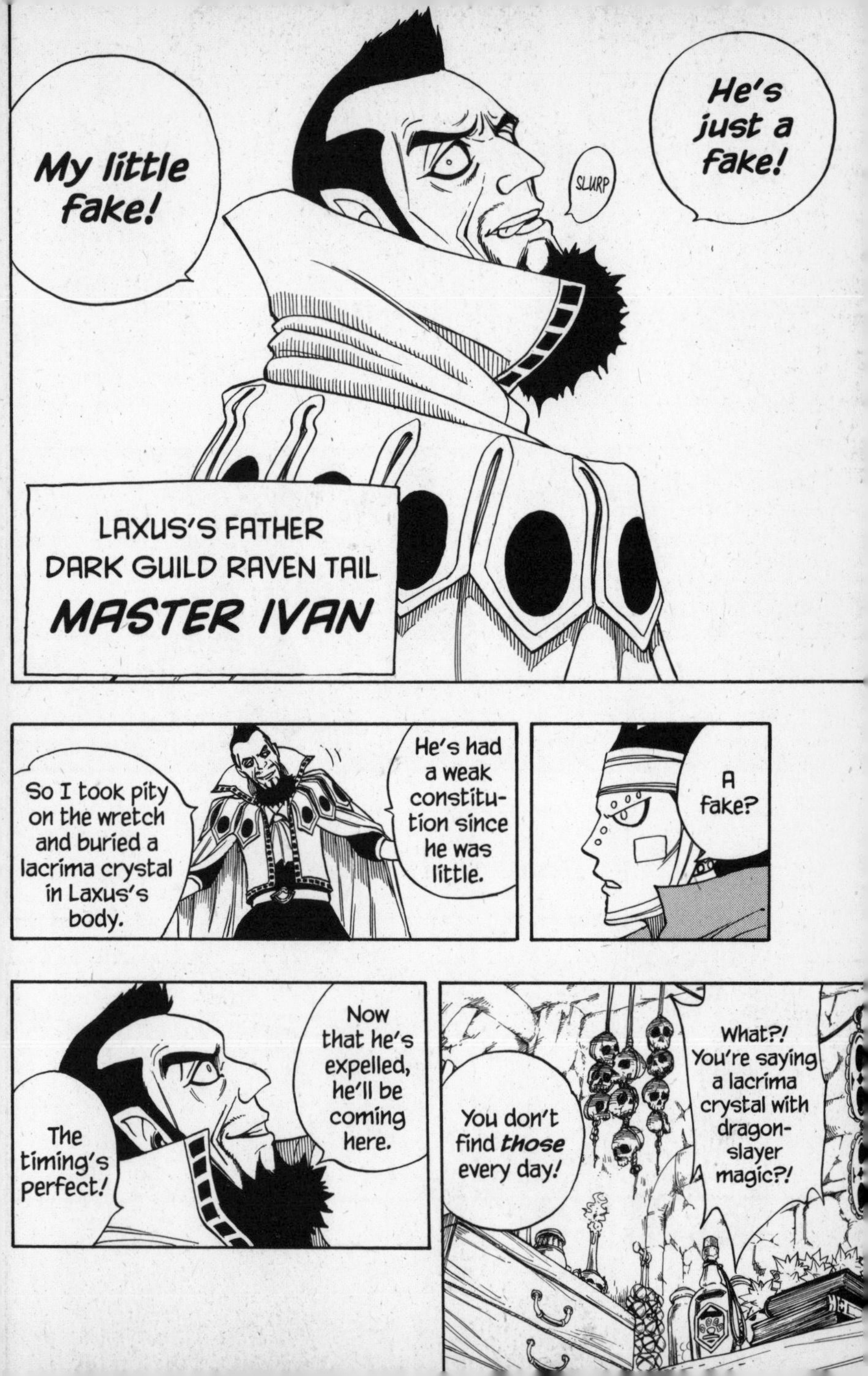
He's just a fake!
SLURP
My little fake!
LAXUS'S FATHER
DARK GUILD RAVEN TAIL
MASTER IVAN
A fake?
He's had a weak constitution since he was little.
So I took pity on the wretch and buried a lacrima crystal in Laxus's body.
What?! You're saying a lacrima crystal with dragon-slayer magic?!
You don't find *those* every day!
Now that he's expelled, he'll be coming here.
The timing's perfect!

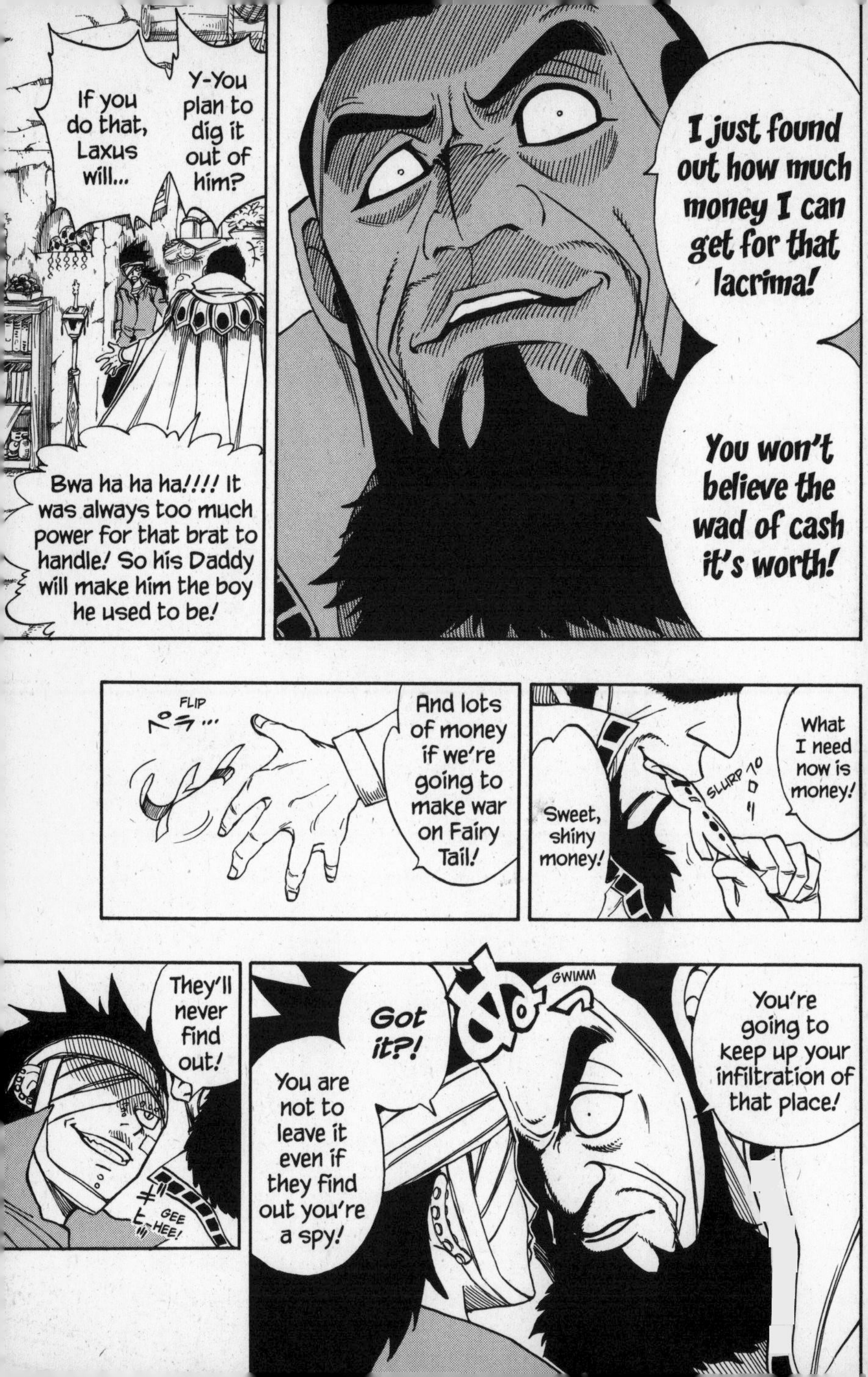
I just found out how much money I can get for that lacrima!
You won't believe the wad of cash it's worth!
Y-You plan to dig it out of him?
If you do that, Laxus will...
Bwa ha ha ha!!!! It was always too much power for that brat to handle! So his Daddy will make him the boy he used to be!
What I need now is money!
SLURP
Sweet, shiny money!
And lots of money if we're going to make war on Fairy Tail!
FLIP
You're going to keep up your infiltration of that place!
GWIMM
Got it?!
You are not to leave it even if they find out you're a spy!
They'll never find out!
GEE HEE!

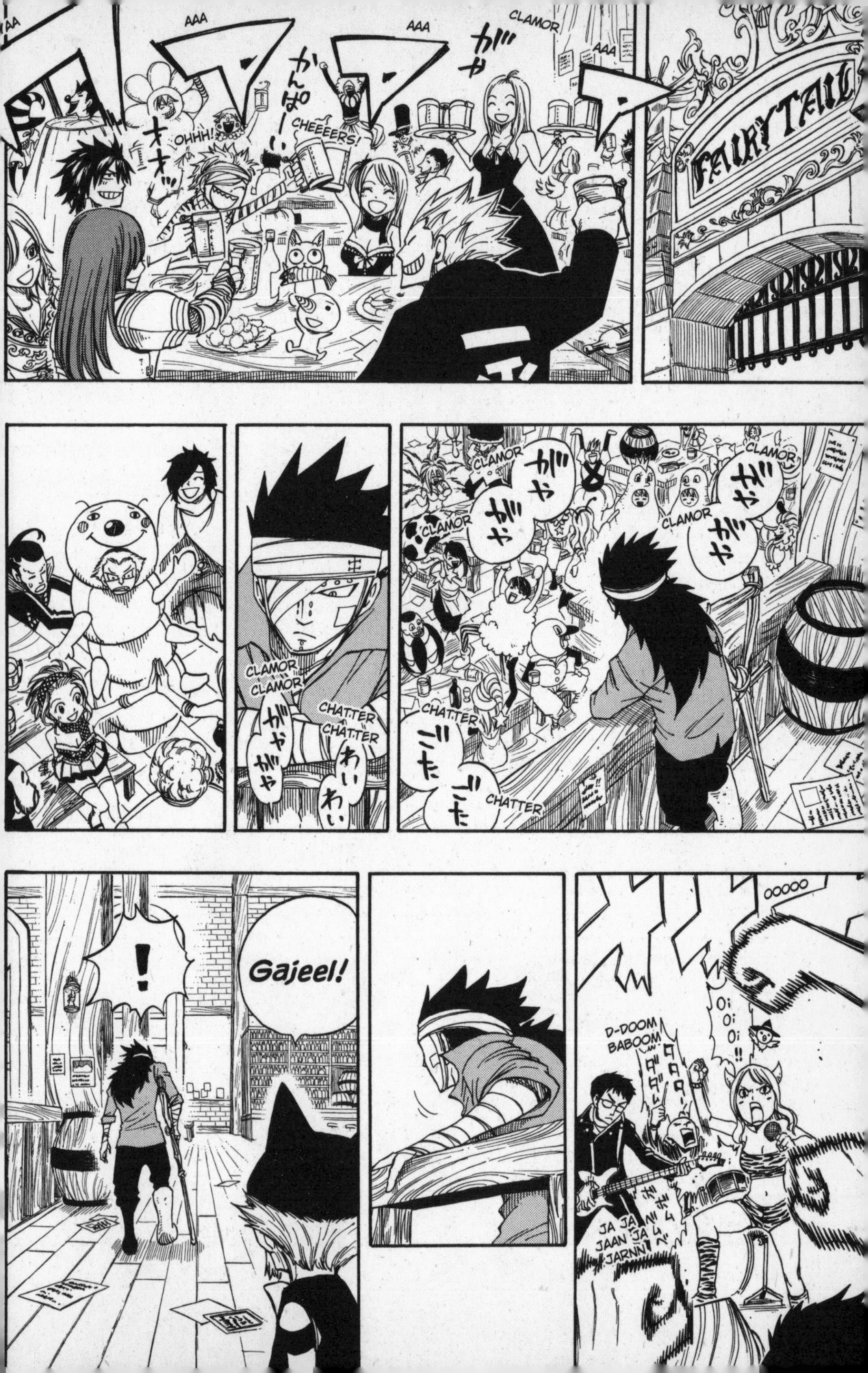

FAIRY TAIL
AAA
CLAMOR
ガヤ
AAA
かんぱーい
CHEEEERS!
AAA
オオッ
OHHH!
AA
CLAMOR
ガヤ
CLAMOR
ガヤ
CLAMOR
ガヤ
CLAMOR
ガヤ
CHATTER
ごた
ごた
CHATTER
CLAMOR
CLAMOR
ガヤガヤ
CHATTER
CHATTER
わいわい
OOOOO
Oi Oi Oi!!
D-DOOM BABOOM
JA JA JAAN JA JARNN
!
Gajeel!

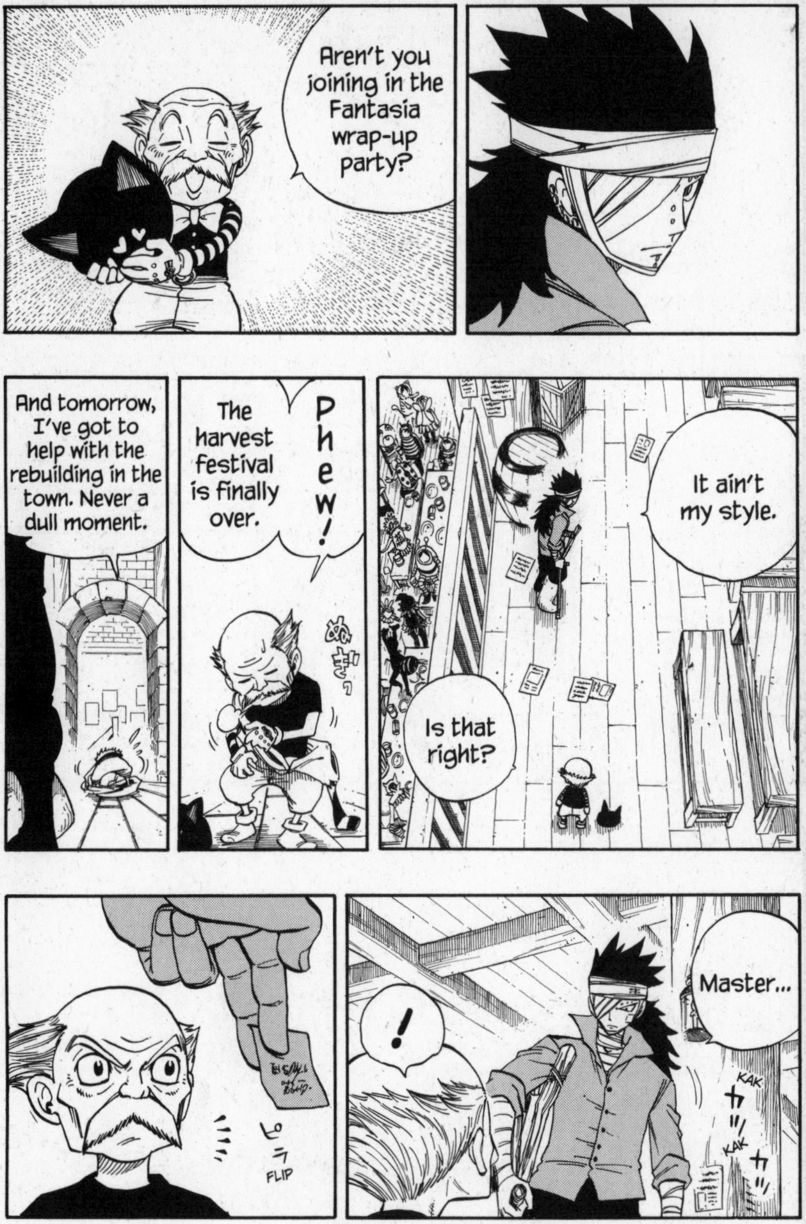
Aren't you joining in the Fantasia wrap-up party?
It ain't my style.
Is that right?
Phew!
The harvest festival is finally over.
And tomorrow, I've got to help with the rebuilding in the town. Never a dull moment.
Master...
!
KAK
KAK
FLIP

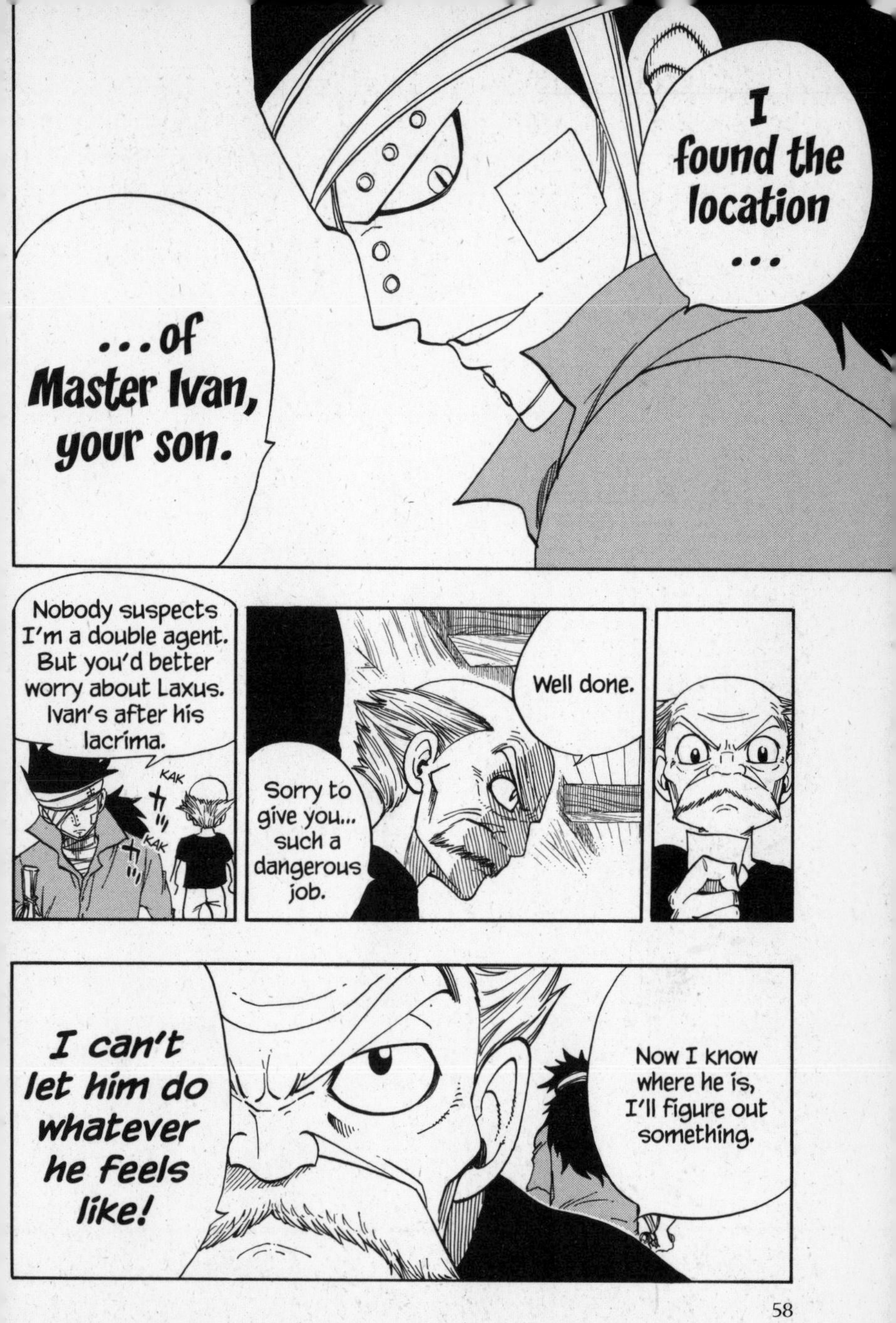
I found the location ...
...of Master Ivan, your son.
Well done.
Sorry to give you... such a dangerous job.
Nobody suspects I'm a double agent. But you'd better worry about Laxus. Ivan's after his lacrima.
KAK
KAK
Now I know where he is, I'll figure out something.
I can't let him do whatever he feels like!

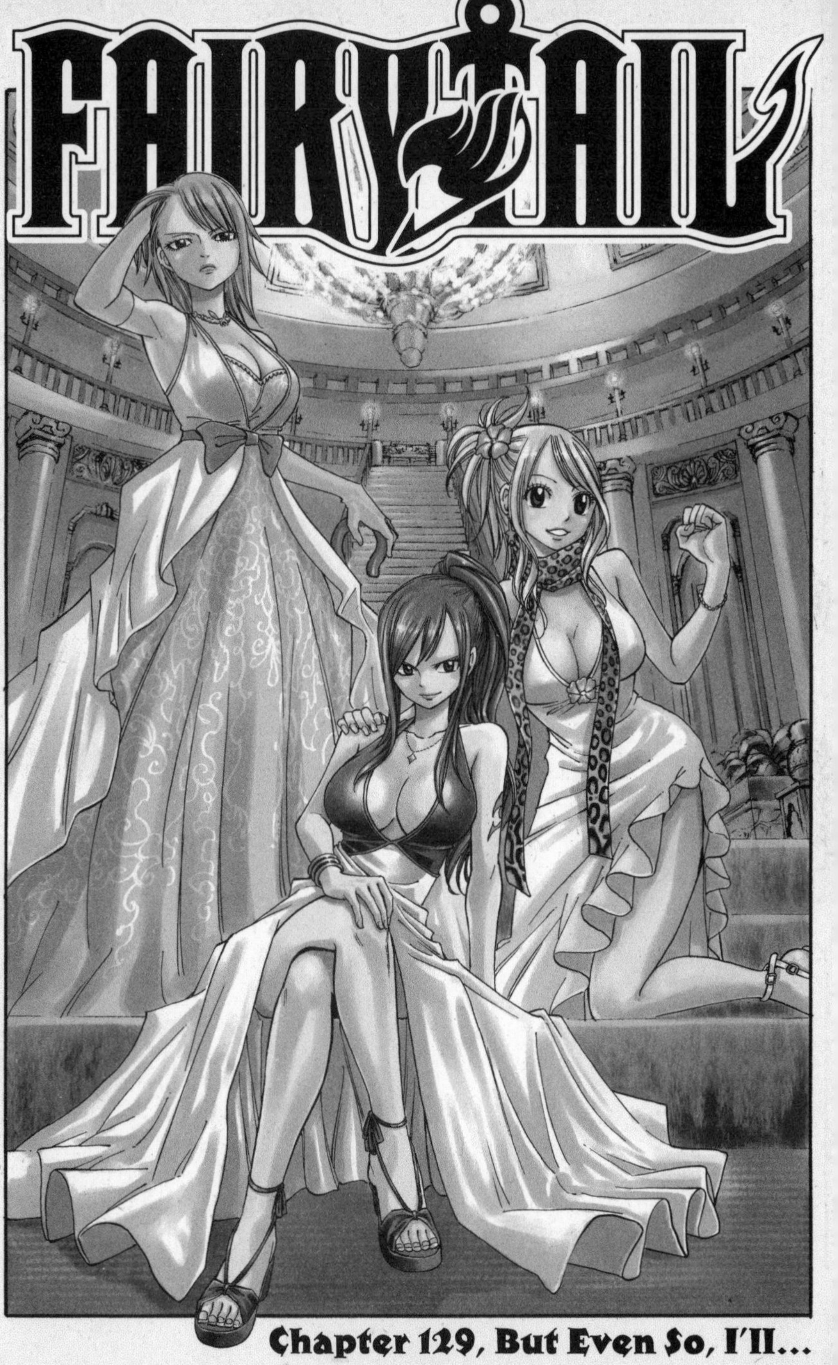
FAIRY TAIL

Chapter 129, But Even So, I'll...

FAIRYTAIL
フェアリーテイル

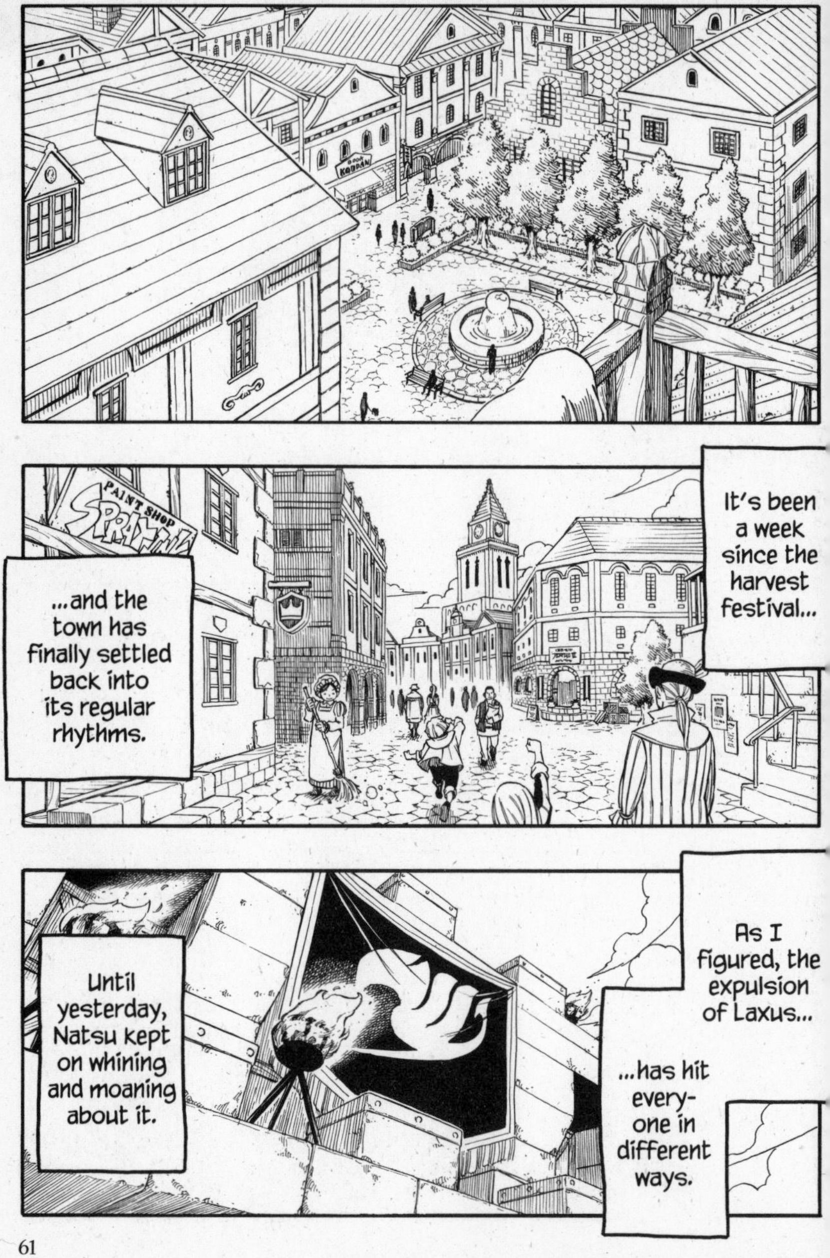
It's been a week since the harvest festival...
...and the town has finally settled back into its regular rhythms.
As I figured, the expulsion of Laxus...
...has hit every-one in different ways.
Until yesterday, Natsu kept on whining and moaning about it.

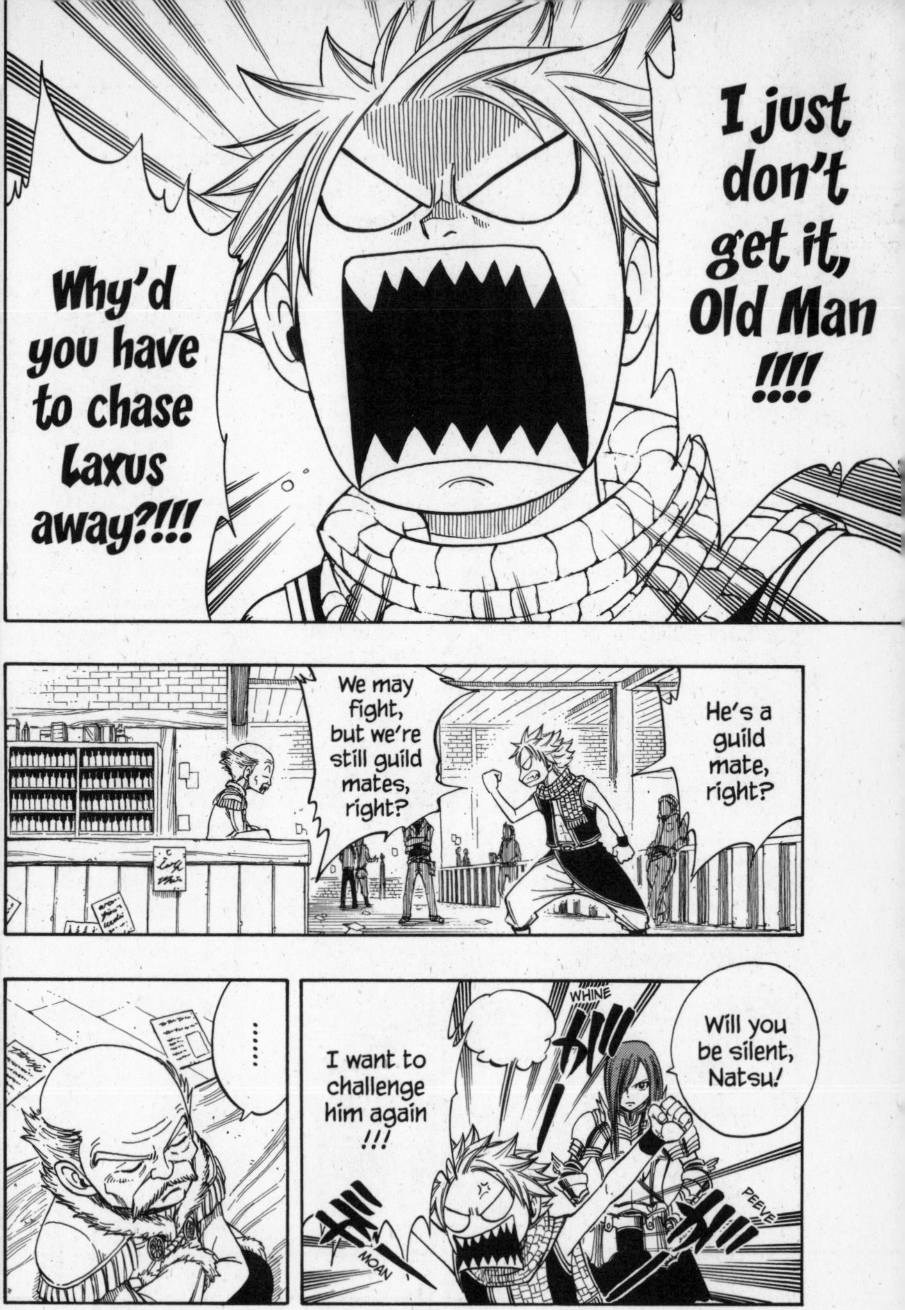
I just don't get it, Old Man !!!!
Why'd you have to chase Laxus away?!!!
He's a guild mate, right?
We may fight, but we're still guild mates, right?
Will you be silent, Natsu!
WHINE
I want to challenge him again !!!
PEEVE
MOAN
......

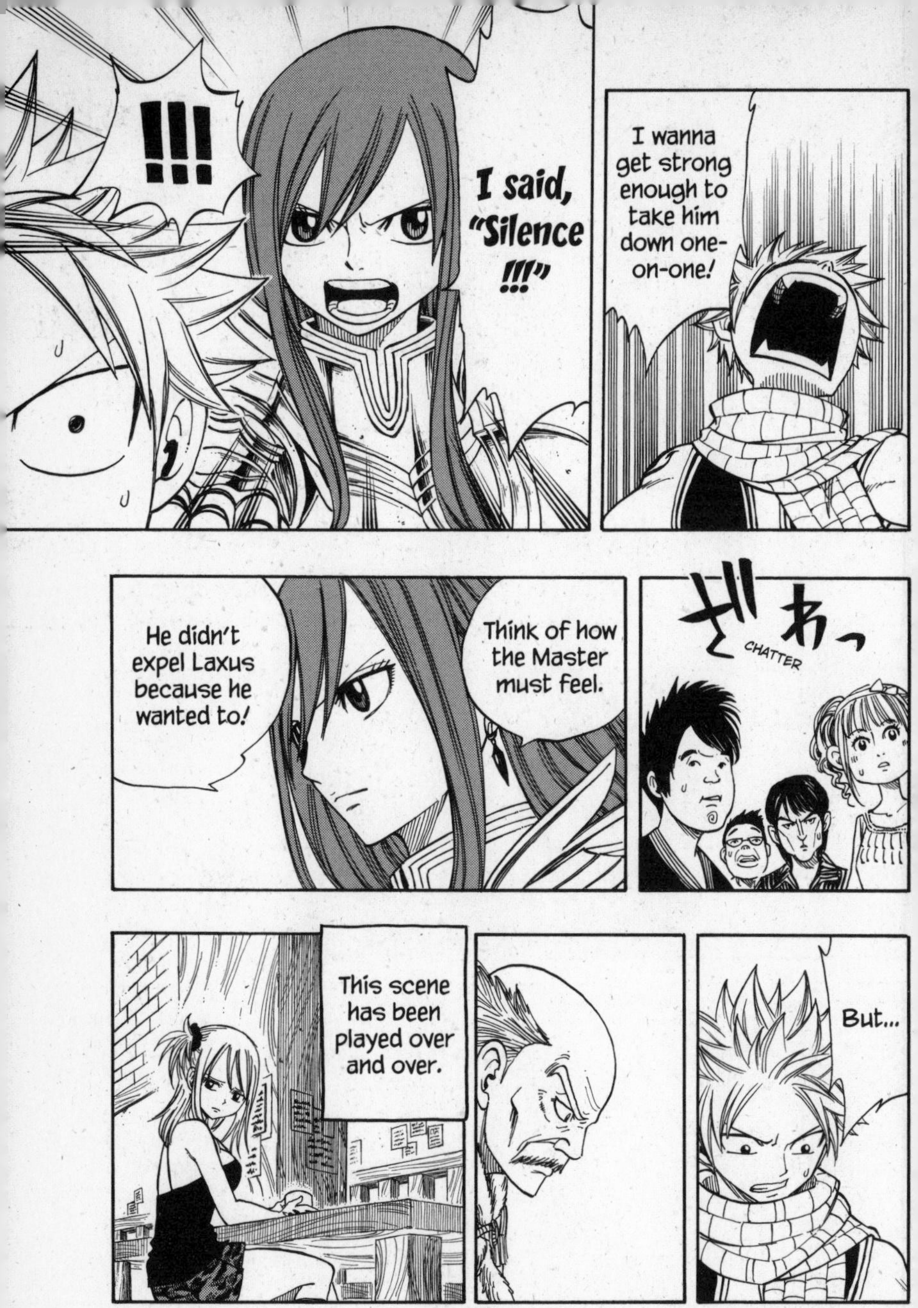

I wanna get strong enough to take him down one-on-one!
I said, "Silence!!!"
!!!
ざわっ
CHATTER
Think of how the Master must feel.
He didn't expel Laxus because he wanted to!
But...
This scene has been played over and over.

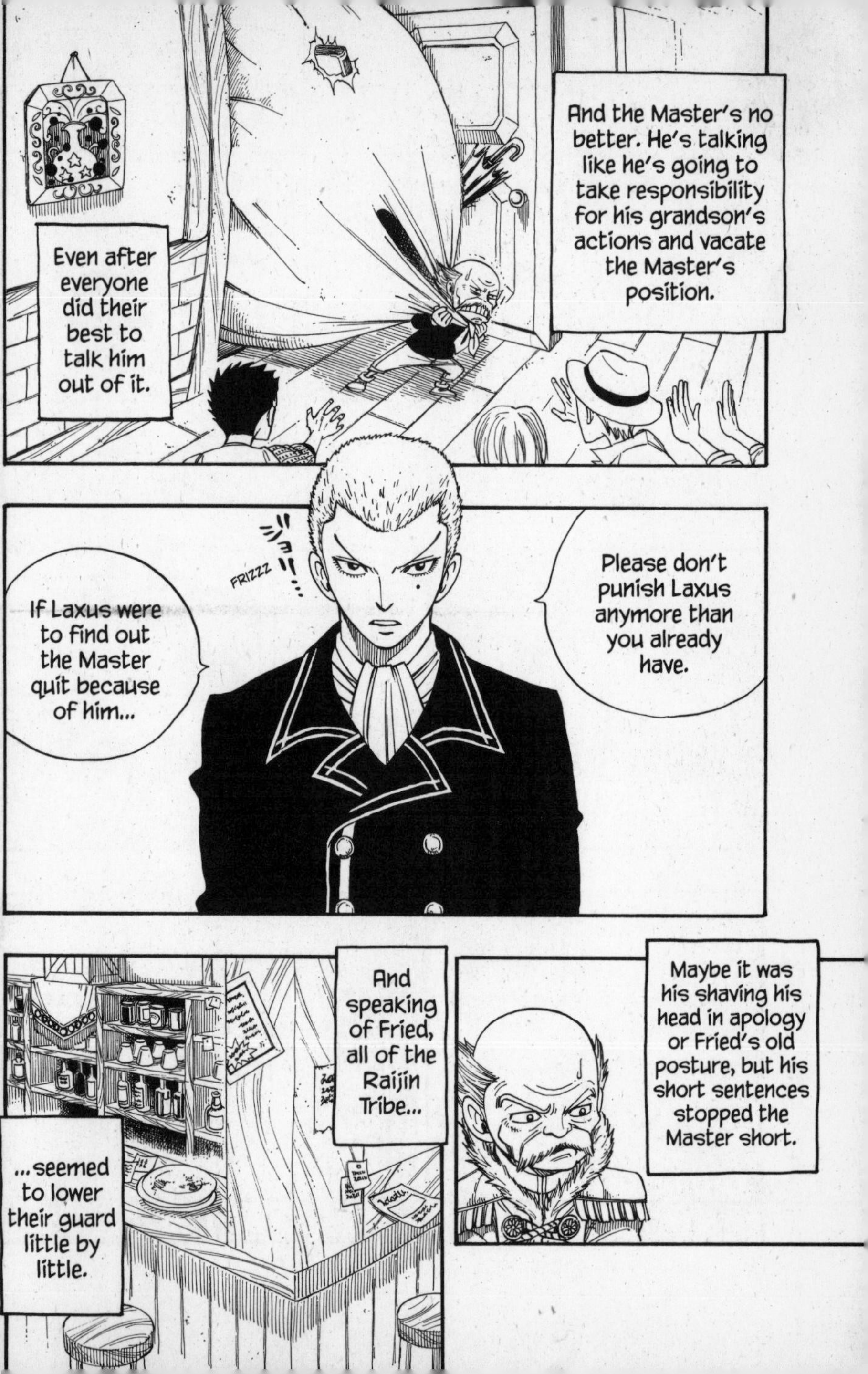
And the Master's no better. He's talking like he's going to take responsibility for his grandson's actions and vacate the Master's position.
Even after everyone did their best to talk him out of it.
Please don't punish Laxus anymore than you already have.
FRIZZZ
If Laxus were to find out the Master quit because of him...
Maybe it was his shaving his head in apology or Fried's old posture, but his short sentences stopped the Master short.
And speaking of Fried, all of the Raijin Tribe...
...seemed to lower their guard little by little.

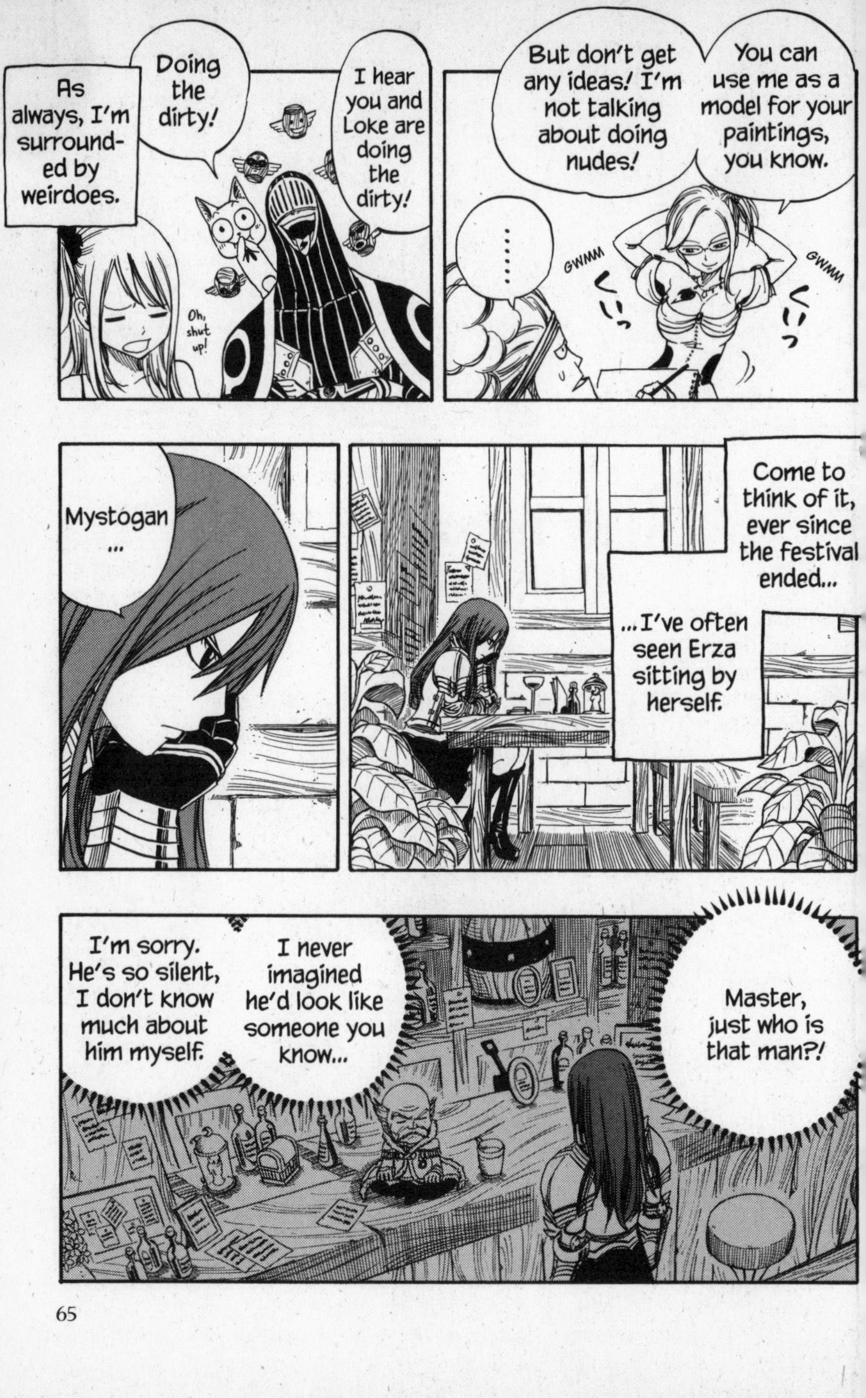

You can use me as a model for your paintings, you know.
But don't get any ideas! I'm not talking about doing nudes!
GWMM
GWMM
......
I hear you and Loke are doing the dirty!
Doing the dirty!
As always, I'm surround-ed by weirdoes.
Oh, shut up!
Come to think of it, ever since the festival ended...
...I've often seen Erza sitting by herself.
Mystogan ...
Master, just who is that man?!
I never imagined he'd look like someone you know...
I'm sorry. He's so silent, I don't know much about him myself.

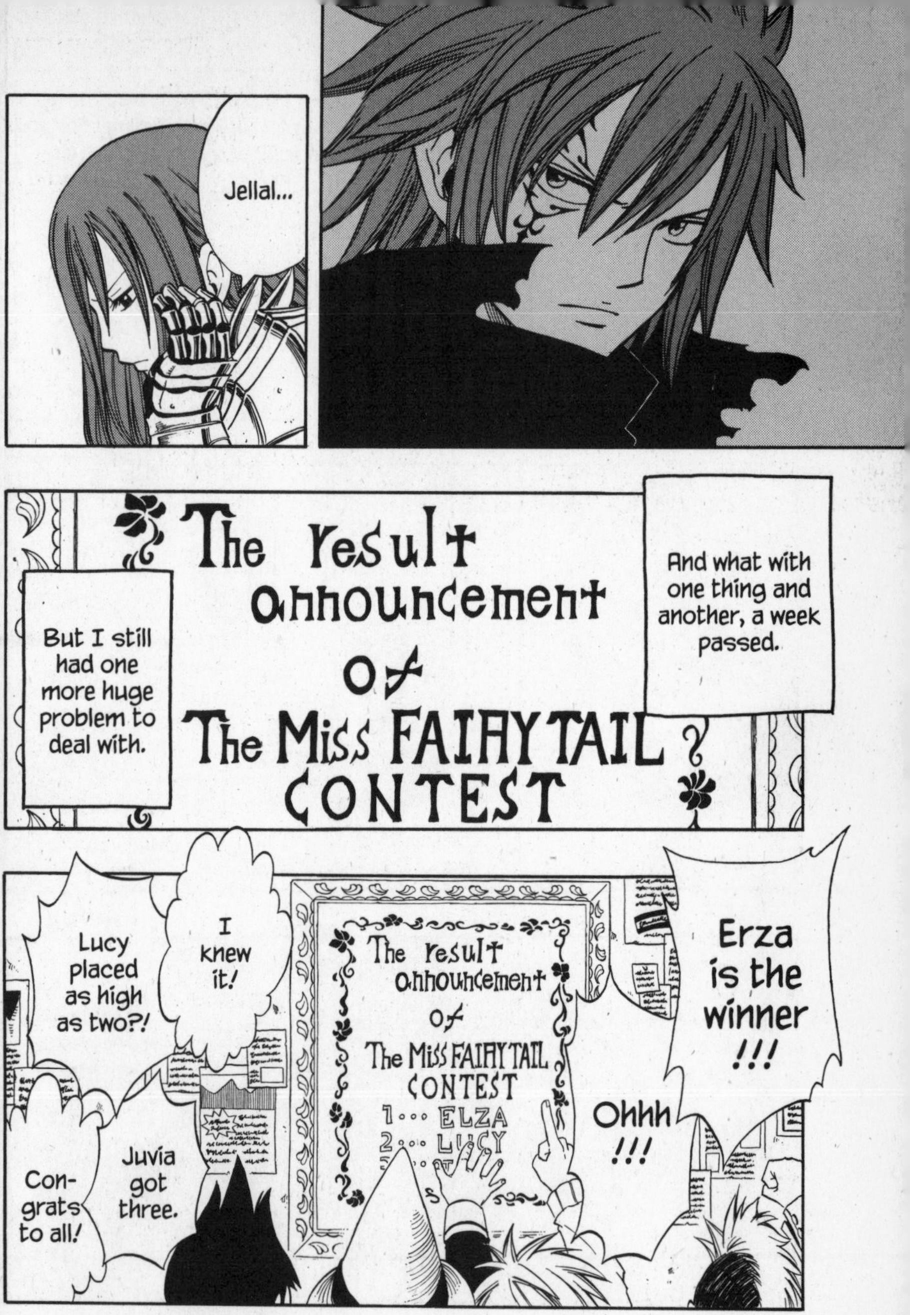
Jellal...
And what with one thing and another, a week passed.
The result announcement of The Miss FAIRY TAIL CONTEST
But I still had one more huge problem to deal with.
Erza is the winner!!!
Ohhh!!!
The result announcement of The Miss FAIRY TAIL CONTEST
1... ELZA
2... LUCY
I knew it!
Lucy placed as high as two?!
Juvia got three.
Con-grats to all!

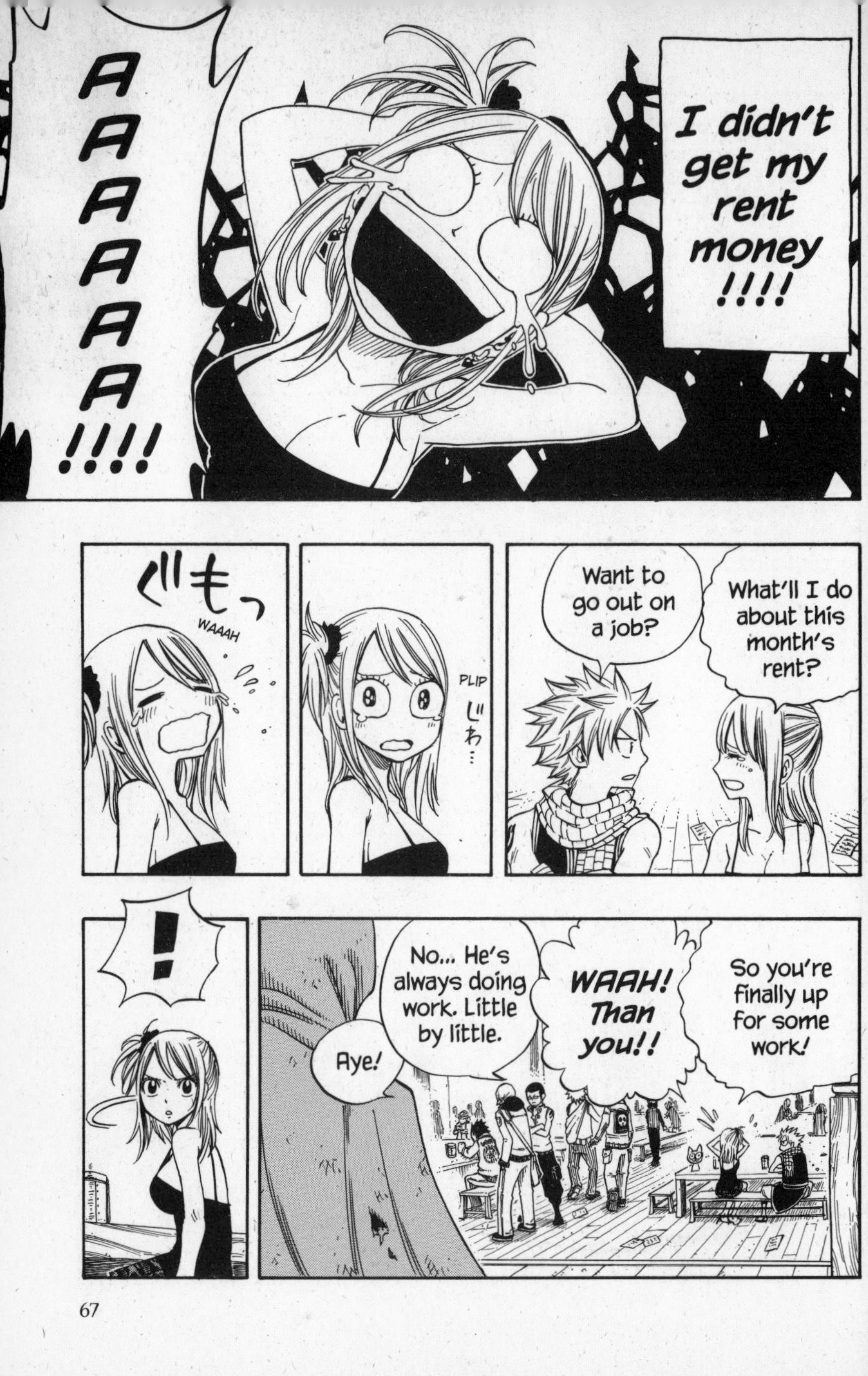
I didn't get my rent money!!!!
AAAAAA!!!!
What'll I do about this month's rent?
Want to go out on a job?
PLIP
じわ…
ぐもっ
WAAAH
So you're finally up for some work!
WAAH! Than you!!
No... He's always doing work. Little by little.
Aye!
!

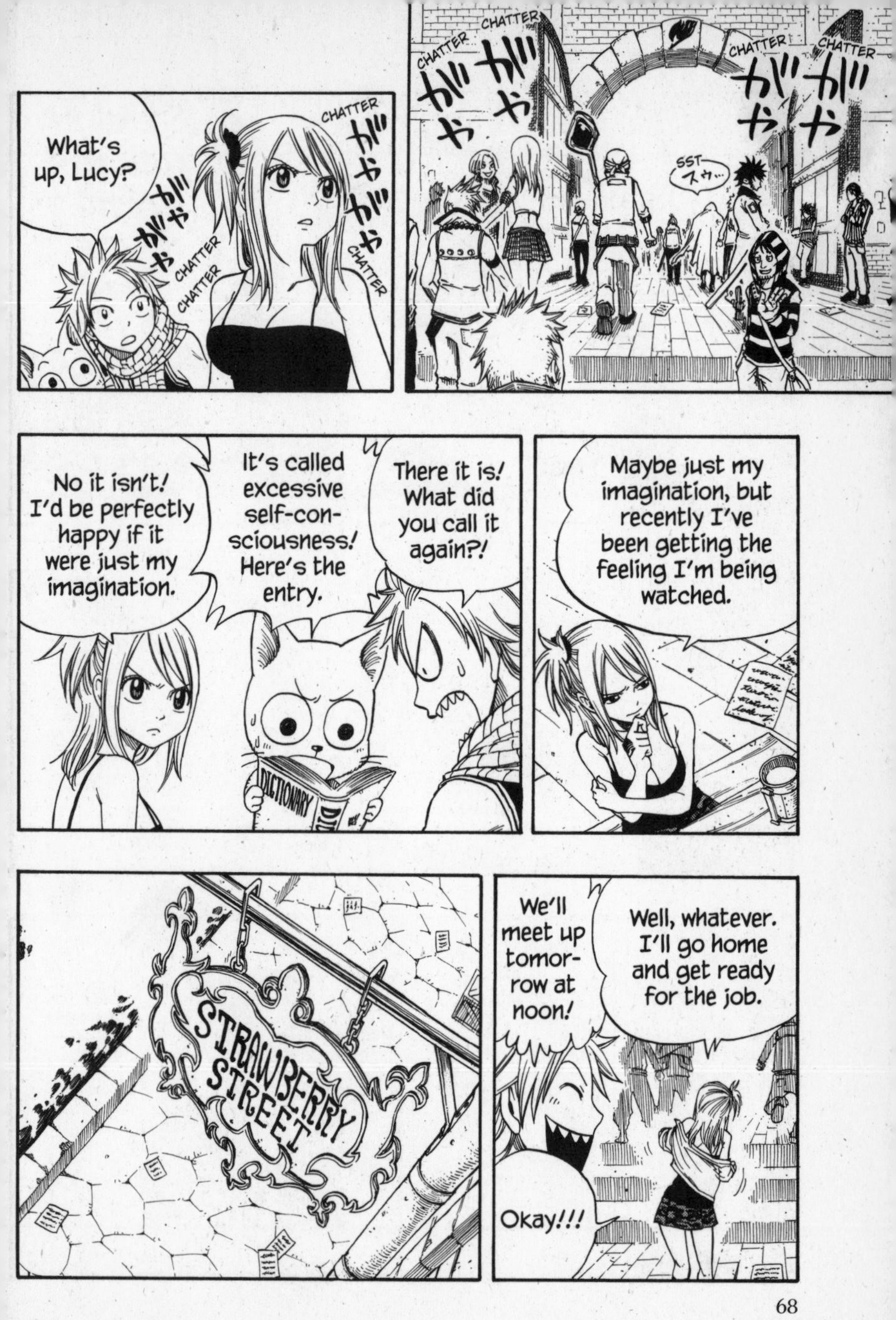
CHATTER
CHATTER
ガヤ
ガヤ
CHATTER
CHATTER
ガヤ
ガヤ
SST
スゥ…
What's up, Lucy?
CHATTER
ガヤガヤ
CHATTER
ガヤガヤ
CHATTER
CHATTER
Maybe just my imagination, but recently I've been getting the feeling I'm being watched.
There it is! What did you call it again?!
It's called excessive self-consciousness! Here's the entry.
No it isn't! I'd be perfectly happy if it were just my imagination.
DICTIONARY
Well, whatever. I'll go home and get ready for the job.
We'll meet up tomorrow at noon!
Okay!!!
STRAWBERRY STREET

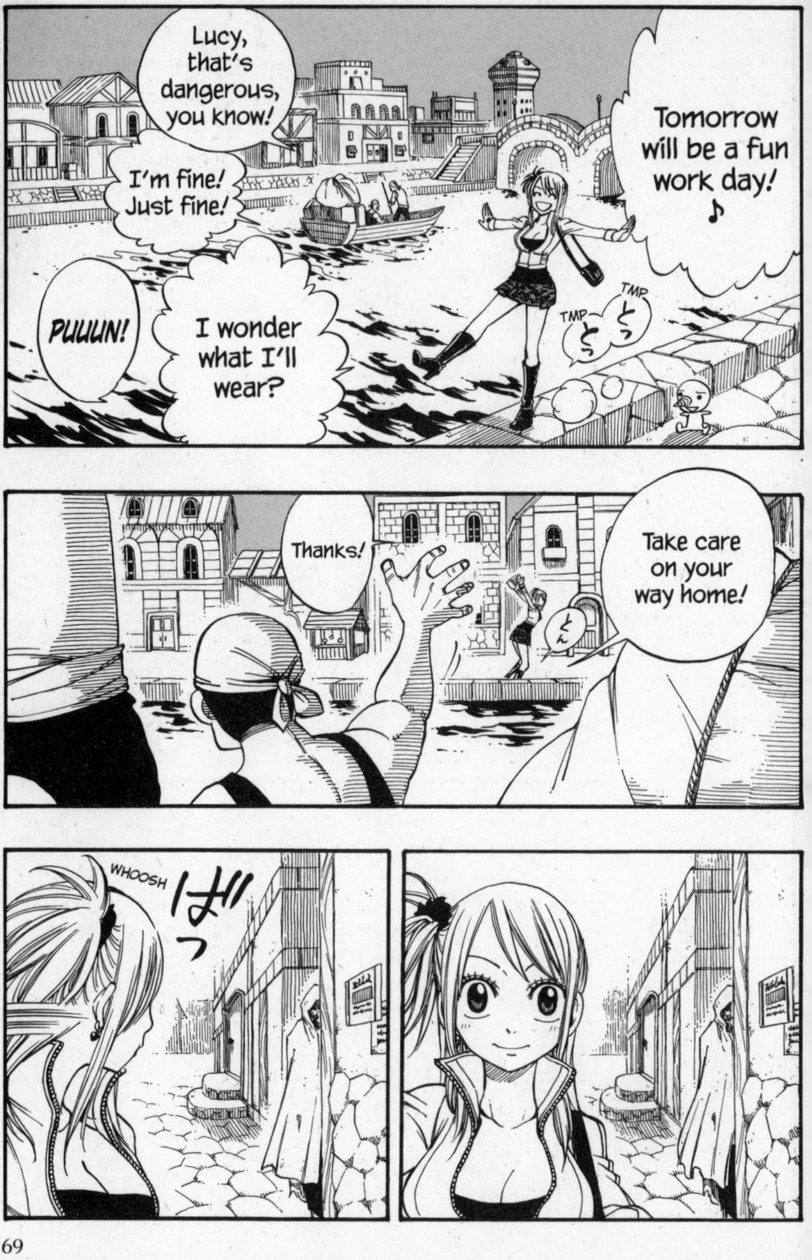

Tomorrow will be a fun work day! ♪
Lucy, that's dangerous, you know!
I'm fine! Just fine!
TMP とっ
TMP とっ
I wonder what I'll wear?
PUUUN!
Take care on your way home!
とん
Thanks!
WHOOSH ばっ

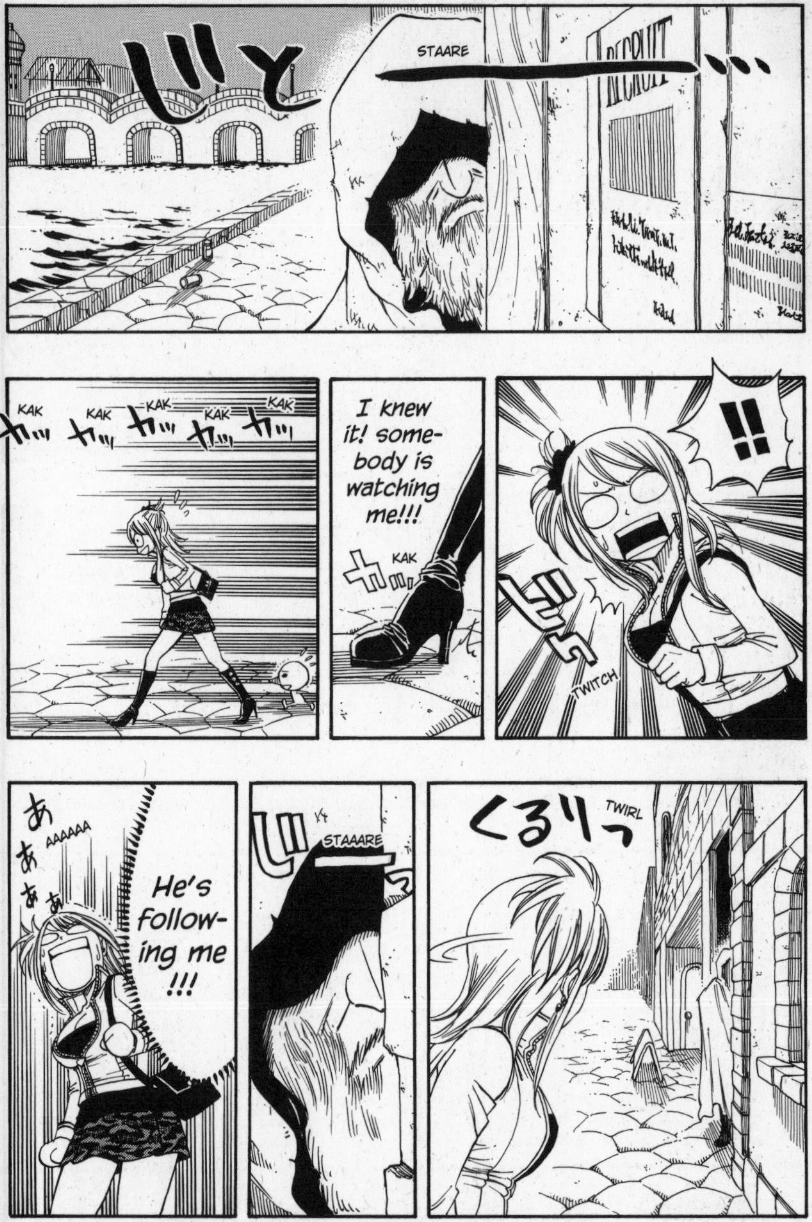
STAARE
!!
TWITCH
I knew it! some-body is watching me!!!
KAK
KAK
KAK
KAK
KAK
KAK
くるりっ
TWIRL
STAAARE
ああああ
AAAAAA
He's follow-ing me !!!

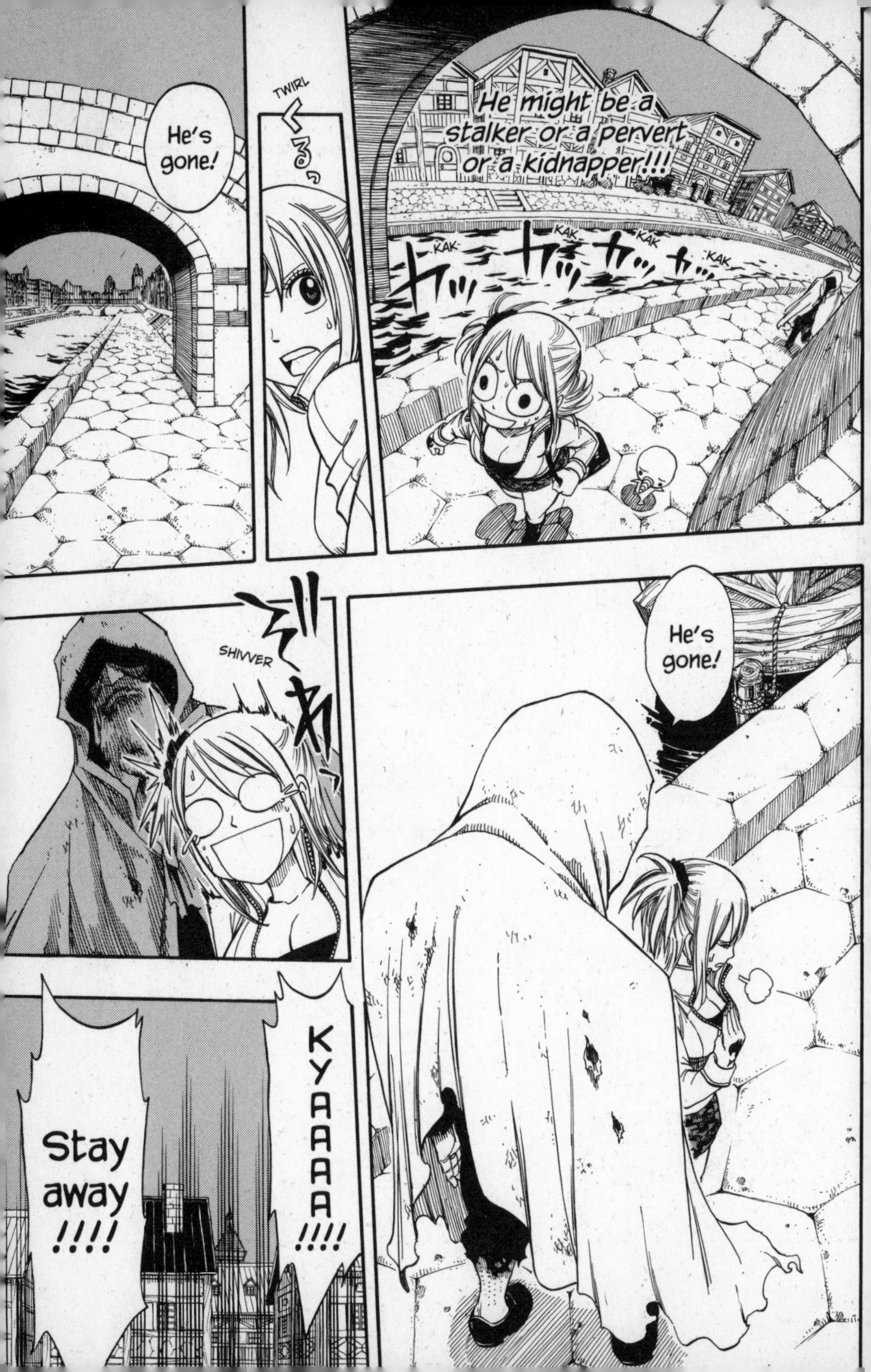

He might be a stalker or a pervert or a kidnapper!!!
KAK
KAK
KAK
KAK
TWIRL
He's gone!
He's gone!
SHIVVER
KYAAAAA!!!!
Stay away!!!!

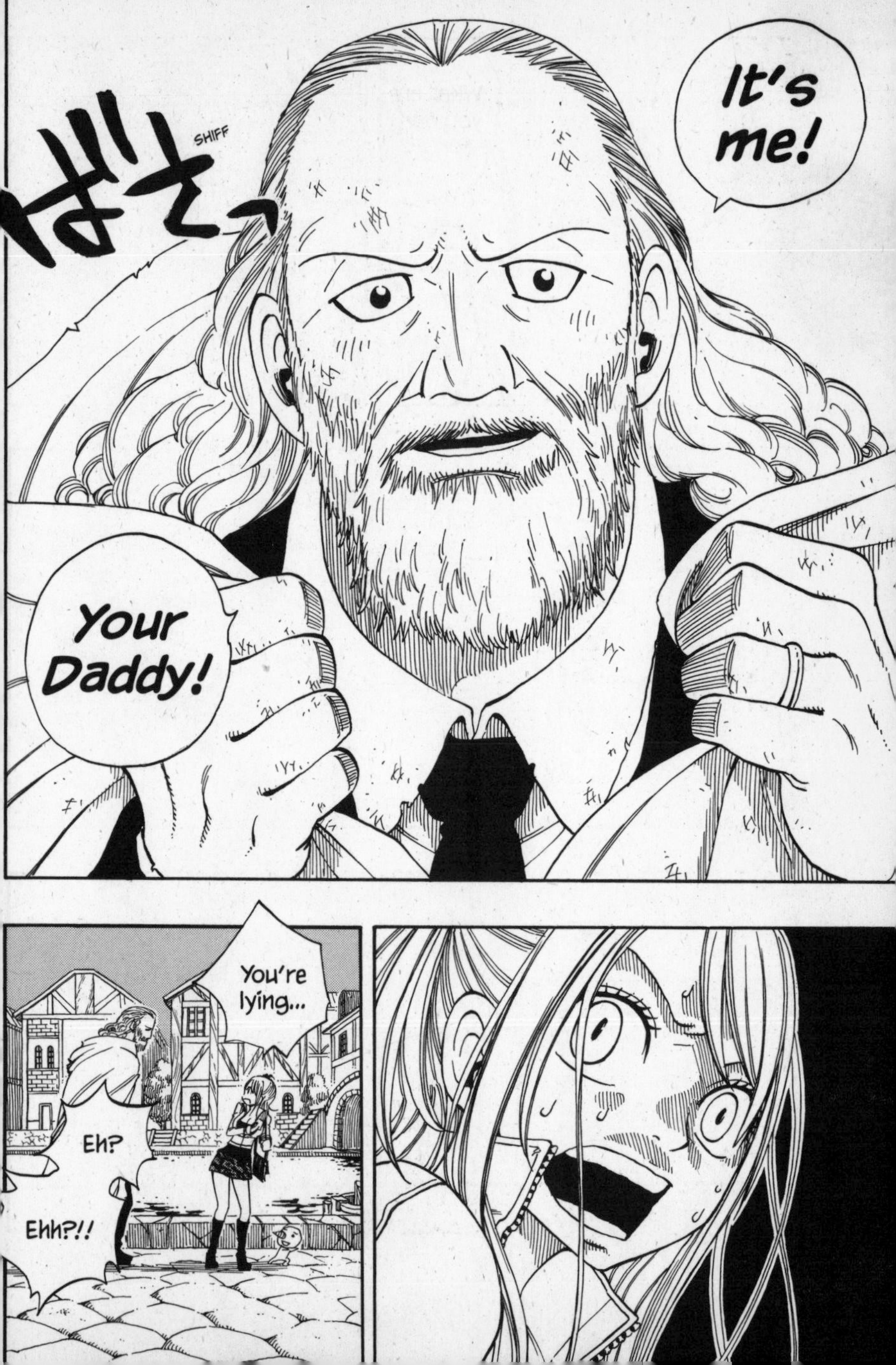
It's me!
ばさっ
SHIFF
Your Daddy!
You're lying...
Eh?
Ehh?!!

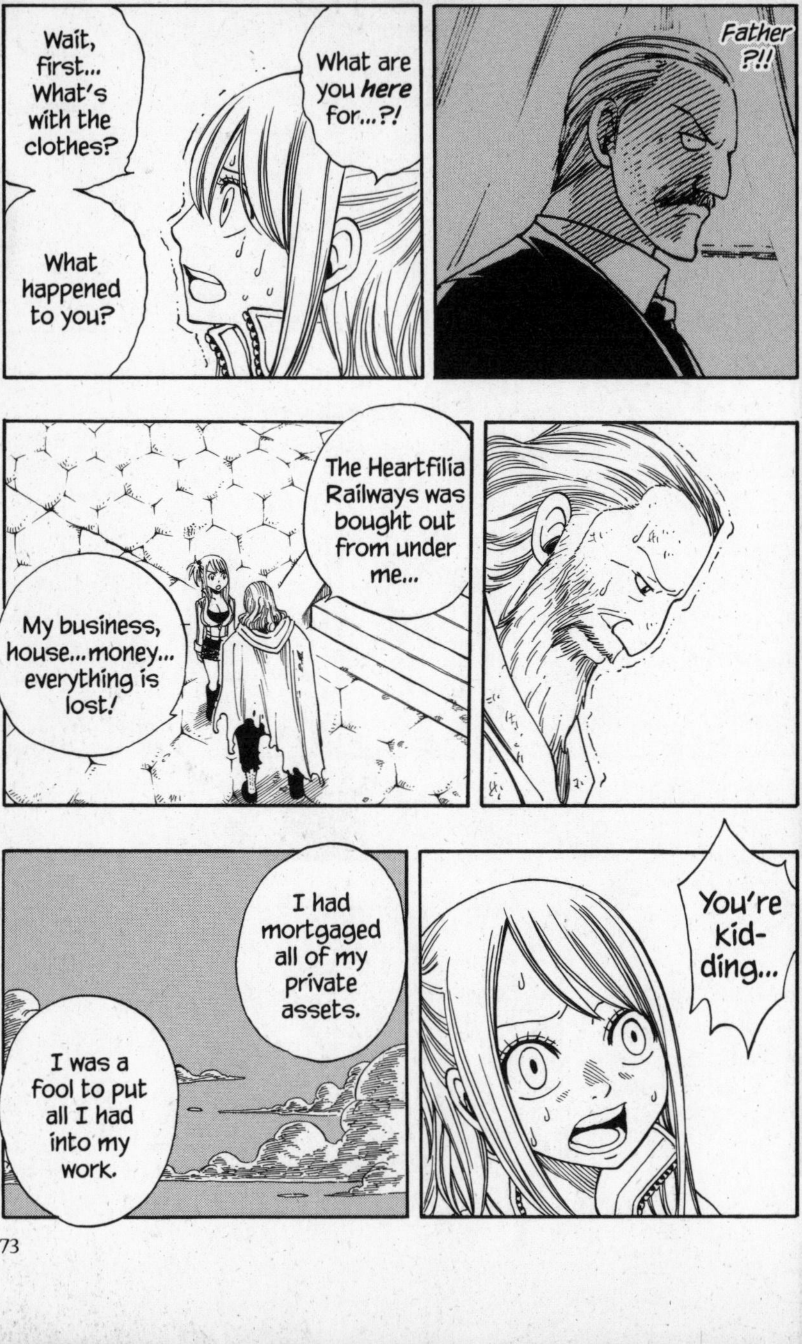
Father?!!
What are you *here* for...?!
Wait, first... What's with the clothes?
What happened to you?
The Heartfilia Railways was bought out from under me...
My business, house...money... everything is lost!
You're kid-ding...
I had mortgaged all of my private assets.
I was a fool to put all I had into my work.

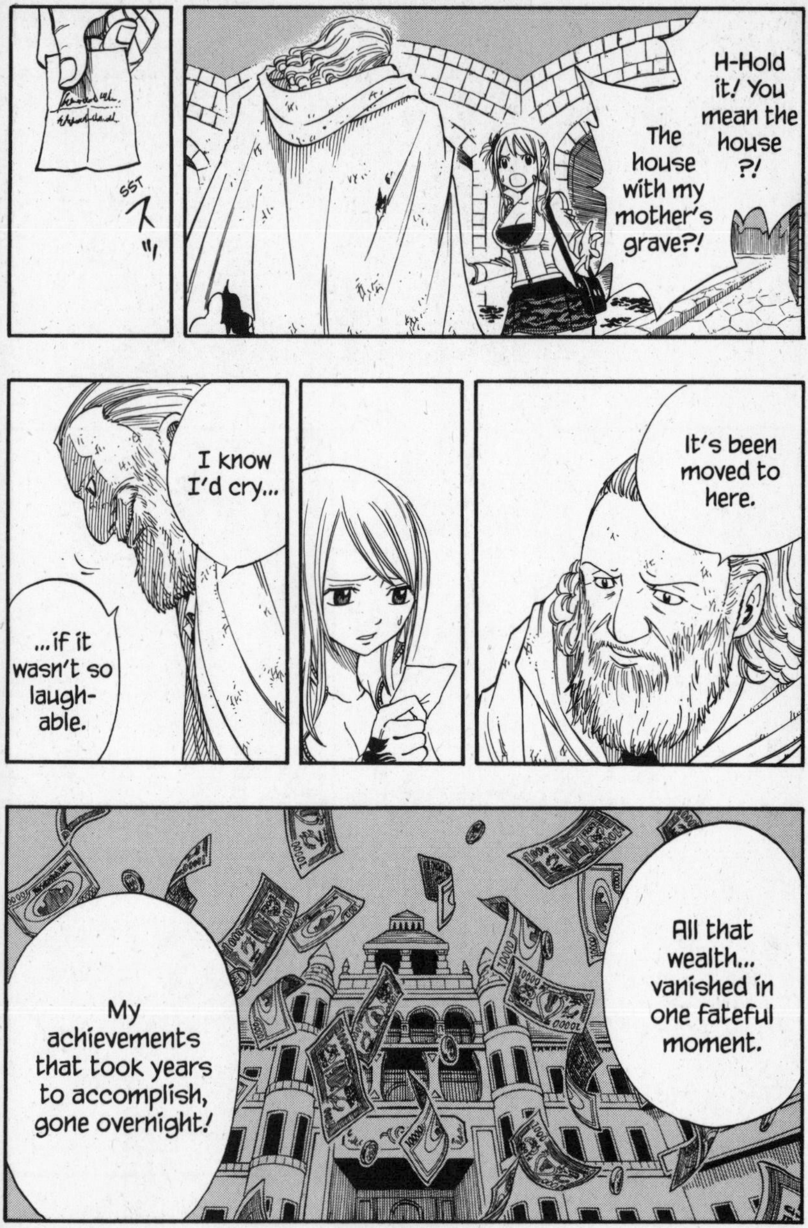
H-Hold it! You mean the house?!
The house with my mother's grave?!
SST
It's been moved to here.
I know I'd cry...
...if it wasn't so laughable.
All that wealth... vanished in one fateful moment.
My achievements that took years to accomplish, gone overnight!

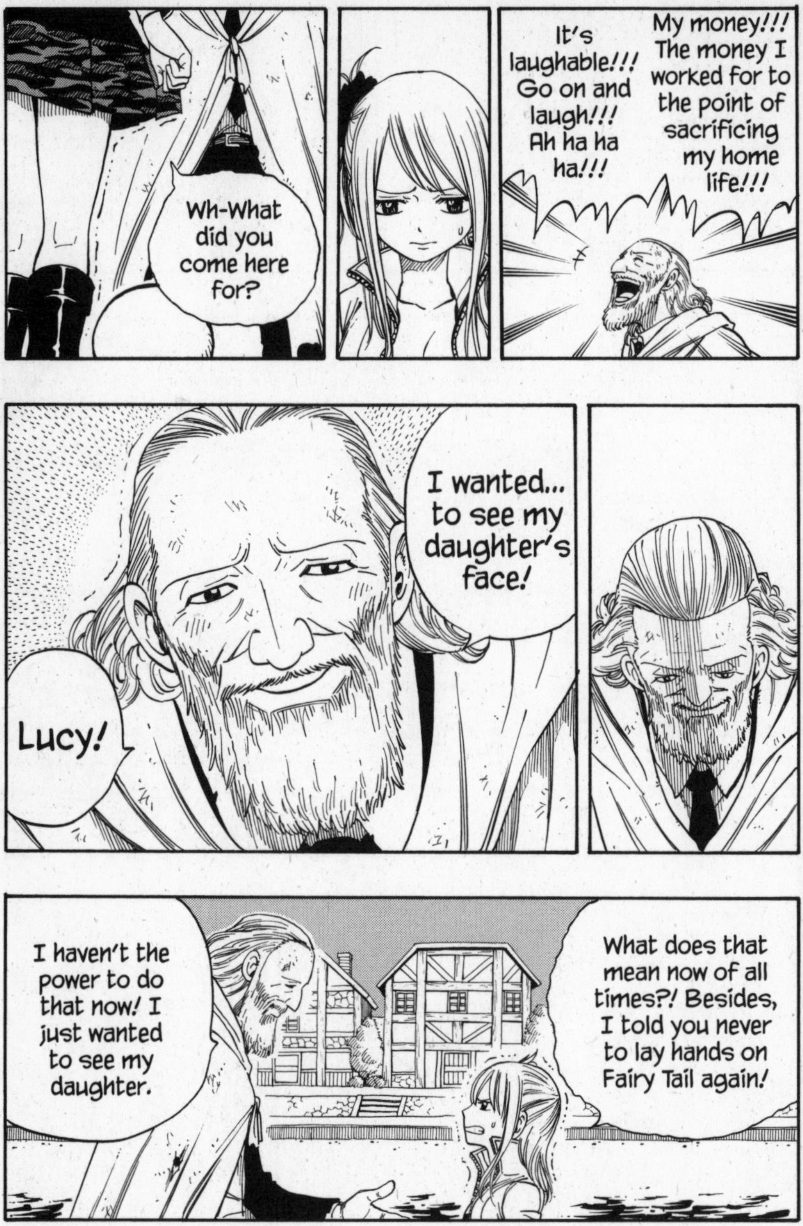
My money!!! The money I worked for to the point of sacrificing my home life!!!
It's laughable!!! Go on and laugh!!! Ah ha ha ha!!!
Wh-What did you come here for?
I wanted... to see my daughter's face!
Lucy!
What does that mean now of all times?! Besides, I told you never to lay hands on Fairy Tail again!
I haven't the power to do that now! I just wanted to see my daughter.

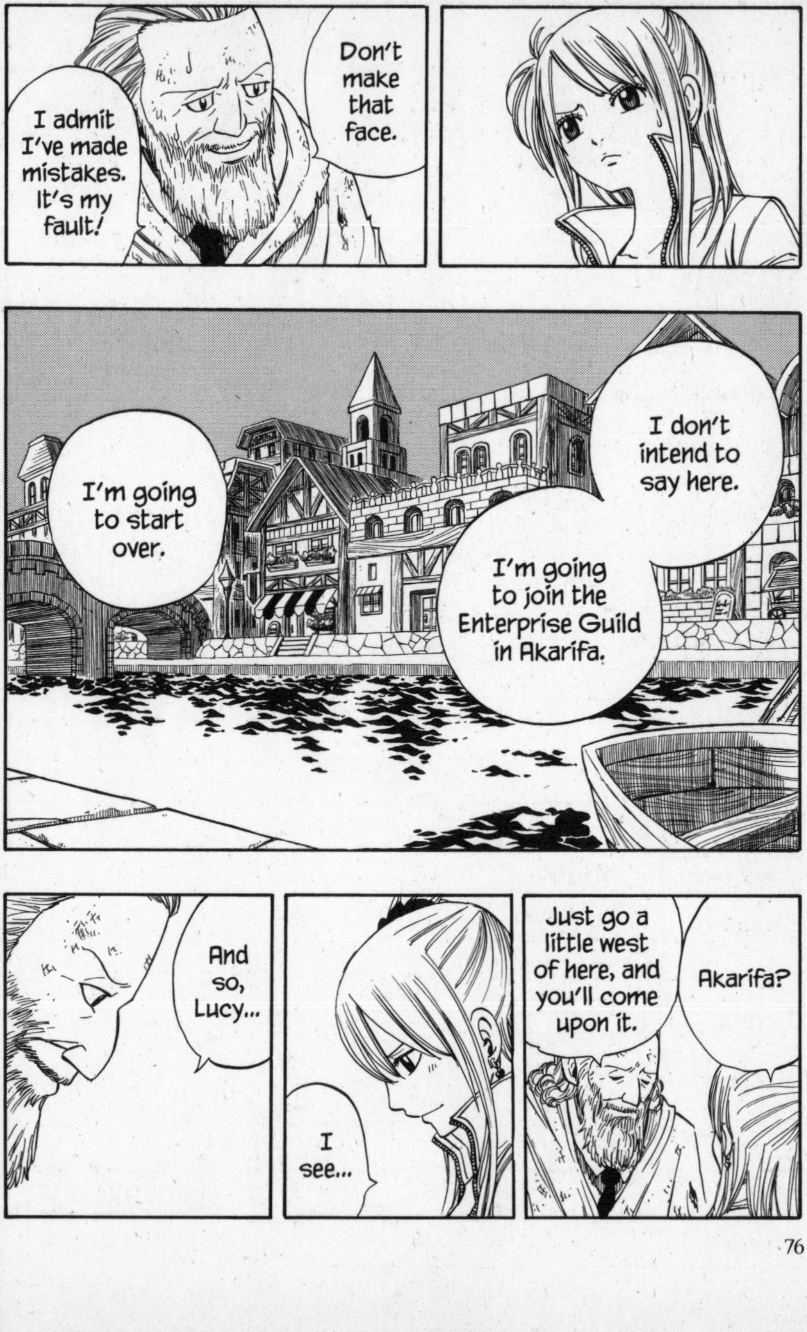
Don't make that face.
I admit I've made mistakes. It's my fault!
I don't intend to say here.
I'm going to join the Enterprise Guild in Akarifa.
I'm going to start over.
Akarifa?
Just go a little west of here, and you'll come upon it.
I see...
And so, Lucy...

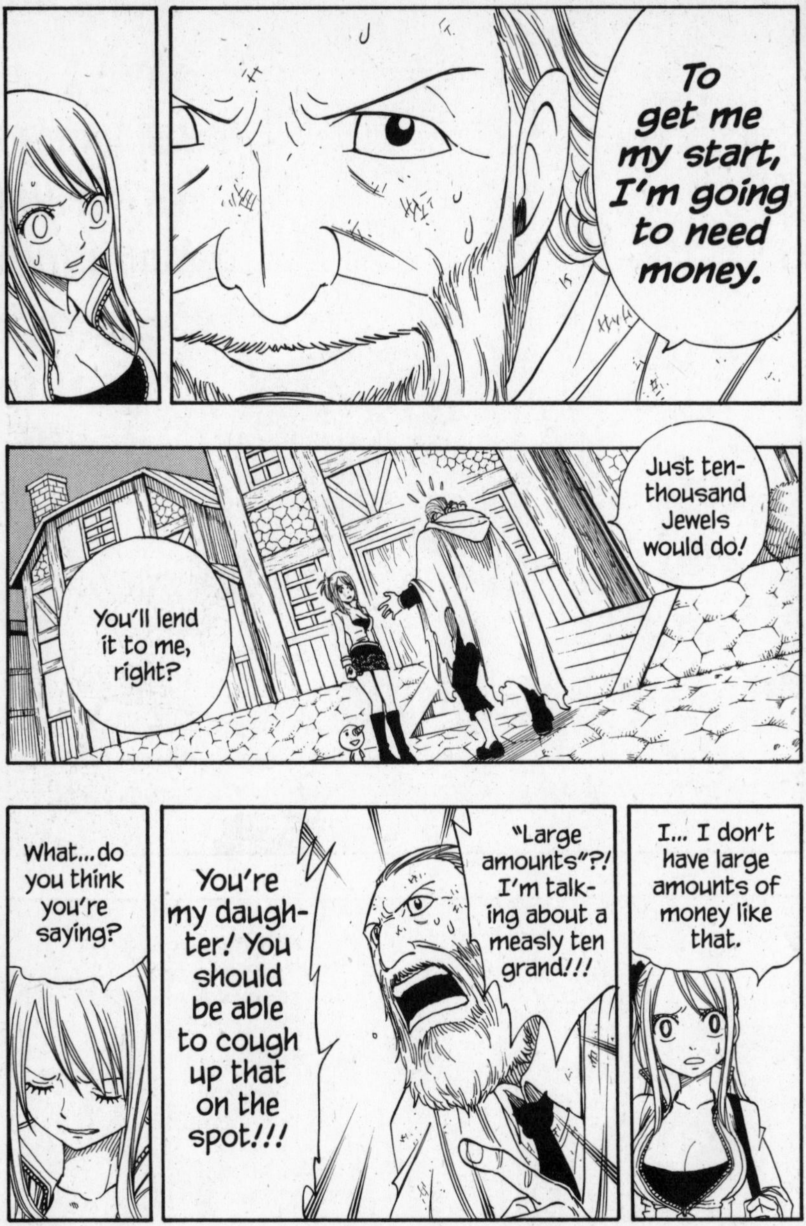
To get me my start, I'm going to need money.
Just ten-thousand Jewels would do!
You'll lend it to me, right?
I... I don't have large amounts of money like that.
"Large amounts"?! I'm talk-ing about a measly ten grand!!!
You're my daugh-ter! You should be able to cough up that on the spot!!!
What...do you think you're saying?

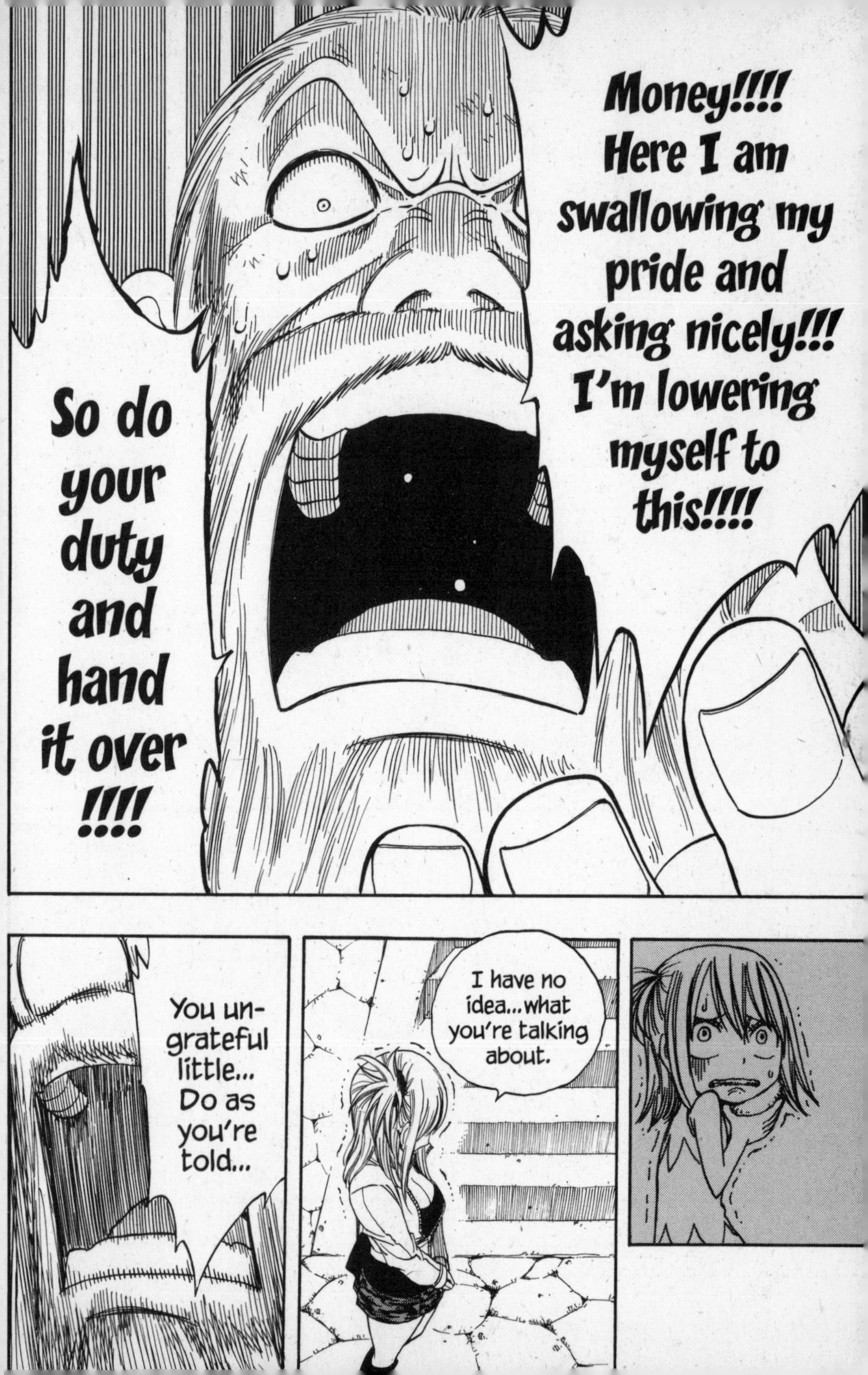
Money!!!! Here I am swallowing my pride and asking nicely!!! I'm lowering myself to this!!!!
So do your duty and hand it over !!!!
I have no idea...what you're talking about.
You un-grateful little... Do as you're told...

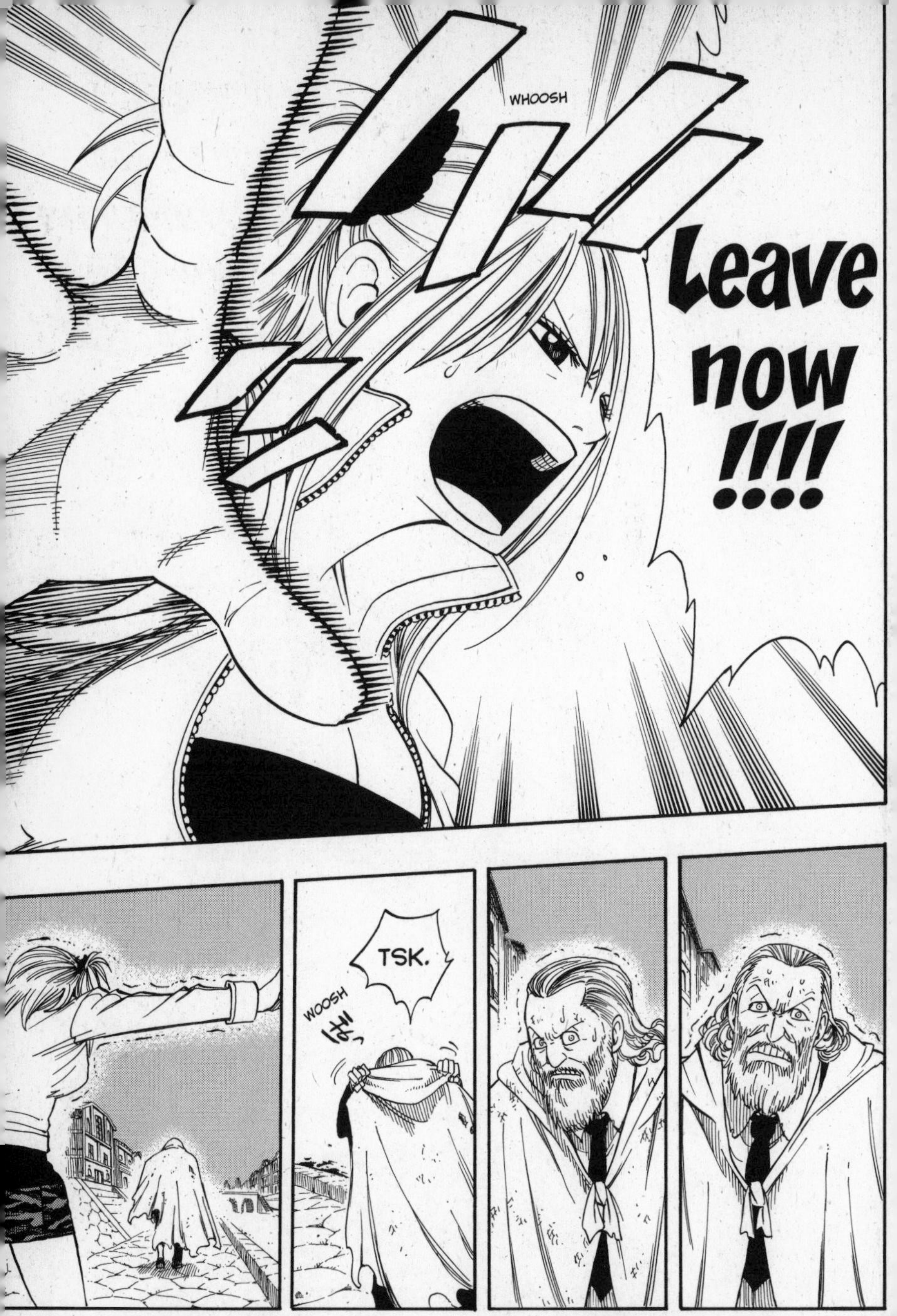
WHOOSH
Leave now!!!!
TSK.
WOOSH

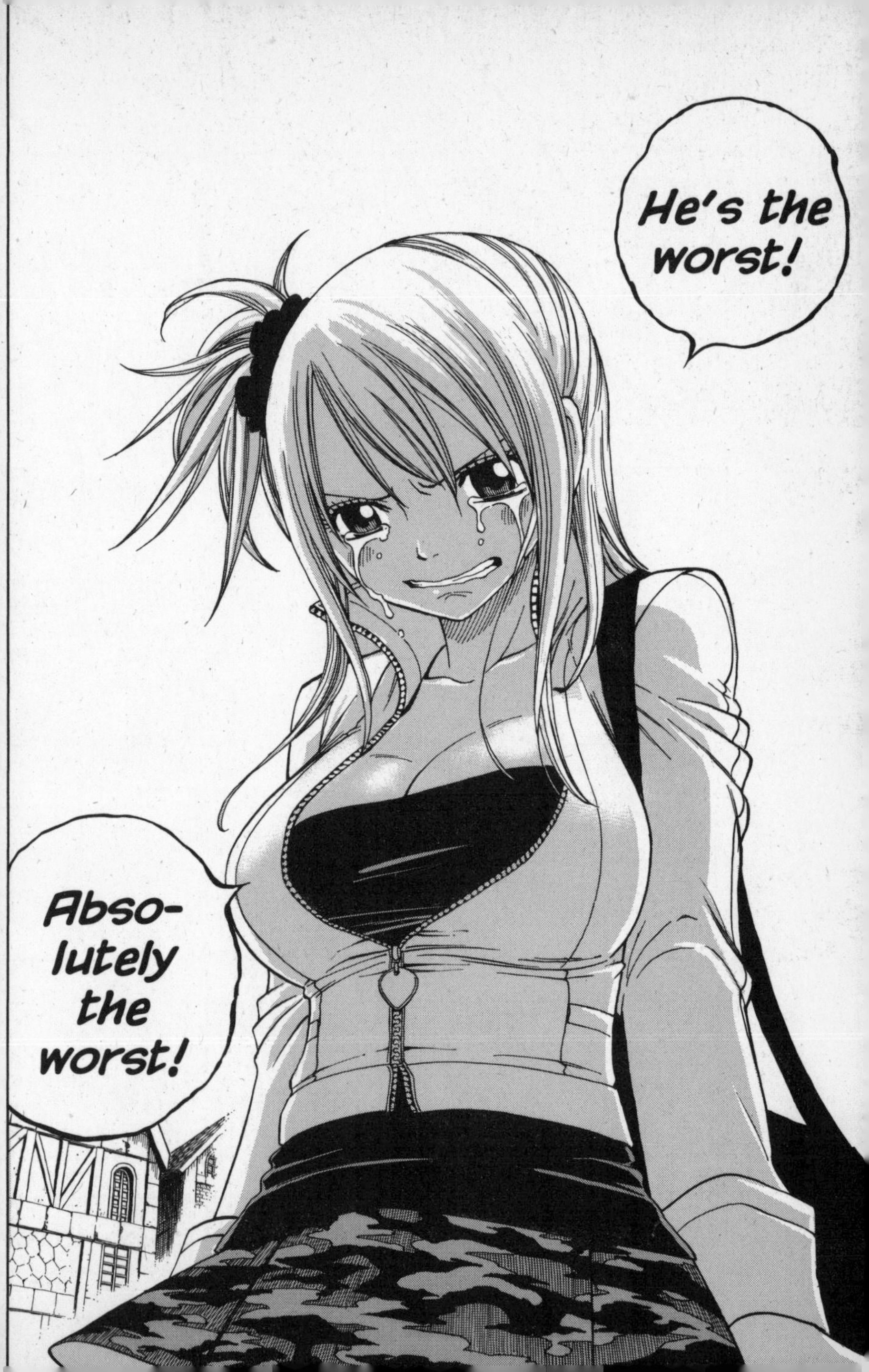
He's the worst!
Abso-lutely the worst!

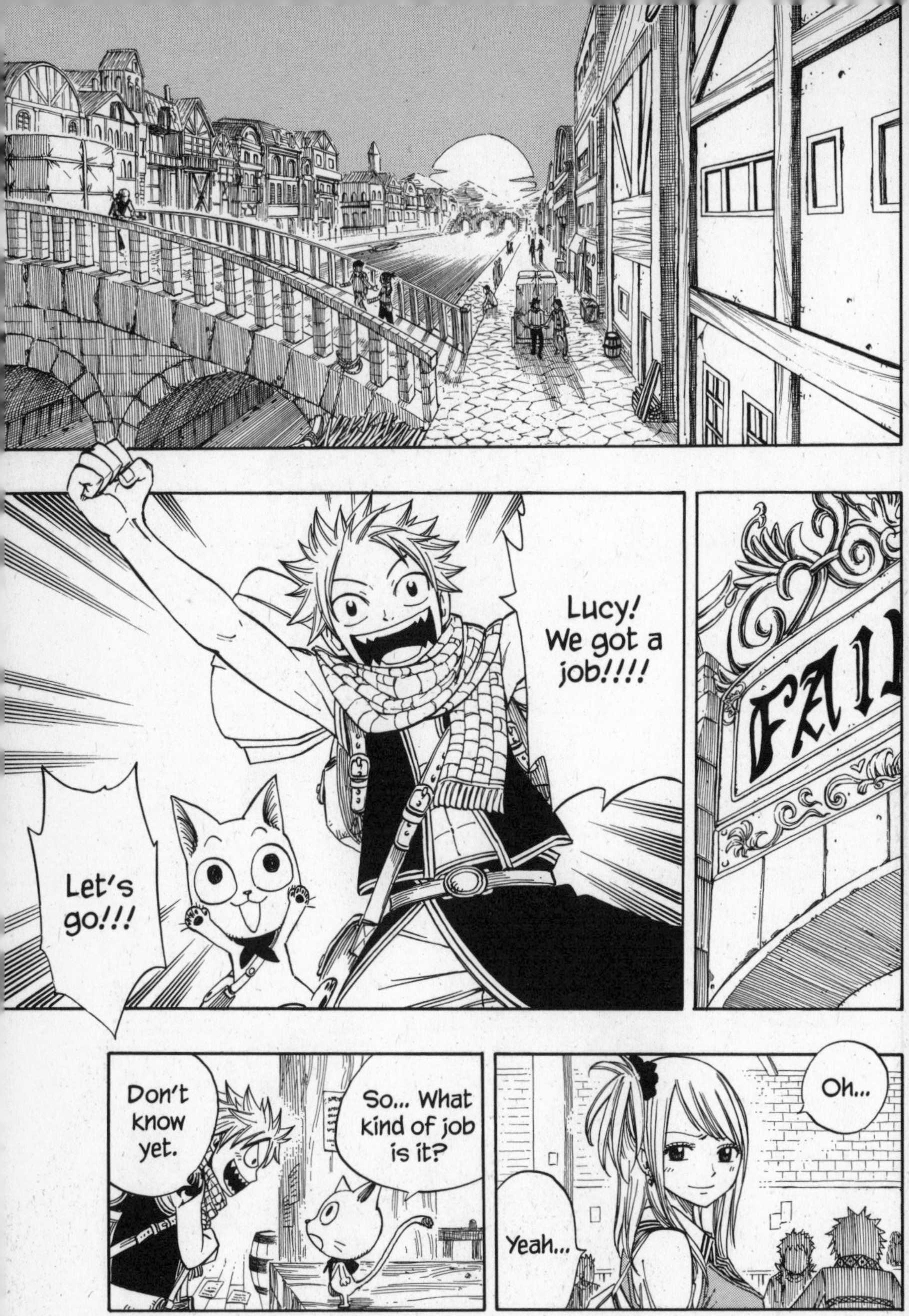
Lucy! We got a job!!!!
Let's go!!!
Oh...
Yeah...
So... What kind of job is it?
Don't know yet.

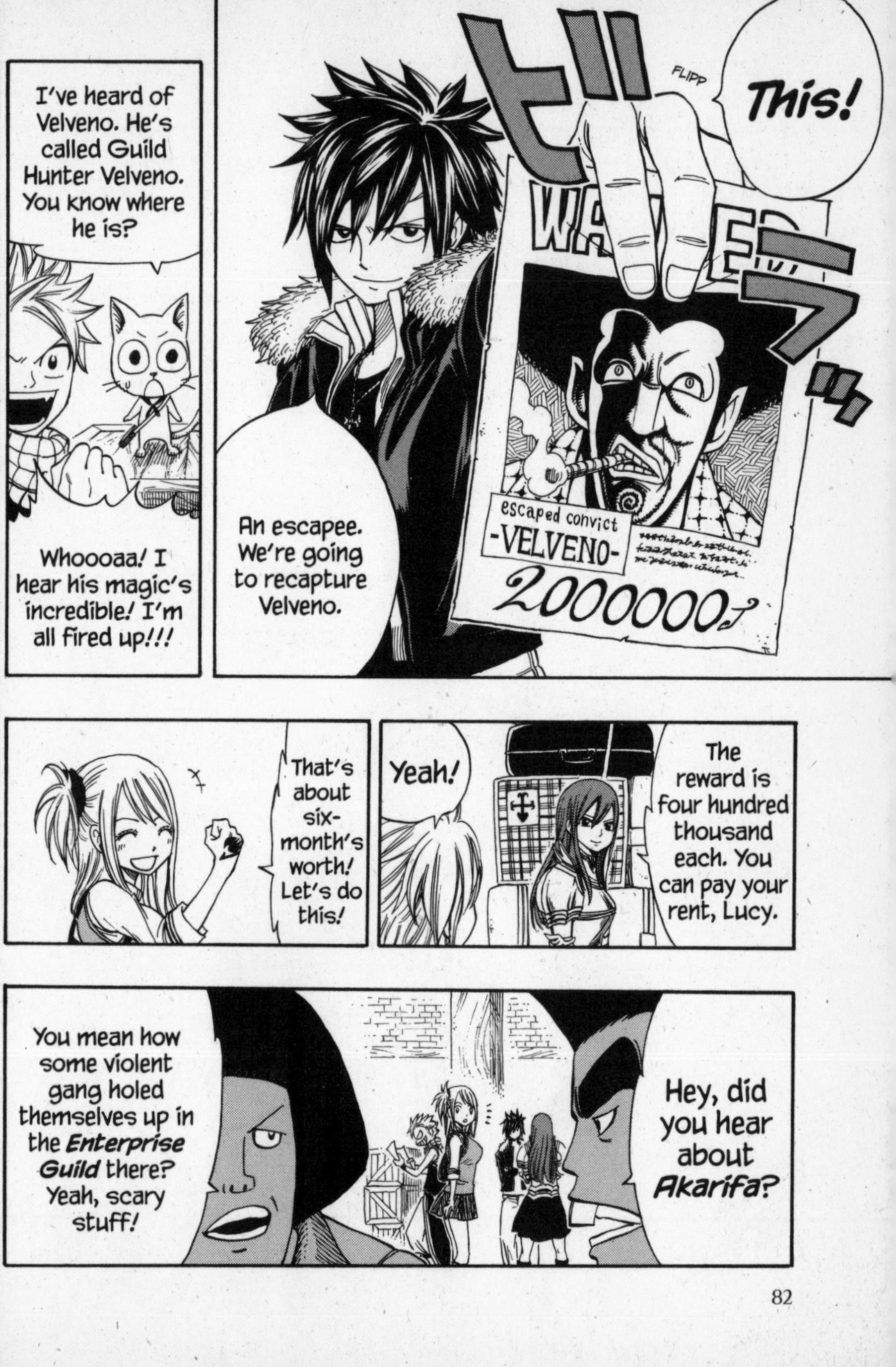
This!
FLIPP
escaped convict
-VELVENO-
2000000
An escapee. We're going to recapture Velveno.
I've heard of Velveno. He's called Guild Hunter Velveno. You know where he is?
Whoooaa! I hear his magic's incredible! I'm all fired up!!!
The reward is four hundred thousand each. You can pay your rent, Lucy.
Yeah!
That's about six-month's worth! Let's do this!
Hey, did you hear about *Akarifa*?
You mean how some violent gang holed themselves up in the *Enterprise Guild* there? Yeah, scary stuff!

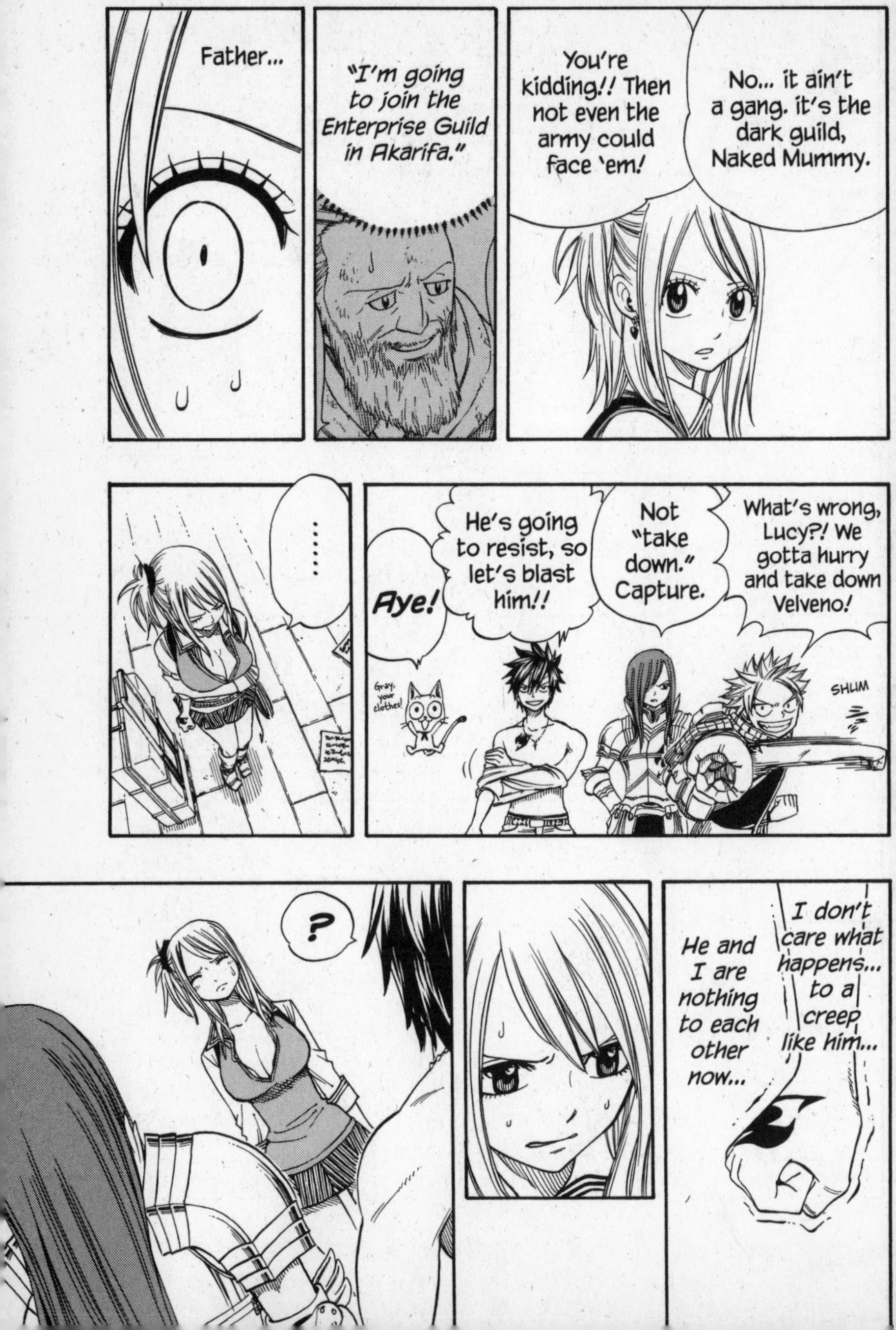
No... it ain't a gang. it's the dark guild, Naked Mummy.
You're kidding!! Then not even the army could face 'em!
"I'm going to join the Enterprise Guild in Akarifa."
Father...
What's wrong, Lucy?! We gotta hurry and take down Velveno!
SHUM
Not "take down." Capture.
He's going to resist, so let's blast him!!
Aye!
Gray, your clothes!
......
I don't care what happens... to a creep like him...
He and I are nothing to each other now...
?

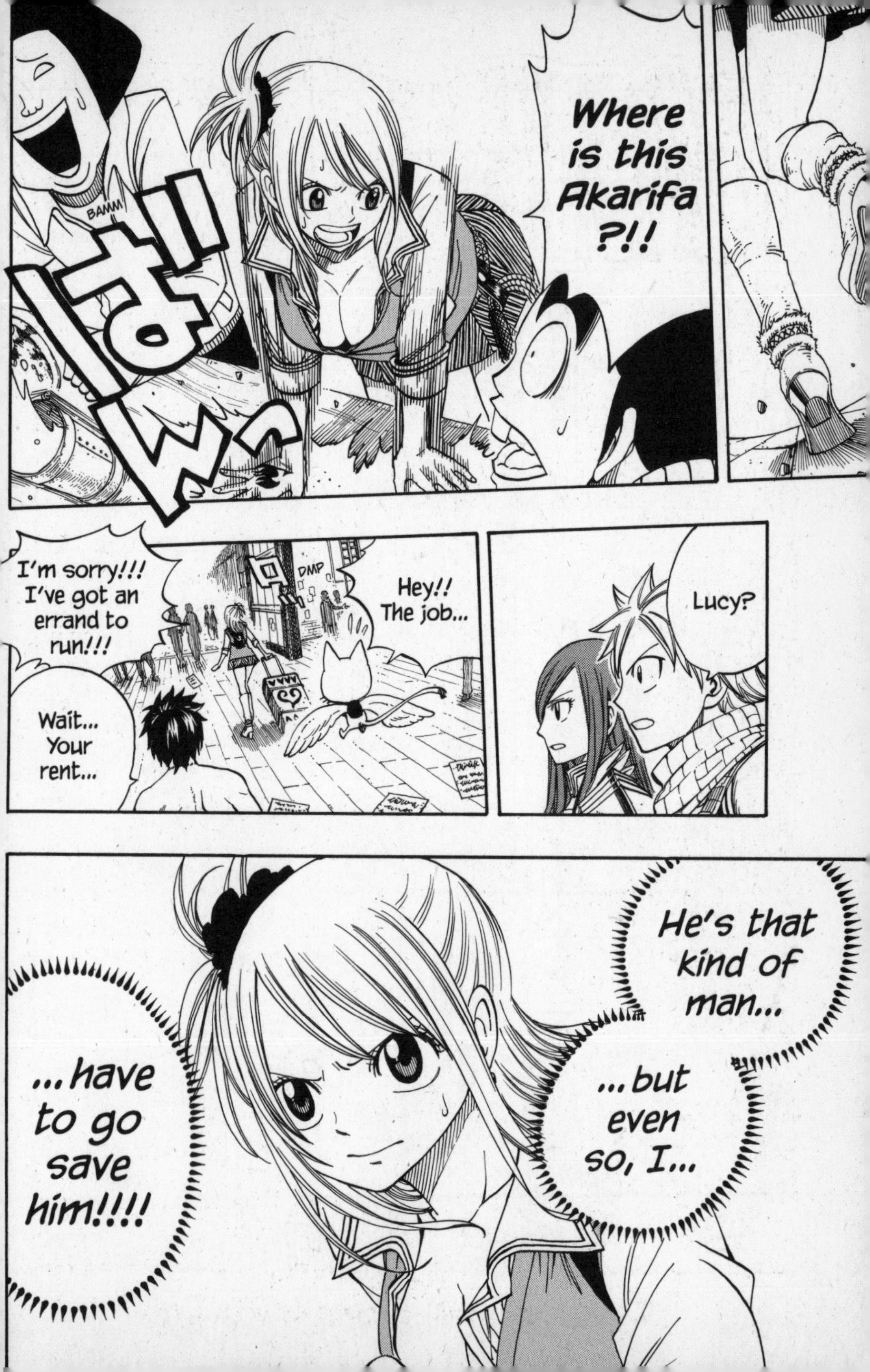
Where is this Akarifa ?!!
BAMM
Lucy?
Hey!! The job...
DMP
I'm sorry!!! I've got an errand to run!!!
Wait... Your rent...
He's that kind of man...
...but even so, I...
...have to go save him!!!!

FAIRY TAIL

Chapter 130, Love & Lucky

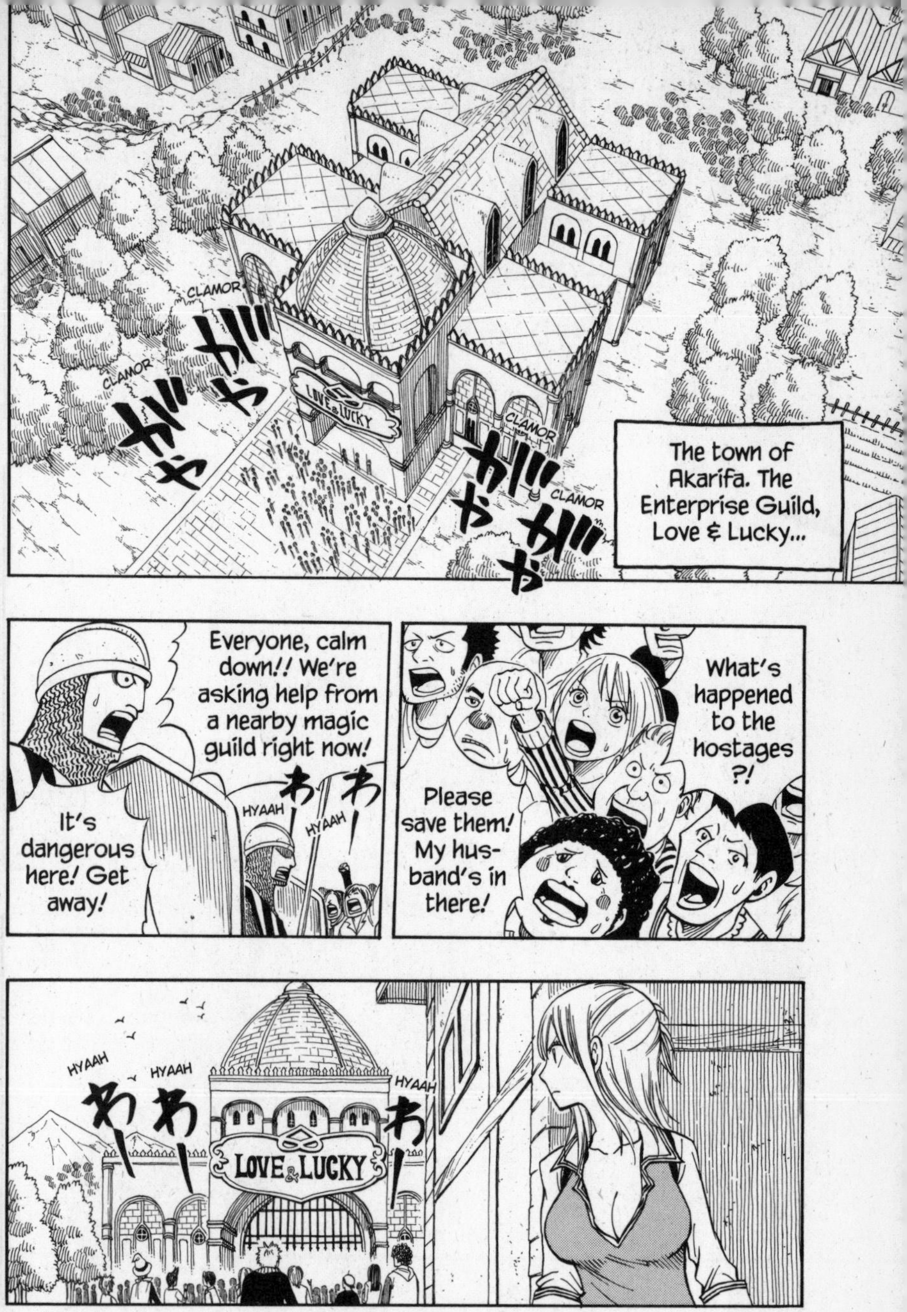
The town of Akarifa. The Enterprise Guild, Love & Lucky...
CLAMOR
CLAMOR
CLAMOR
CLAMOR
LOVE & LUCKY
What's happened to the hostages?!
Please save them! My hus-band's in there!
Everyone, calm down!! We're asking help from a nearby magic guild right now!
It's dangerous here! Get away!
HYAAH
HYAAH
HYAAH
HYAAH
HYAAH
LOVE & LUCKY

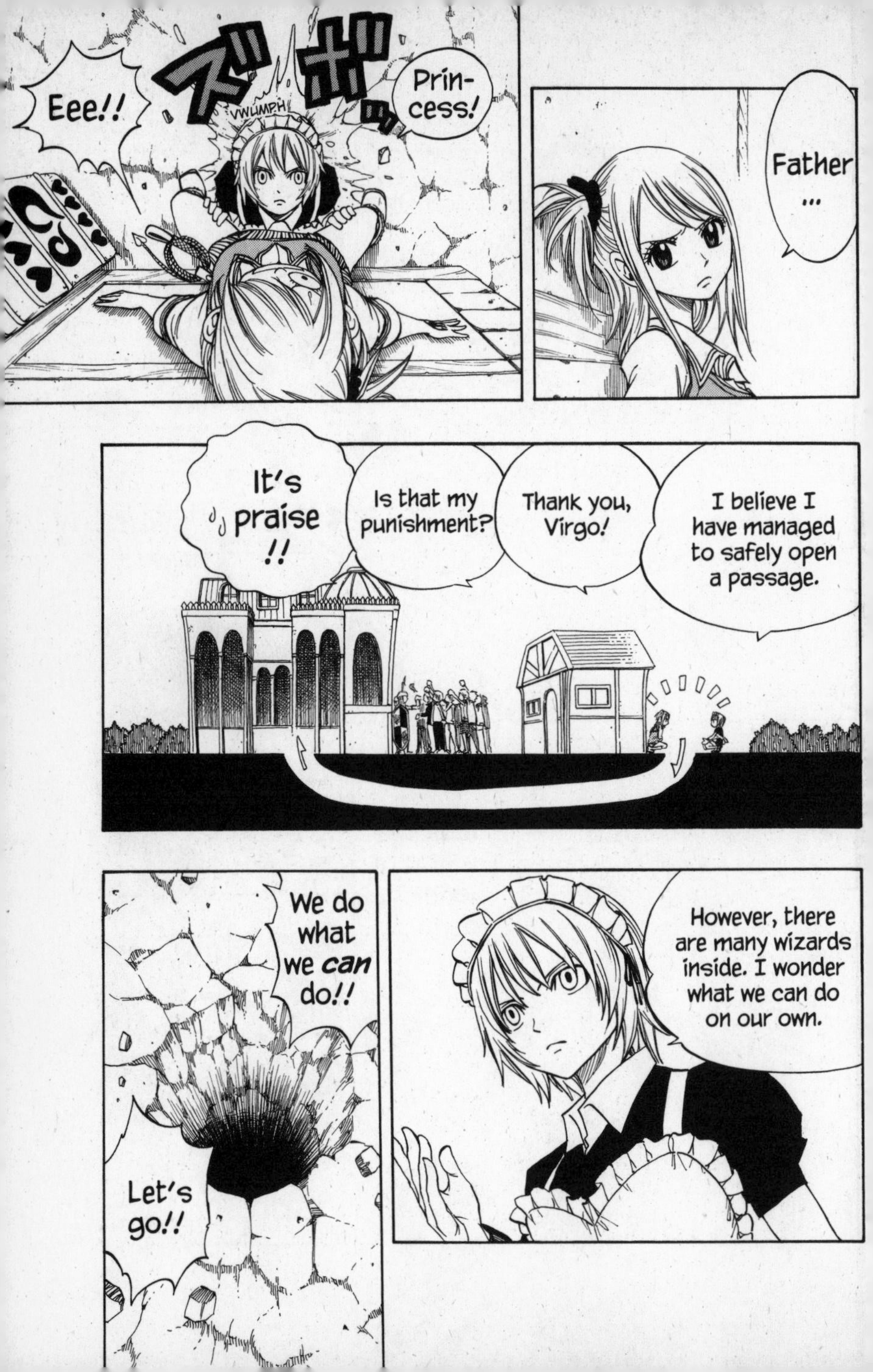
Father ...
Prin- cess!
ズボッ
VWUMPH
Eee!!
I believe I have managed to safely open a passage.
Thank you, Virgo!
Is that my punishment?
It's praise!!
However, there are many wizards inside. I wonder what we can do on our own.
We do what we *can* do!!
Let's go!!

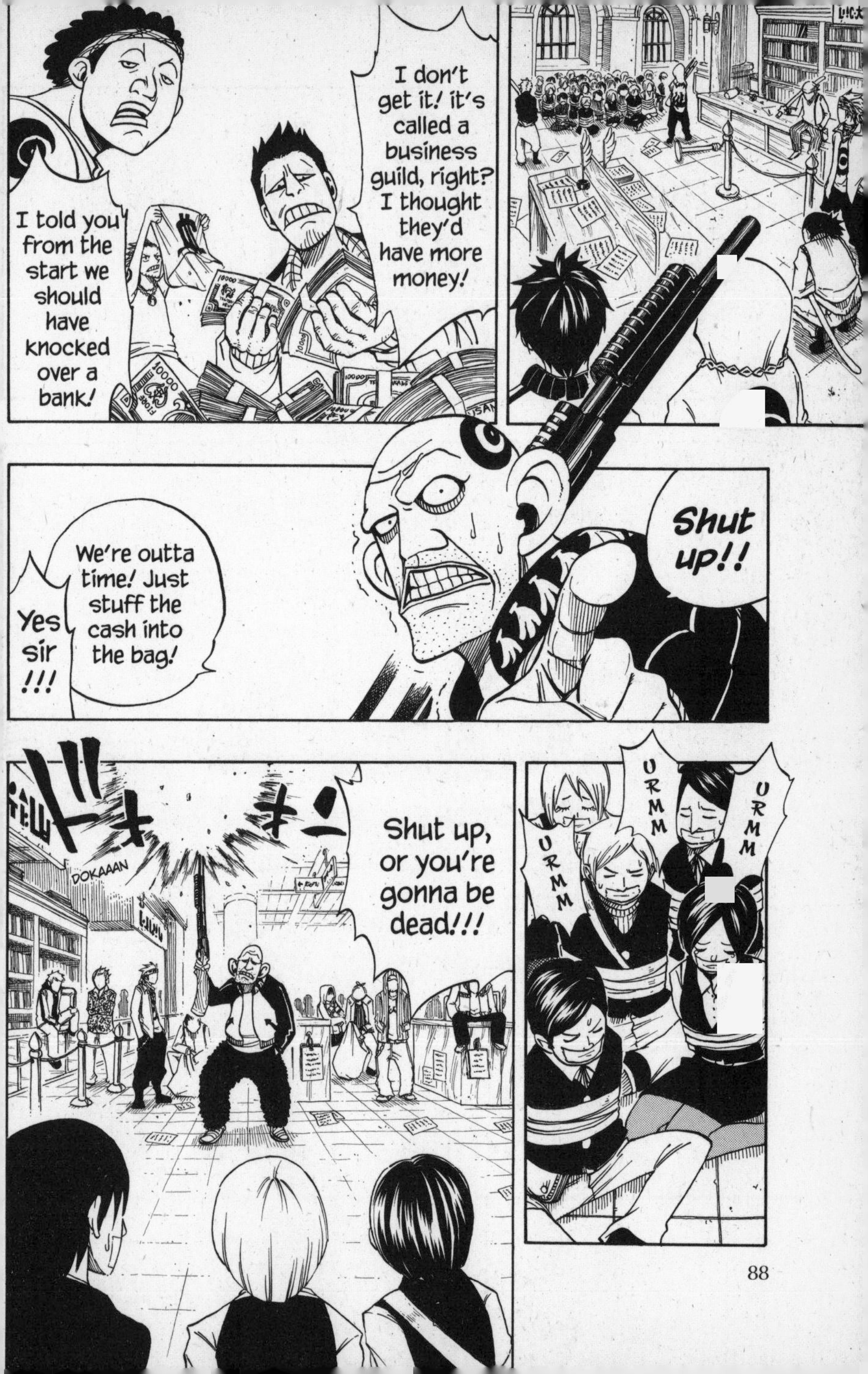

I don't get it! it's called a business guild, right? I thought they'd have more money!
I told you from the start we should have knocked over a bank!
Shut up!!
We're outta time! Just stuff the cash into the bag!
Yes sir!!!
URMM
URMM
URMM
Shut up, or you're gonna be dead!!!
DOKAAAN

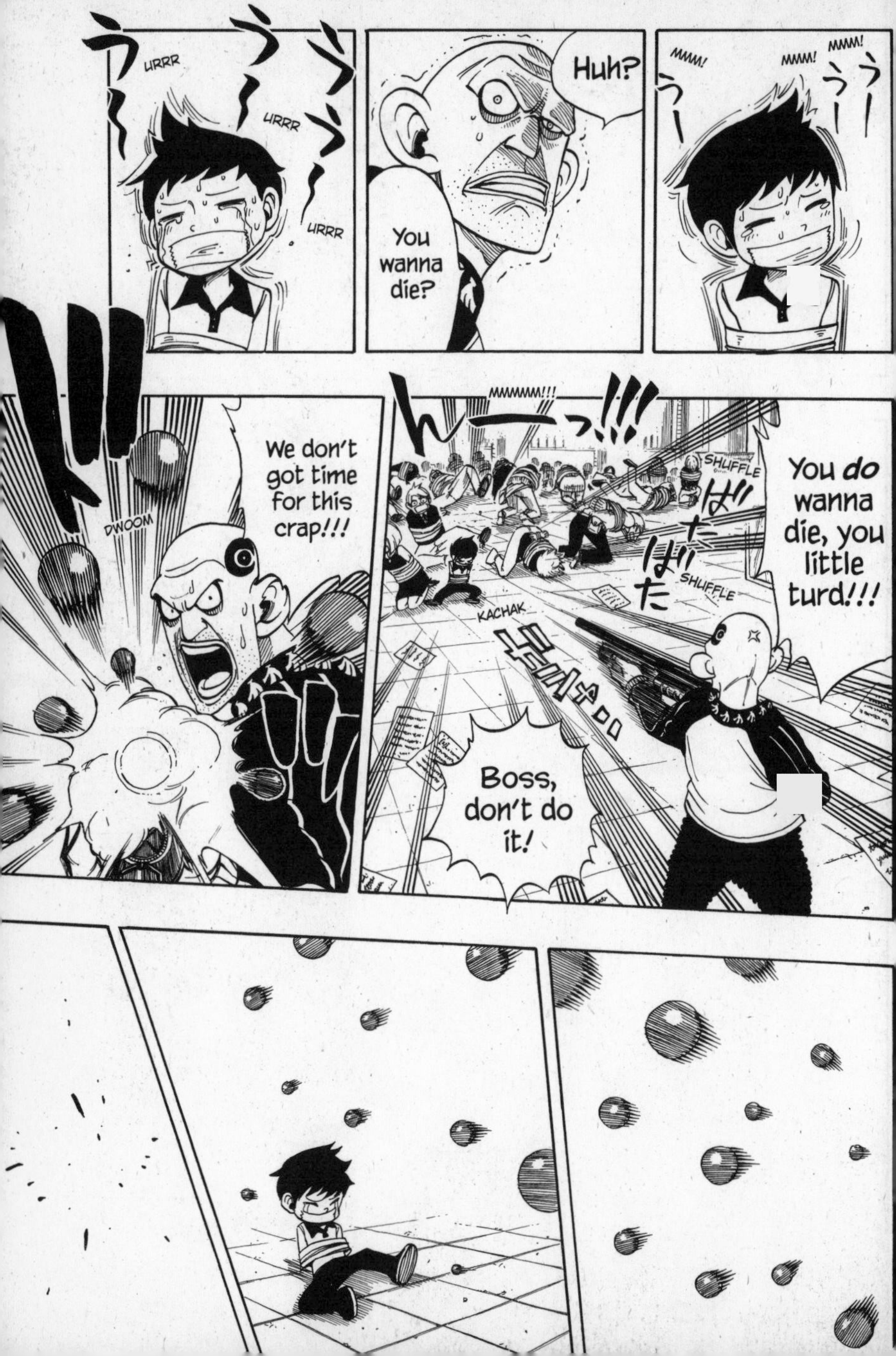
MMM!
MMM!
MMM!
Huh?
You wanna die?
URRR
URRR
URRR
MMMMMM!!!
SHUFFLE
SHUFFLE
You do wanna die, you little turd!!!
KACHAK
Boss, don't do it!
We don't got time for this crap!!!
DWOOM

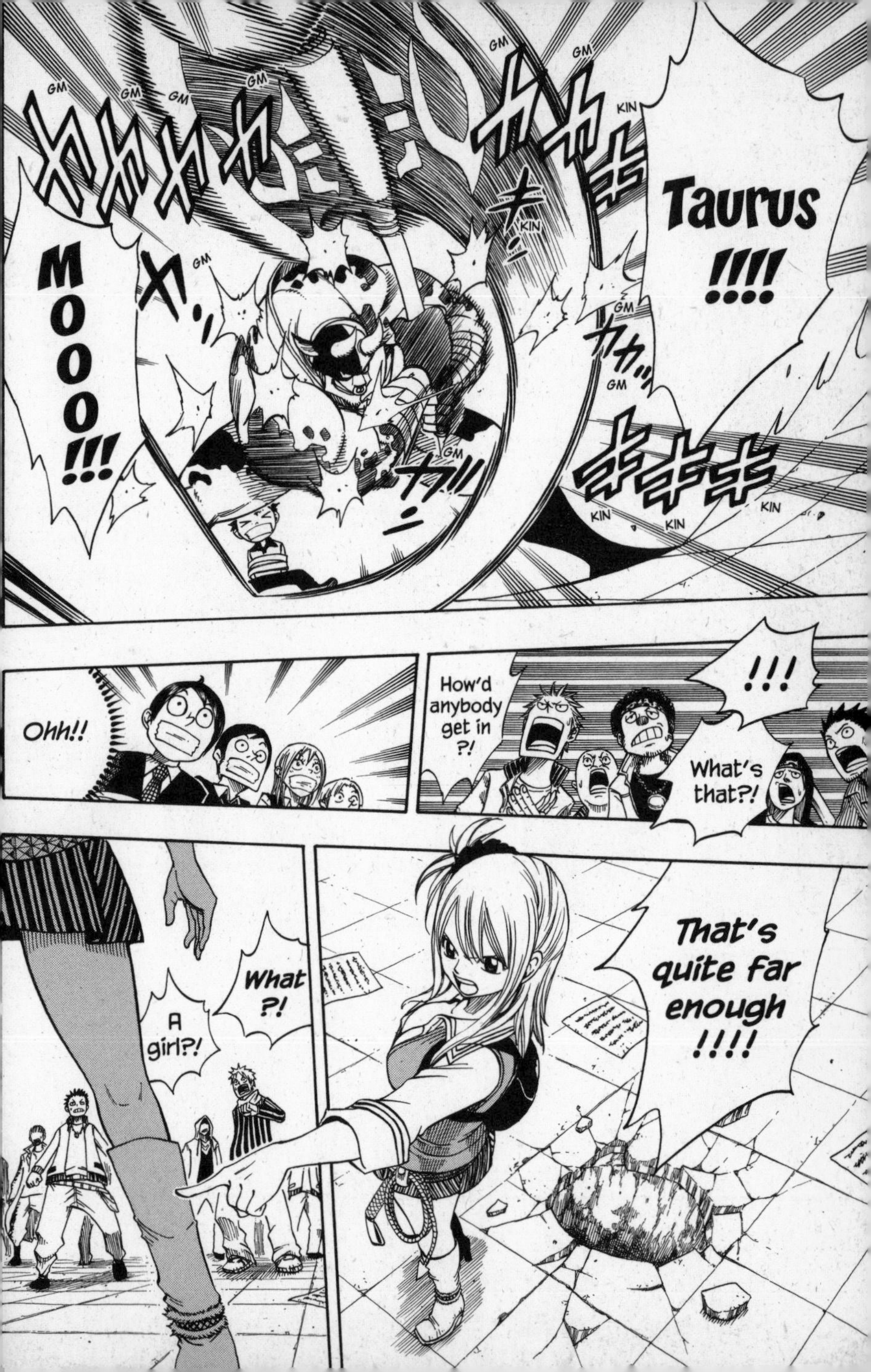

Taurus !!!!
KIN
GM
MOOOO!!!
!!!
What's that?!
How'd anybody get in ?!
Ohh!!
That's quite far enough !!!!
What ?!
A girl?!

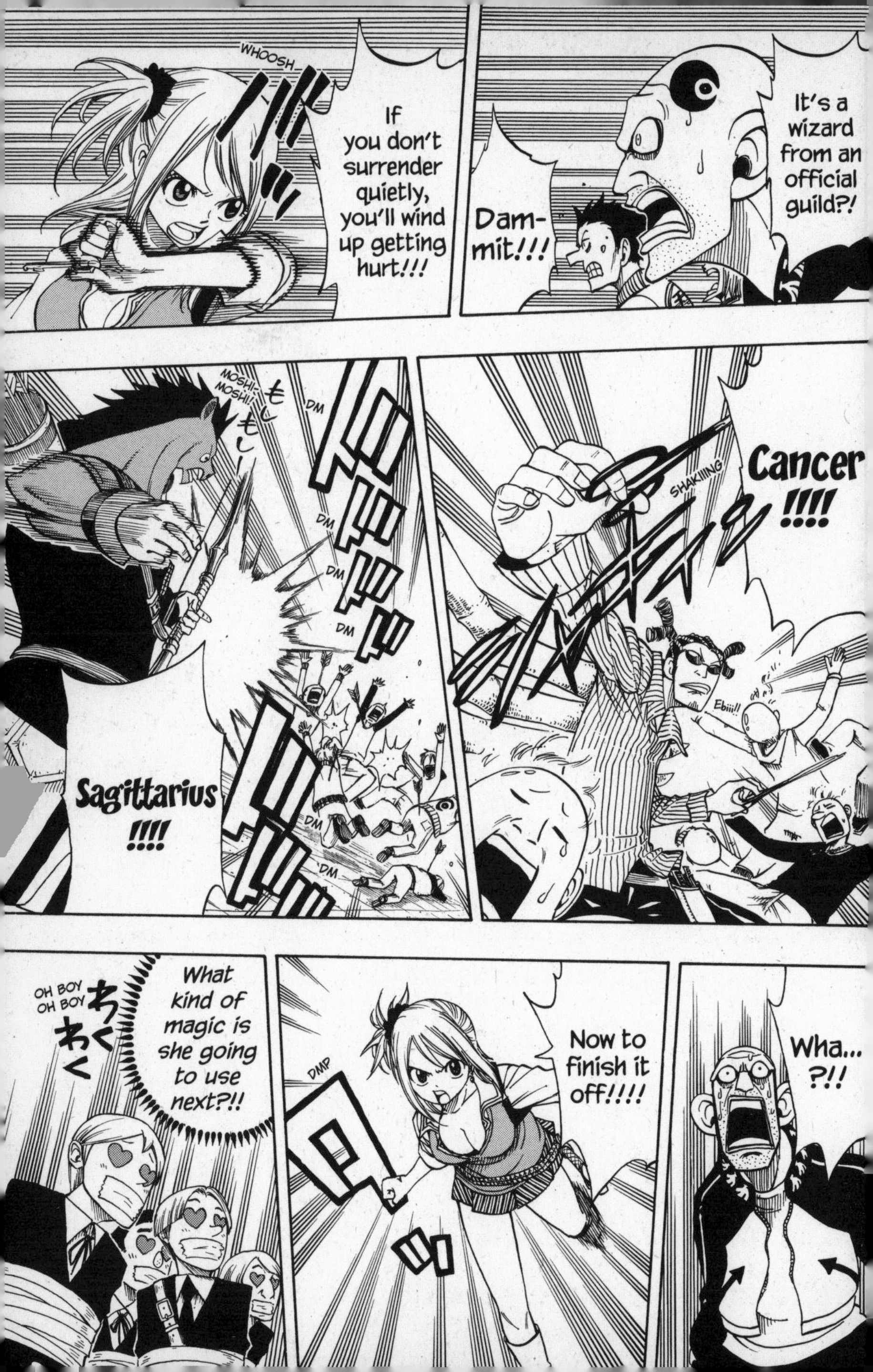
It's a wizard from an official guild?!
Dam-mit!!!
WHOOSH
If you don't surrender quietly, you'll wind up getting hurt!!!
Cancer!!!!
SHAKIIING
Ebiii!!
MOSHI-MOSHI!
もしもし
DM
DM
DM
DM
DM
DM
Sagittarius!!!!
Wha...?!!
Now to finish it off!!!!
DMP
OH BOY OH BOY
わくわく
What kind of magic is she going to use next?!!

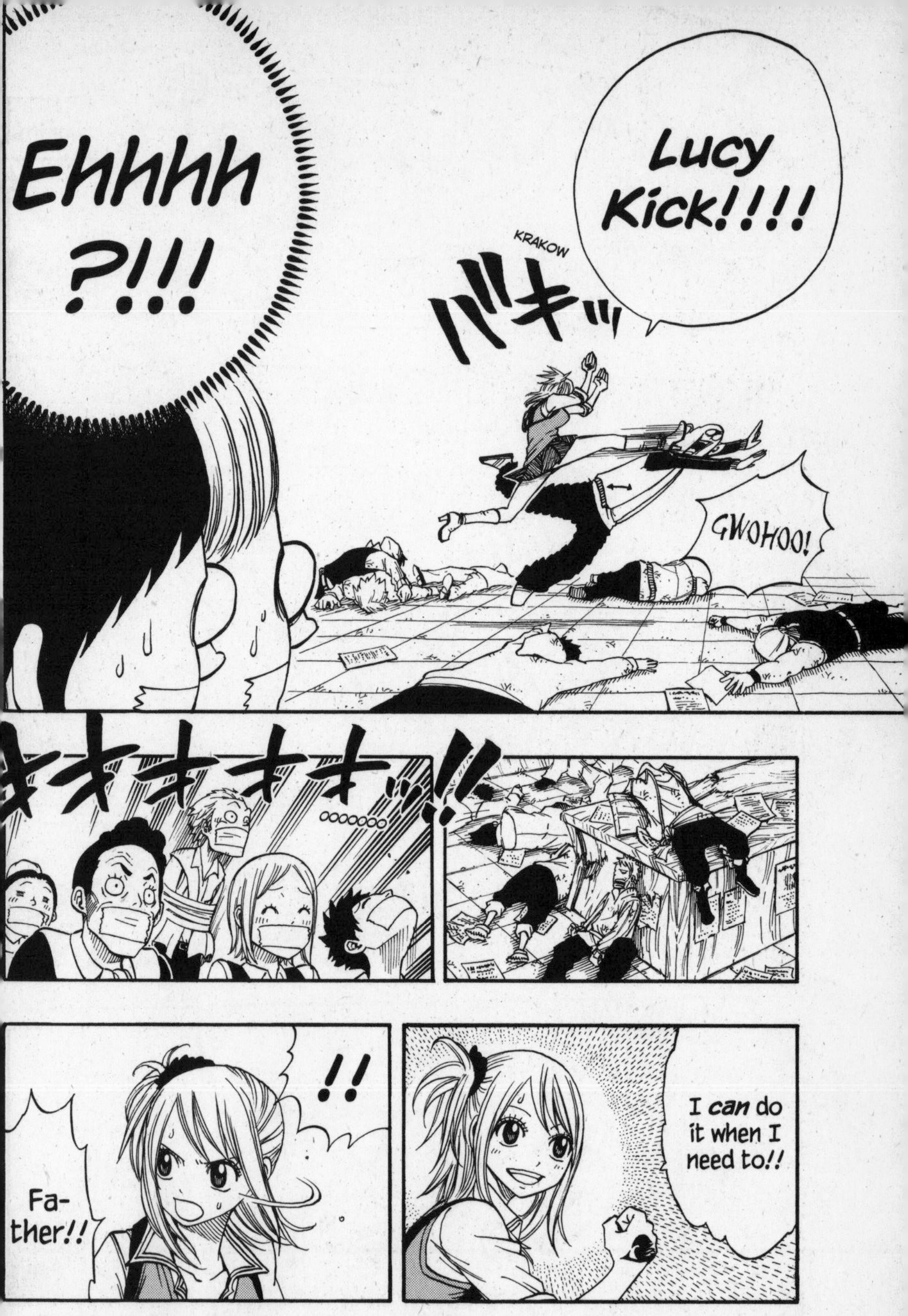
Lucy Kick!!!!
Ehhhh ?!!!
KRAKOW
GWOHOO!
ooooooo
I *can* do it when I need to!!
!!
Fa-ther!!

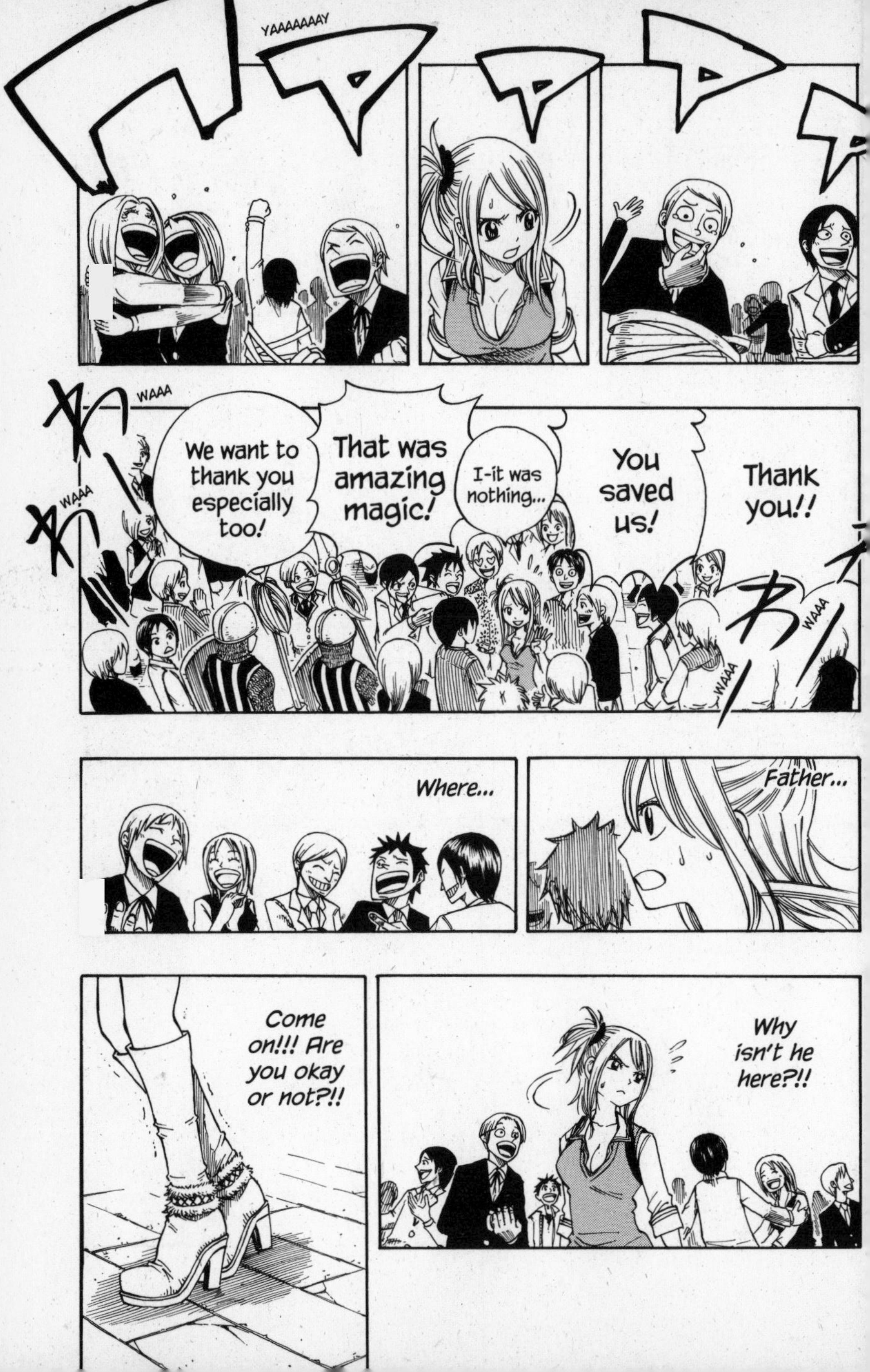
YAAAAAAAY
Thank you!!
You saved us!
I-it was nothing...
That was amazing magic!
We want to thank you especially too!
WAAA
WAAA
WAAA
WAAA
Father...
Where...
Why isn't he here?!!
Come on!!! Are you okay or not?!!

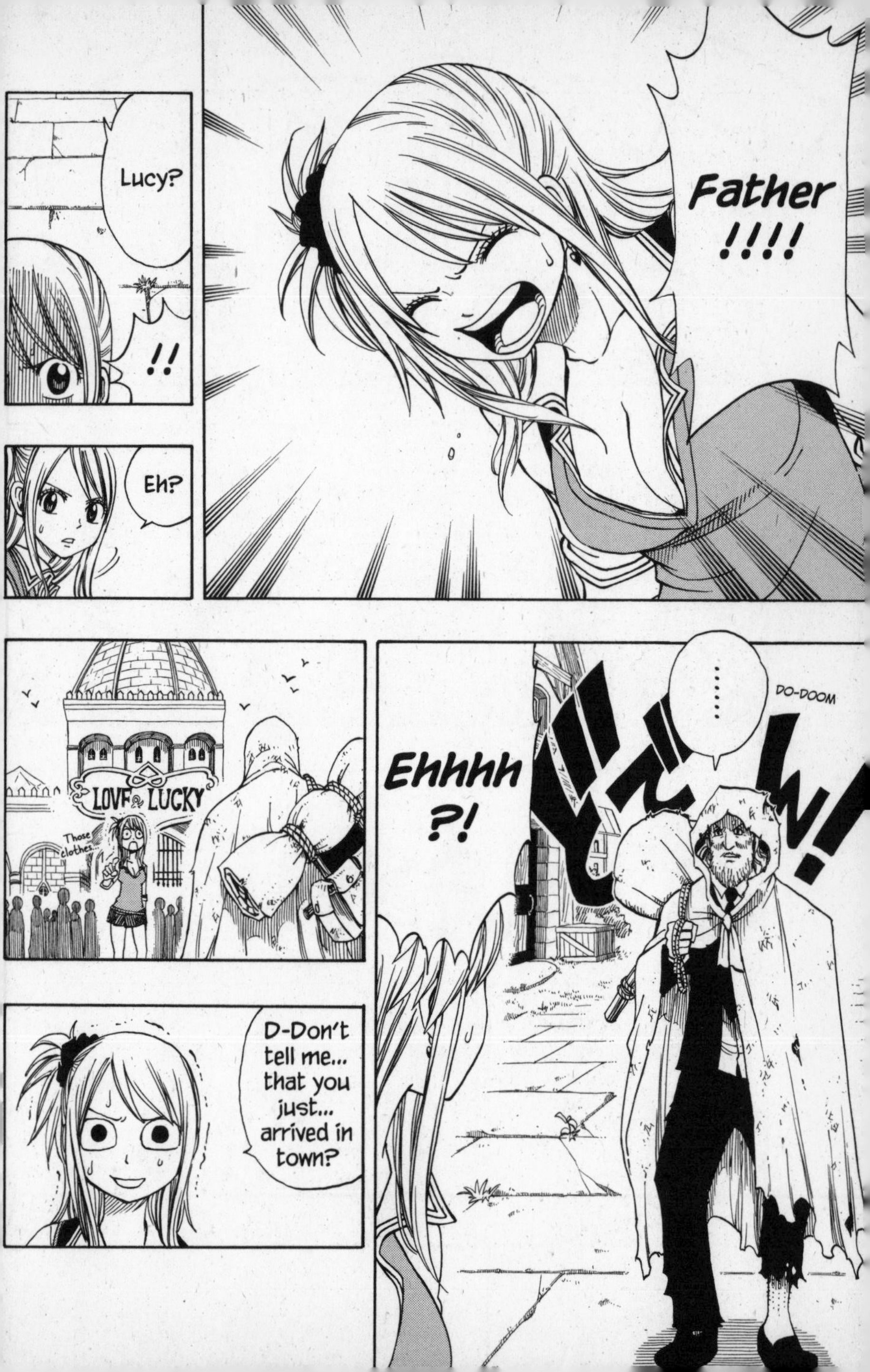
Father !!!!
Lucy?
!!
Eh?
......
DO-DOOM
Ehhhh ?!
LOVE & LUCKY
Those clothes...
D-Don't tell me... that you just... arrived in town?

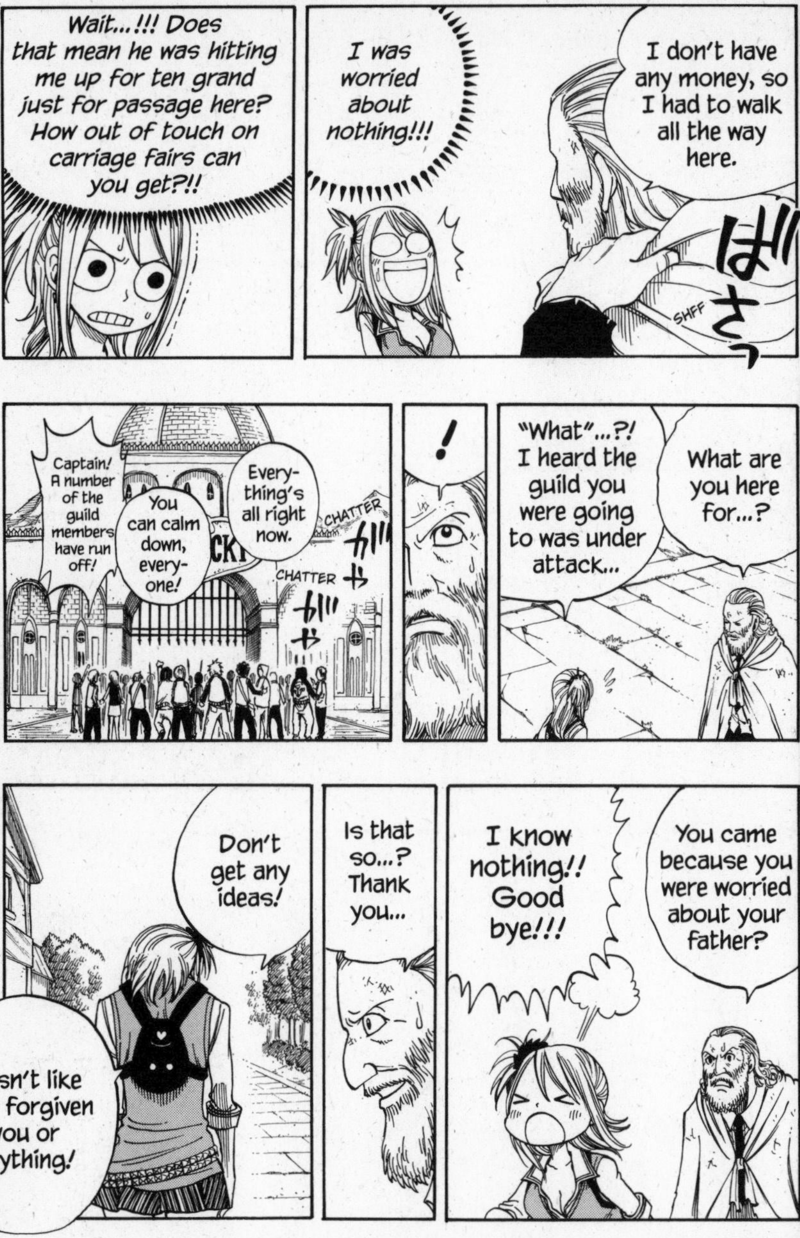
I don't have any money, so I had to walk all the way here.
ばさっ
SHFF
I was worried about nothing!!!
Wait...!!! Does that mean he was hitting me up for ten grand just for passage here? How out of touch on carriage fairs can you get?!!
What are you here for...?
"What"...?! I heard the guild you were going to was under attack...
!
Every-thing's all right now.
CHATTER
がや
Captain! A number of the guild members have run off!
You can calm down, every-one!
CHATTER
がや
You came because you were worried about your father?
I know nothing!! Good bye!!!
Is that so...? Thank you...
Don't get any ideas!
It isn't like I've forgiven you or anything!

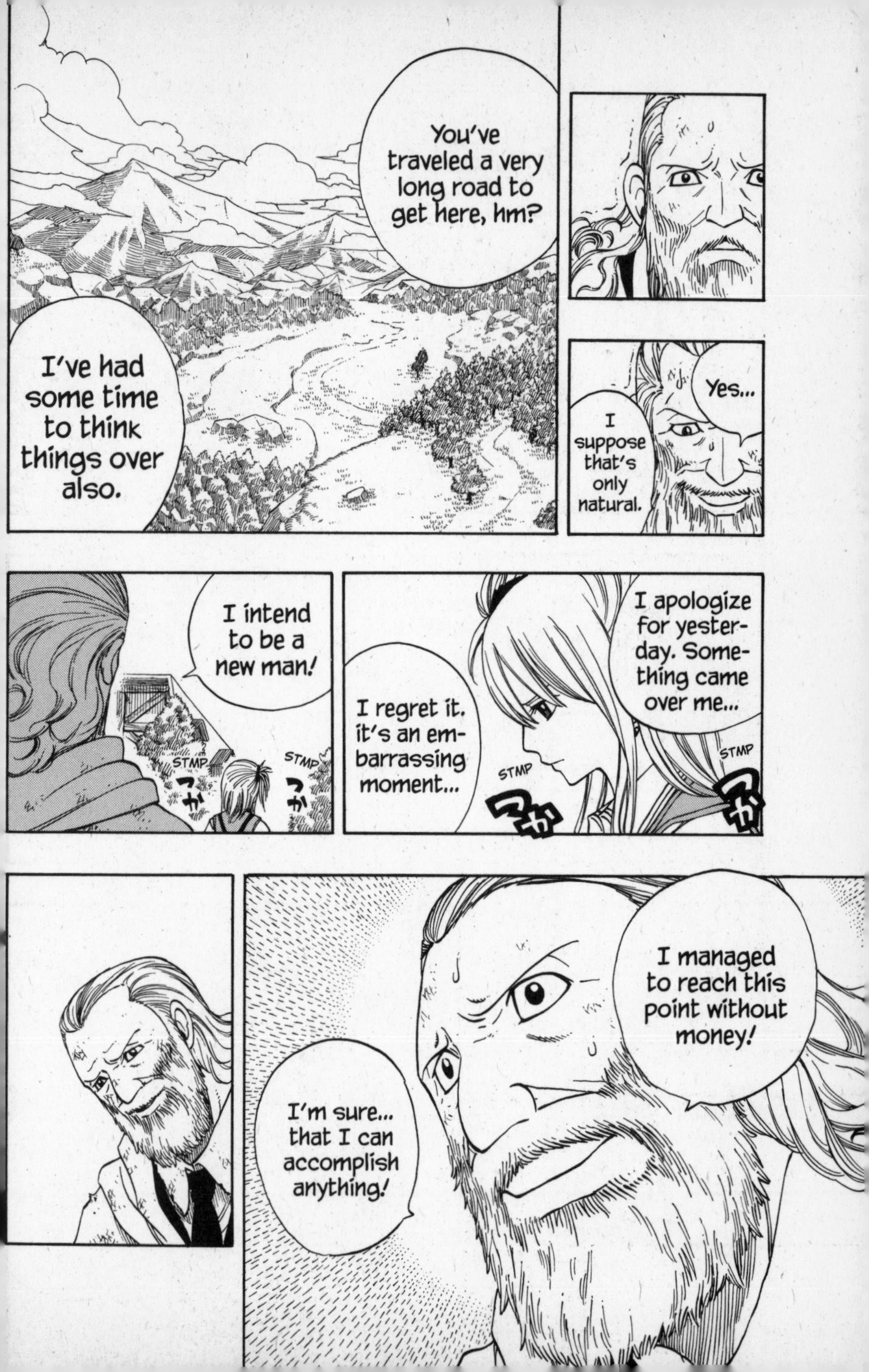
Yes...
I suppose that's only natural.
You've traveled a very long road to get here, hm?
I've had some time to think things over also.
I apologize for yester-day. Some-thing came over me...
STMP
I regret it. it's an em-barrassing moment...
STMP
I intend to be a new man!
STMP
STMP
I managed to reach this point without money!
I'm sure... that I can accomplish anything!

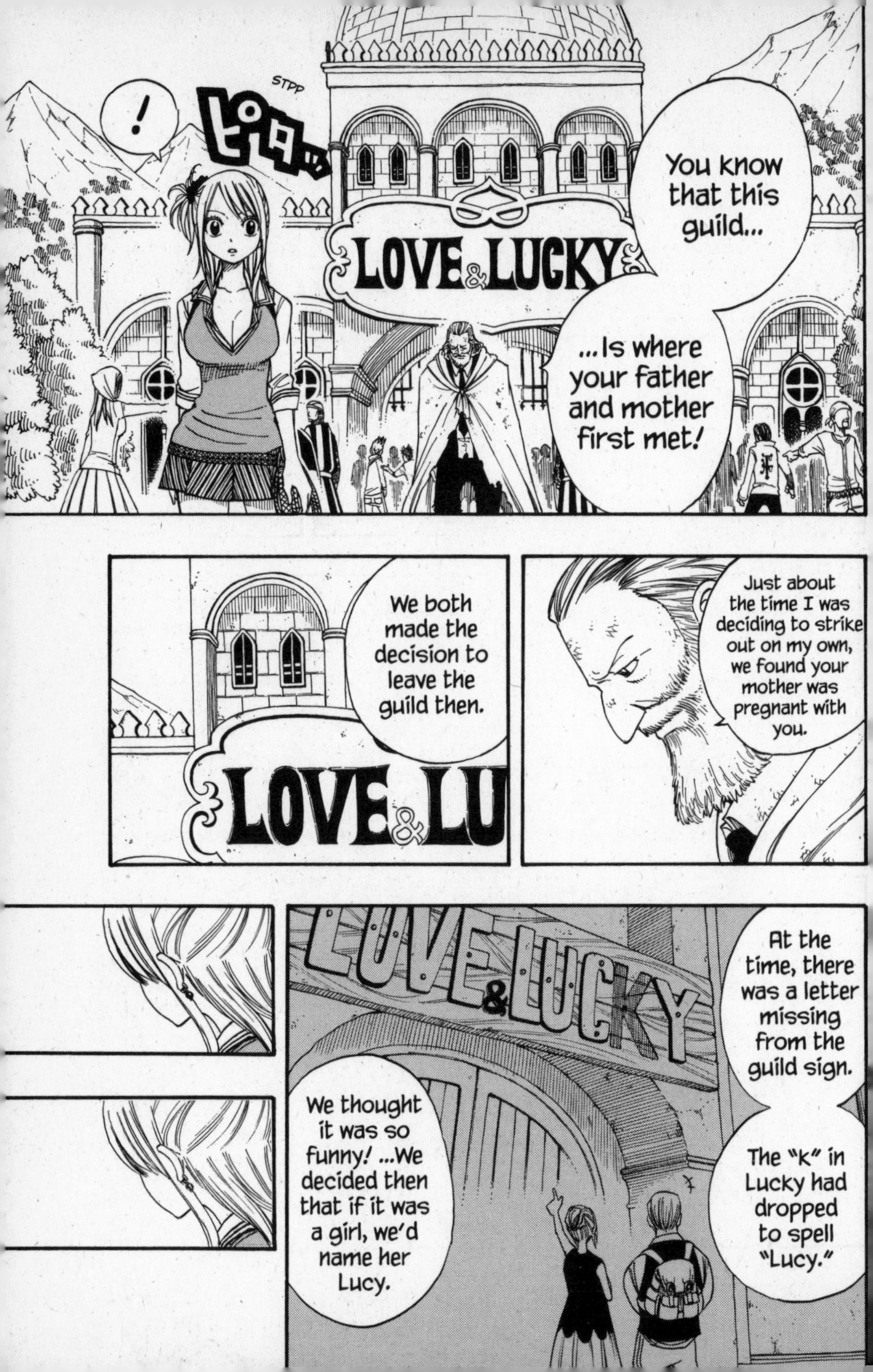
You know that this guild...
...Is where your father and mother first met!
LOVE & LUCKY
STPP
!
Just about the time I was deciding to strike out on my own, we found your mother was pregnant with you.
We both made the decision to leave the guild then.
LOVE & LU
At the time, there was a letter missing from the guild sign.
The "K" in Lucky had dropped to spell "Lucy."
LOVE & LUCKY
We thought it was so funny! ...We decided then that if it was a girl, we'd name her Lucy.

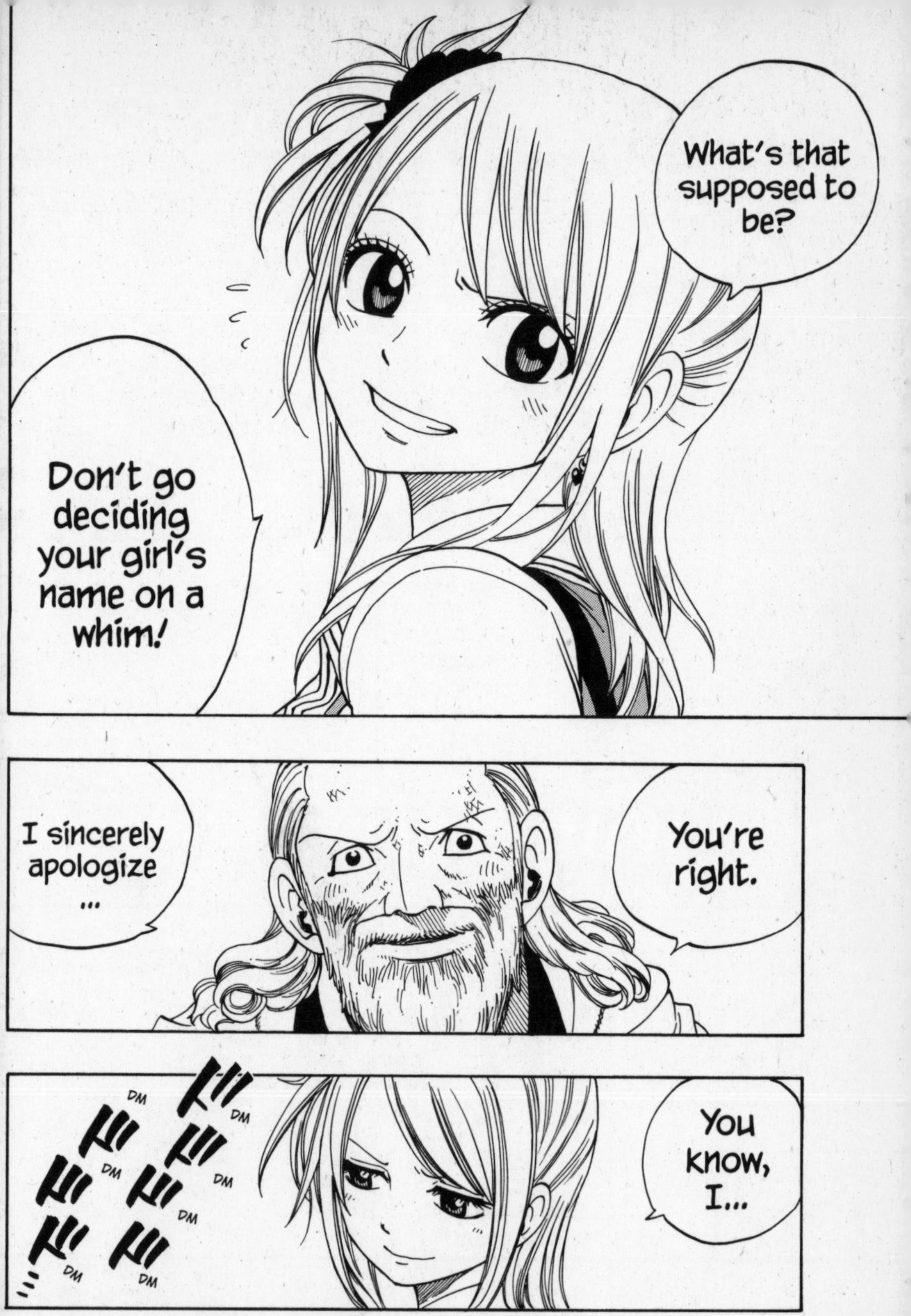
What's that supposed to be?
Don't go deciding your girl's name on a whim!
You're right.
I sincerely apologize ...
You know, I...
DM DM DM DM DM DM DM

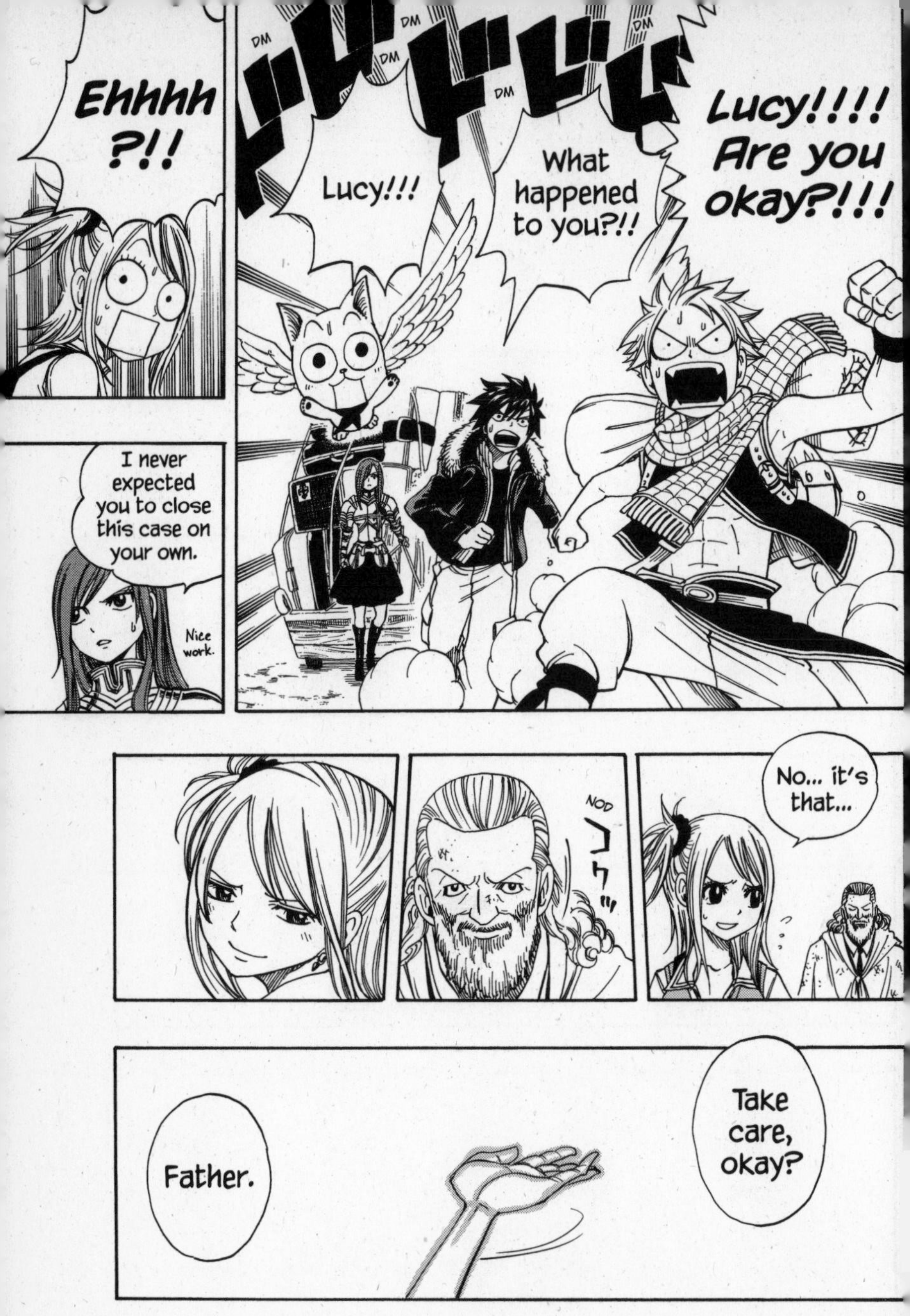
DM DM DM DM DM
Lucy!!!! Are you okay?!!!
What happened to you?!!
Lucy!!!
Ehhhh ?!!
I never expected you to close this case on your own.
Nice work.
No... it's that...
NOD
Take care, okay?
Father.

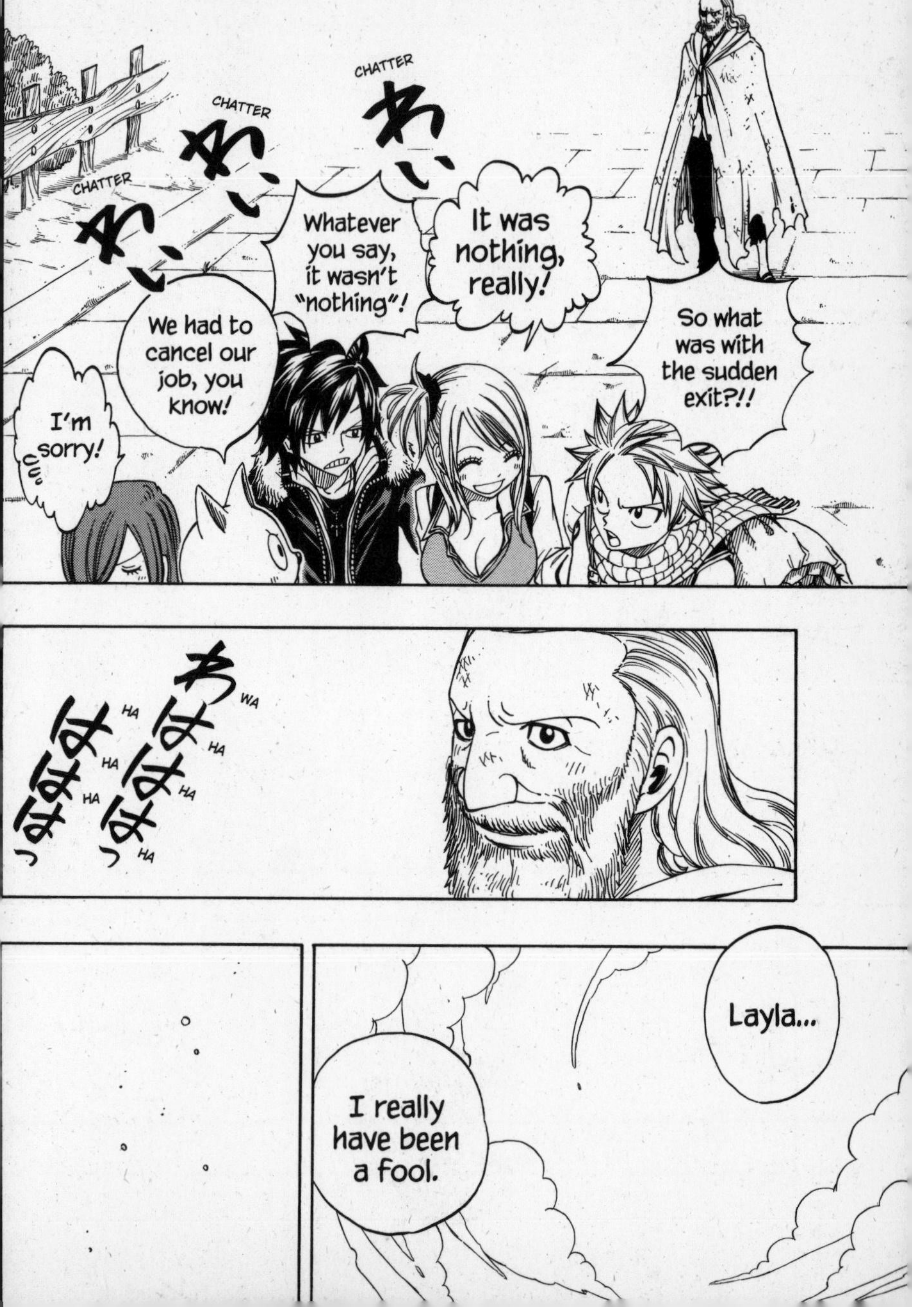
CHATTER
わい
CHATTER
わい
CHATTER
わい
So what was with the sudden exit?!!
It was nothing, really!
Whatever you say, it wasn't "nothing"!
We had to cancel our job, you know!
I'm sorry!
わははははっ
WA HA HA HA HA HA
Layla...
I really have been a fool.

Main Guild Building of the dark guild, Naked Mummy...
The money!
Where is it?
I'b forry! An official guilf got in da way ...!!!
Dere wath nothig we could do!!!!

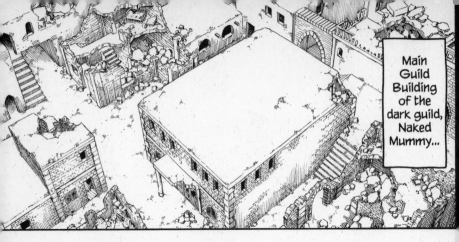

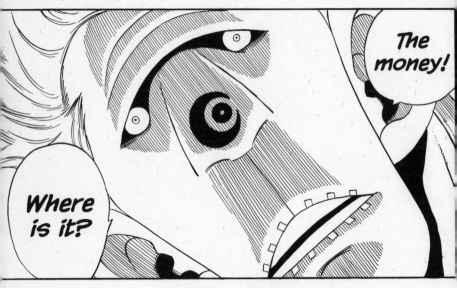

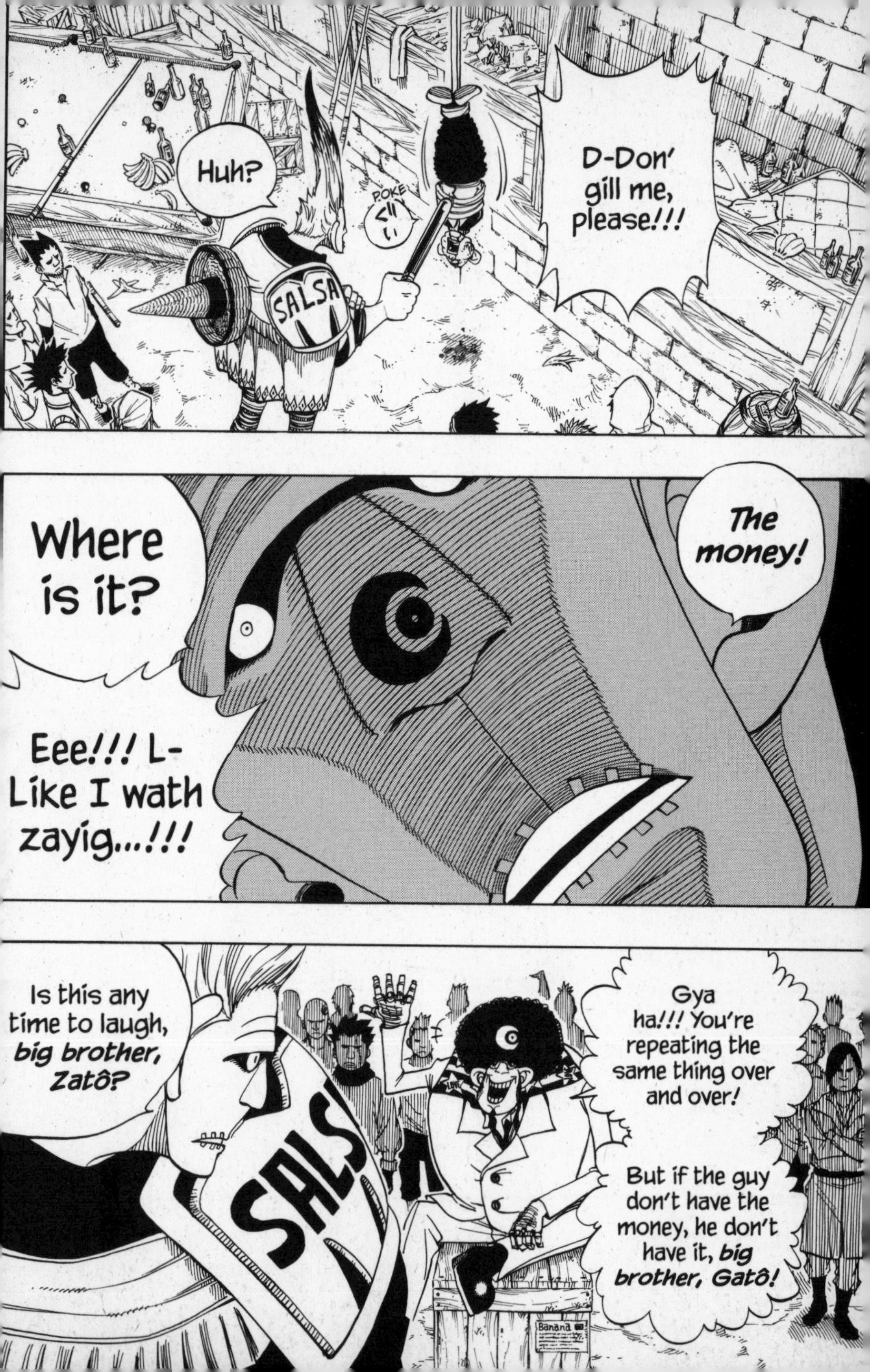
D-Don' gill me, please!!!
POKE
Huh?
SALSA
The money!
Where is it?
Eee!!! L-Like I wath zayig...!!!
Gya ha!!! You're repeating the same thing over and over!
But if the guy don't have the money, he don't have it, *big brother, Gatô!*
Is this any time to laugh, *big brother, Zatô?*
SALS
Banana

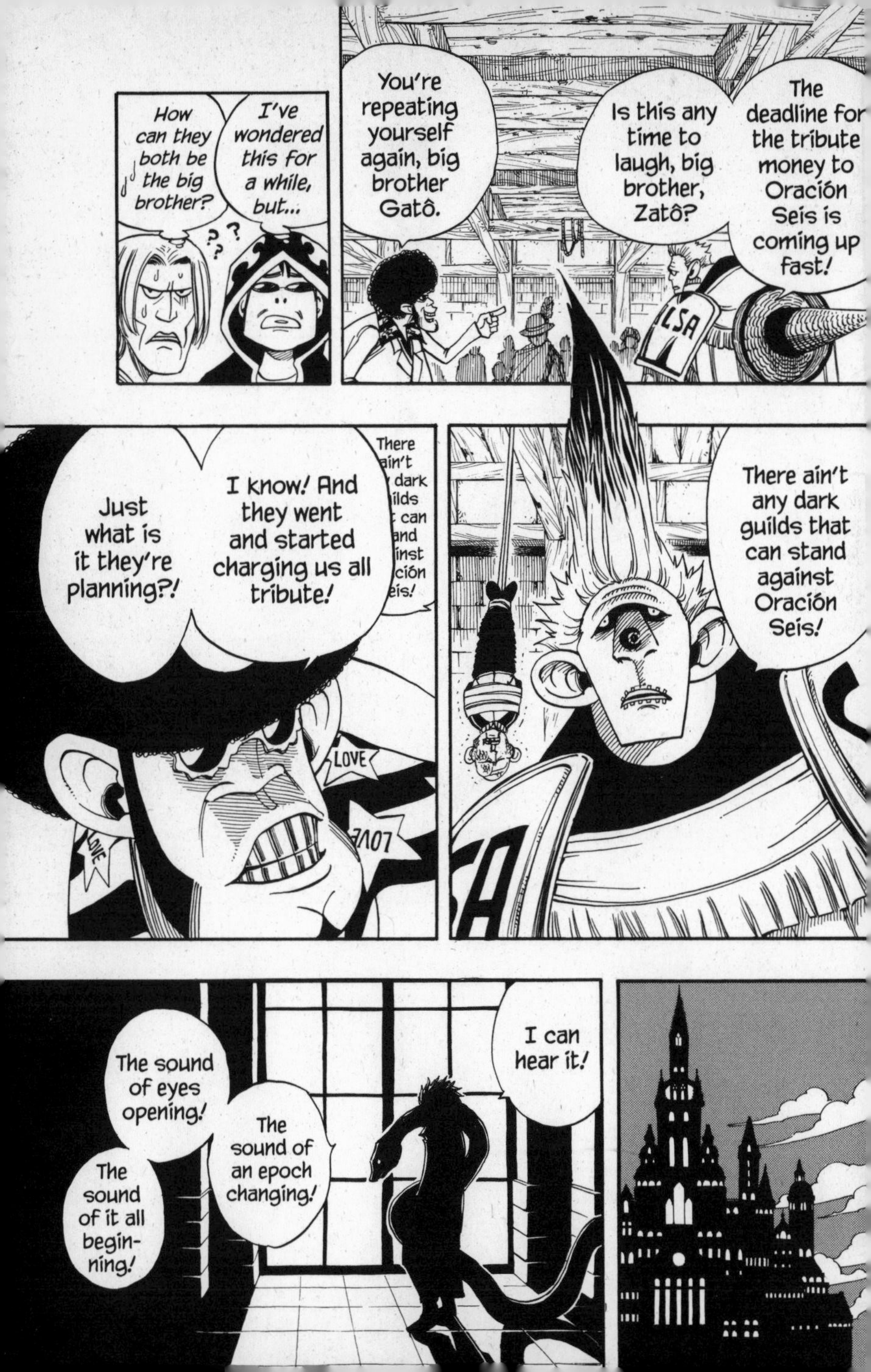
The deadline for the tribute money to Oración Seis is coming up fast!
Is this any time to laugh, big brother, Zatô?
You're repeating yourself again, big brother Gatô.
I've wondered this for a while, but...
How can they both be the big brother?
ELSA
There ain't any dark guilds that can stand against Oración Seis!
I know! And they went and started charging us all tribute!
Just what is it they're planning?!
LOVE
LOVE
LOVE
I can hear it!
The sound of eyes opening!
The sound of an epoch changing!
The sound of it all beginning!

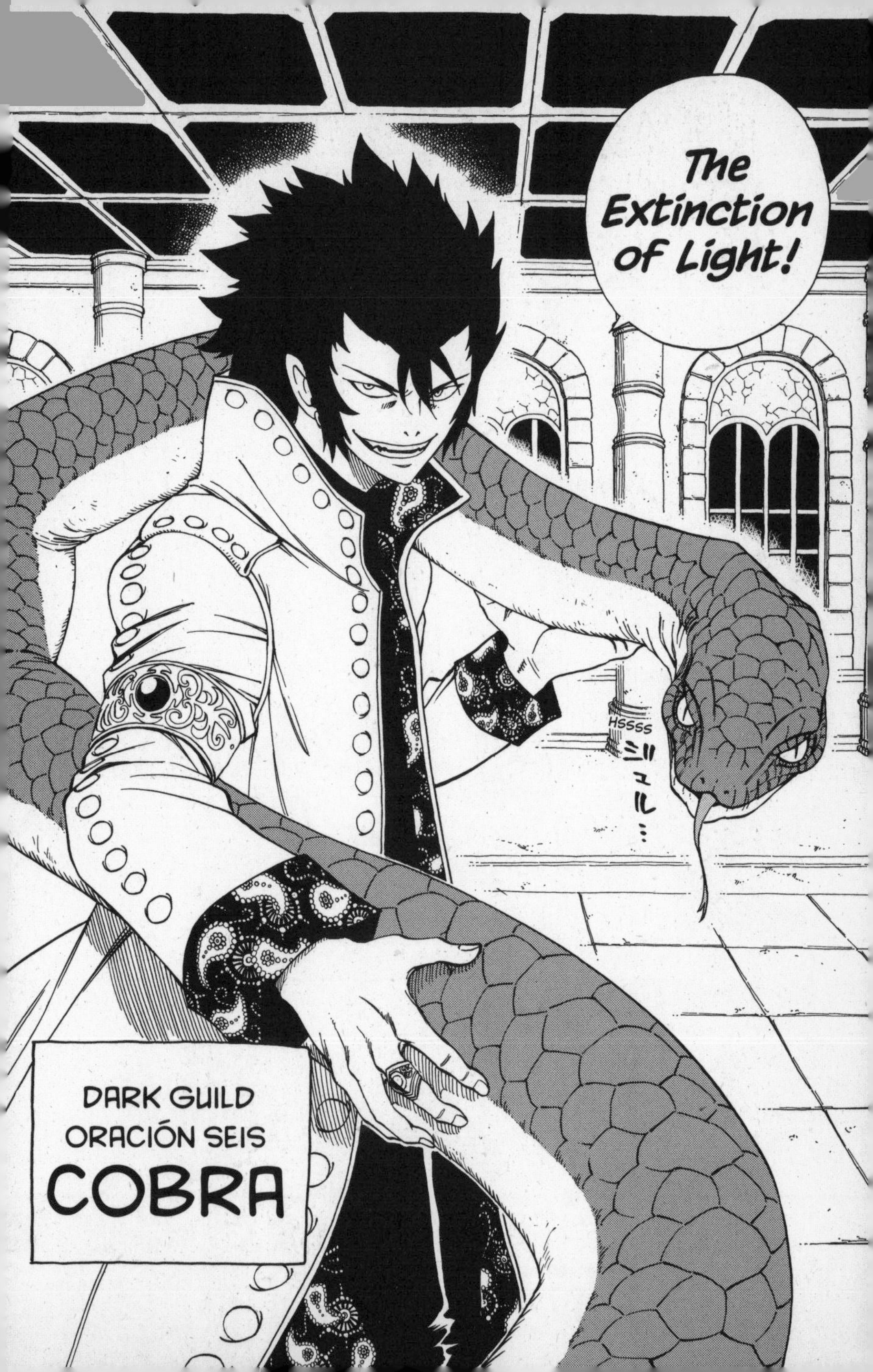
The Extinction of Light!
HSSSS
ジュル…
DARK GUILD
ORACIÓN SEIS
COBRA

FAIRY TAIL

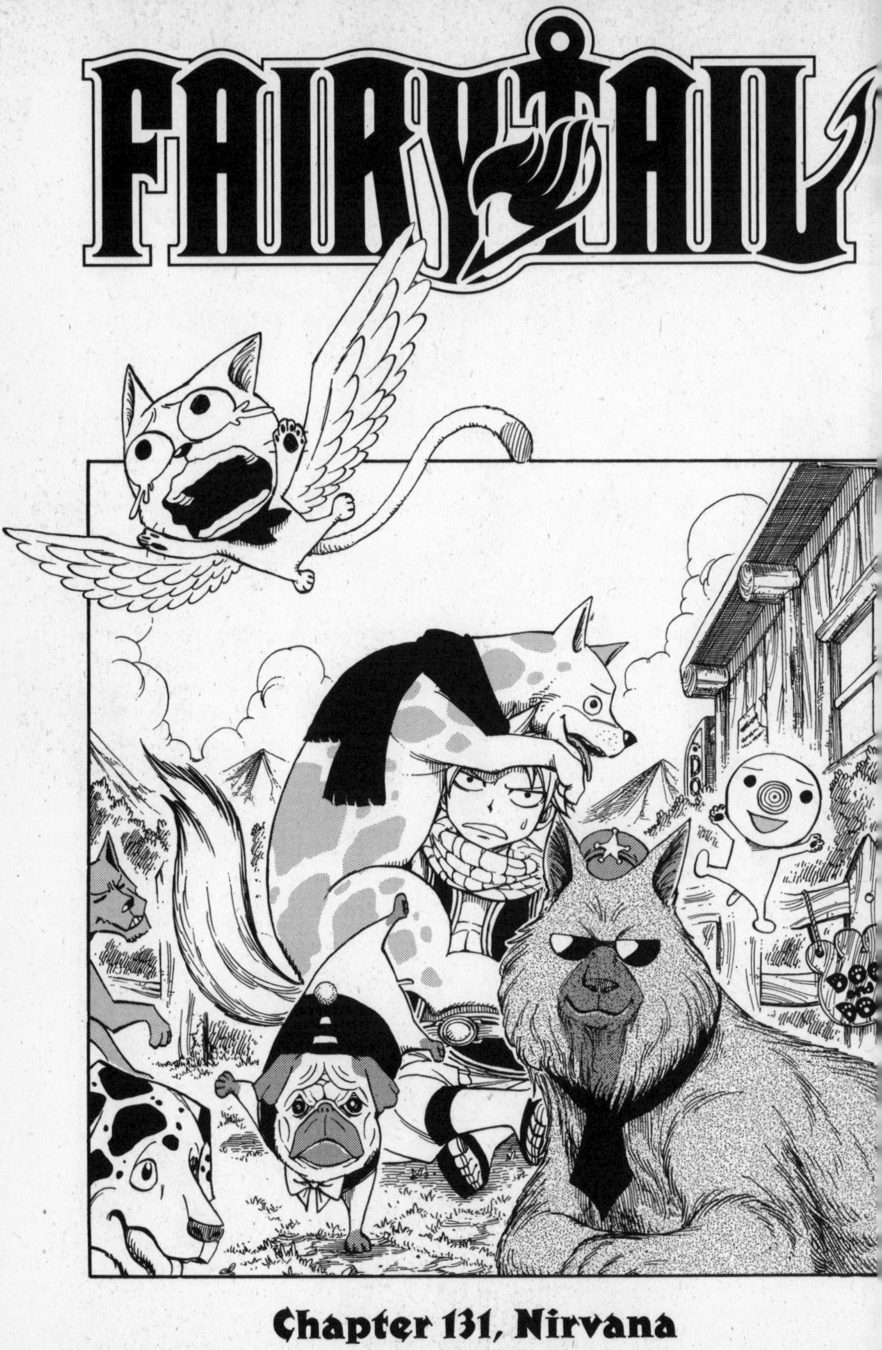

Chapter 131, Nirvana

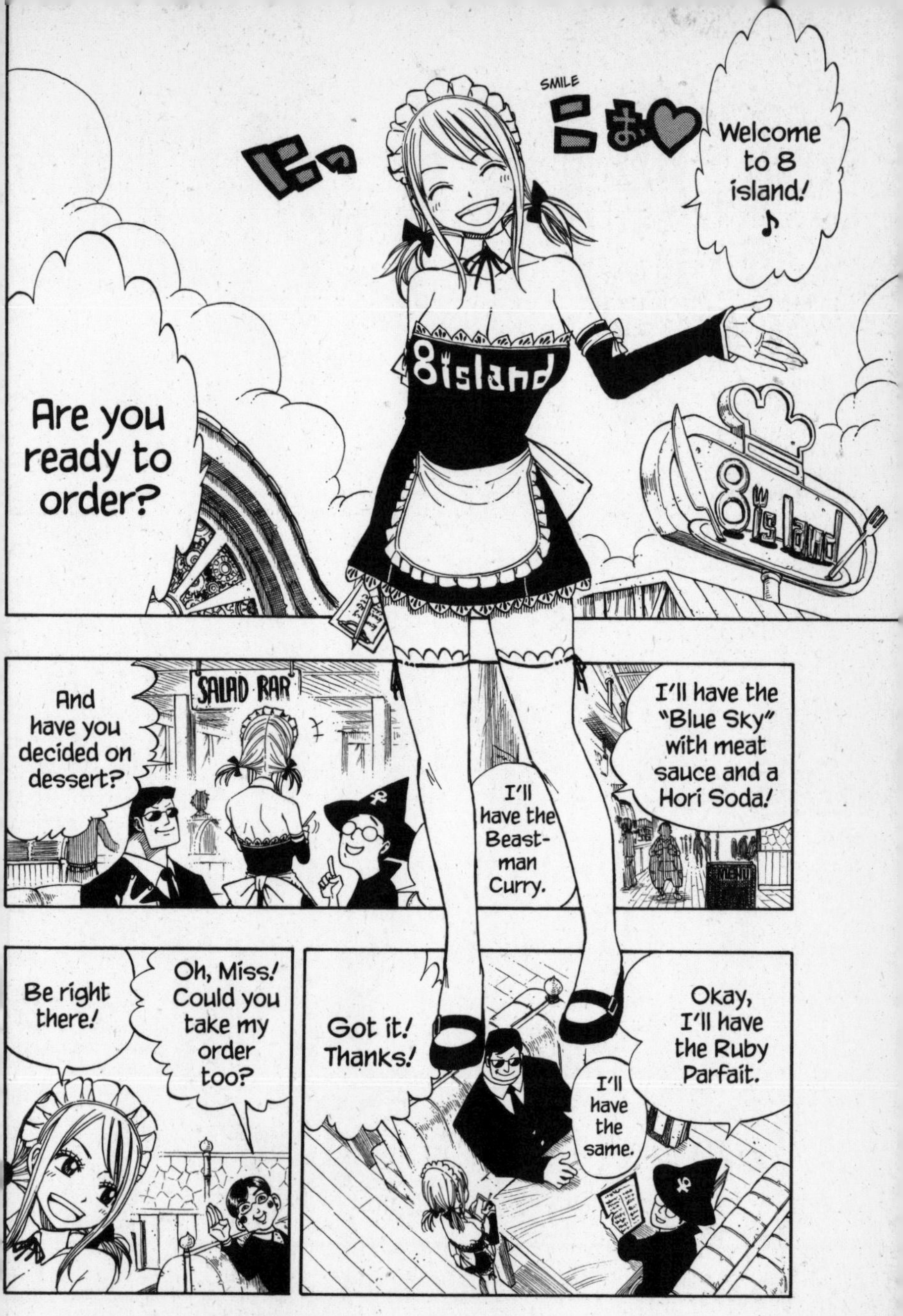
SMILE
Welcome to 8 island! ♪
8 island
8 island
Are you ready to order?
I'll have the "Blue Sky" with meat sauce and a Hori Soda!
I'll have the Beast-man Curry.
SALAD BAR
And have you decided on dessert?
Okay, I'll have the Ruby Parfait.
I'll have the same.
Got it! Thanks!
Oh, Miss! Could you take my order too?
Be right there!

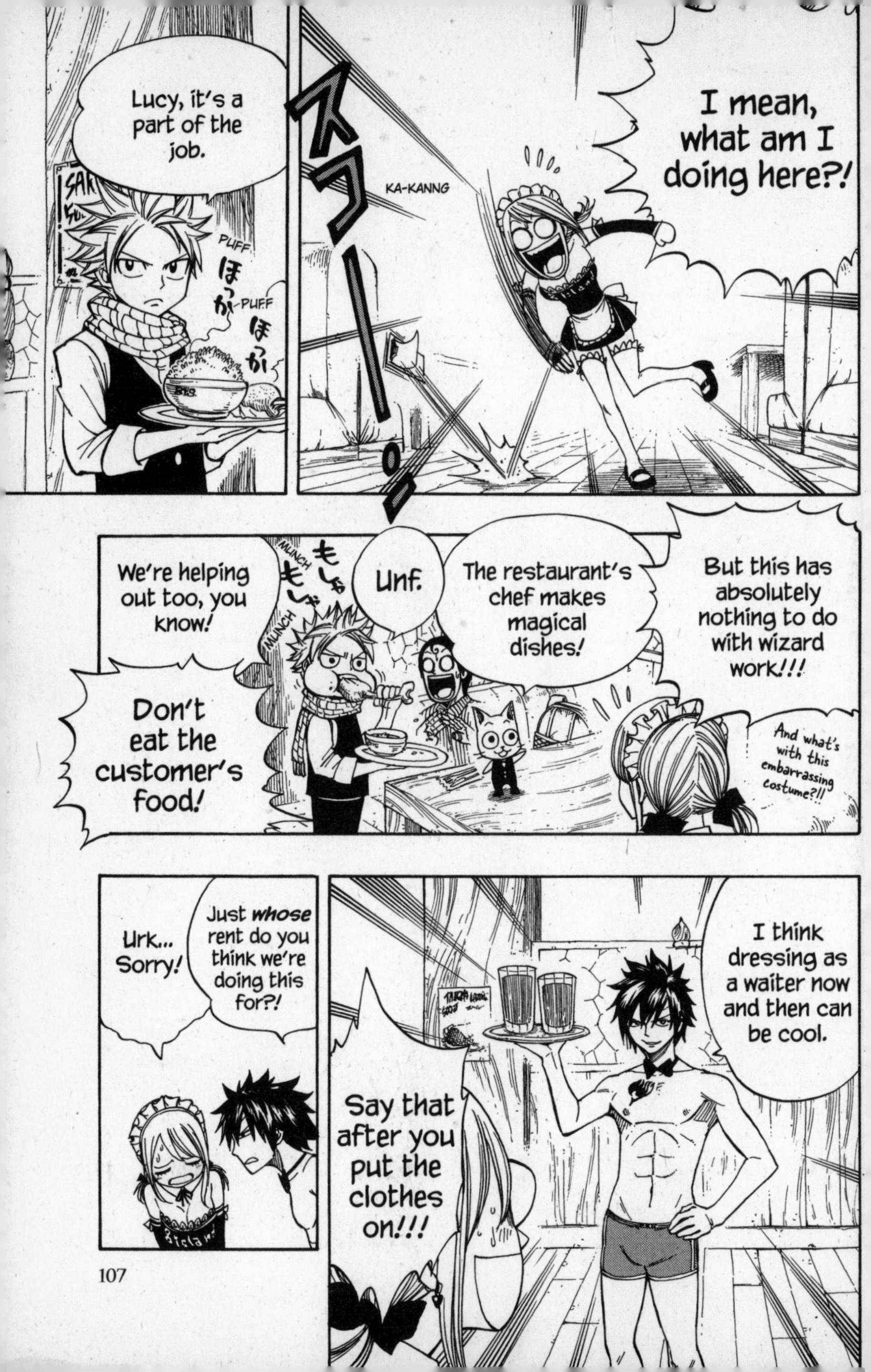
I mean, what am I doing here?!
スコーン
KA-KANNG
Lucy, it's a part of the job.
PUFF
ほっか
PUFF
ほっか
But this has absolutely nothing to do with wizard work!!!
And what's with this embarrassing costume?!!
The restaurant's chef makes magical dishes!
Unf.
MUNCH
もしゃ
MUNCH
もしゃ
We're helping out too, you know!
Don't eat the customer's food!
I think dressing as a waiter now and then can be cool.
Say that after you put the clothes on!!!
Just *whose* rent do you think we're doing this for?!
Urk... Sorry!

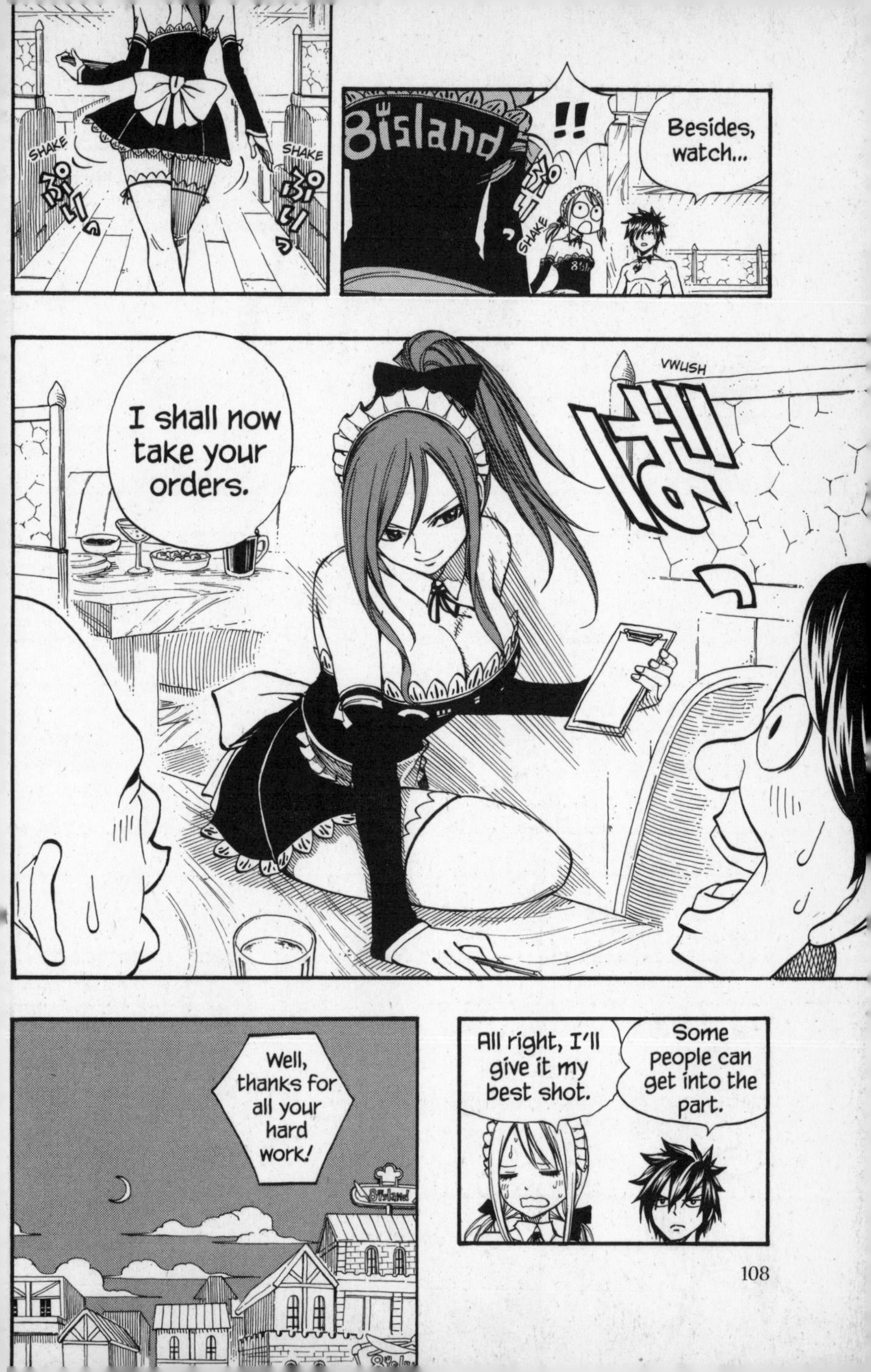

Besides, watch...
!!
SHAKE
8island
SHAKE
SHAKE
VWUSH
I shall now take your orders.
Some people can get into the part.
All right, I'll give it my best shot.
Well, thanks for all your hard work!

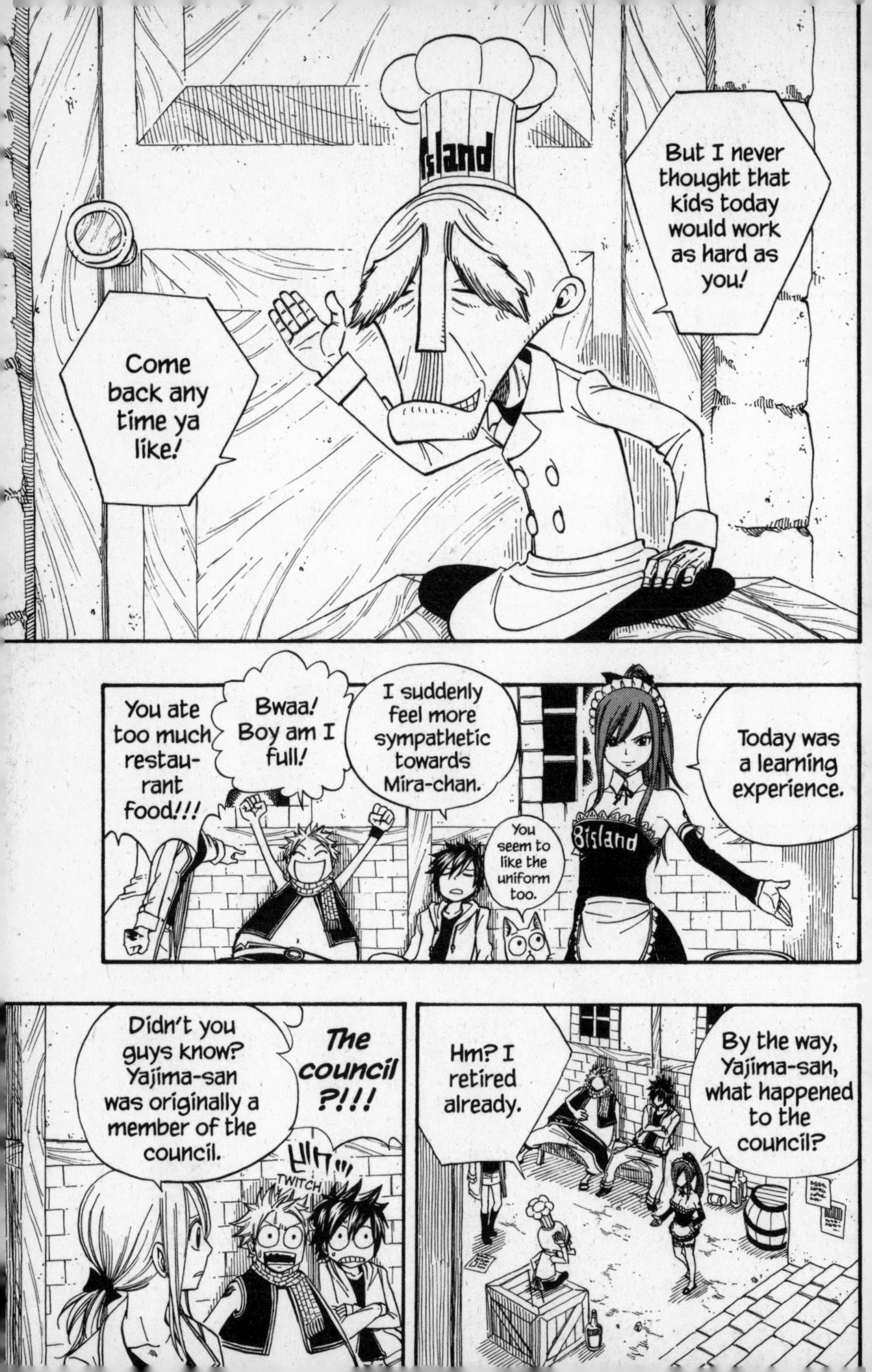
But I never thought that kids today would work as hard as you!
Come back any time ya like!
Today was a learning experience.
You seem to like the uniform too.
I suddenly feel more sympathetic towards Mira-chan.
Bwaa! Boy am I full!
You ate too much restaurant food!!!
By the way, Yajima-san, what happened to the council?
Hm? I retired already.
The council ?!!!
Didn't you guys know? Yajima-san was originally a member of the council.
TWITCH

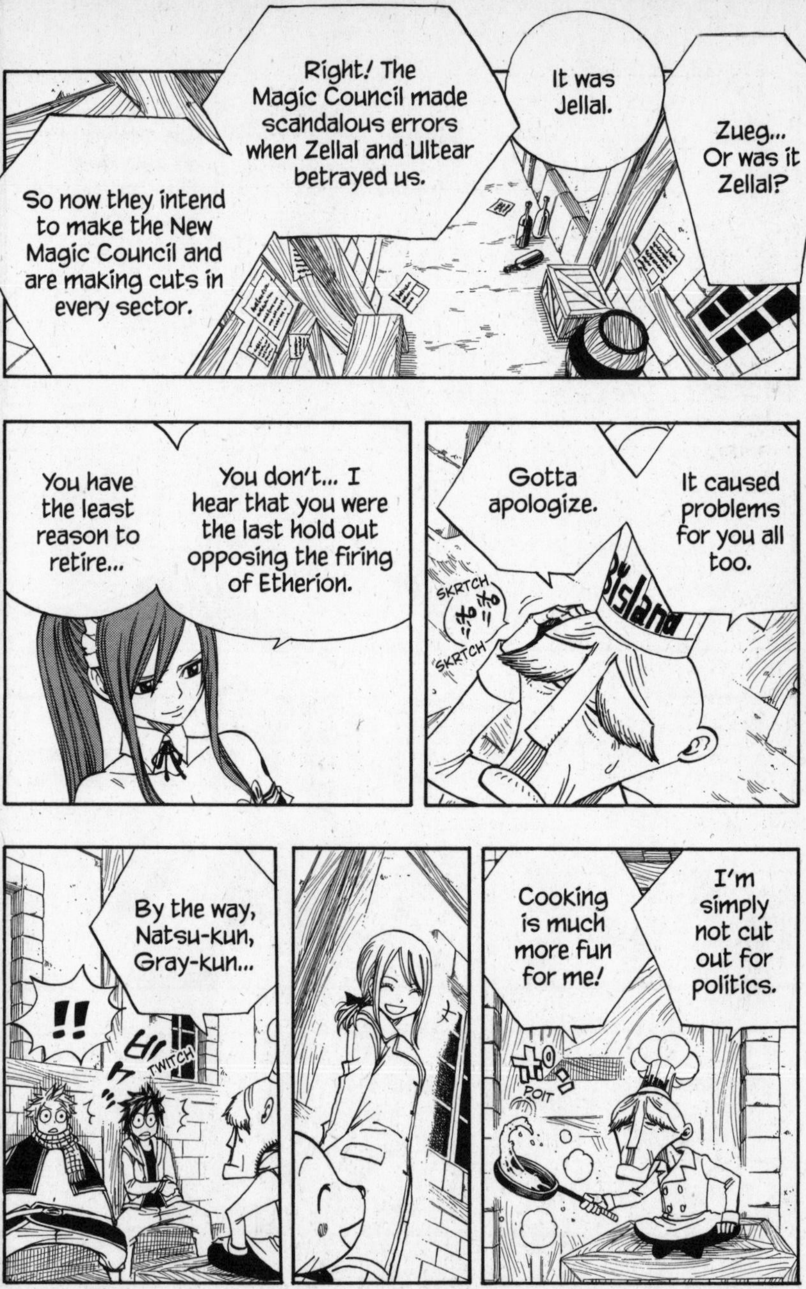
Zueg... Or was it Zellal?
It was Jellal.
Right! The Magic Council made scandalous errors when Zellal and Ultear betrayed us.
So now they intend to make the New Magic Council and are making cuts in every sector.
It caused problems for you all too.
Gotta apologize.
Bisland
SKRTCH
SKRTCH
You don't... I hear that you were the last hold out opposing the firing of Etherion.
You have the least reason to retire...
I'm simply not cut out for politics.
Cooking is much more fun for me!
POIT
By the way, Natsu-kun, Gray-kun...
!!
TWITCH

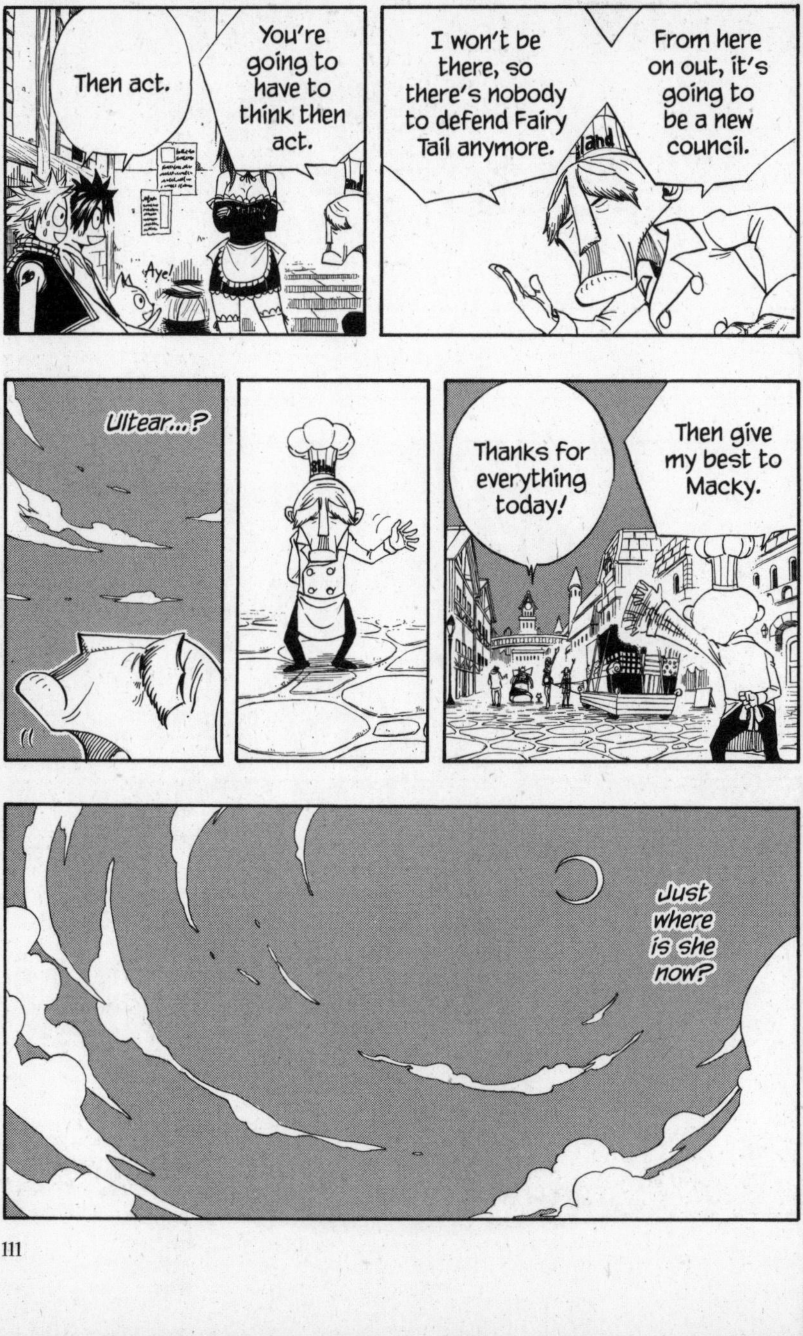
From here on out, it's going to be a new council.
I won't be there, so there's nobody to defend Fairy Tail anymore.
You're going to have to think then act.
Then act.
Aye!
Then give my best to Macky.
Thanks for everything today!
Ultear...?
Just where is she now?

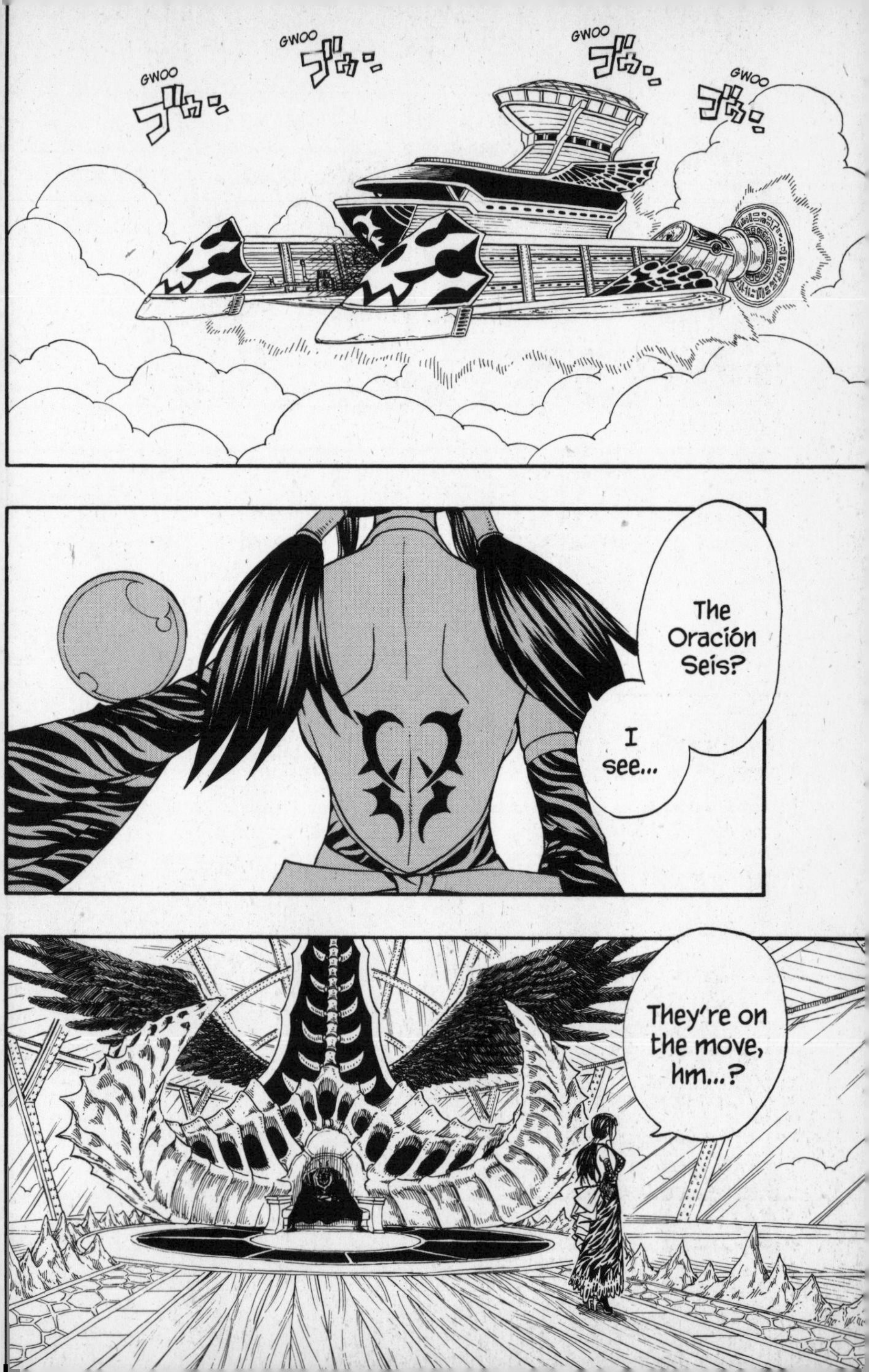
GWOO
ブゥ〜
GWOO
ブゥ〜
GWOO
ブゥ〜
GWOO
ブゥ〜
The Oración Seis?
I see...
They're on the move, hm...?

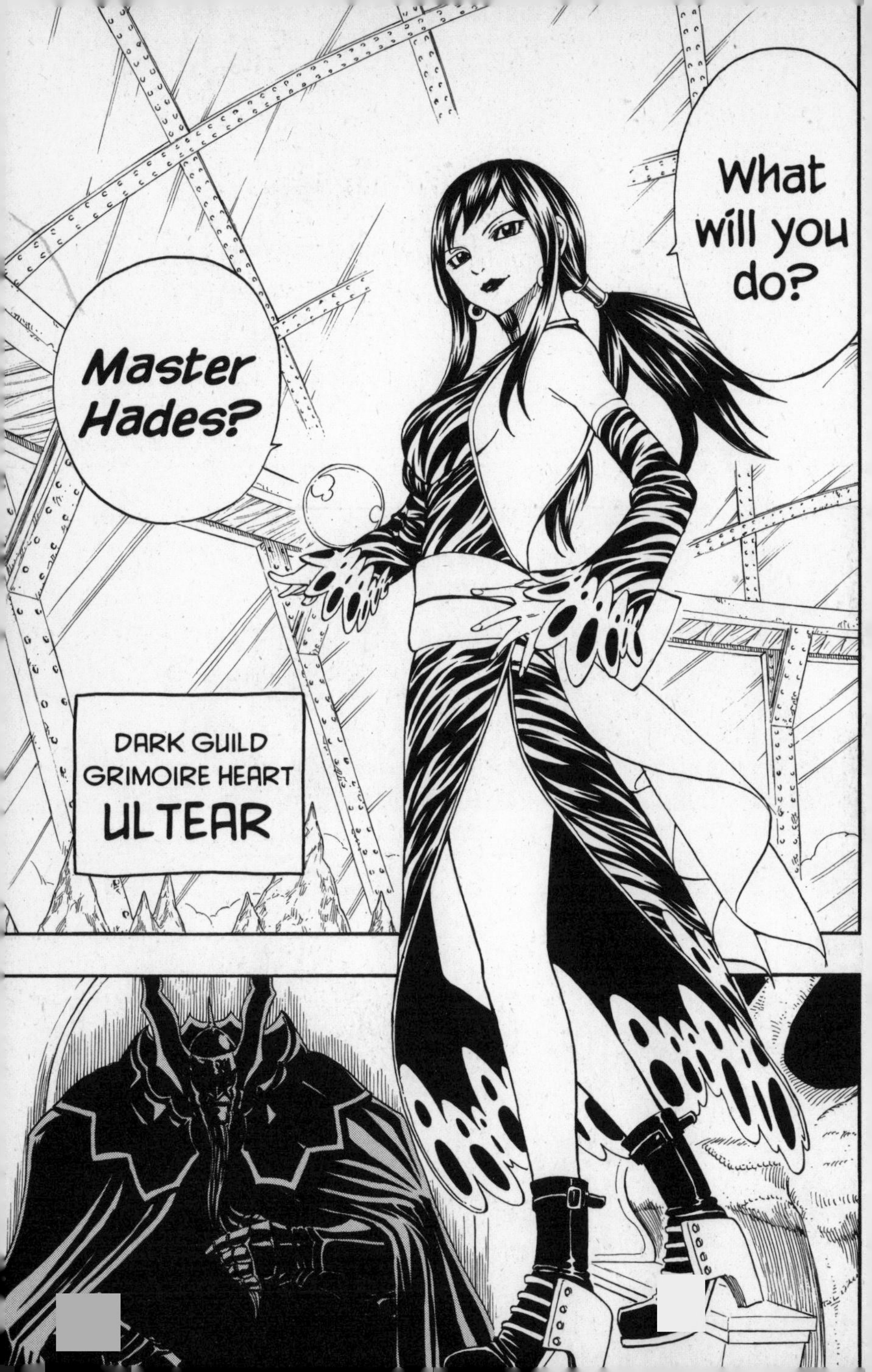
What will you do?
Master Hades?
DARK GUILD GRIMOIRE HEART ULTEAR

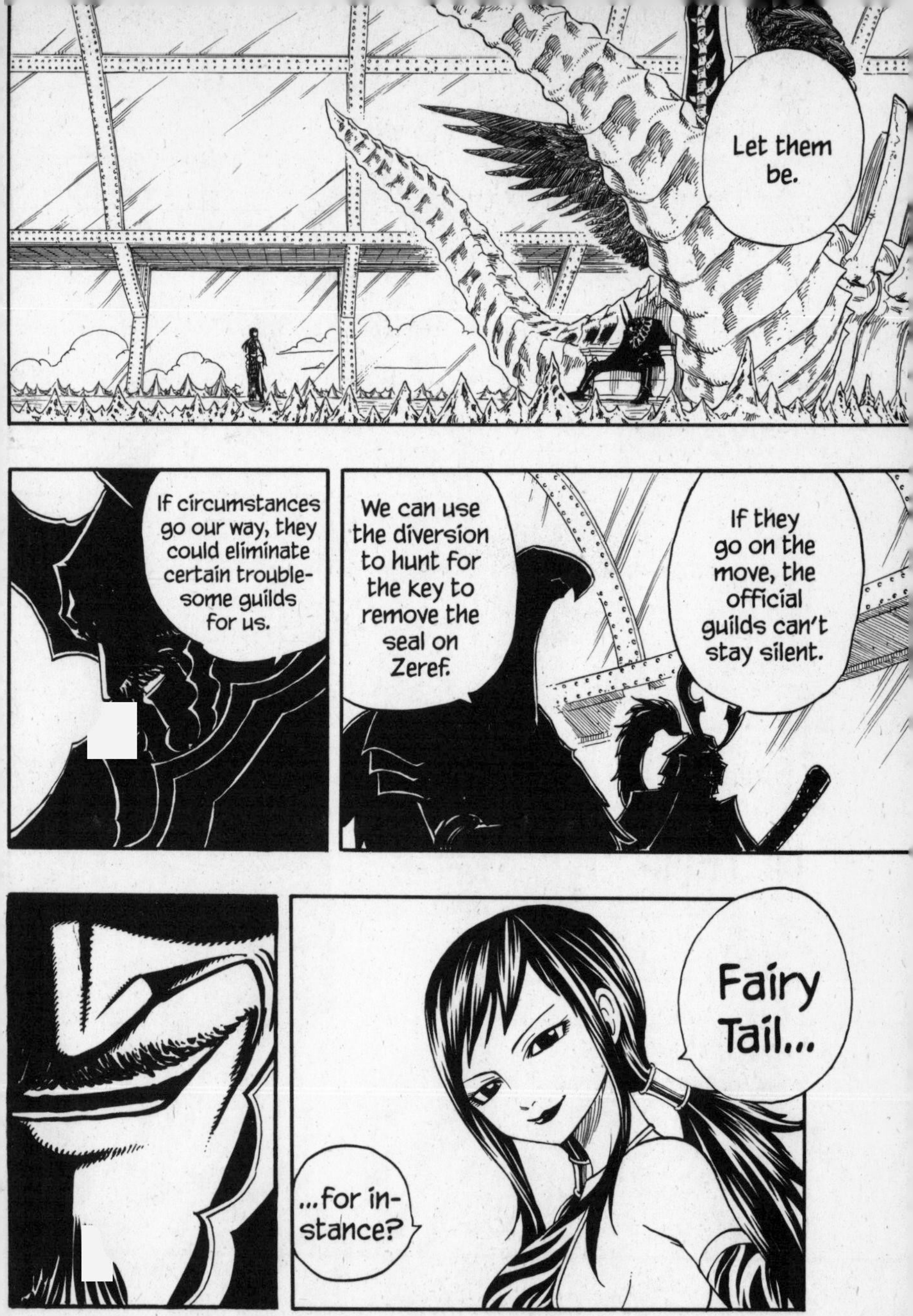
Let them be.
If they go on the move, the official guilds can't stay silent.
We can use the diversion to hunt for the key to remove the seal on Zeref.
If circumstances go our way, they could eliminate certain trouble-some guilds for us.
Fairy Tail...
...for in-stance?

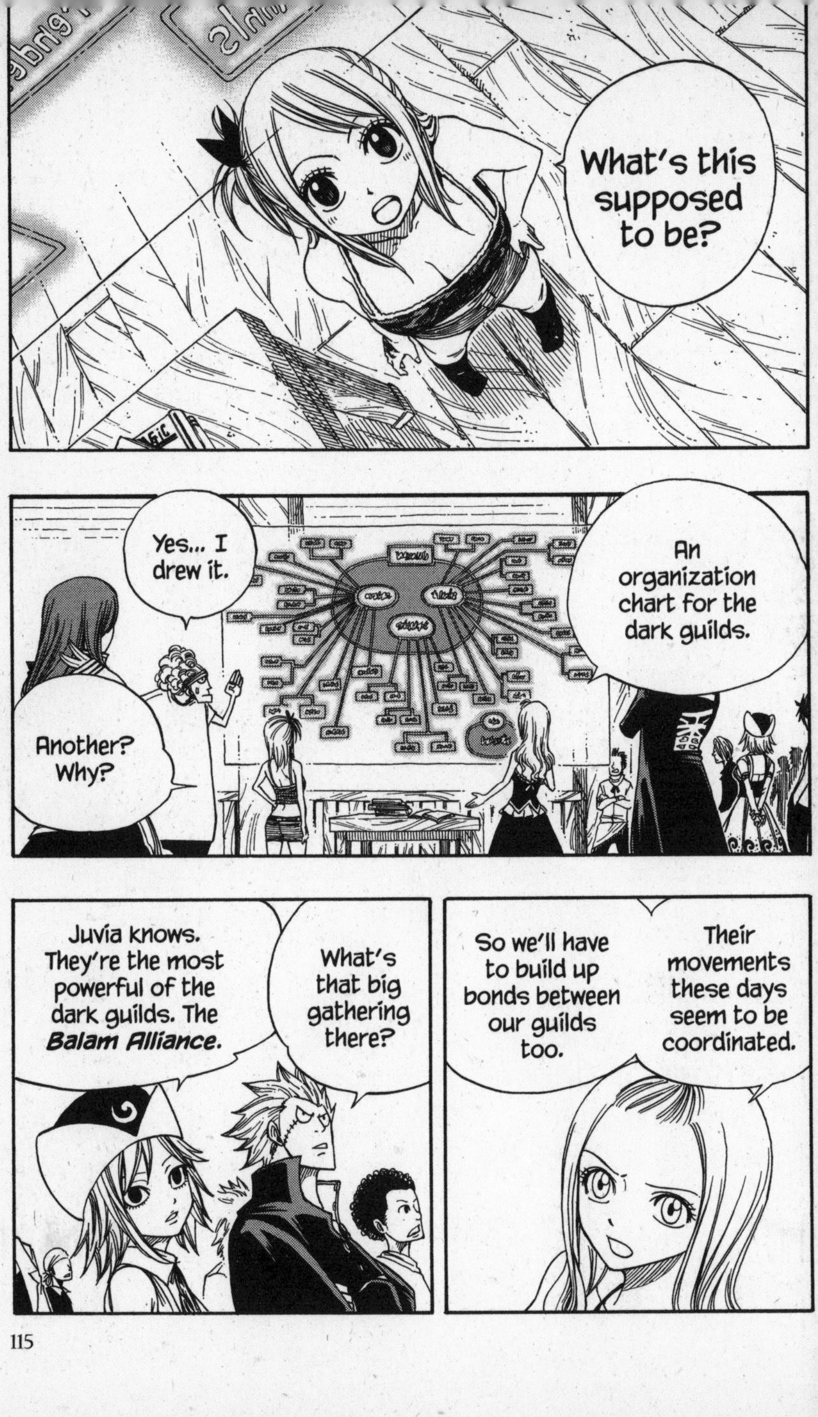
What's this supposed to be?
An organization chart for the dark guilds.
Yes... I drew it.
Another? Why?
Their movements these days seem to be coordinated.
So we'll have to build up bonds between our guilds too.
What's that big gathering there?
Juvia knows. They're the most powerful of the dark guilds. The *Balam Alliance*.

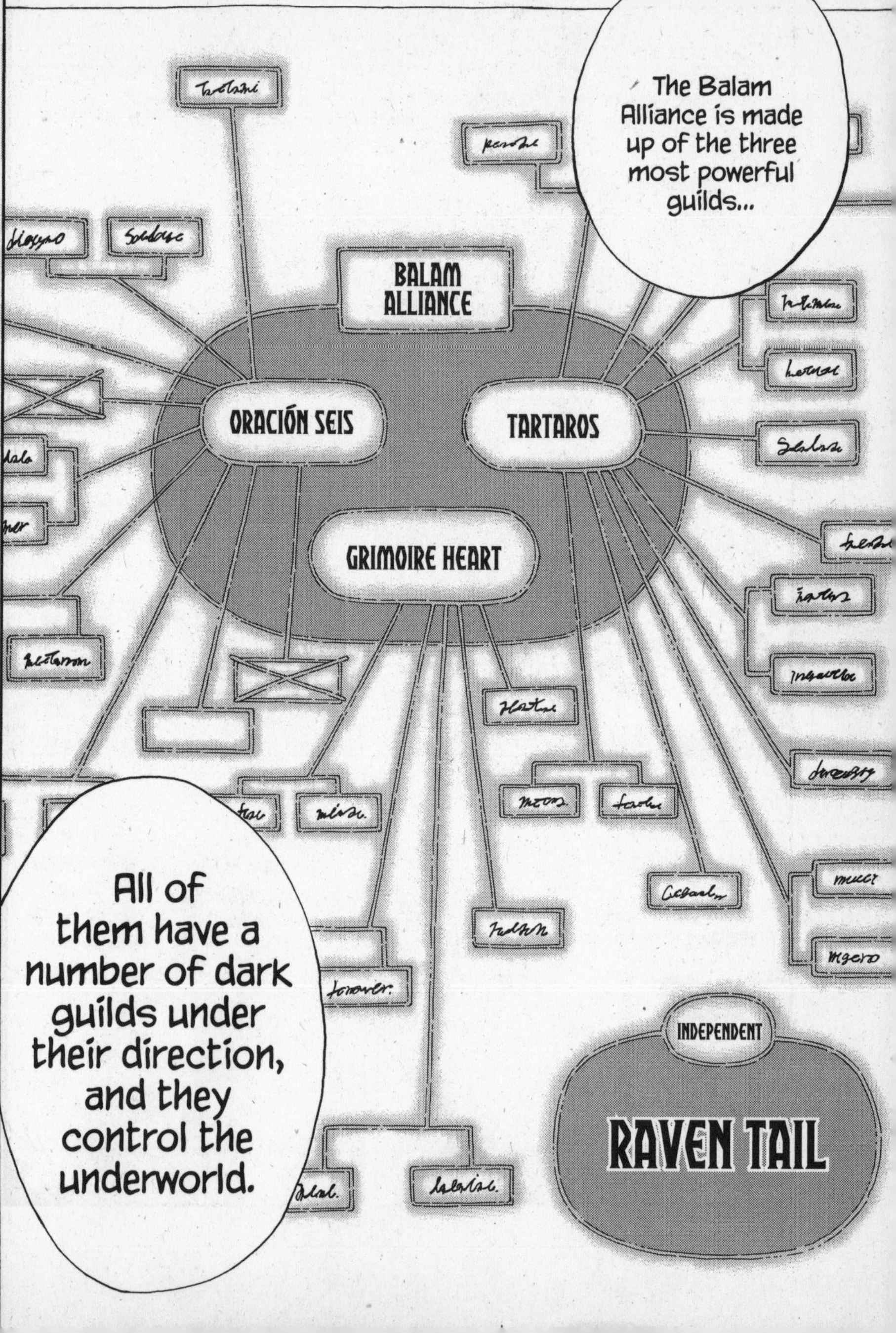
The Balam Alliance is made up of the three most powerful guilds...
BALAM ALLIANCE
ORACIÓN SEIS
TARTAROS
GRIMOIRE HEART
INDEPENDENT
RAVEN TAIL
All of them have a number of dark guilds under their direction, and they control the underworld.

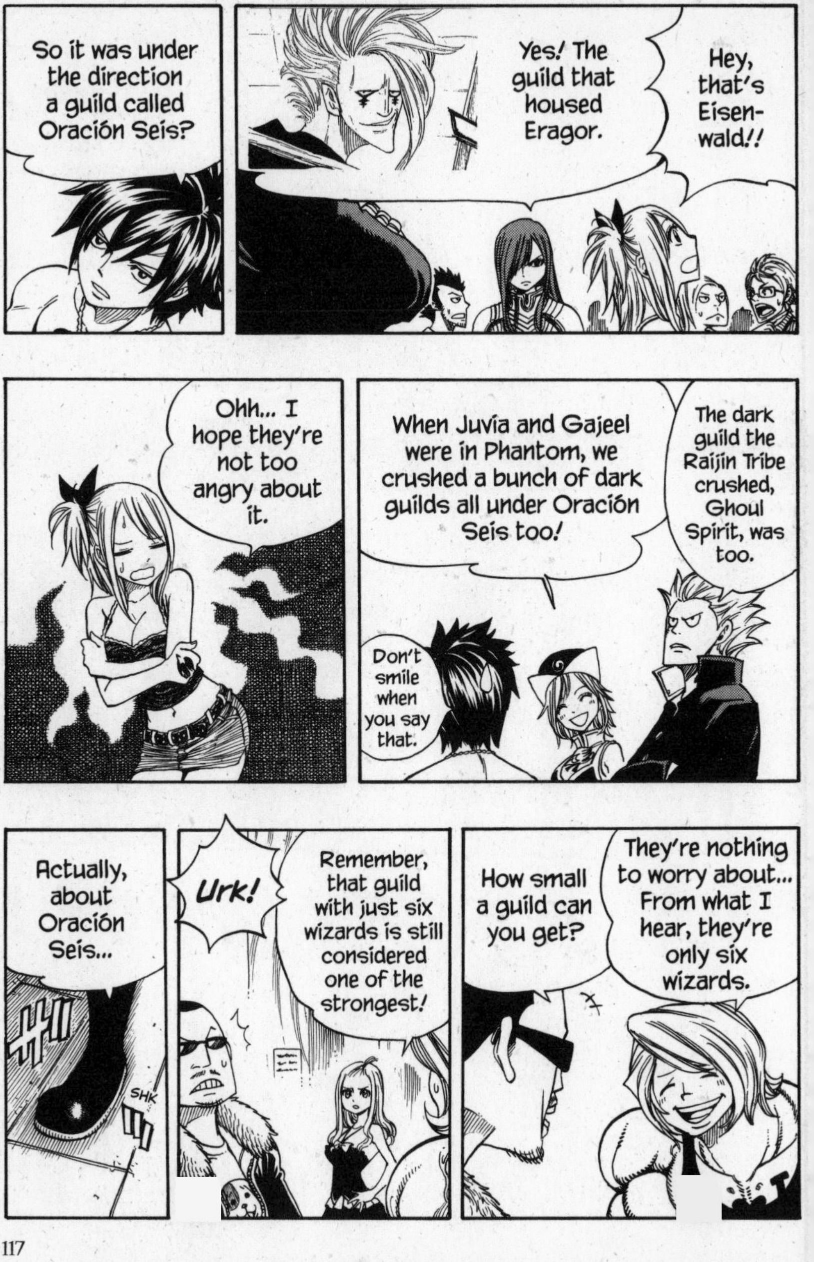
Hey, that's Eisen-wald!!
Yes! The guild that housed Eragor.
So it was under the direction a guild called Oración Seis?
The dark guild the Raijin Tribe crushed, Ghoul Spirit, was too.
When Juvia and Gajeel were in Phantom, we crushed a bunch of dark guilds all under Oración Seis too!
Don't smile when you say that.
Ohh... I hope they're not too angry about it.
They're nothing to worry about... From what I hear, they're only six wizards.
How small a guild can you get?
Remember, that guild with just six wizards is still considered one of the strongest!
Urk!
Actually, about Oración Seis...
SHK

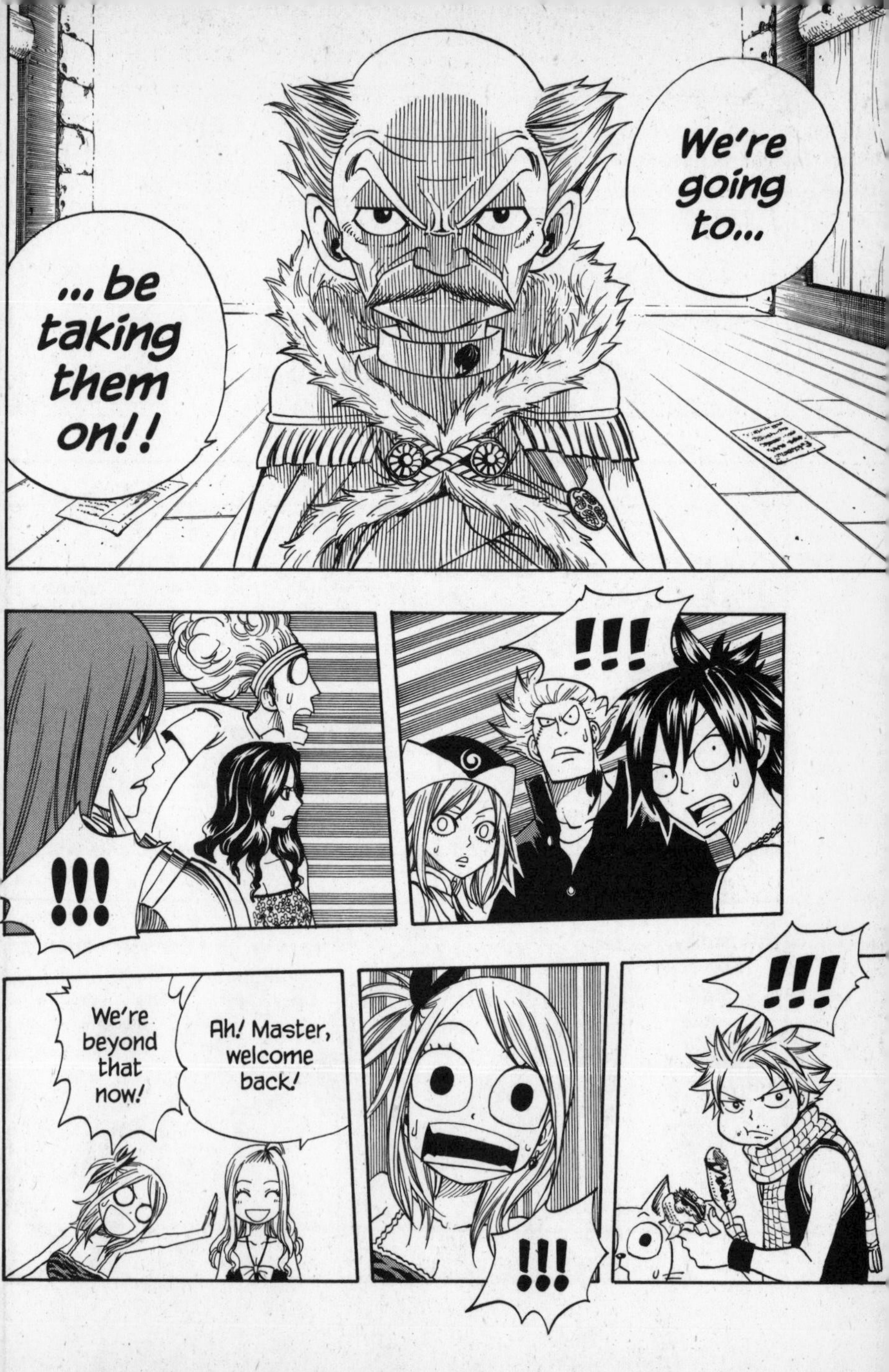
We're going to...
...be taking them on!!
!!!
!!!
!!!
!!!
Ah! Master, welcome back!
We're beyond that now!

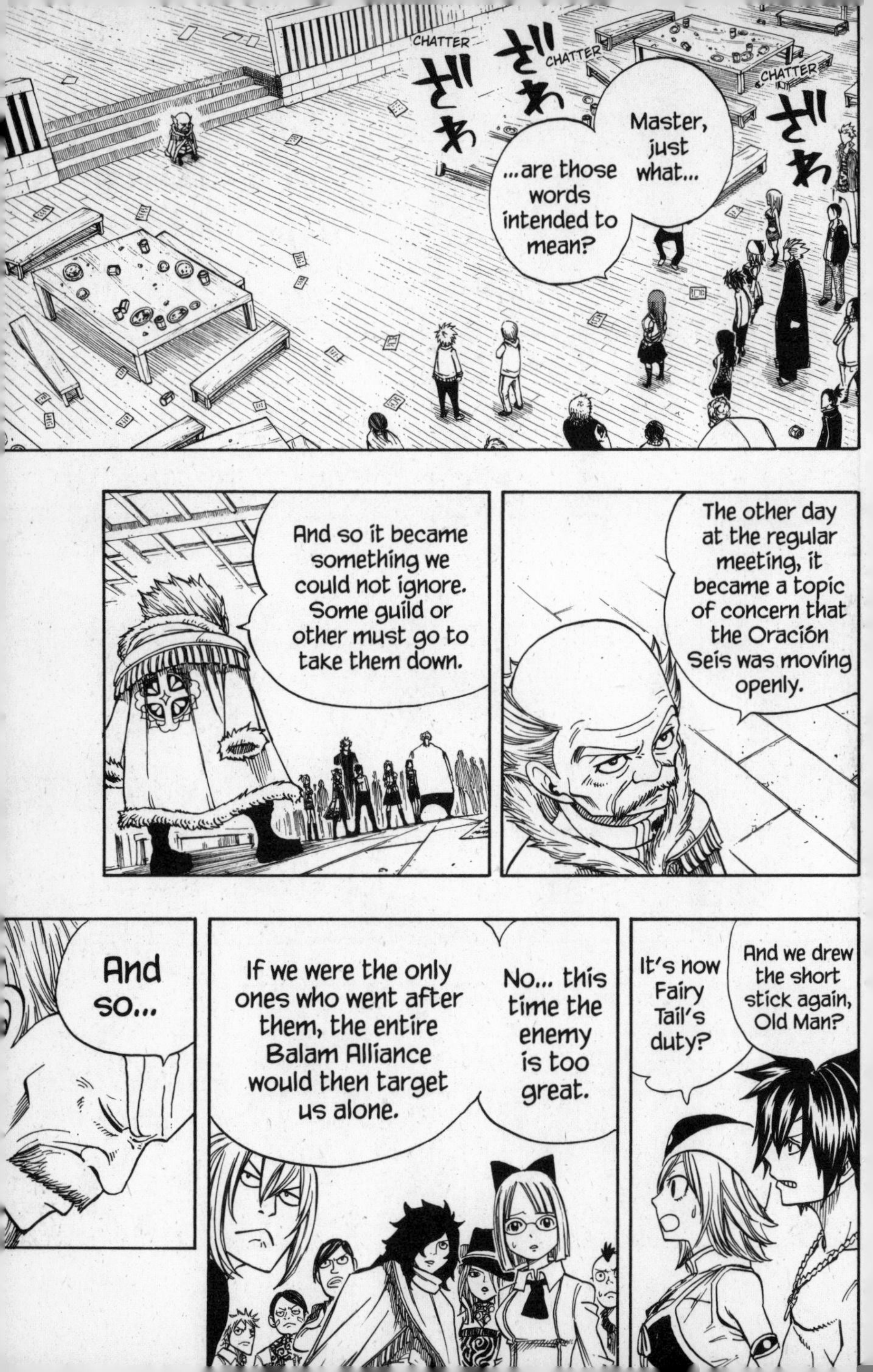
ざわ
CHATTER
ざわ
CHATTER
ざわ
CHATTER
Master, just what...
...are those words intended to mean?
The other day at the regular meeting, it became a topic of concern that the Oración Seis was moving openly.
And so it became something we could not ignore. Some guild or other must go to take them down.
And we drew the short stick again, Old Man?
It's now Fairy Tail's duty?
No... this time the enemy is too great.
If we were the only ones who went after them, the entire Balam Alliance would then target us alone.
And so...

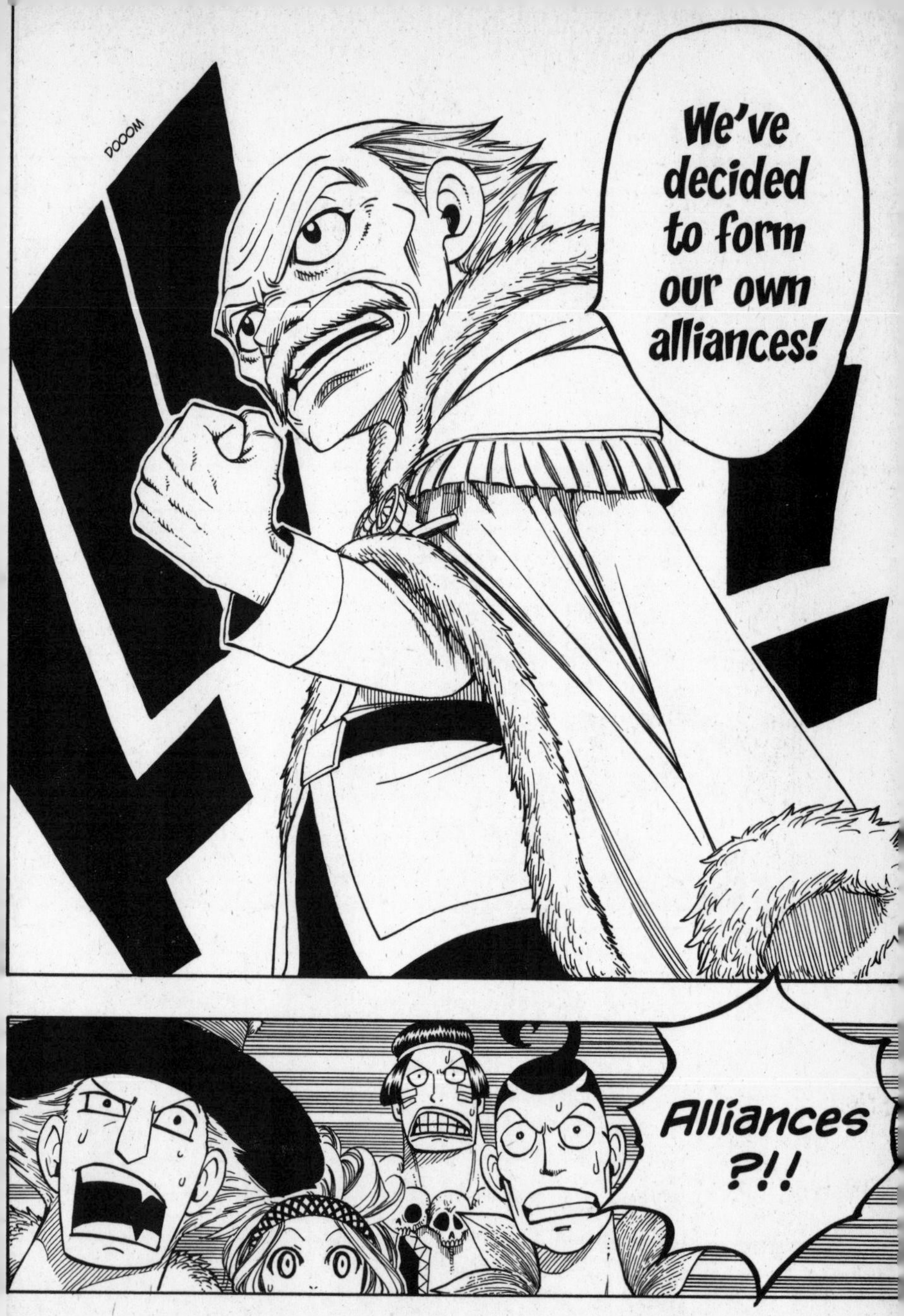
We've decided to form our own alliances!
DOOOM
Alliances ?!!

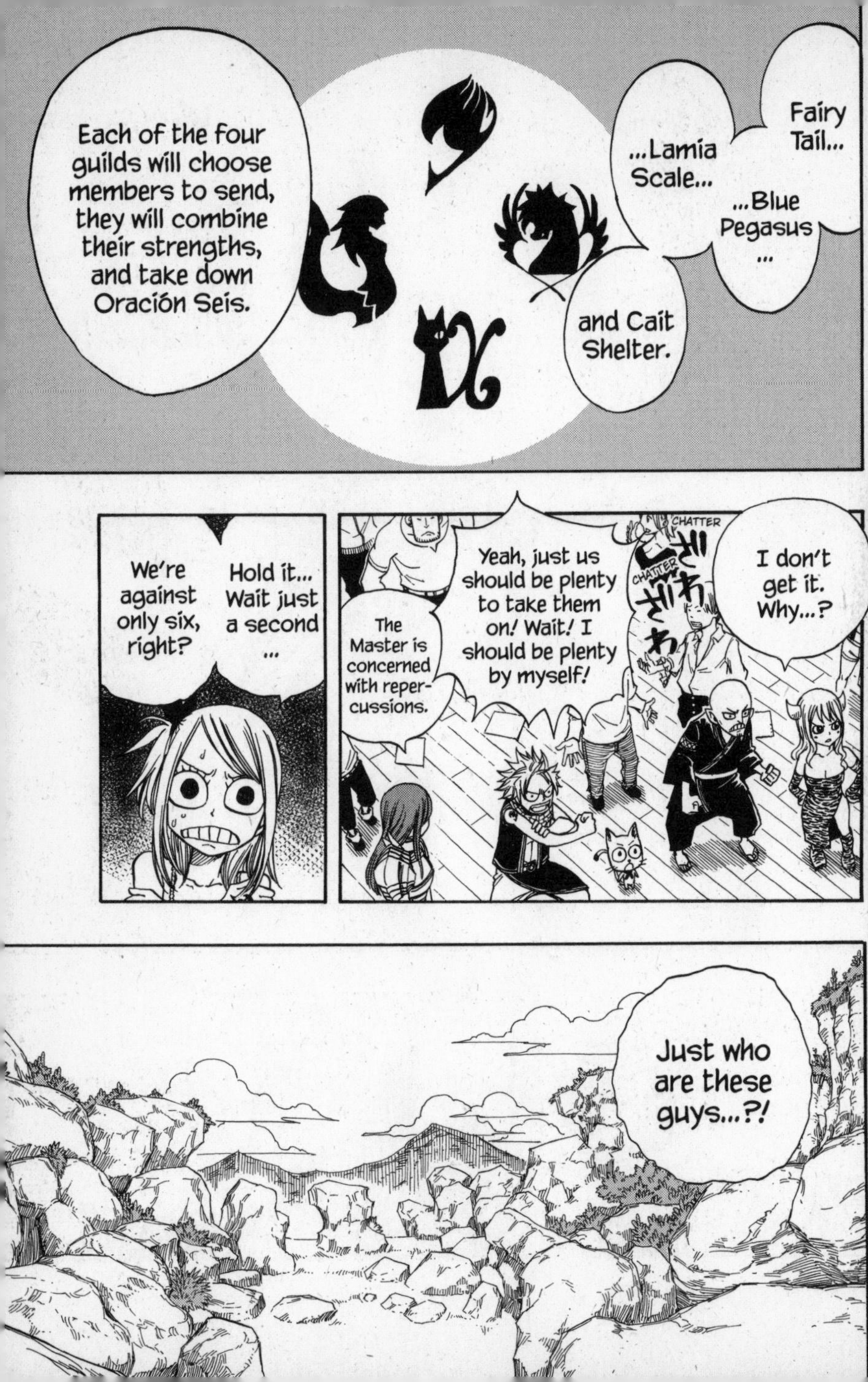
Fairy Tail...
...Lamia Scale...
...Blue Pegasus ...
and Cait Shelter.
Each of the four guilds will choose members to send, they will combine their strengths, and take down Oración Seis.
I don't get it. Why...?
CHATTER
CHATTER
Yeah, just us should be plenty to take them on! Wait! I should be plenty by myself!
The Master is concerned with repercussions.
Hold it... Wait just a second ...
We're against only six, right?
Just who are these guys...?!

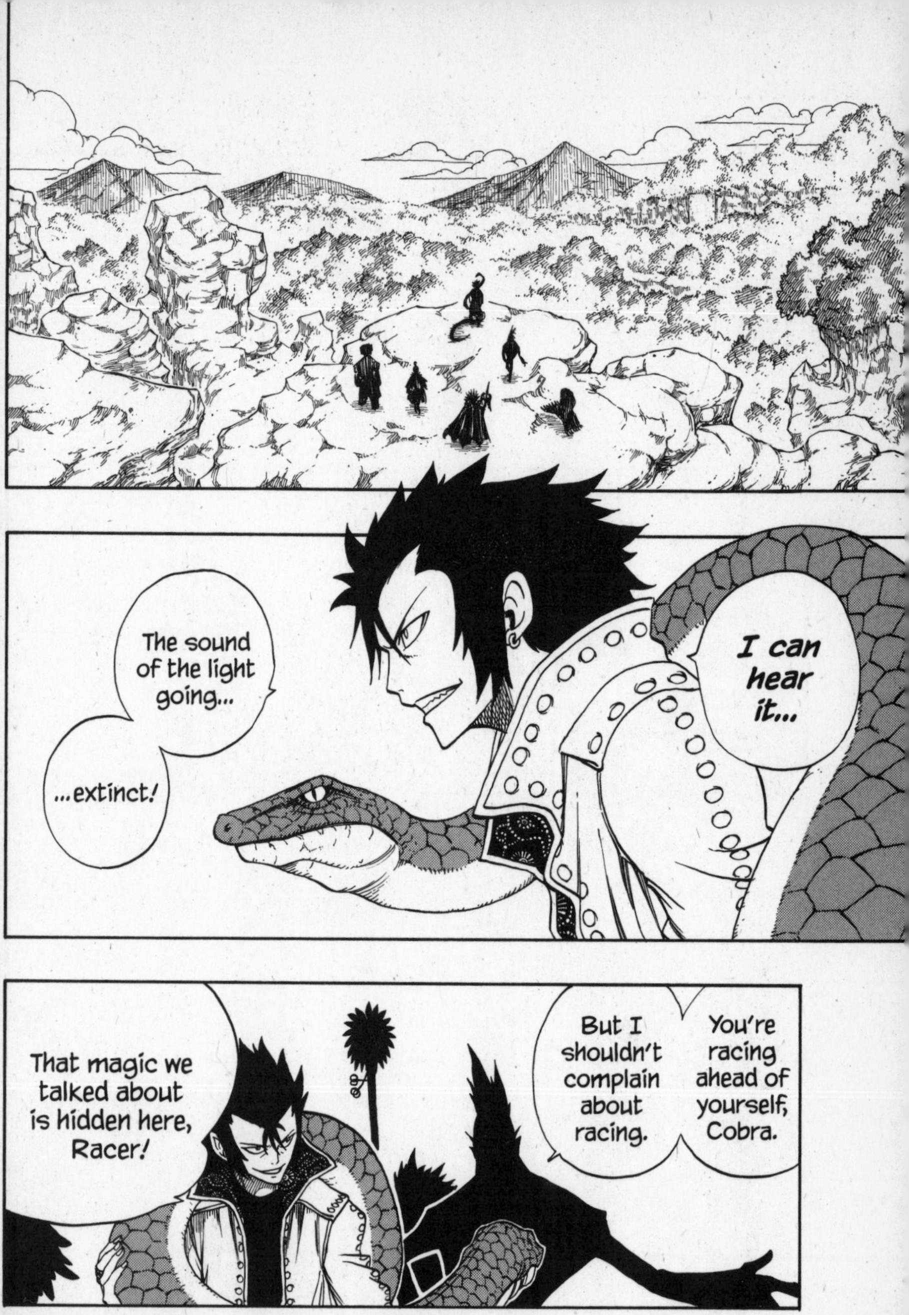
I can hear it...
The sound of the light going...
...extinct!
You're racing ahead of yourself, Cobra.
But I shouldn't complain about racing.
That magic we talked about is hidden here, Racer!

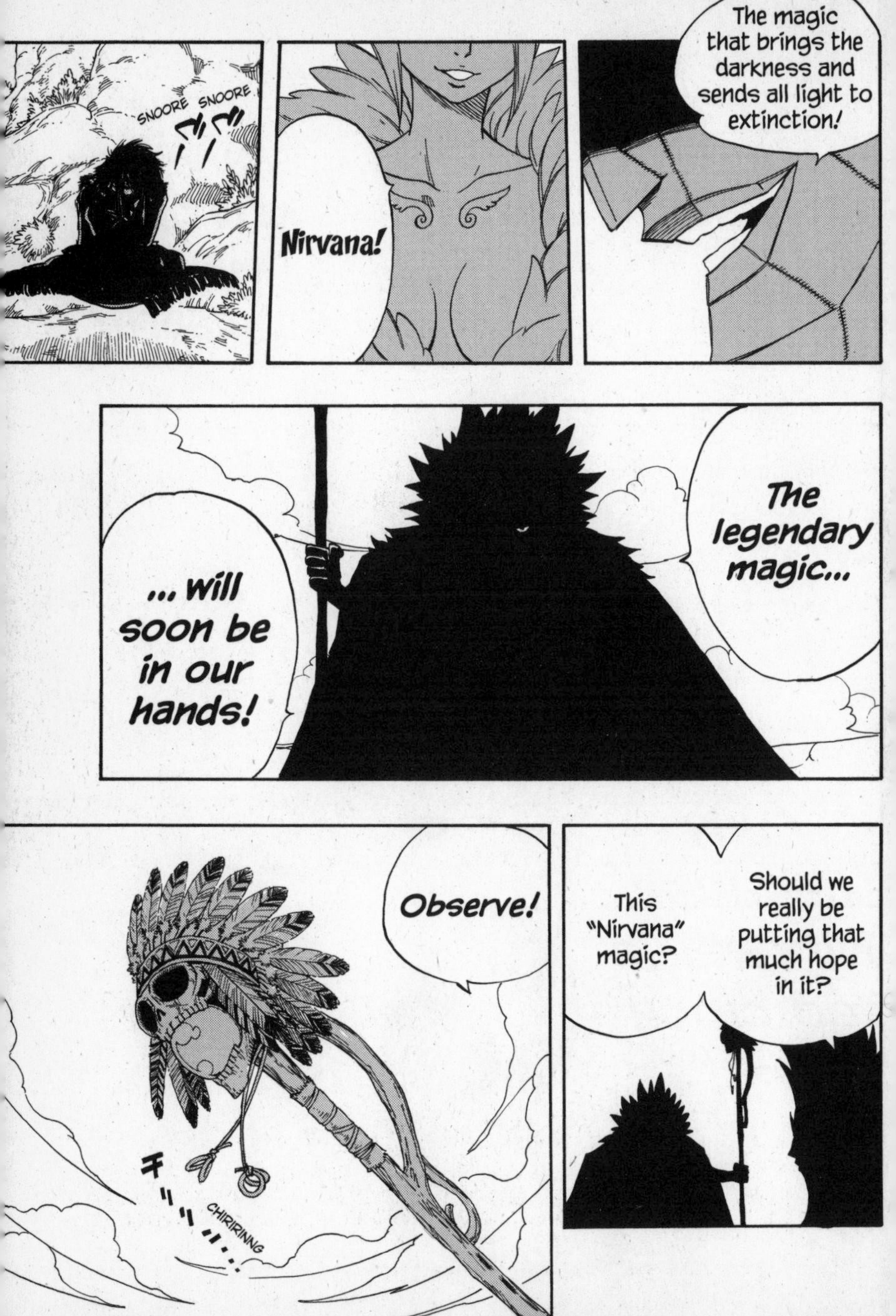
The magic that brings the darkness and sends all light to extinction!
Nirvana!
SNOORE SNOORE
The legendary magic...
... will soon be in our hands!
Should we really be putting that much hope in it?
This "Nirvana" magic?
Observe!
CHIRIRINNG

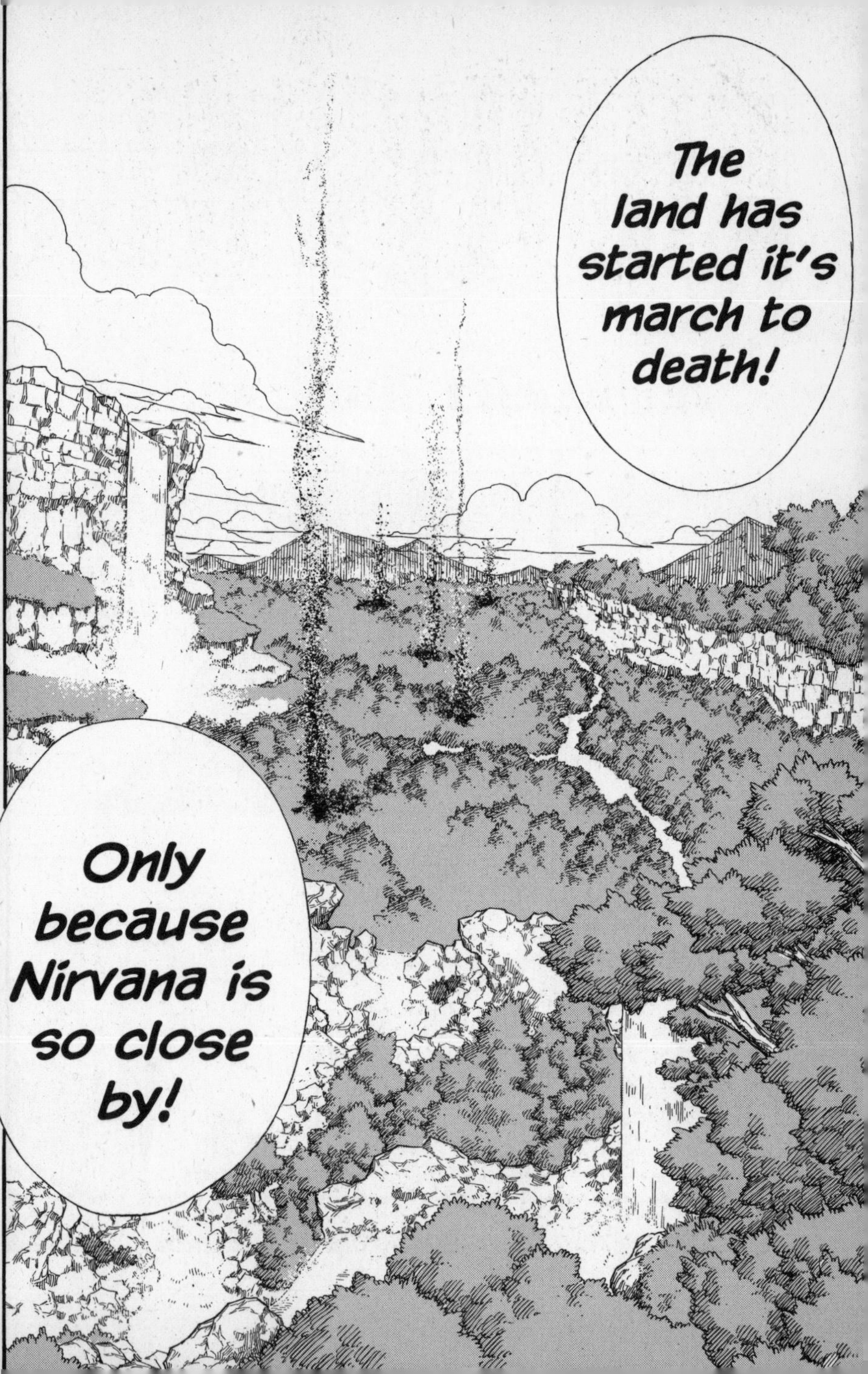
The land has started it's march to death!
Only because Nirvana is so close by!

FAIRY TAIL

Chapter 132, Allies, Unite!

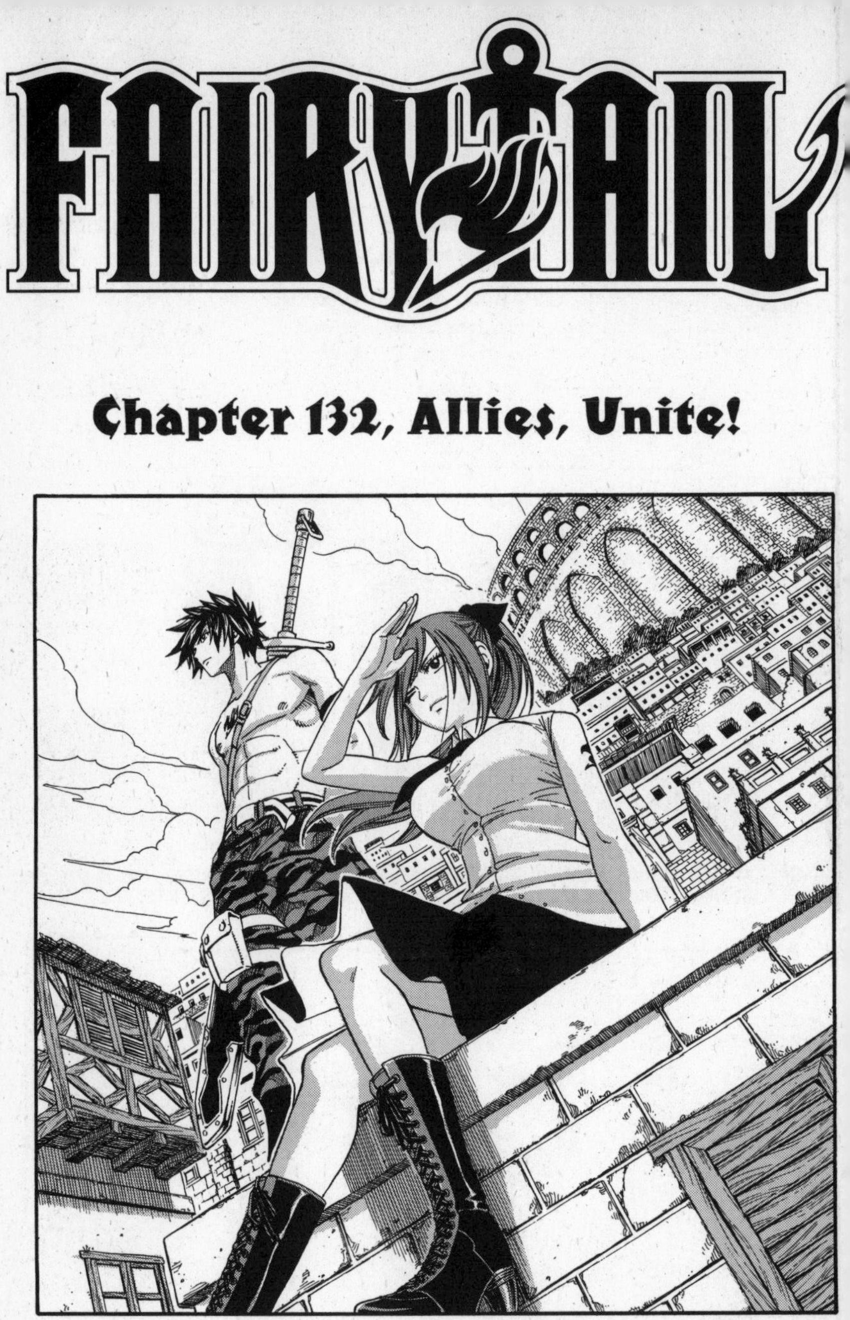

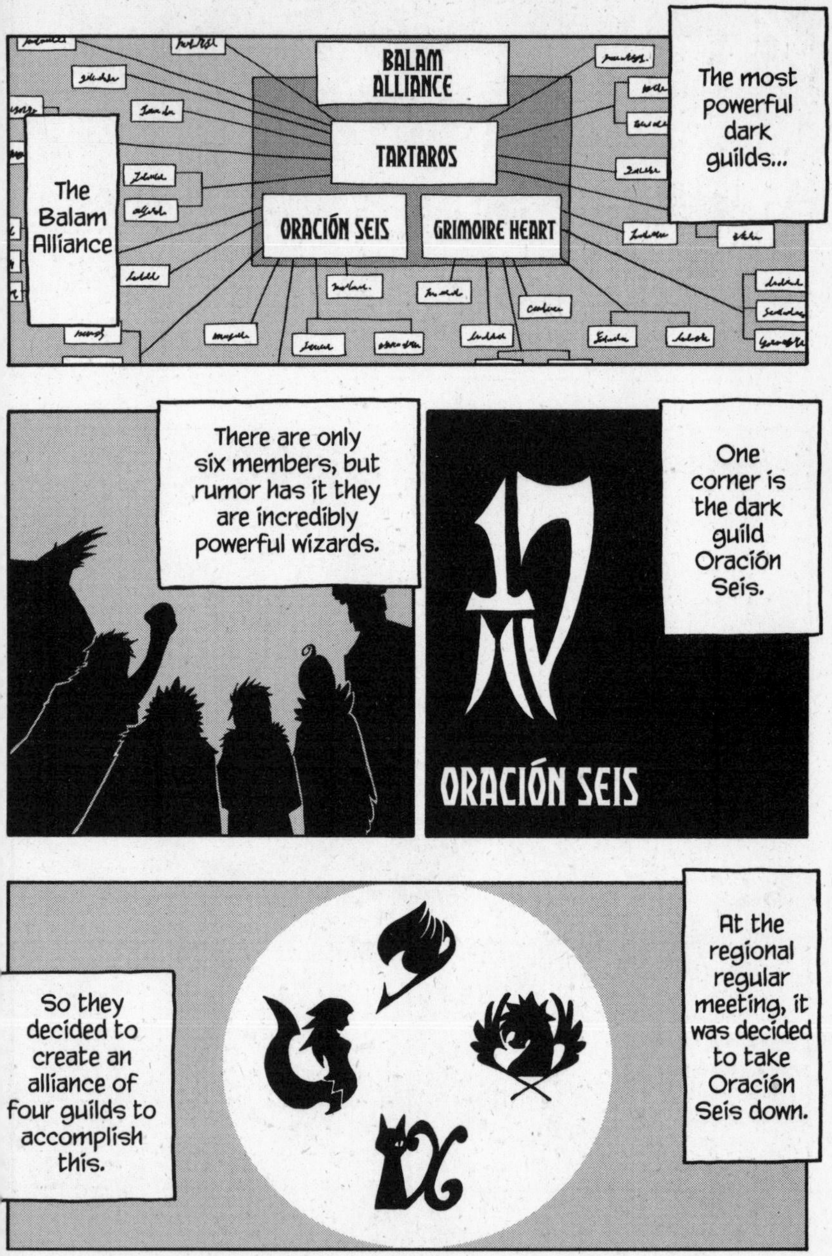
The most powerful dark guilds...
BALAM ALLIANCE
TARTAROS
GRIMOIRE HEART
ORACIÓN SEIS
The Balam Alliance
One corner is the dark guild Oración Seis.
ORACIÓN SEIS
There are only six members, but rumor has it they are incredibly powerful wizards.
At the regional regular meeting, it was decided to take Oración Seis down.
So they decided to create an alliance of four guilds to accomplish this.

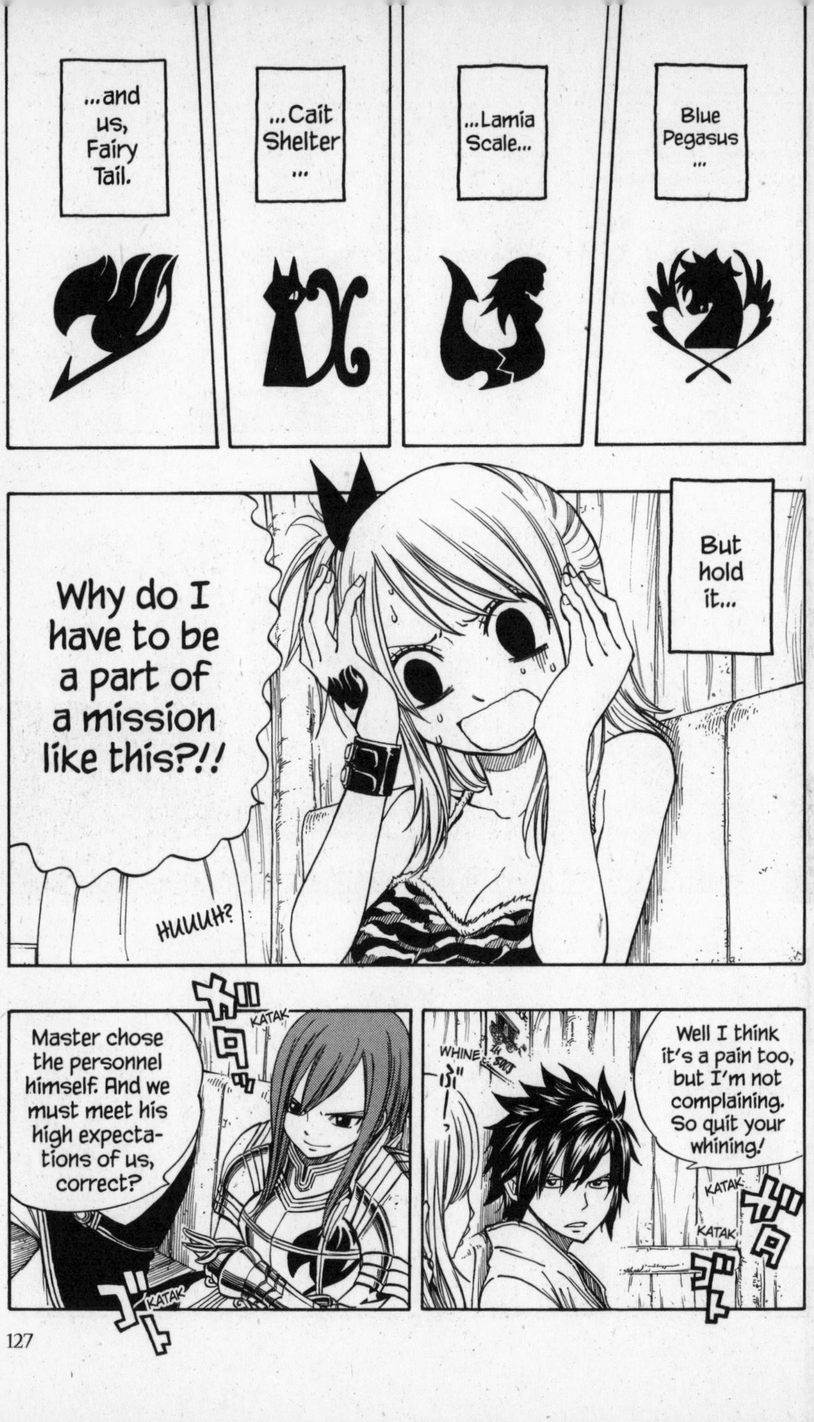
Blue Pegasus ...
...Lamia Scale...
...Cait Shelter ...
...and us, Fairy Tail.
But hold it...
Why do I have to be a part of a mission like this?!!
HUUUH?
WHINE
Well I think it's a pain too, but I'm not complaining. So quit your whining!
KATAK
KATAK
KATAK
Master chose the personnel himself. And we must meet his high expectations of us, correct?
KATAK

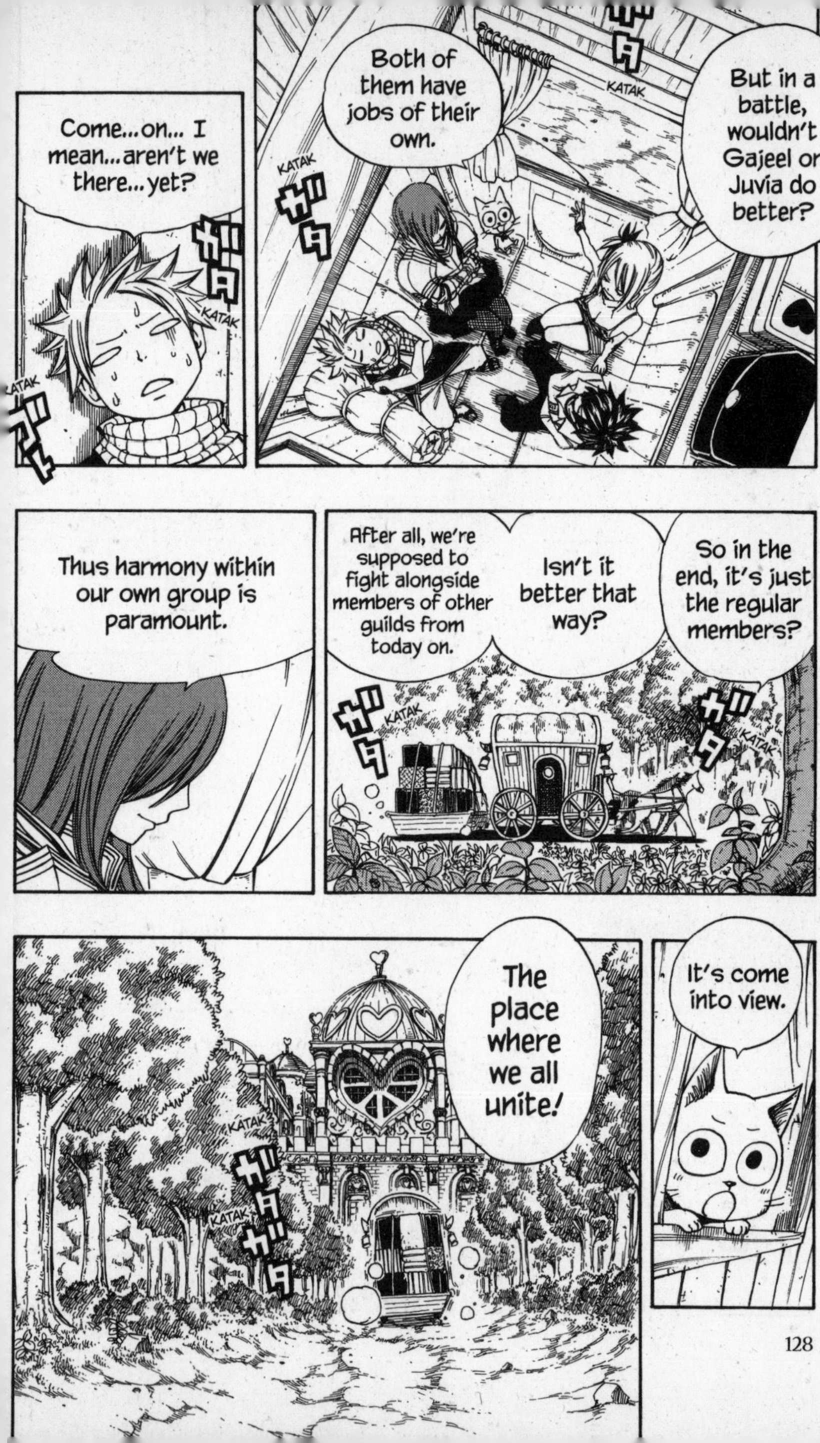
KATAK
But in a battle, wouldn't Gajeel or Juvia do better?
Both of them have jobs of their own.
KATAK
Come...on... I mean...aren't we there...yet?
KATAK
KATAK
So in the end, it's just the regular members?
KATAK
Isn't it better that way?
After all, we're supposed to fight alongside members of other guilds from today on.
KATAK
Thus harmony within our own group is paramount.
It's come into view.
The place where we all unite!
KATAK
KATAK

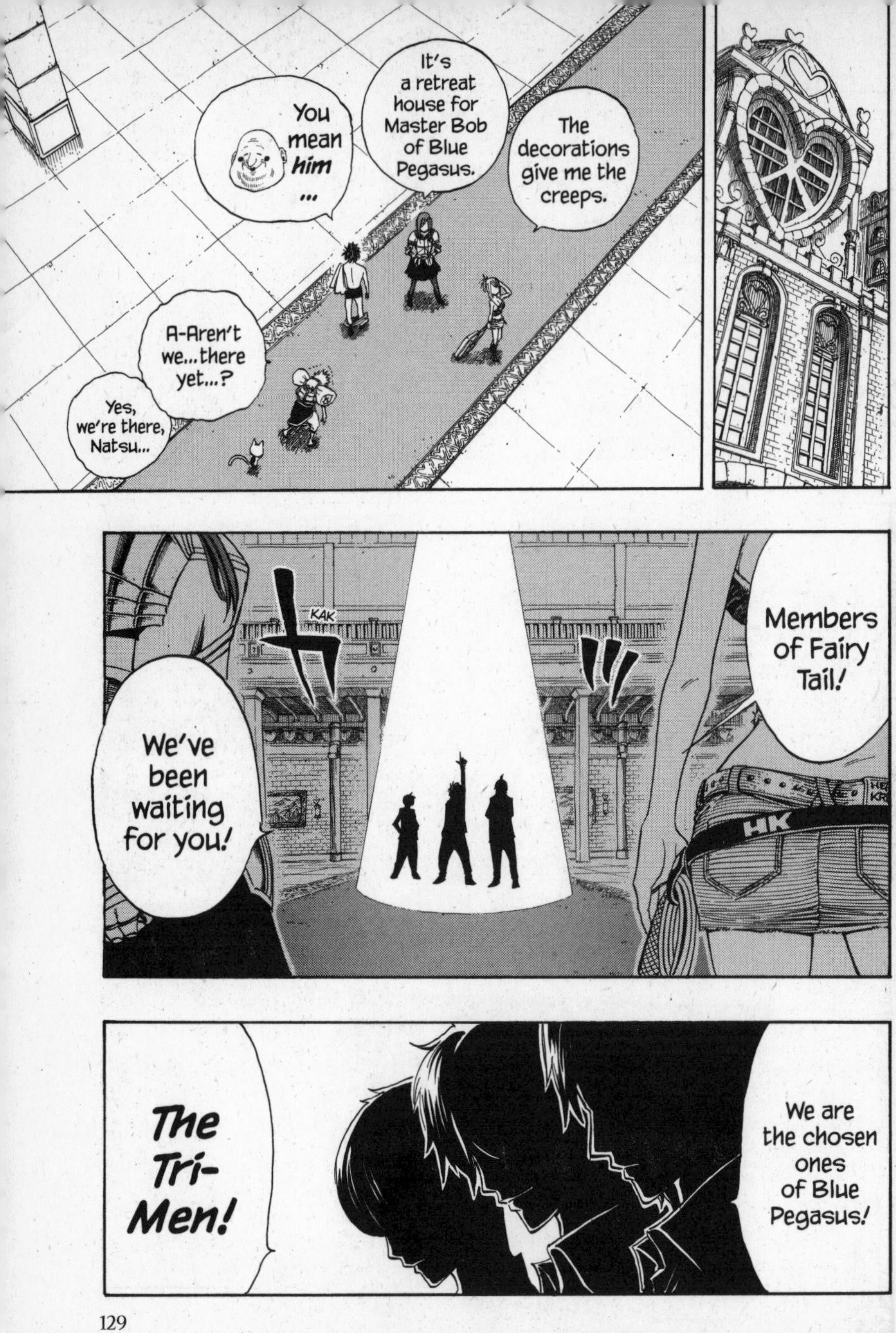
The decorations give me the creeps.
It's a retreat house for Master Bob of Blue Pegasus.
You mean him ...
A-Aren't we...there yet...?
Yes, we're there, Natsu...
Members of Fairy Tail!
KAK
We've been waiting for you!
We are the chosen ones of Blue Pegasus!
The Tri-Men!

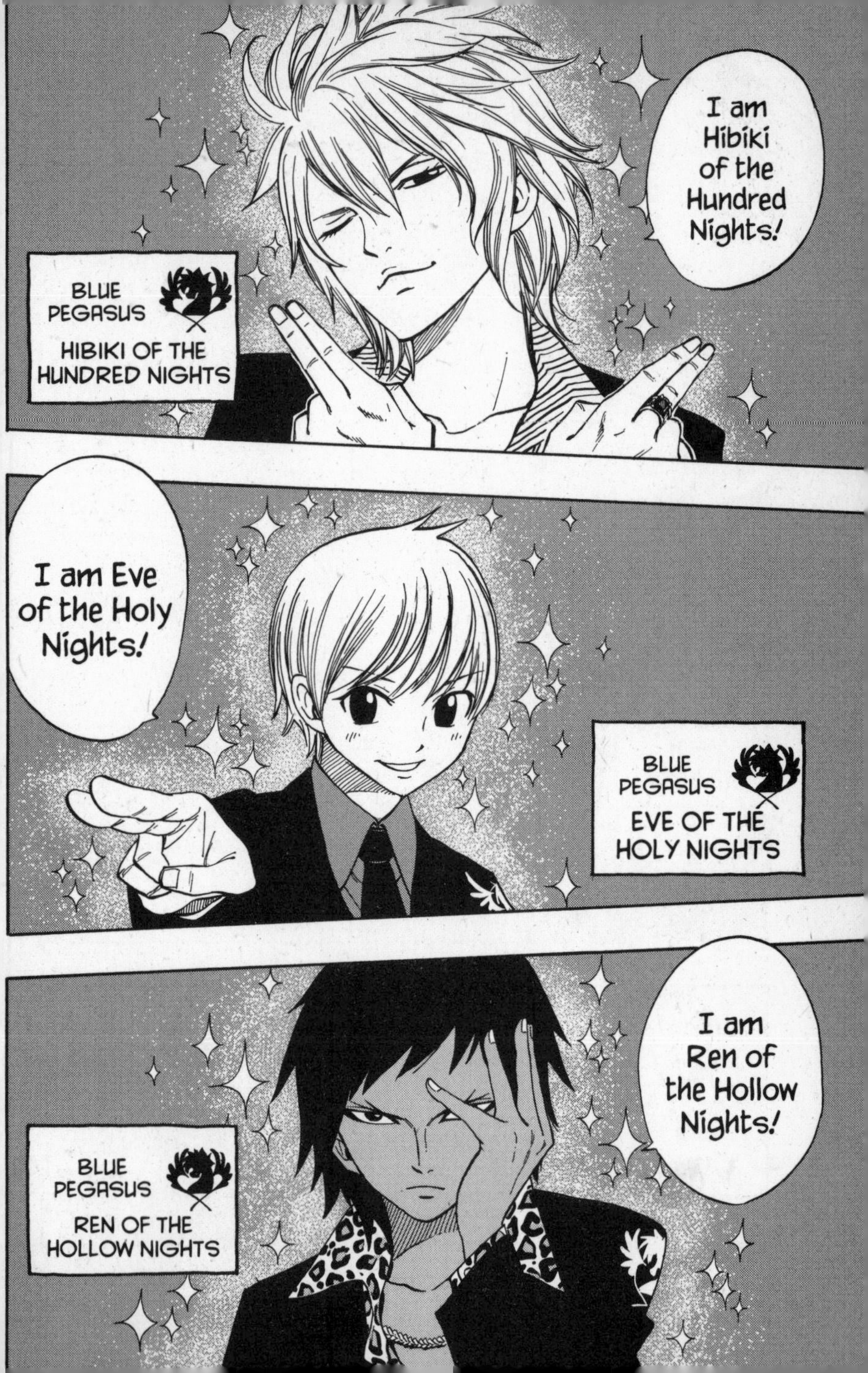
I am Hibiki of the Hundred Nights!
BLUE PEGASUS
HIBIKI OF THE HUNDRED NIGHTS
I am Eve of the Holy Nights!
BLUE PEGASUS
EVE OF THE HOLY NIGHTS
I am Ren of the Hollow Nights!
BLUE PEGASUS
REN OF THE HOLLOW NIGHTS

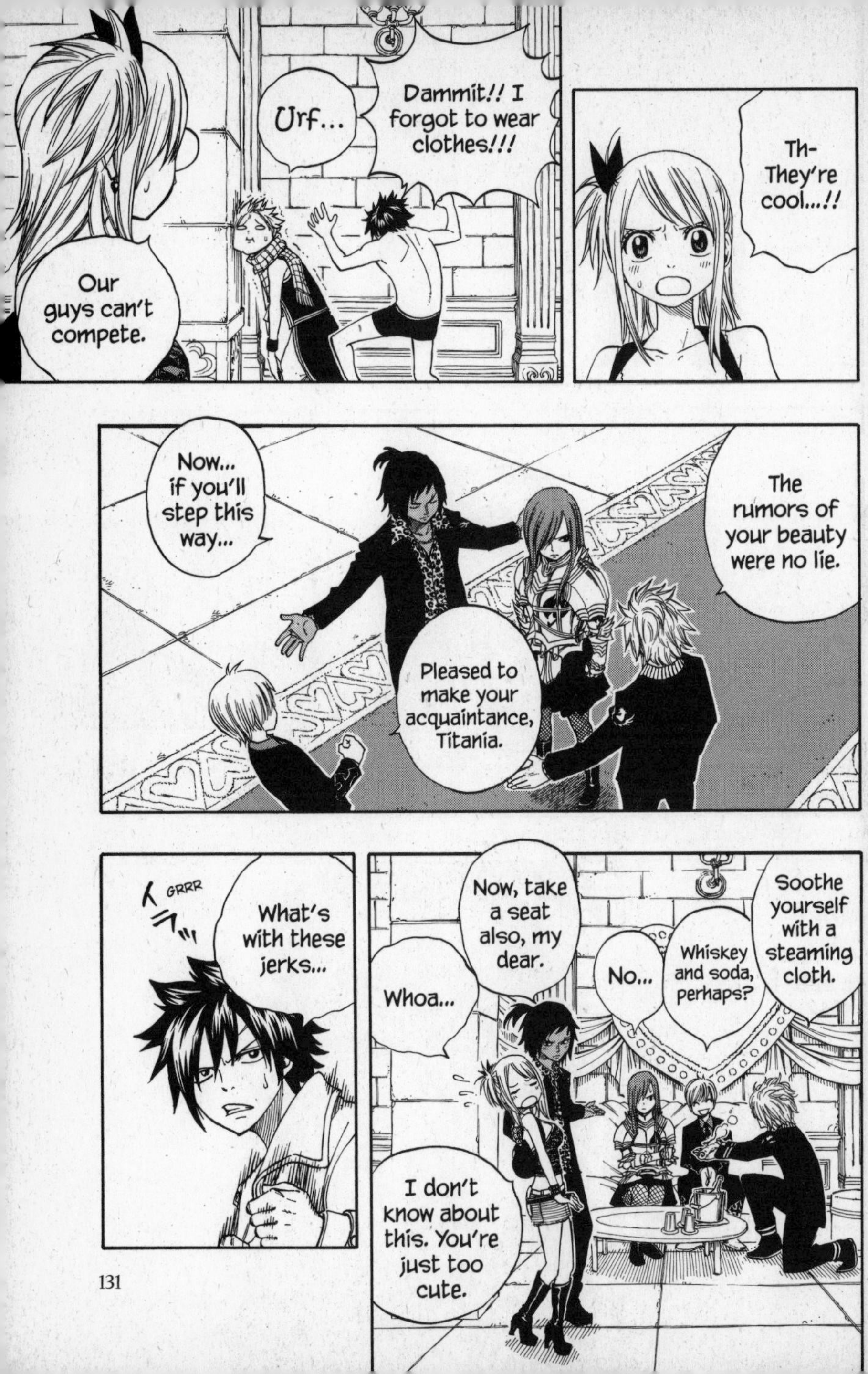

Th- They're cool...!!
Dammit!! I forgot to wear clothes!!!
Urf...
Our guys can't compete.
The rumors of your beauty were no lie.
Pleased to make your acquaintance, Titania.
Now... if you'll step this way...
Soothe yourself with a steaming cloth.
Whiskey and soda, perhaps?
No...
Now, take a seat also, my dear.
Whoa...
I don't know about this. You're just too cute.
GRRR
What's with these jerks...

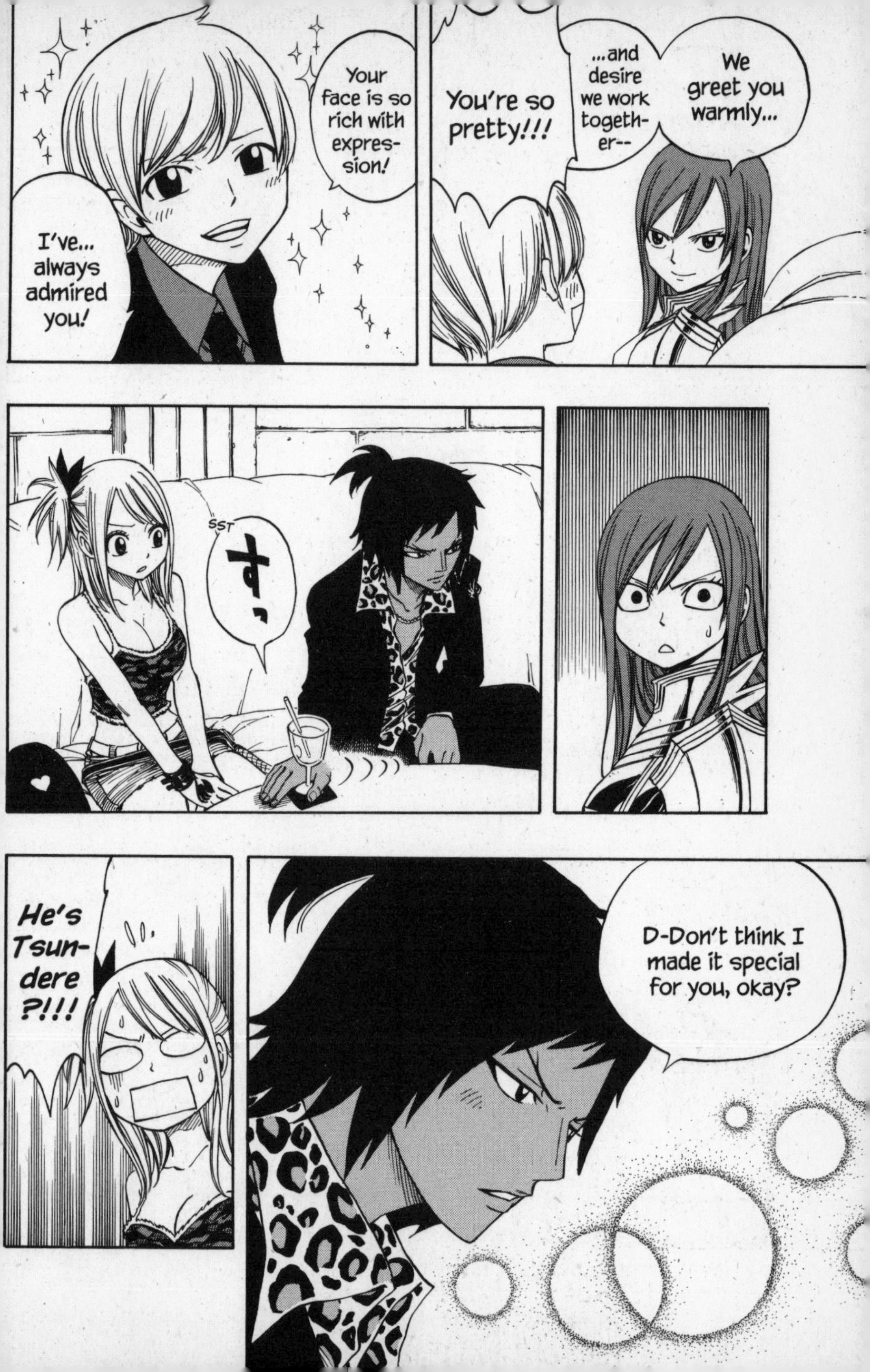
We greet you warmly...
...and desire we work togeth-er--
You're so pretty!!!
Your face is so rich with expres-sion!
I've... always admired you!
SST
す、
D-Don't think I made it special for you, okay?
He's Tsun-dere ?!!!

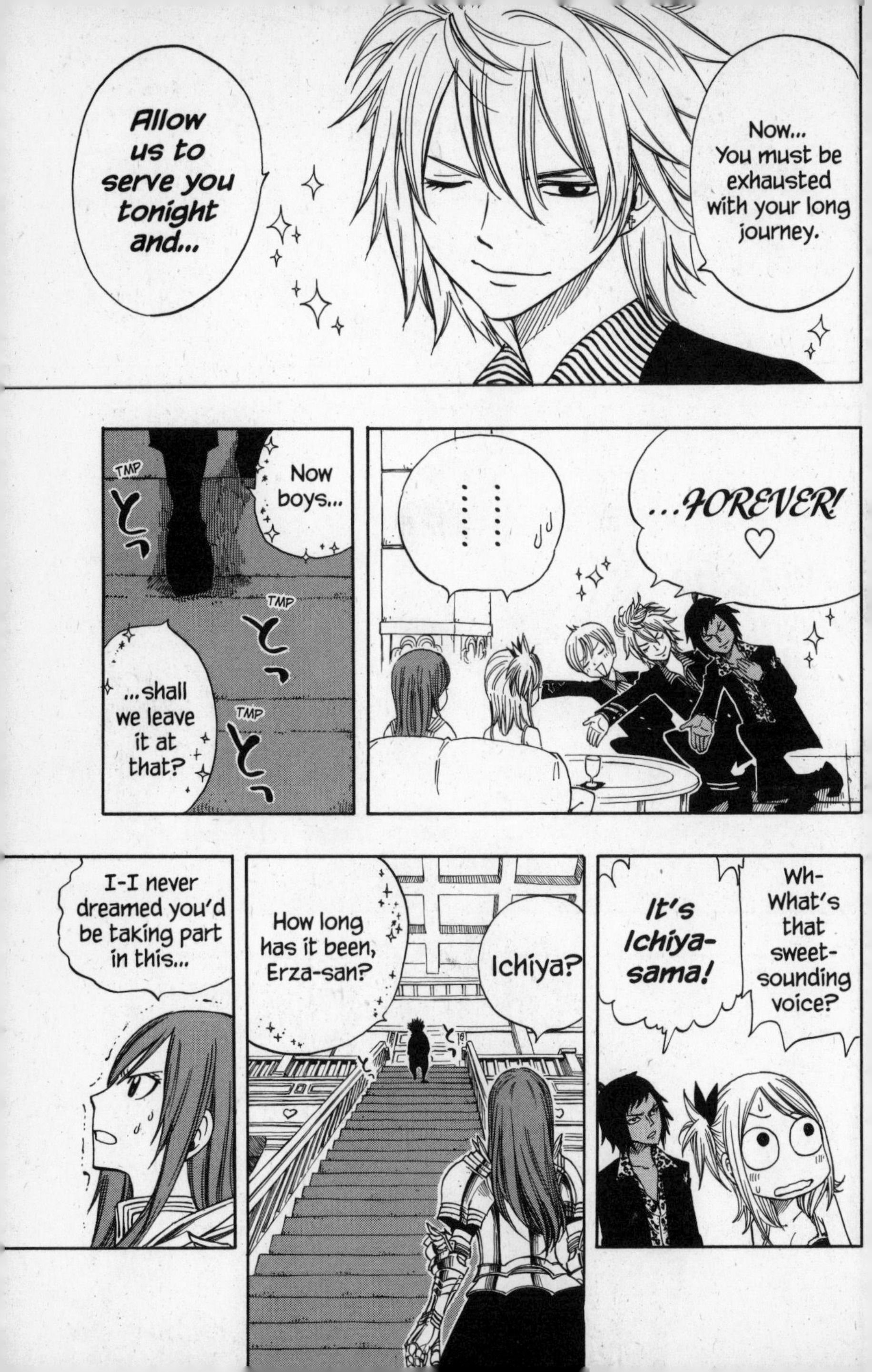
Now... You must be exhausted with your long journey.
Allow us to serve you tonight and...
...FOREVER! ♡
......
Now boys...
TMP
TMP
...shall we leave it at that?
TMP
Wh- What's that sweet-sounding voice?
It's Ichiya-sama!
Ichiya?
How long has it been, Erza-san?
I-I never dreamed you'd be taking part in this...

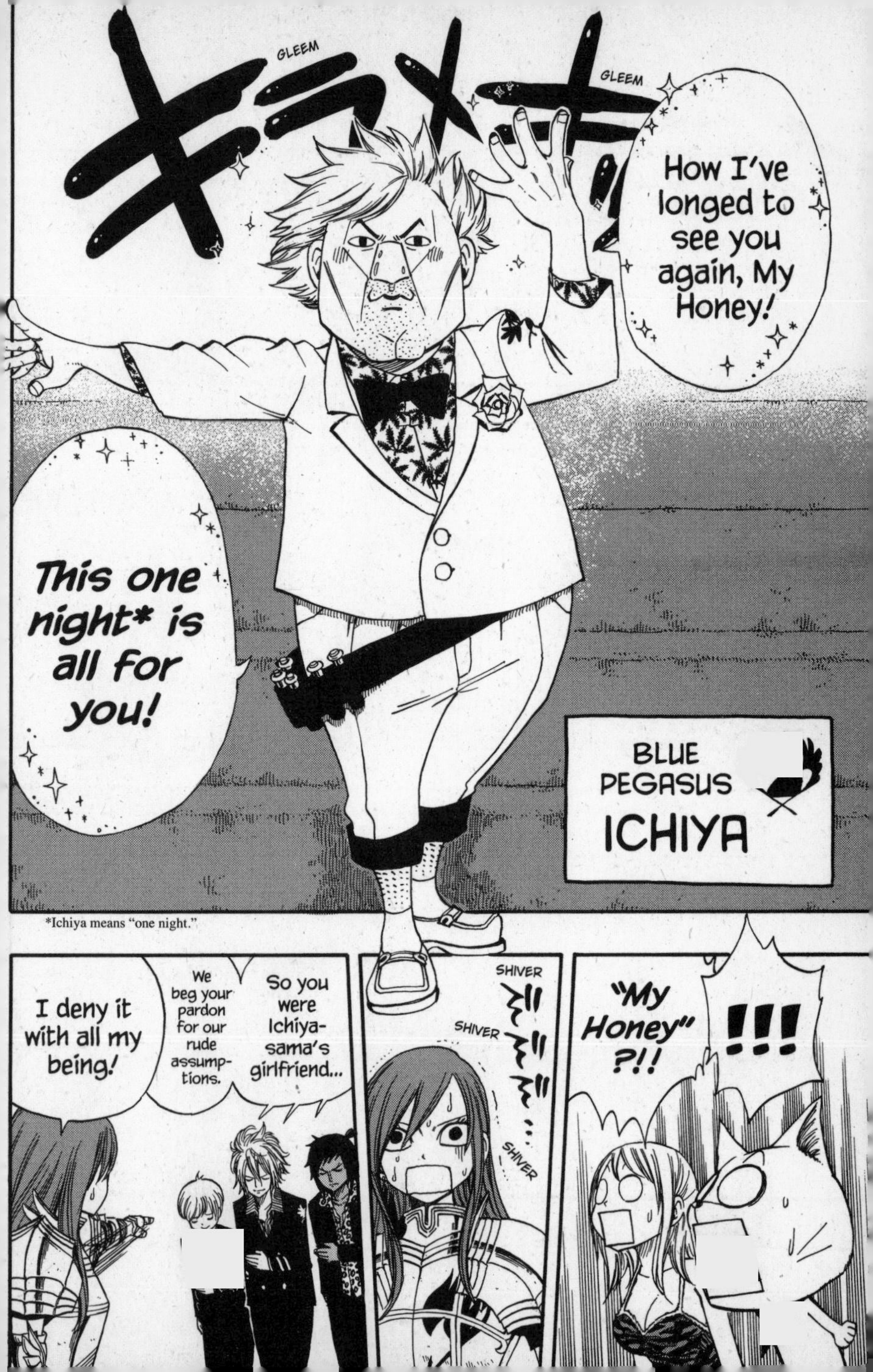
GLEEM
GLEEM
How I've longed to see you again, My Honey!
This one night* is all for you!
BLUE PEGASUS
ICHIYA
"My Honey"?!!
!!!
SHIVER
SHIVER
SHIVER
So you were Ichiya-sama's girlfriend...
We beg your pardon for our rude assumptions.
I deny it with all my being!

*Ichiya means "one night."

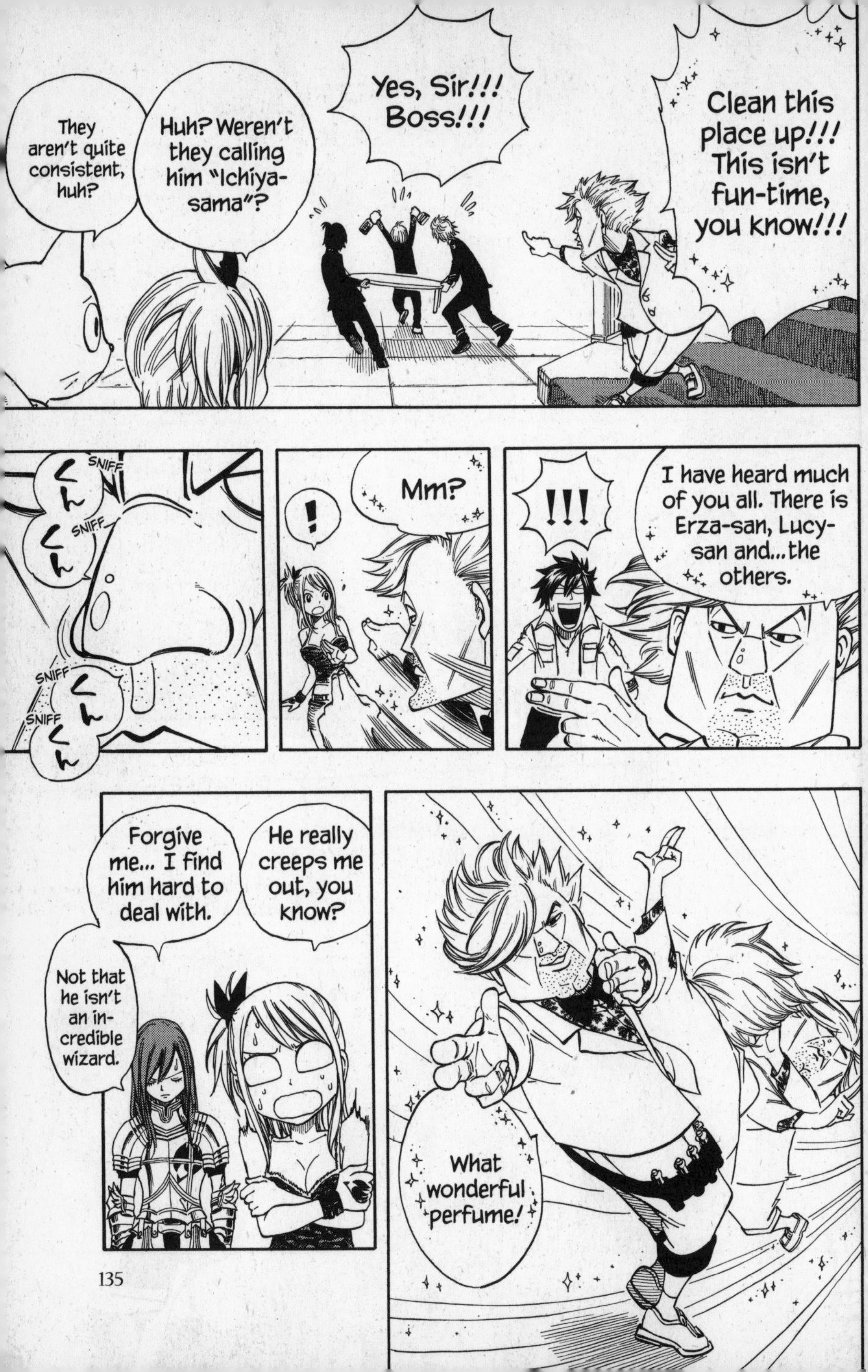
Clean this place up!!! This isn't fun-time, you know!!!
Yes, Sir!!! Boss!!!
Huh? Weren't they calling him "Ichiya-sama"?
They aren't quite consistent, huh?
I have heard much of you all. There is Erza-san, Lucy-san and...the others.
!!!
Mm?
!
くん SNIFF
くん SNIFF
くん SNIFF
くん SNIFF
What wonderful perfume!
He really creeps me out, you know?
Forgive me... I find him hard to deal with.
Not that he isn't an incredible wizard.

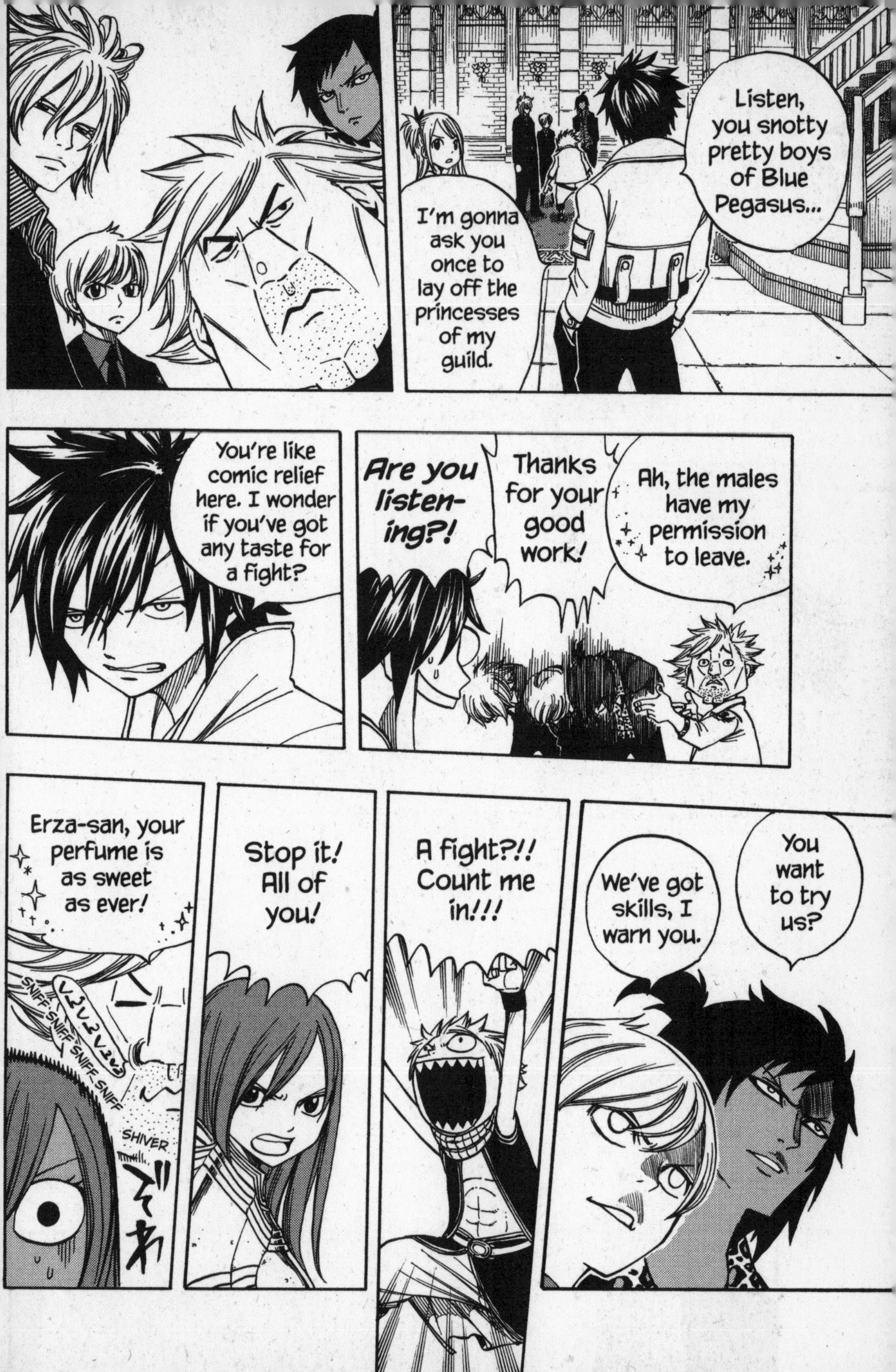
Listen, you snotty pretty boys of Blue Pegasus...
I'm gonna ask you once to lay off the princesses of my guild.
Ah, the males have my permission to leave.
Thanks for your good work!
Are you listen-ing?!
You're like comic relief here. I wonder if you've got any taste for a fight?
You want to try us?
We've got skills, I warn you.
A fight?!! Count me in!!!
Stop it! All of you!
Erza-san, your perfume is as sweet as ever!
SNIFF SNIFF SNIFF SNIFF
SHIVER
ぞわ

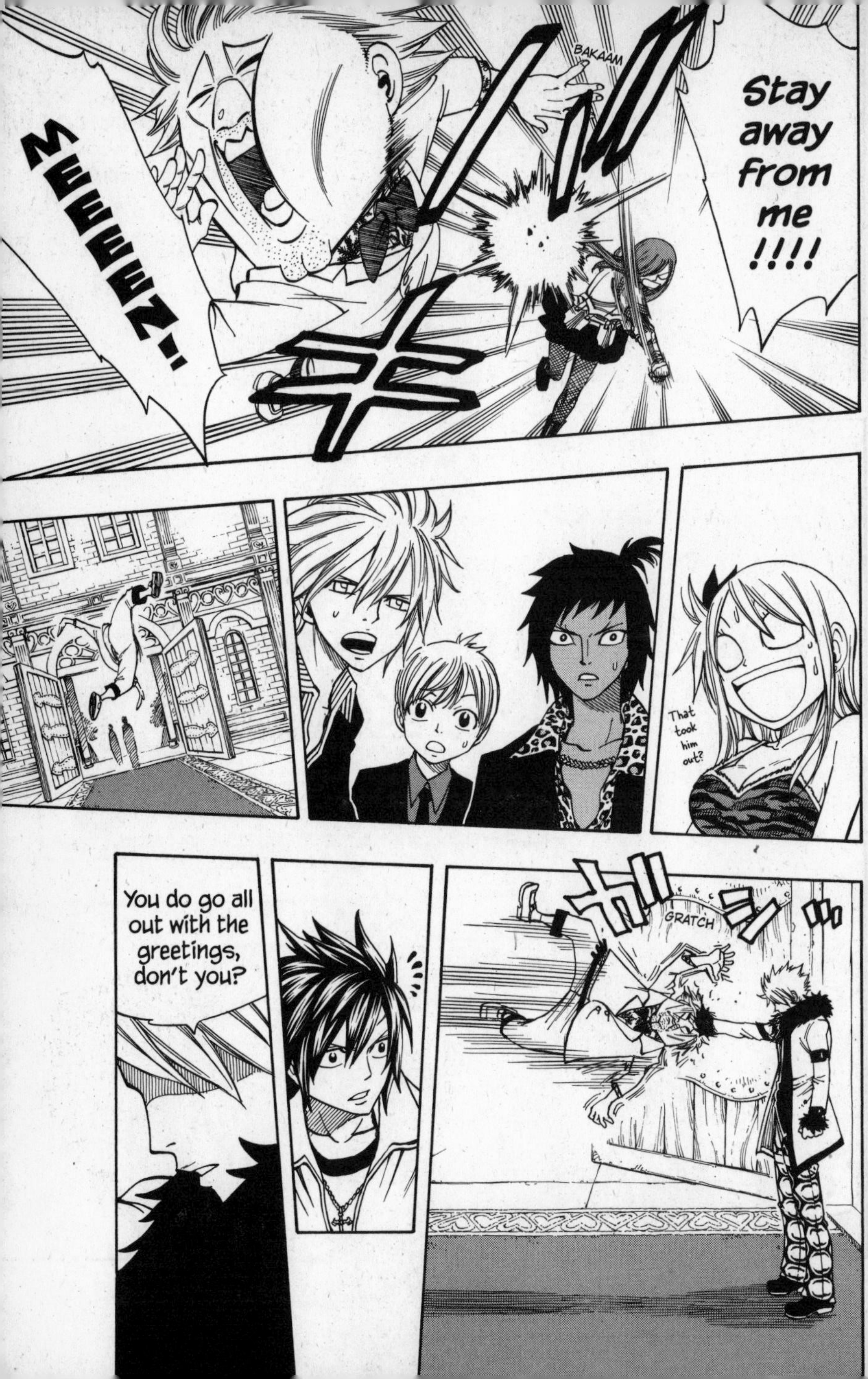
Stay away from me !!!!
BAKAAM
MEEEEN!
That took him out?
GRATCH
You do go all out with the greetings, don't you?

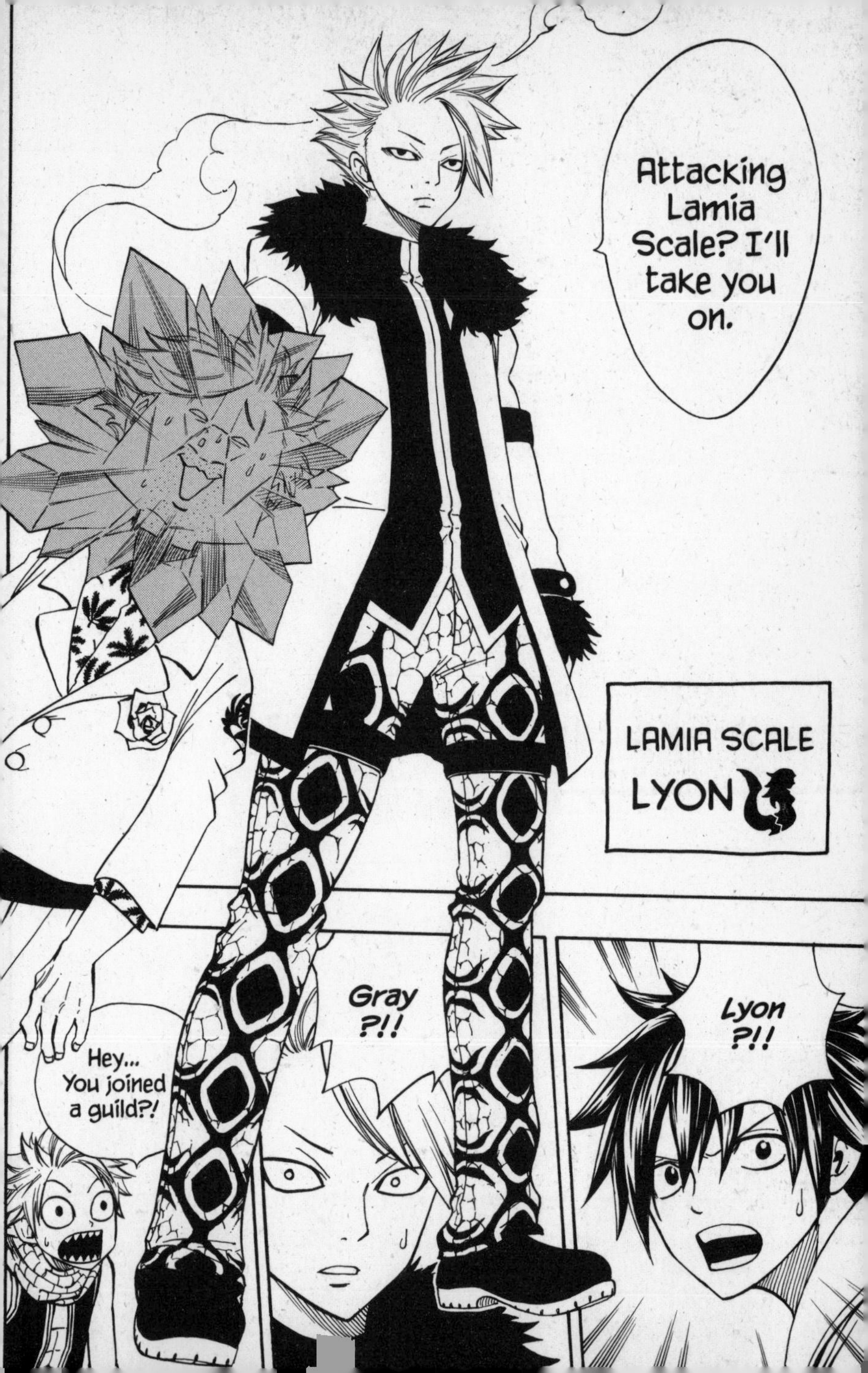
Attacking Lamia Scale? I'll take you on.
LAMIA SCALE
LYON
Lyon ?!!
Gray ?!!
Hey... You joined a guild?!

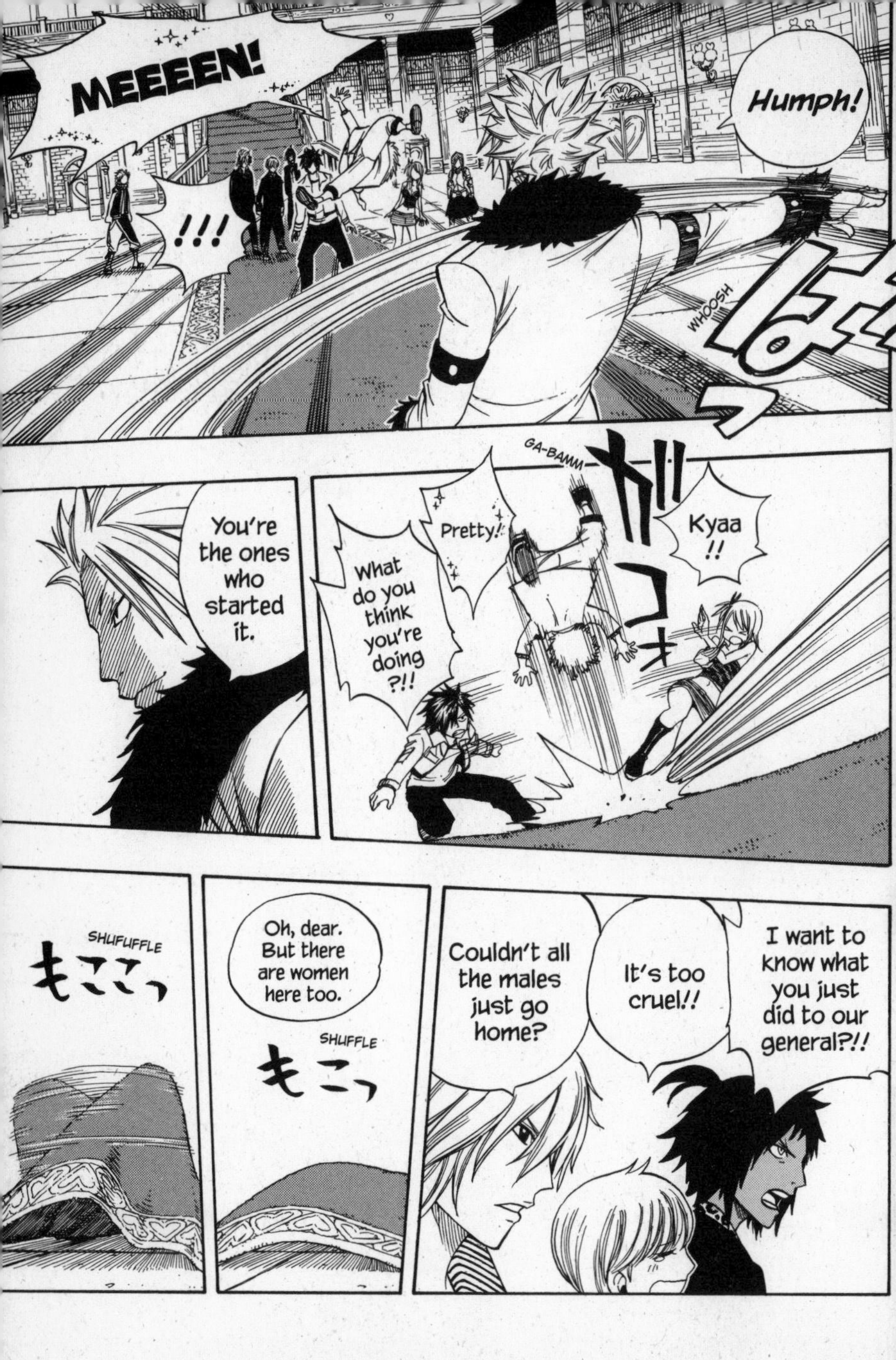
Humph!
WHOOSH
はっ
MEEEEN!
!!!
GA-BAMM
ガゴォ
Kyaa!!
Pretty!
What do you think you're doing?!!
You're the ones who started it.
I want to know what you just did to our general?!!
It's too cruel!!
Couldn't all the males just go home?
Oh, dear. But there are women here too.
SHUFFLE
もこっ
SHUFUFFLE
もここっ

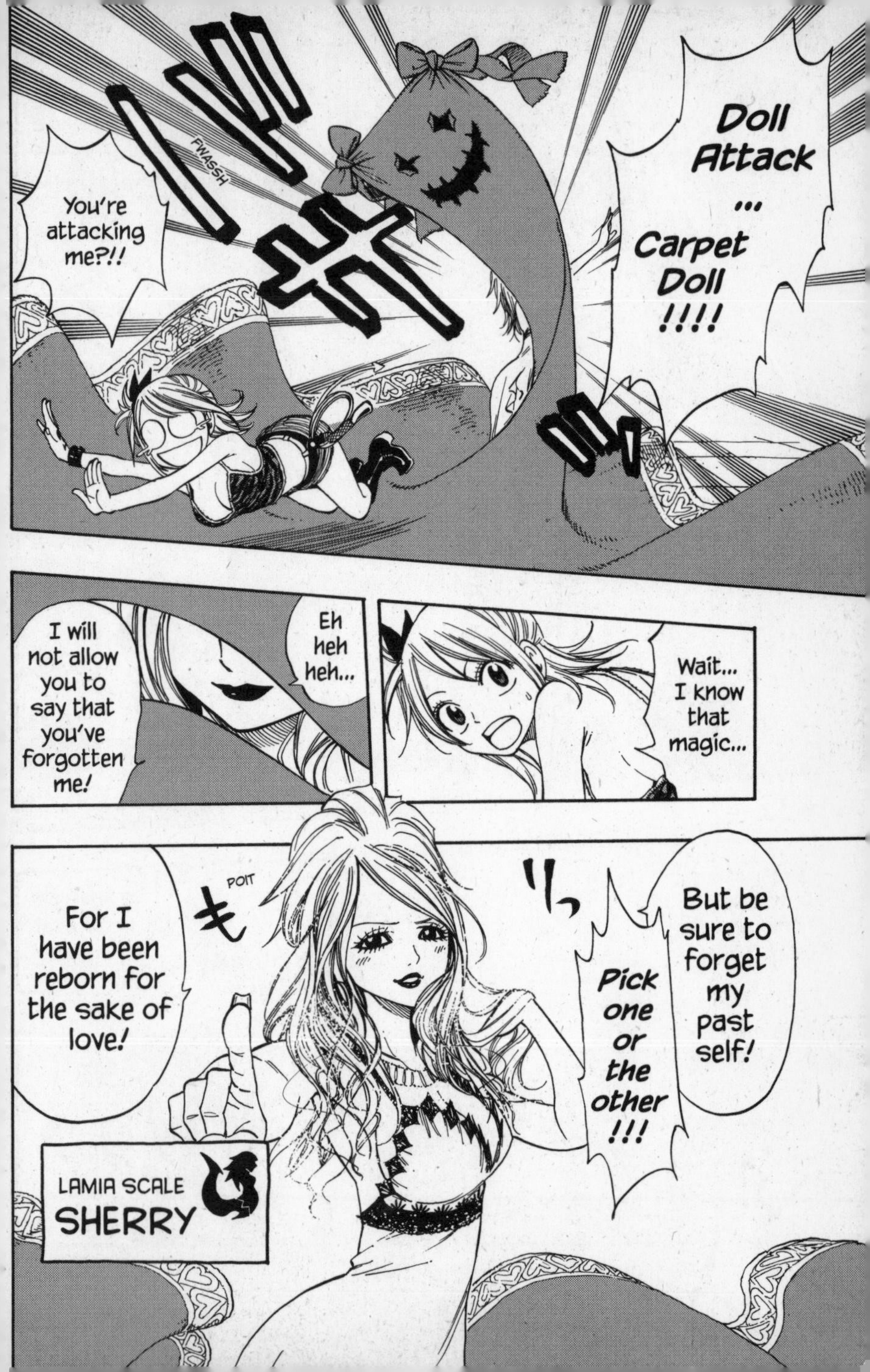
Doll Attack ... Carpet Doll !!!!
FWASSH
You're attacking me?!!
Wait... I know that magic...
Eh heh heh...
I will not allow you to say that you've forgotten me!
But be sure to forget my past self!
Pick one or the other !!!
POIT
For I have been reborn for the sake of love!
LAMIA SCALE
SHERRY

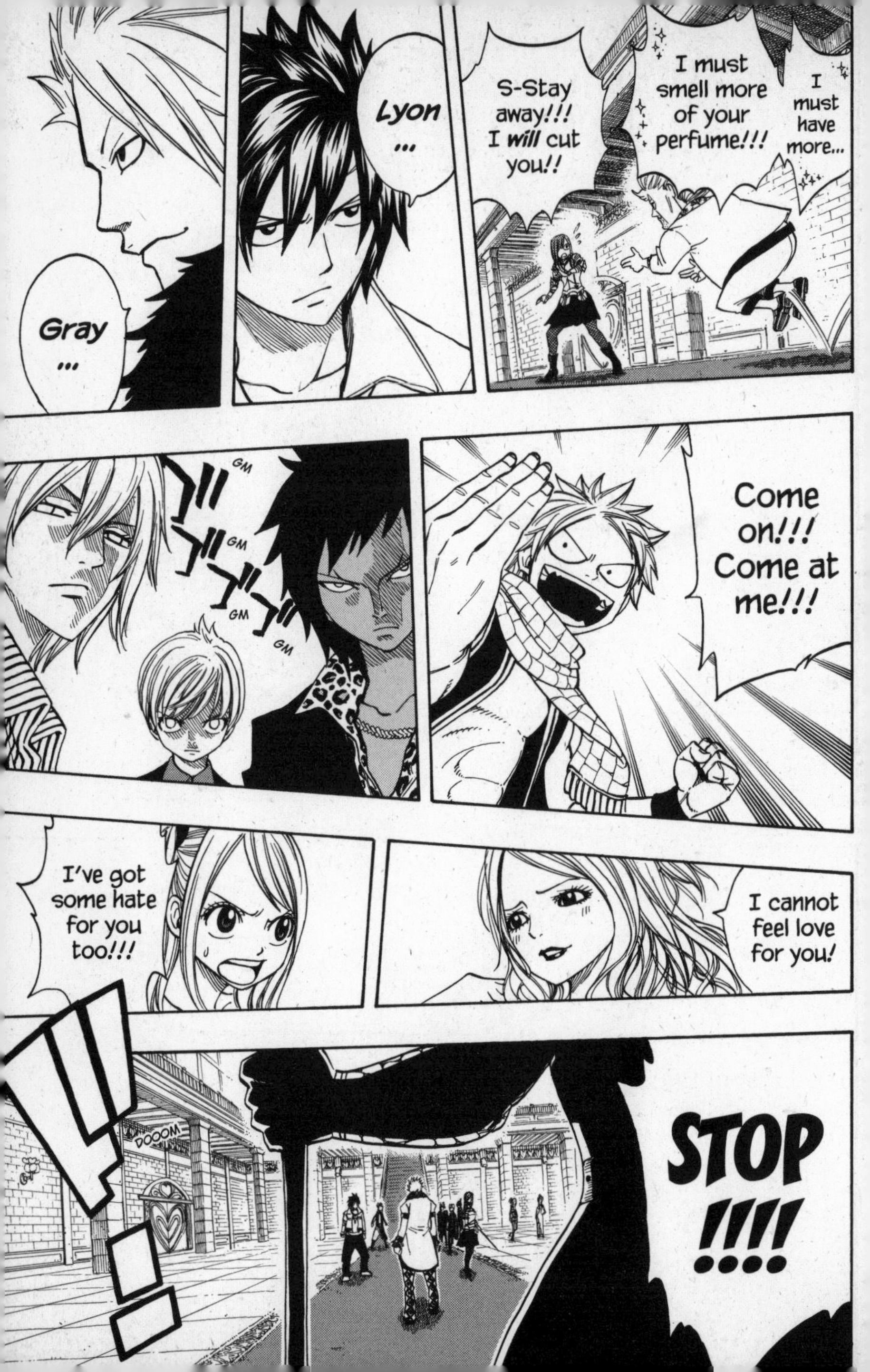
I must have more...
I must smell more of your perfume!!!
S-Stay away!!! I will cut you!!
Lyon ...
Gray ...
Come on!!! Come at me!!!
GM
GM
GM
GM
I cannot feel love for you!
I've got some hate for you too!!!
STOP!!!!
DOOOM
!!

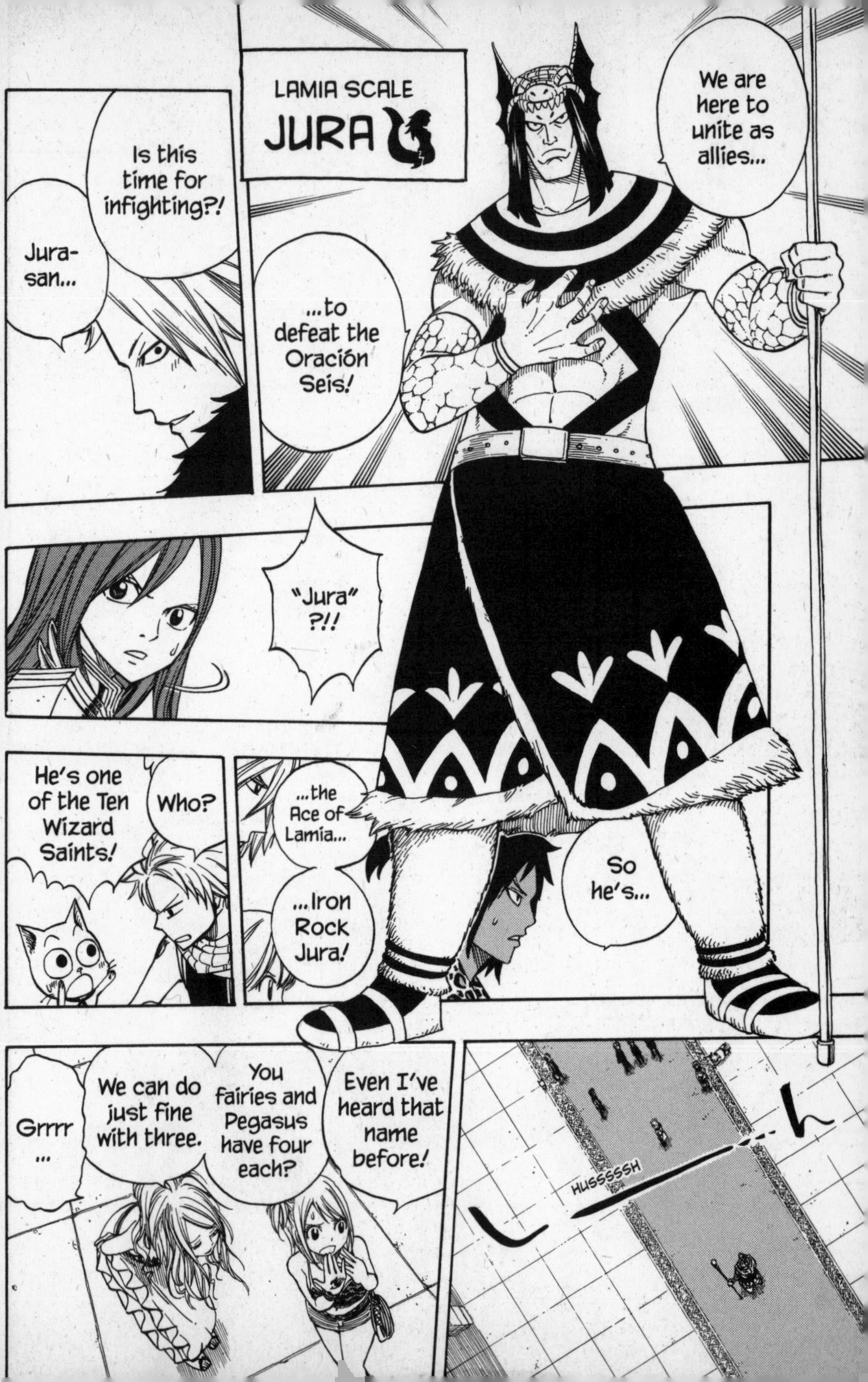
LAMIA SCALE
JURA
We are here to unite as allies...
...to defeat the Oración Seis!
Is this time for infighting?!
Jura-san...
"Jura"?!!
So he's...
...the Ace of Lamia...
...Iron Rock Jura!
Who?
He's one of the Ten Wizard Saints!
HUSSSSSH
Even I've heard that name before!
You fairies and Pegasus have four each?
We can do just fine with three.
Grrrr ...

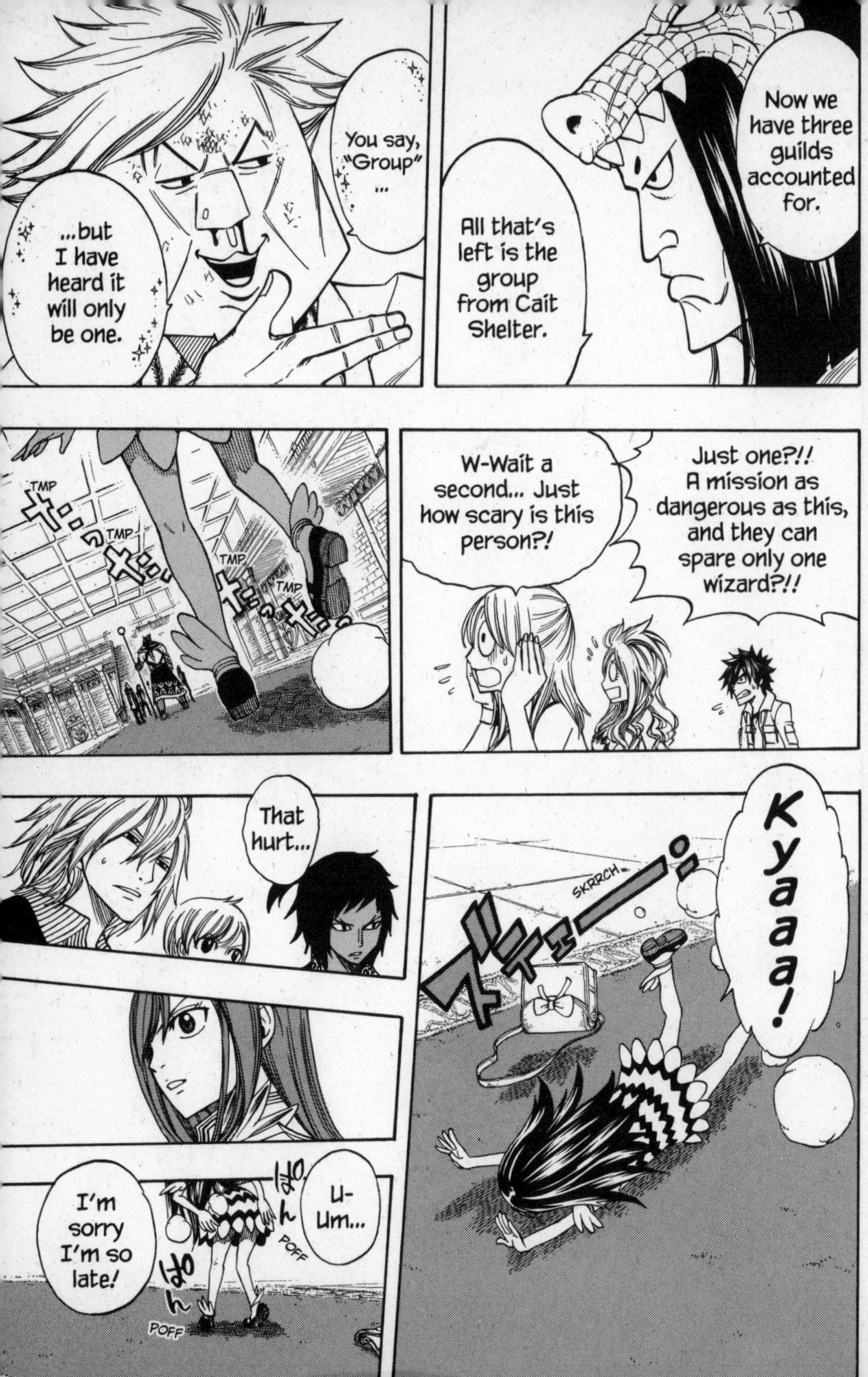
Now we have three guilds accounted for.
All that's left is the group from Cait Shelter.
You say, "Group"...
...but I have heard it will only be one.
Just one?!! A mission as dangerous as this, and they can spare only one wizard?!!
W-Wait a second... Just how scary is this person?!
TMP
TMP
TMP
TMP
Kyaaa!
SKRRCH
That hurt...
U-Um...
POFF
I'm sorry I'm so late!
POFF

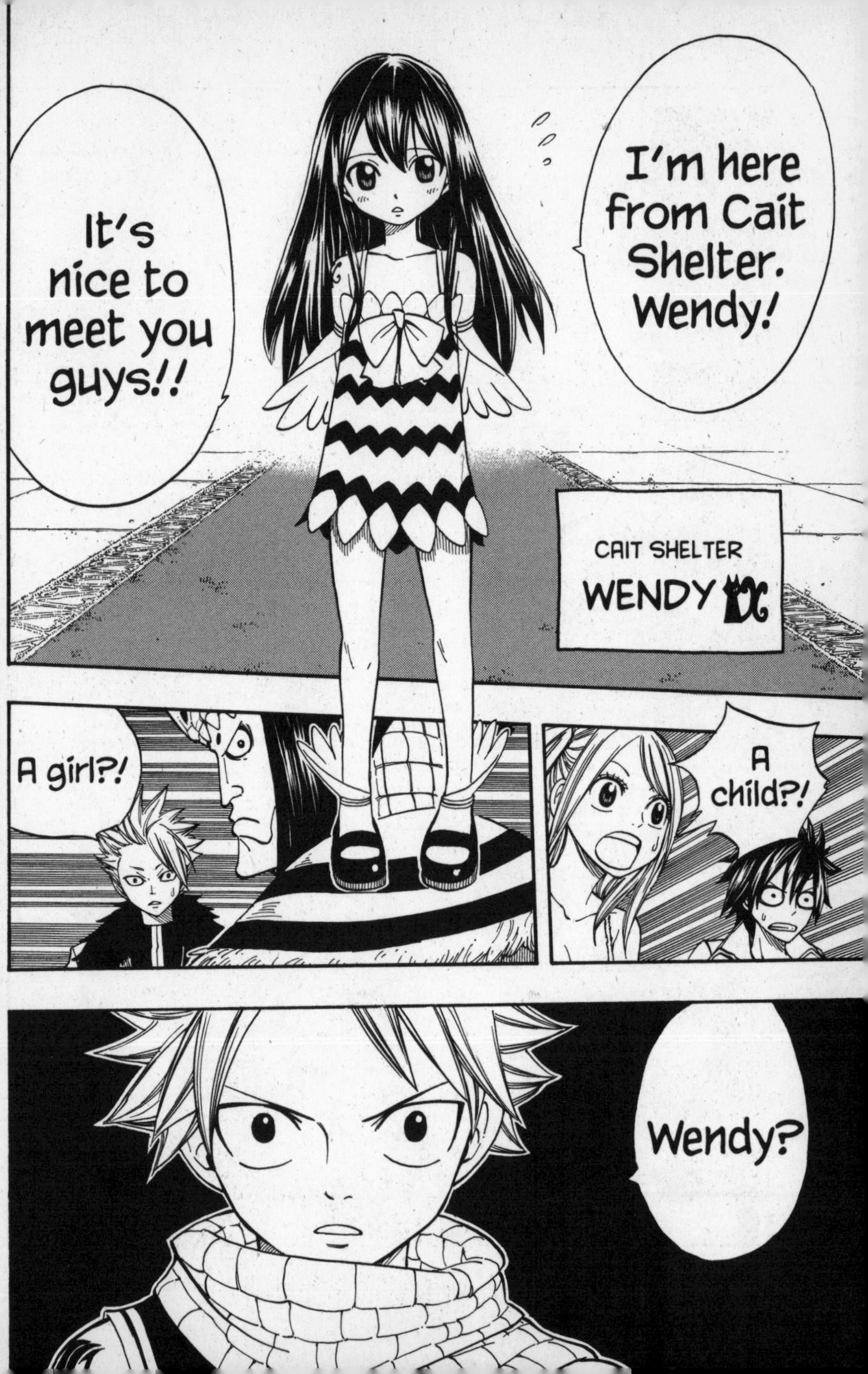
I'm here from Cait Shelter. Wendy!
It's nice to meet you guys!!
CAIT SHELTER
WENDY
A child?!
A girl?!
Wendy?

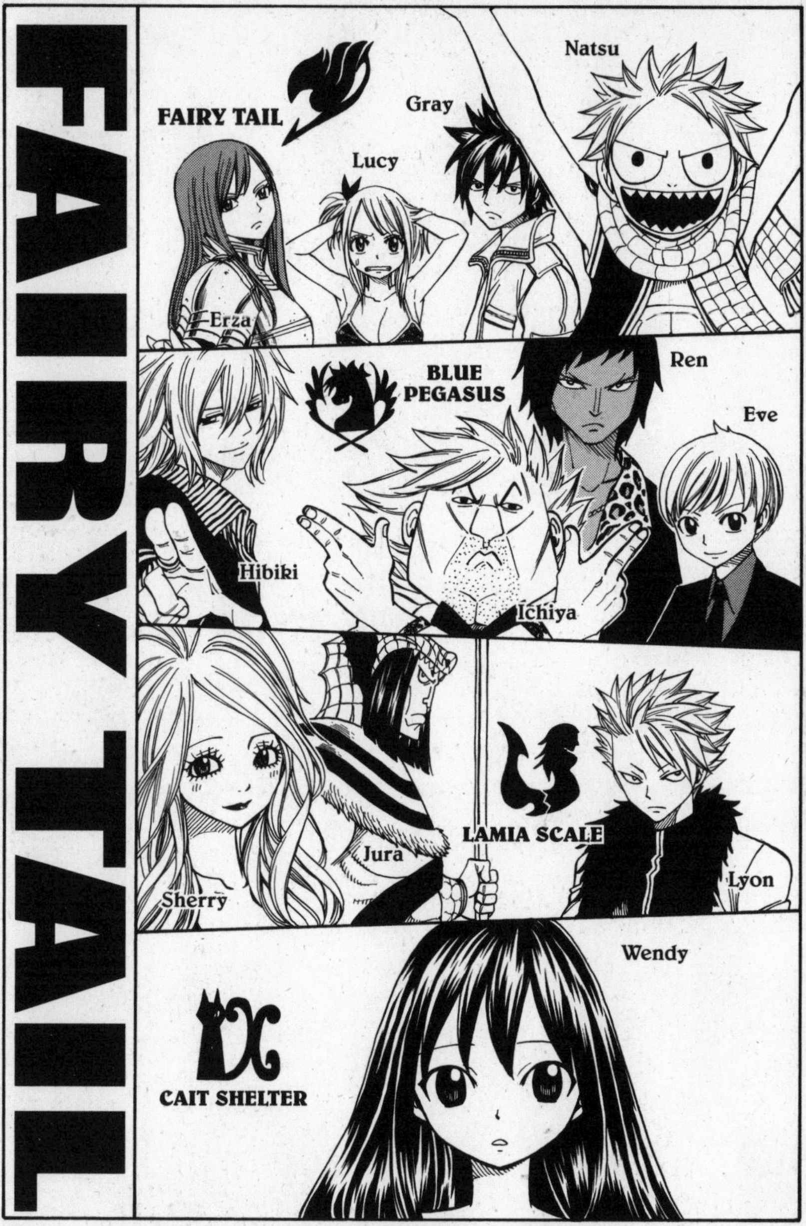
FAIRY TAIL
Natsu
Gray
Lucy
FAIRY TAIL
Erza
Ren
Eve
BLUE PEGASUS
Ichiya
Hibiki
LAMIA SCALE
Lyon
Jura
Sherry
Wendy
CAIT SHELTER

Chapter 133, 12 vs. 6

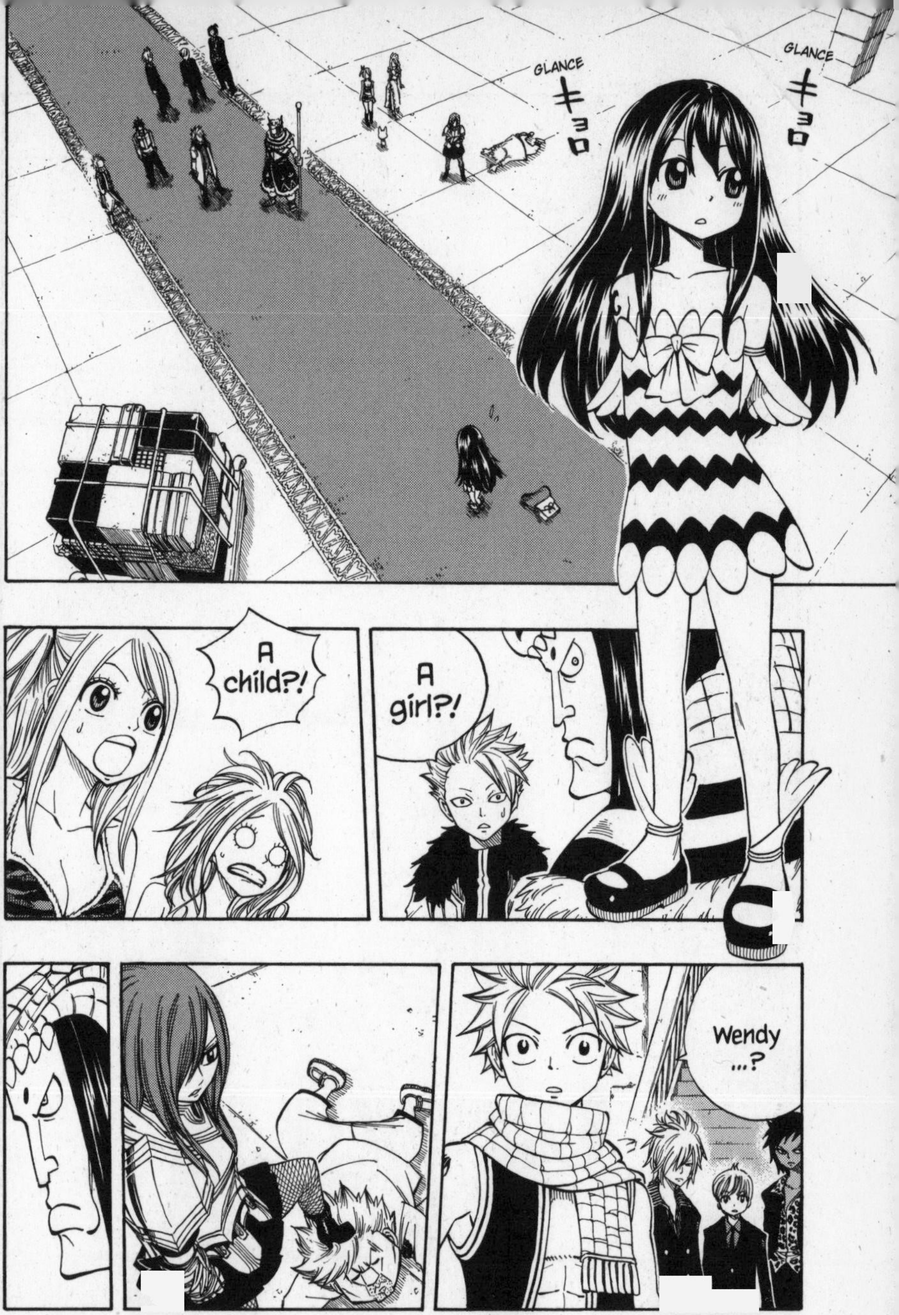
GLANCE
キョロ
GLANCE
キョロ
A girl?!
A child?!
Wendy ...?

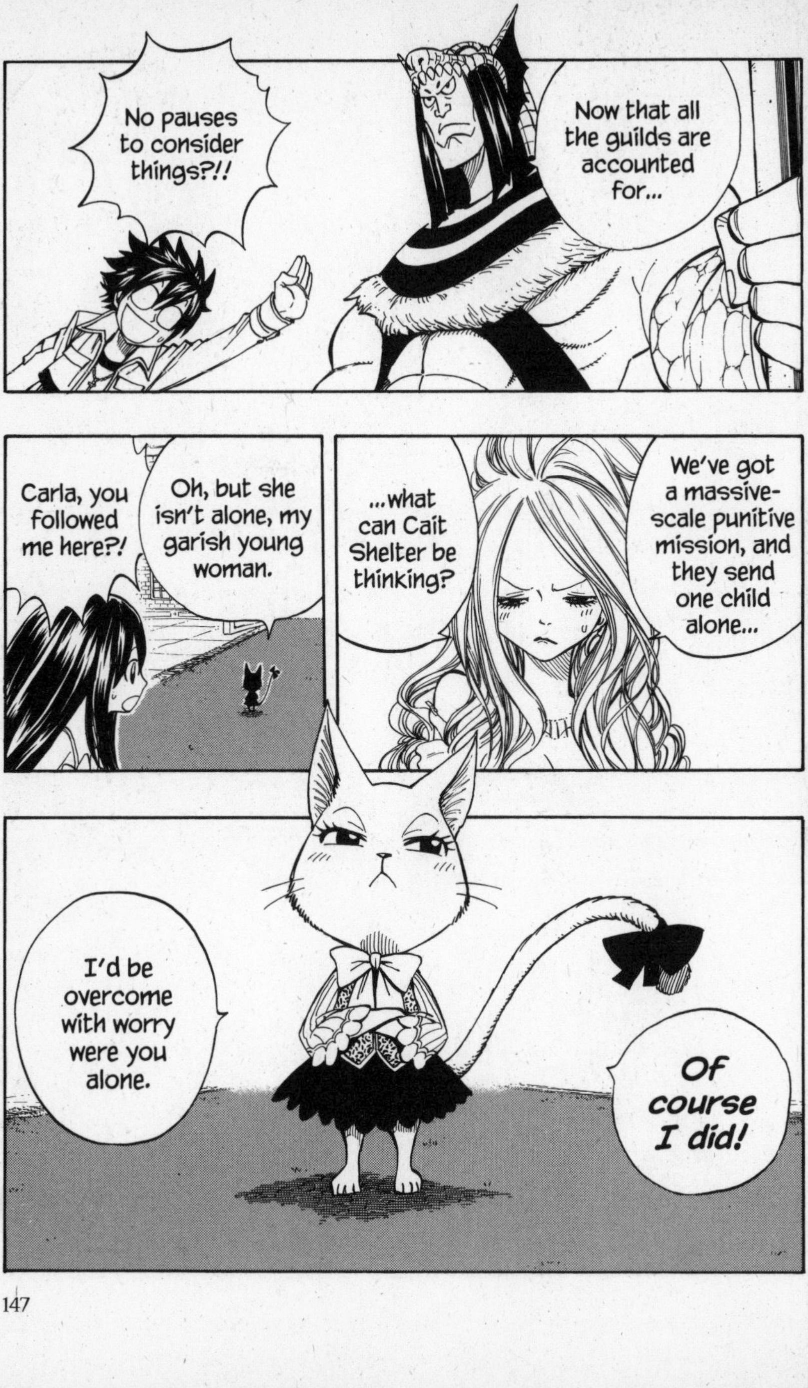
Now that all the guilds are accounted for...
No pauses to consider things?!!
We've got a massive-scale punitive mission, and they send one child alone...
...what can Cait Shelter be thinking?
Oh, but she isn't alone, my garish young woman.
Carla, you followed me here?!
Of course I did!
I'd be overcome with worry were you alone.

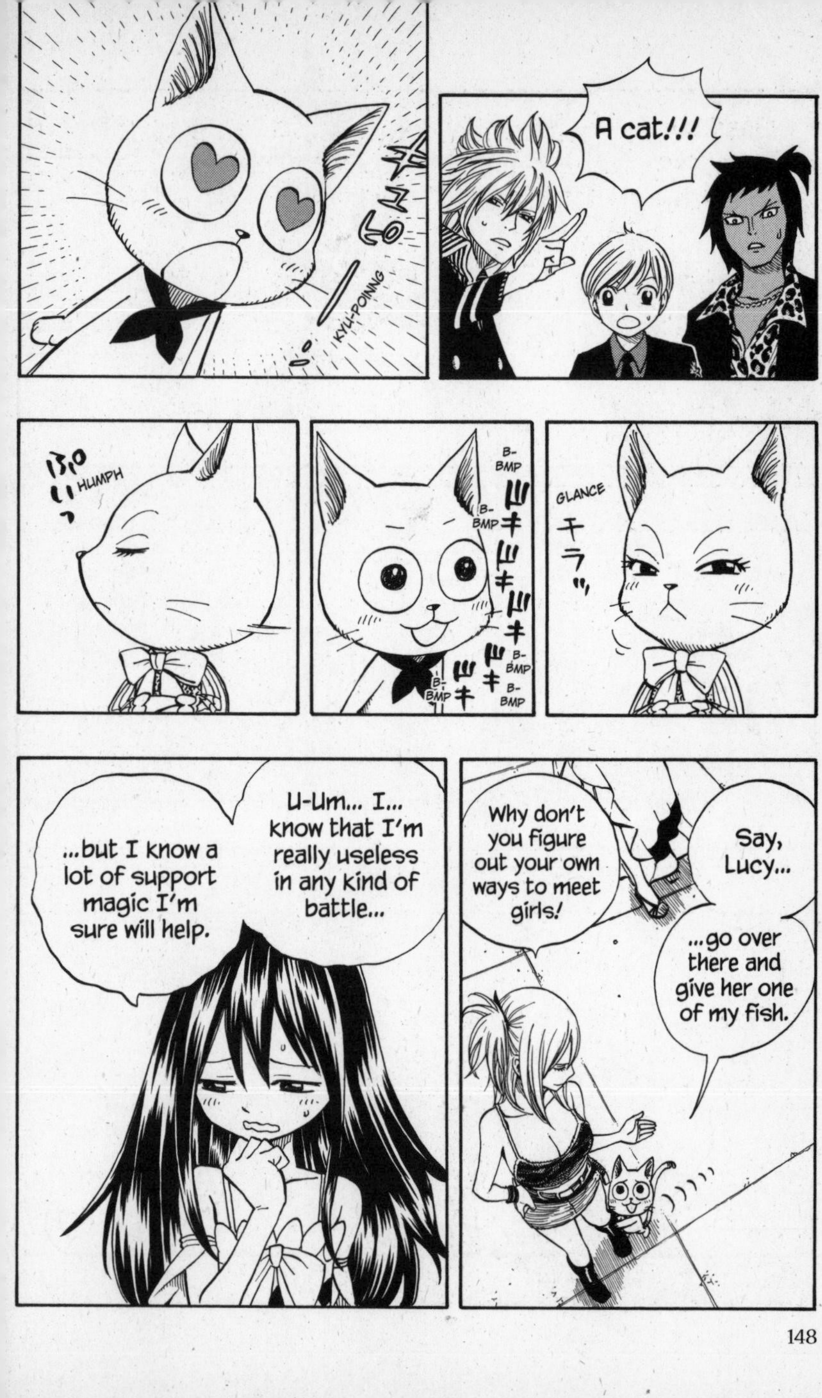
A cat!!!
KYU-POINNG
GLANCE
B-BMP
B-BMP
B-BMP
B-BMP
B-BMP
HUMPH
Say, Lucy...
...go over there and give her one of my fish.
Why don't you figure out your own ways to meet girls!
U-Um... I... know that I'm really useless in any kind of battle...
...but I know a lot of support magic I'm sure will help.

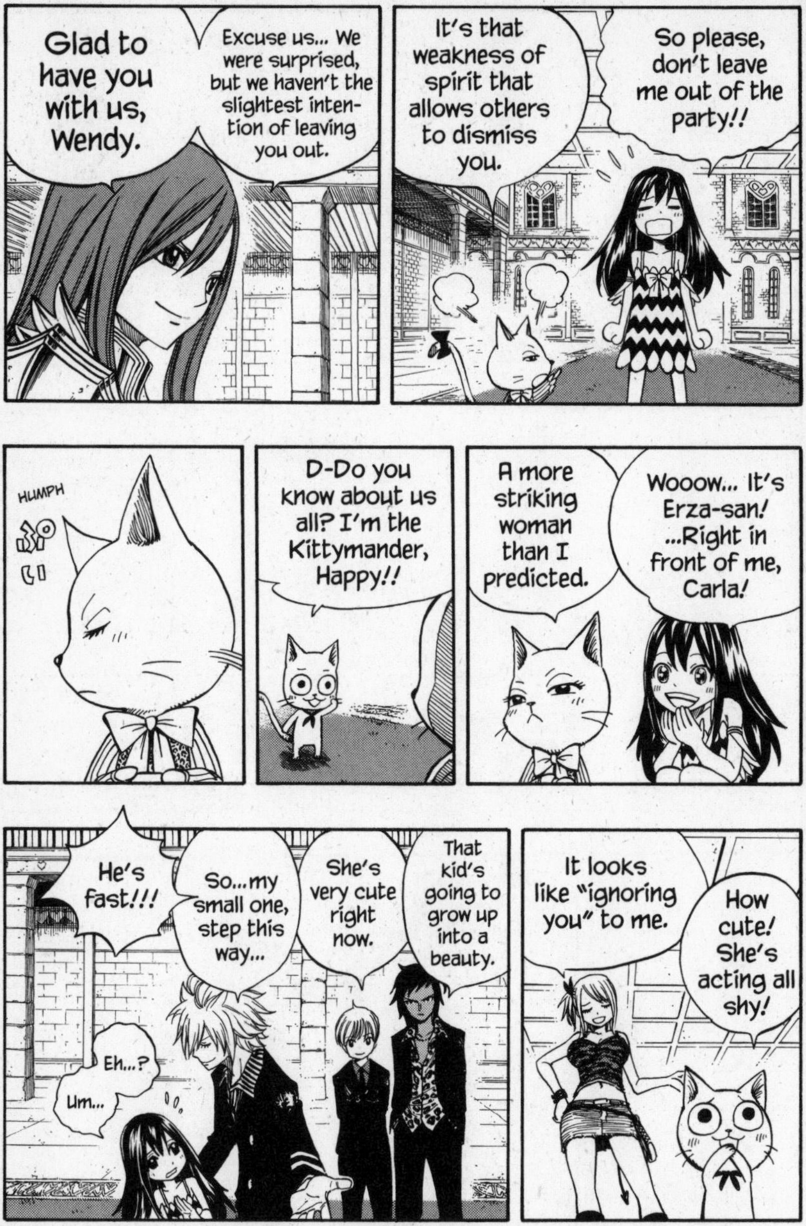
So please, don't leave me out of the party!!
It's that weakness of spirit that allows others to dismiss you.
Excuse us... We were surprised, but we haven't the slightest intention of leaving you out.
Glad to have you with us, Wendy.
Wooow... It's Erza-san! ...Right in front of me, Carla!
A more striking woman than I predicted.
D-Do you know about us all? I'm the Kittymander, Happy!!
HUMPH
How cute! She's acting all shy!
It looks like "ignoring you" to me.
That kid's going to grow up into a beauty.
She's very cute right now.
So...my small one, step this way...
He's fast!!!
Eh...?
Um...

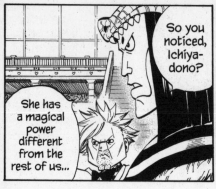

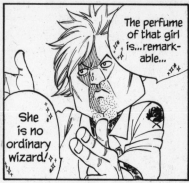

The perfume of that girl is...remark-able...
She is no ordinary wizard!
So you noticed, Ichiya-dono?
She has a magical power different from the rest of us...
And Erza-dono noticed as well.
A-As I sus-pected...
May I interest you in some orange juice?
Um... Uh...
Have a steaming cloth.
What is with these males?!
Wendy...
What is it, Natsu?
I have the feeling I've heard that name somewhere before...
Hmm...

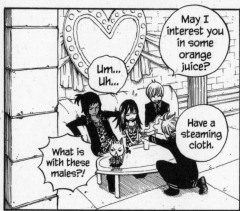

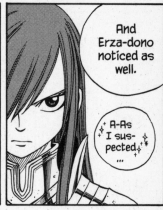

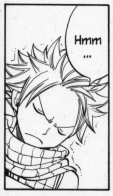

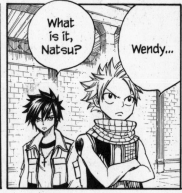

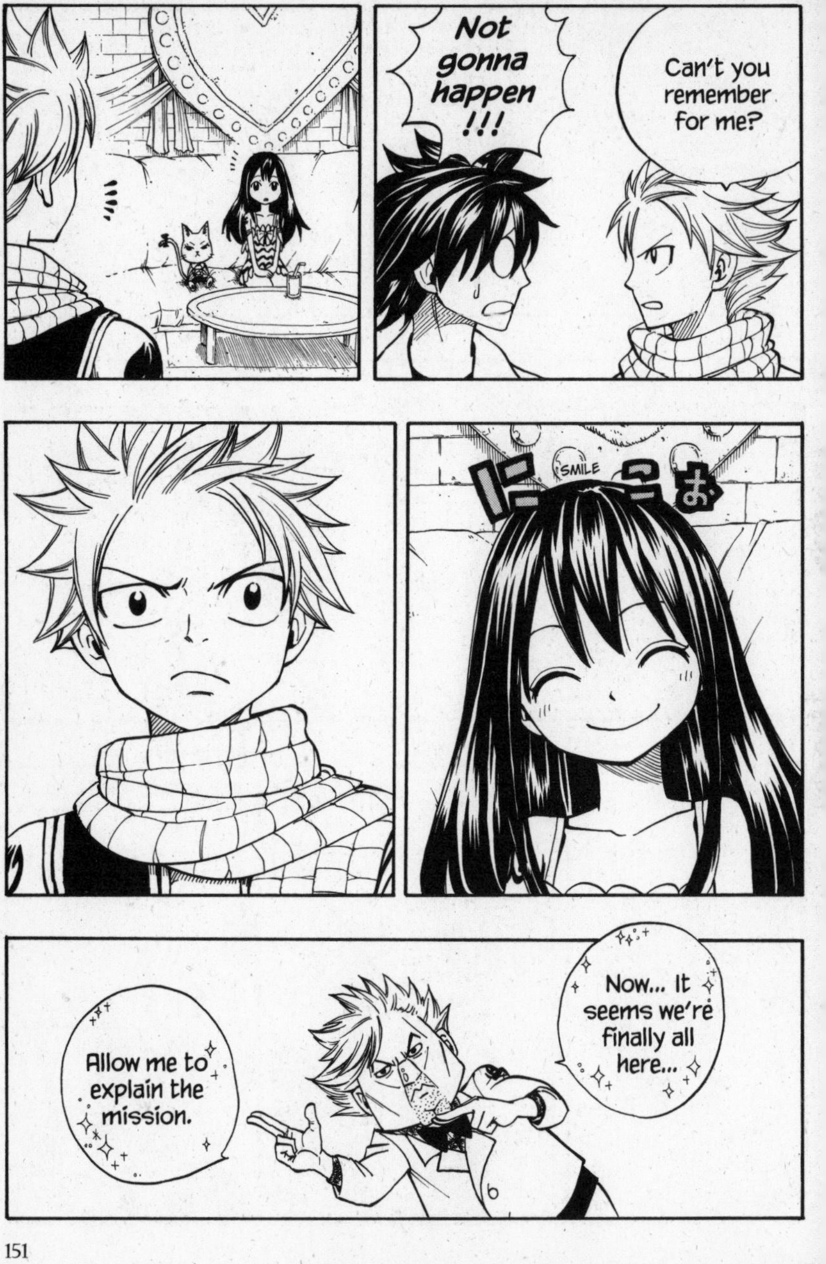
Can't you remember for me?
Not gonna happen!!!
にこお
SMILE
Now... It seems we're finally all here...
Allow me to explain the mission.

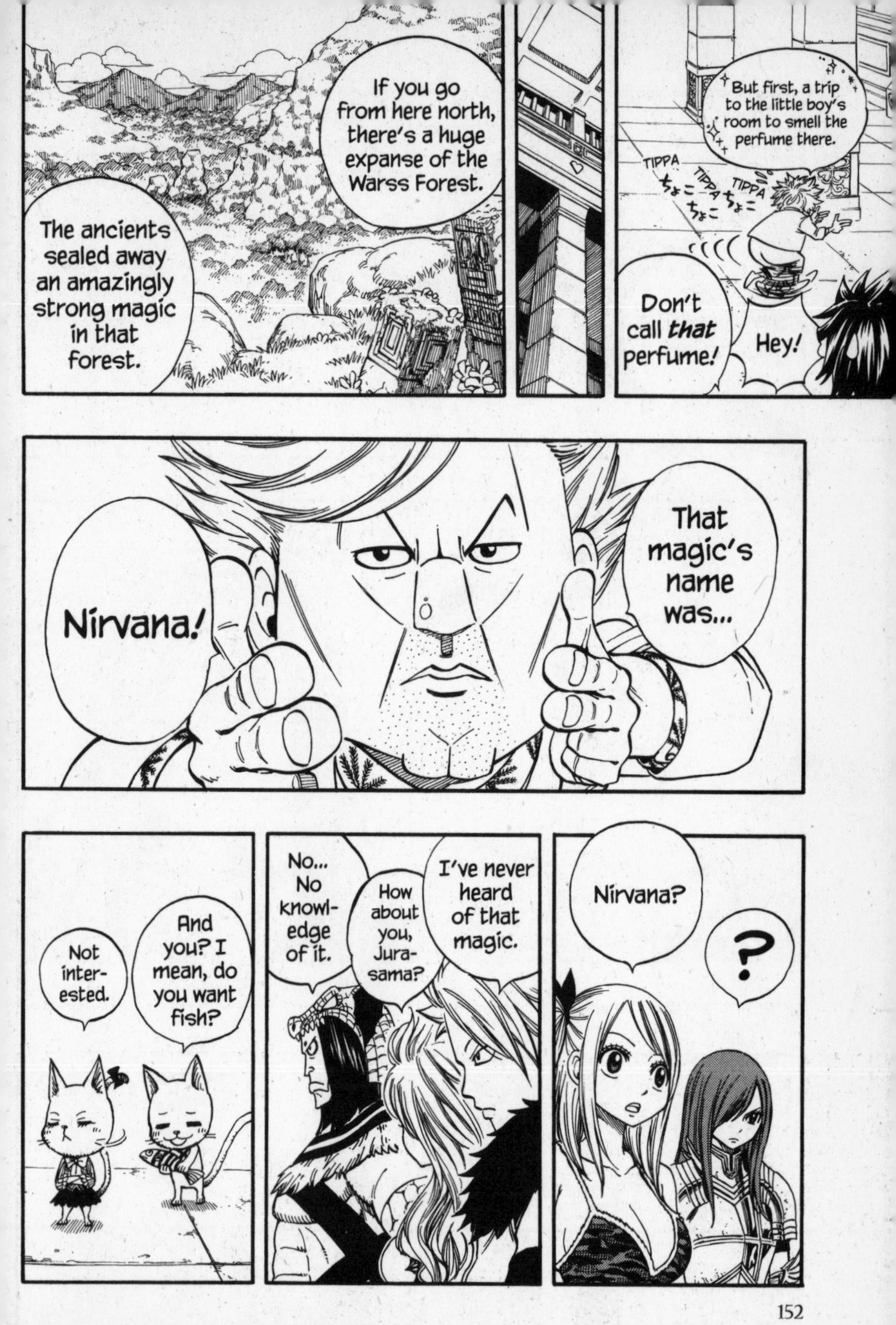
But first, a trip to the little boy's room to smell the perfume there.
TIPPA ちょこ
TIPPA ちょこ
TIPPA ちょこ
Hey!
Don't call *that* perfume!
If you go from here north, there's a huge expanse of the Warss Forest.
The ancients sealed away an amazingly strong magic in that forest.
That magic's name was...
Nirvana!
Nirvana?
?
I've never heard of that magic.
How about you, Jura-sama?
No... No knowledge of it.
And you? I mean, do you want fish?
Not interested.

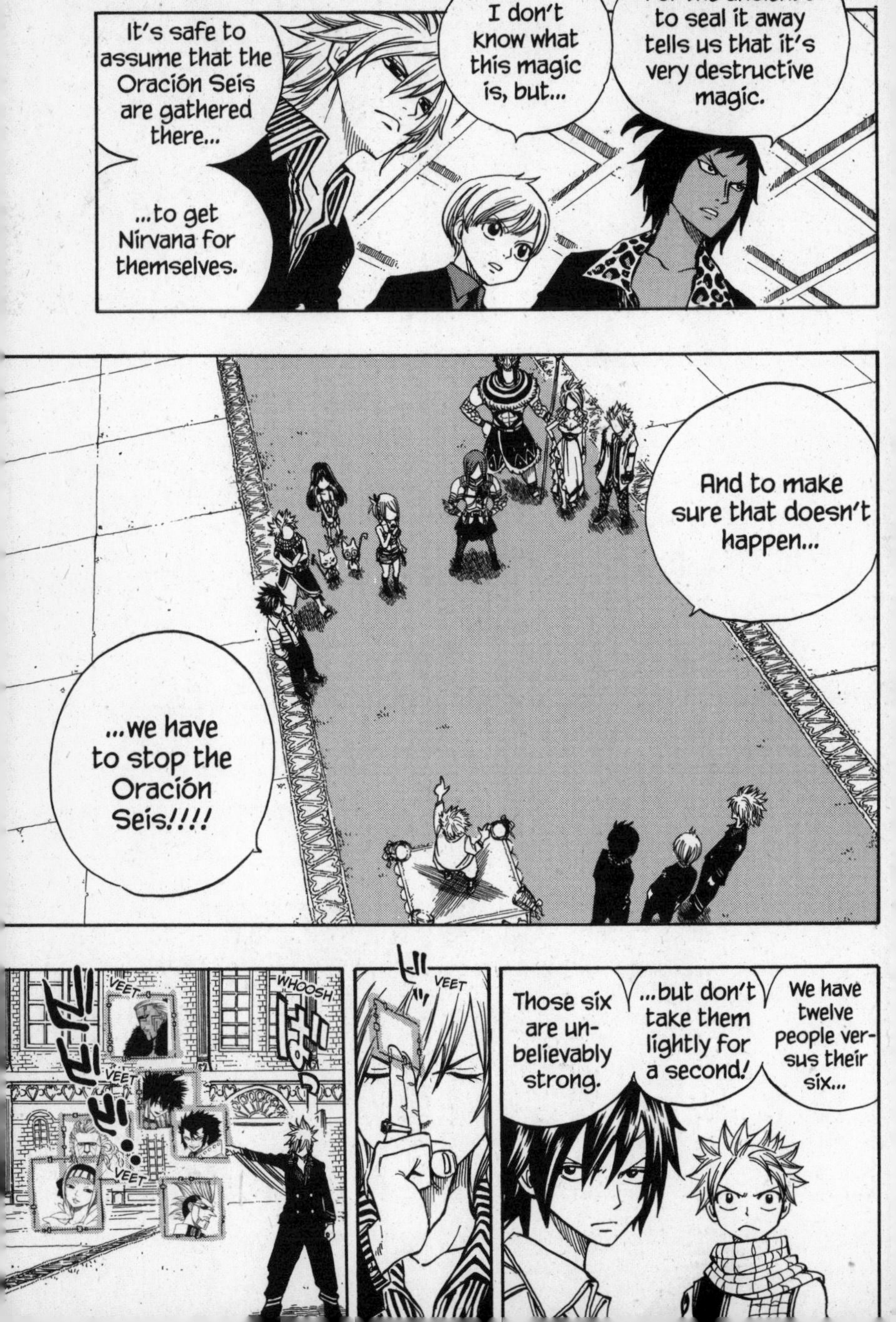
For the ancients to seal it away tells us that it's very destructive magic.
I don't know what this magic is, but...
It's safe to assume that the Oración Seis are gathered there...
...to get Nirvana for themselves.
And to make sure that doesn't happen...
...we have to stop the Oración Seis!!!!
We have twelve people ver-sus their six...
...but don't take them lightly for a second!
Those six are un-believably strong.
VEET
WHOOSH
VEET
VEET
VEET

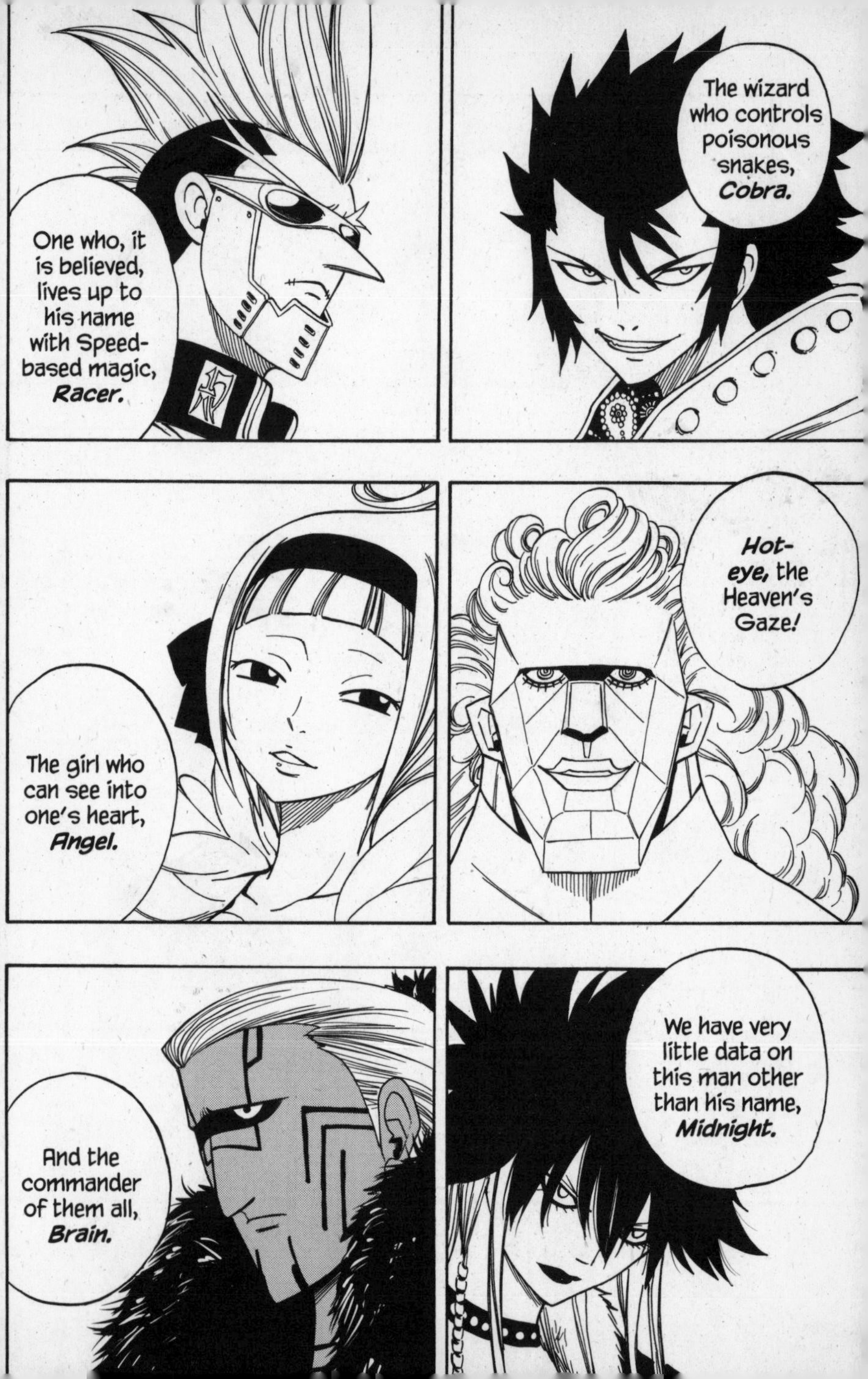
The wizard who controls poisonous snakes, Cobra.
One who, it is believed, lives up to his name with Speed-based magic, Racer.
Hot-eye, the Heaven's Gaze!
The girl who can see into one's heart, Angel.
We have very little data on this man other than his name, Midnight.
And the commander of them all, Brain.

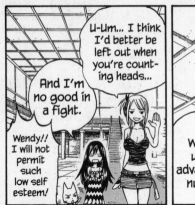

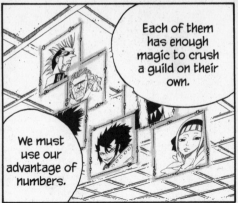

Each of them has enough magic to crush a guild on their own.
We must use our advantage of numbers.
U-Um... I think I'd better be left out when you're counting heads...
And I'm no good in a fight.
Wendy!! I will not permit such low self esteem!
You can relax on that account. We do not simply count fighting strength in our tactical advantages.
As long as we can simply find their base, we'll be fine.
Base?
There is much we don't know about them yet, but one thing we've deduced is they have a stronghold in the forest.
What would be best is to have all of them gathered in that base.
How do we do that?
We brawl until it happens, what else?!
So it *is* just about battle strength.
What will you do after they are gathered?
VSSH

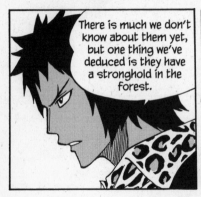

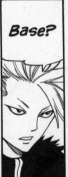

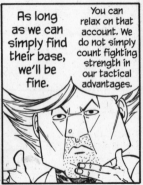

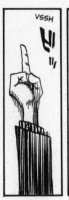

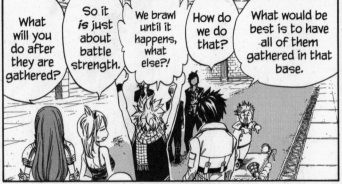

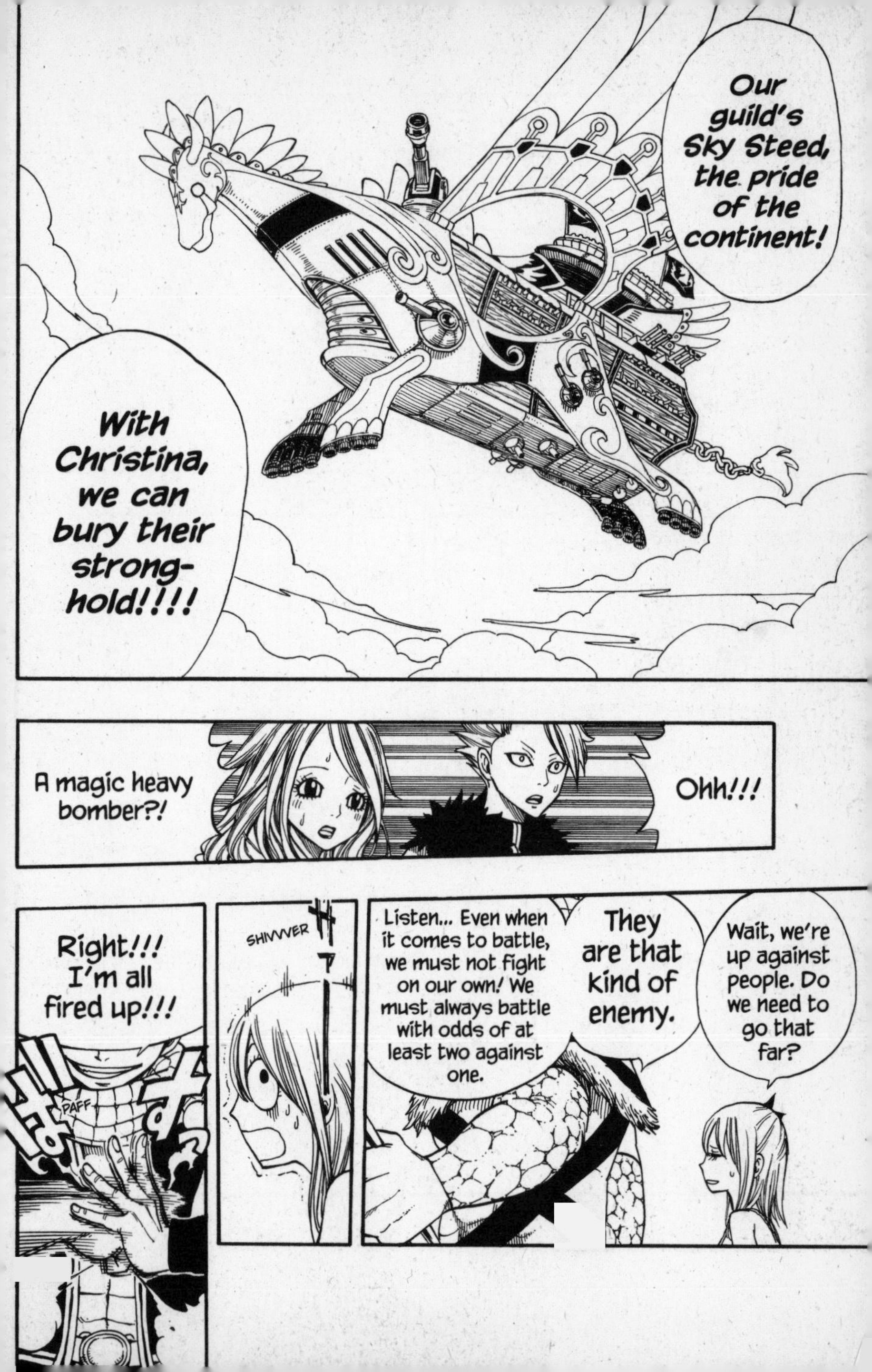
Our guild's Sky Steed, the pride of the continent!
With Christina, we can bury their stronghold!!!!
Ohh!!!
A magic heavy bomber?!
Wait, we're up against people. Do we need to go that far?
They are that kind of enemy.
Listen... Even when it comes to battle, we must not fight on our own! We must always battle with odds of at least two against one.
SHIVVVER
Right!!! I'm all fired up!!!
PAFF

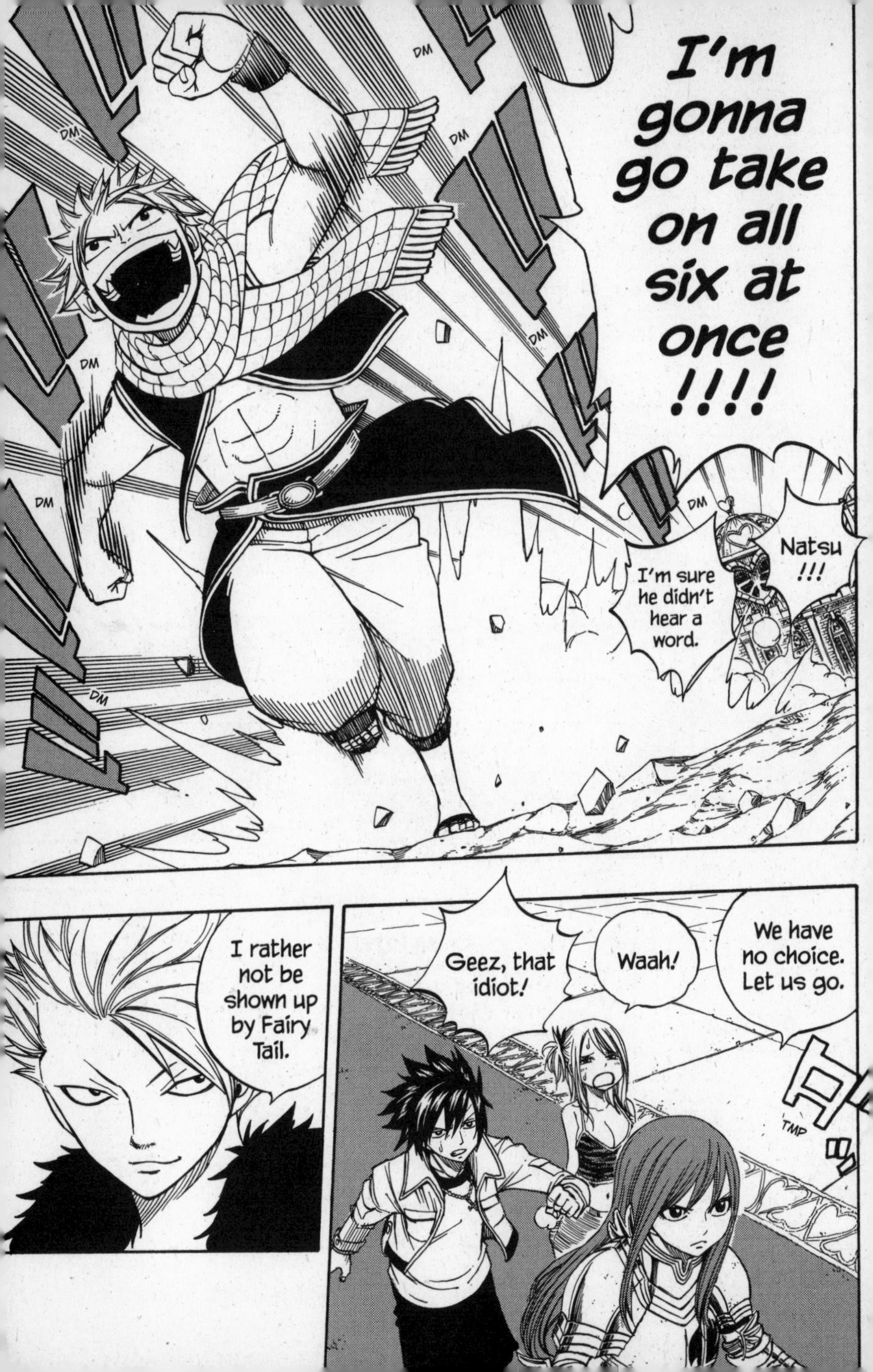
I'm gonna go take on all six at once !!!!
DM
DM
DM
DM
DM
DM
DM
DM
Natsu !!!
I'm sure he didn't hear a word.
We have no choice. Let us go.
TMP
Waah!
Geez, that idiot!
I rather not be shown up by Fairy Tail.

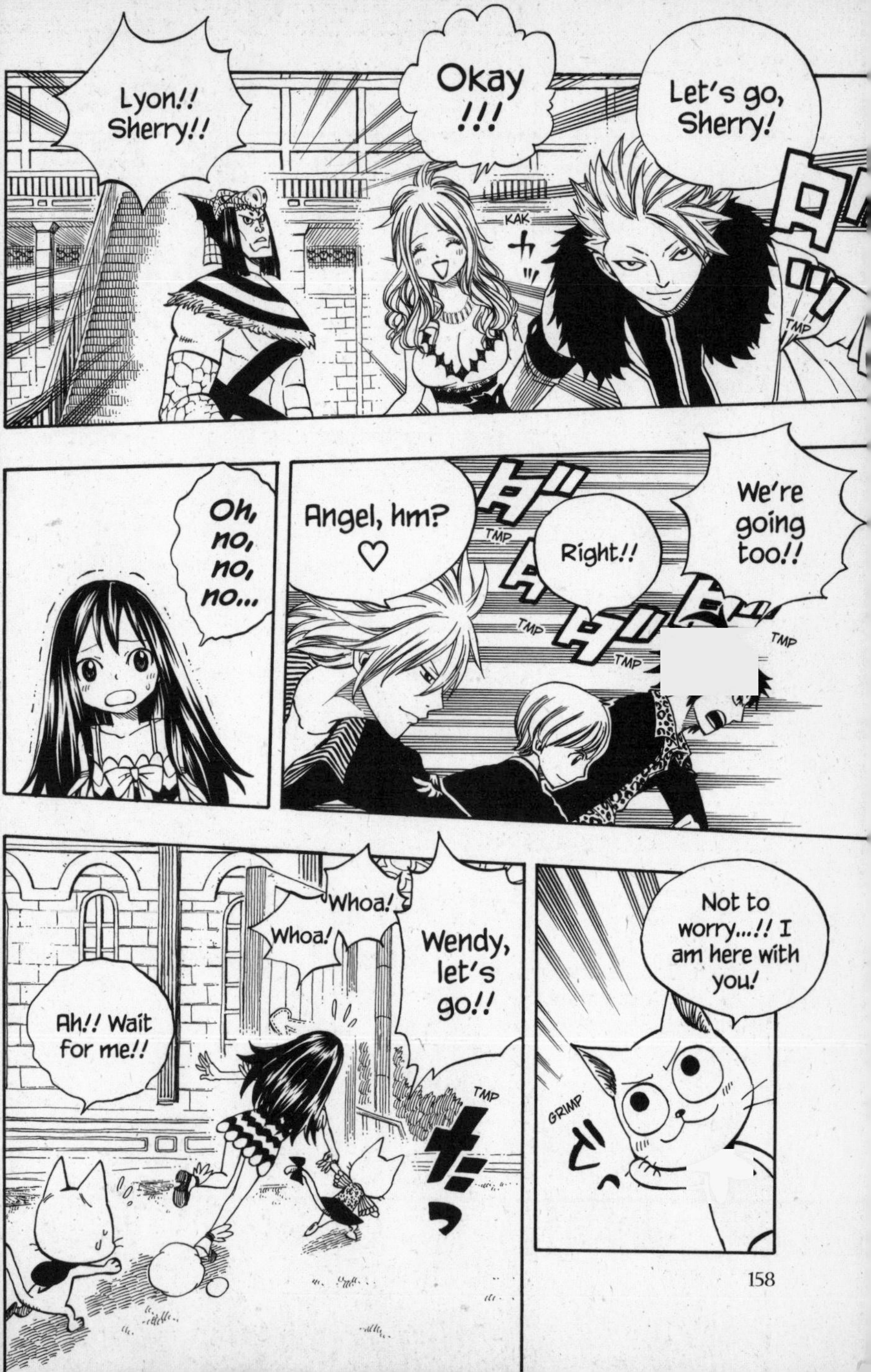
Let's go, Sherry!
TMP
KAK
Okay!!!
Lyon!! Sherry!!
We're going too!!
Right!!
TMP
TMP
TMP
TMP
Angel, hm? ♡
Oh, no, no, no...
Not to worry...!! I am here with you!
GRIMP
TMP
Wendy, let's go!!
Whoa!
Whoa!
Ah!! Wait for me!!

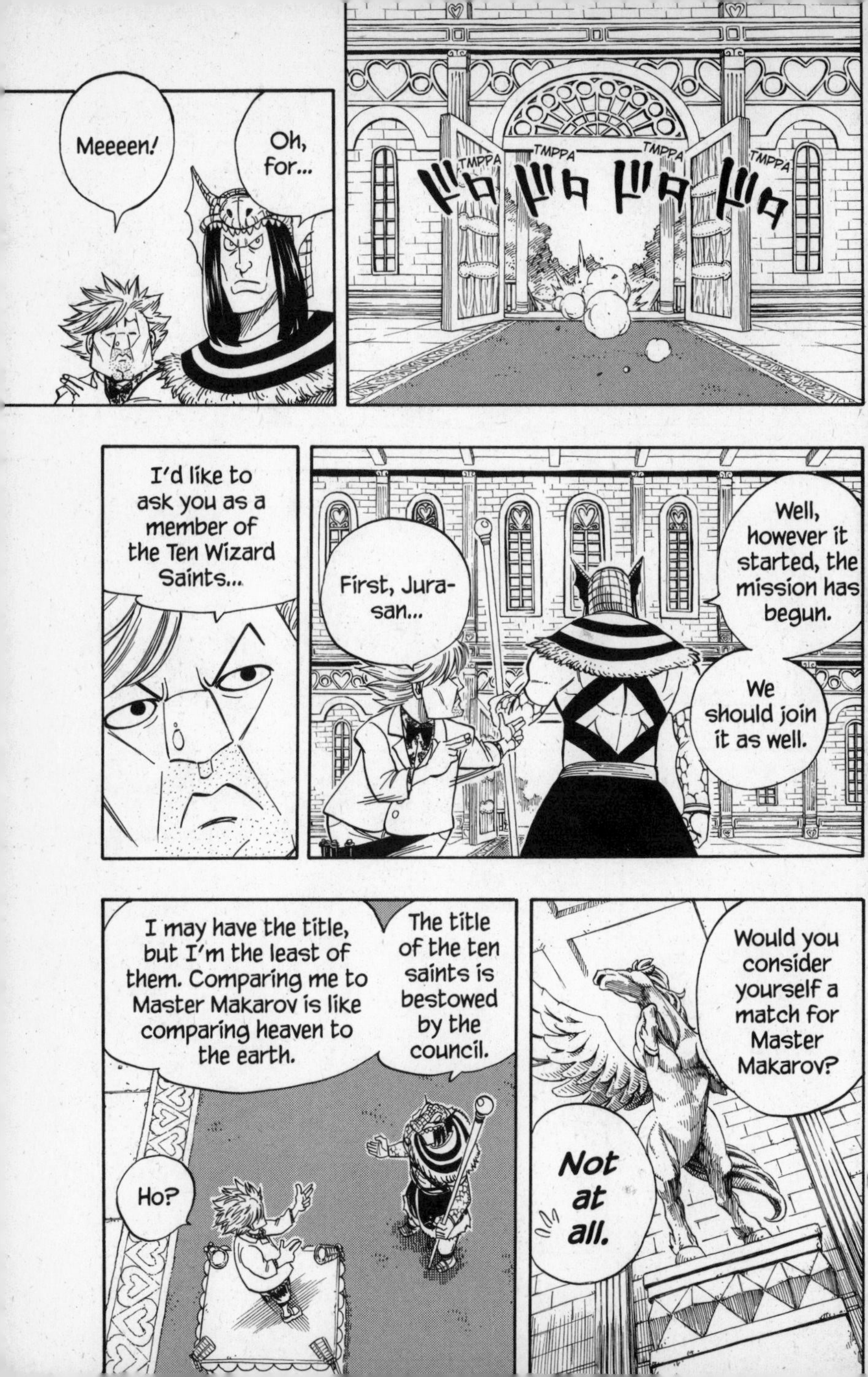
TMPPA
TMPPA
TMPPA
TMPPA
Oh, for...
Meeeen!
Well, however it started, the mission has begun.
We should join it as well.
First, Jura-san...
I'd like to ask you as a member of the Ten Wizard Saints...
Would you consider yourself a match for Master Makarov?
Not at all.
The title of the ten saints is bestowed by the council.
I may have the title, but I'm the least of them. Comparing me to Master Makarov is like comparing heaven to the earth.
Ho?

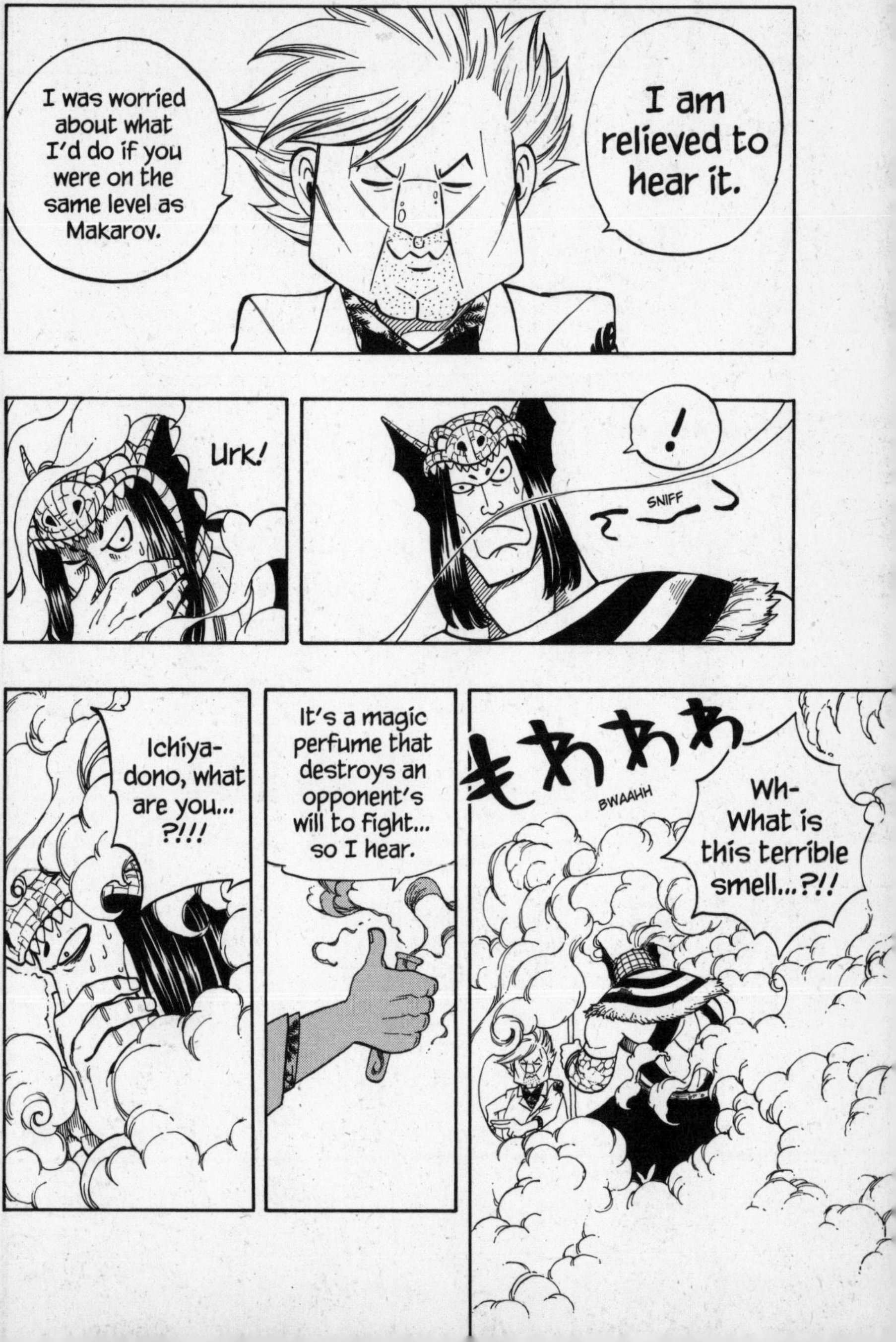
I am relieved to hear it.
I was worried about what I'd do if you were on the same level as Makarov.
!
SNIFF
Urk!
もわわわ
BWAAHH
Wh- What is this terrible smell...?!!
It's a magic perfume that destroys an opponent's will to fight... so I hear.
Ichiya-dono, what are you...?!!!

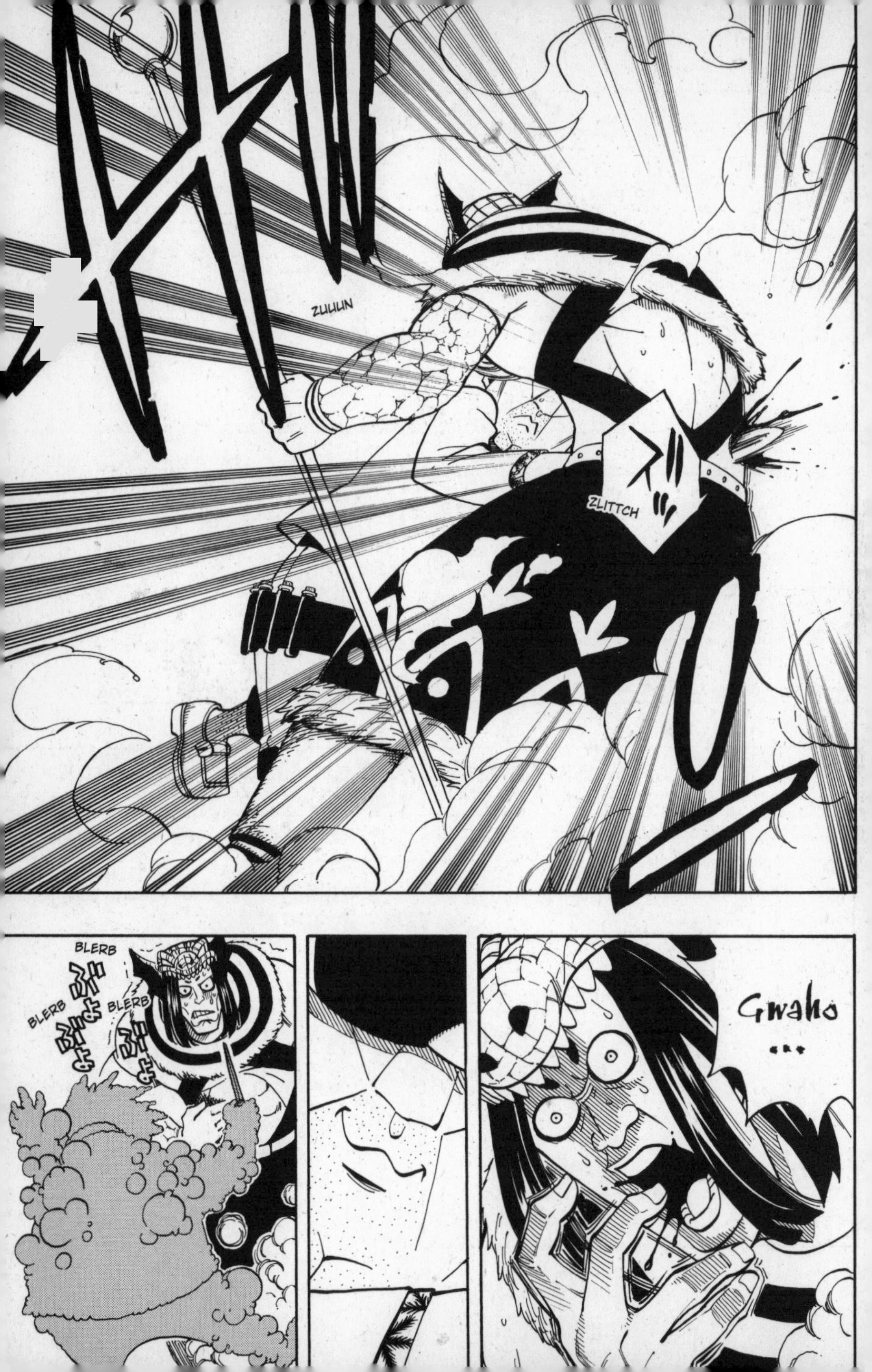
ZUUUN
ZLITTCH
Gwaho ...
BLERB
BLERB
BLERB

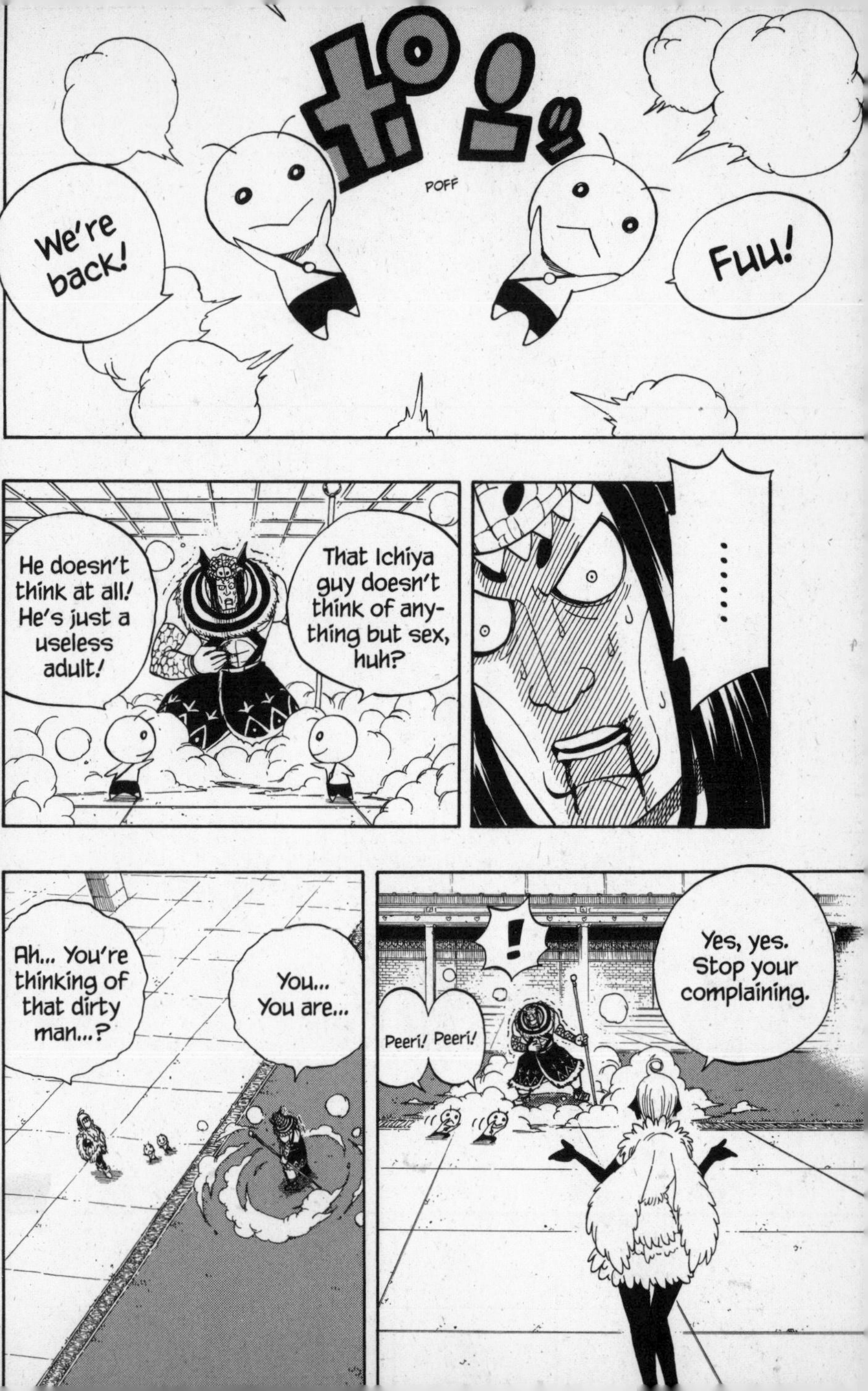
Fuu!
POFF
We're back!
......
That Ichiya guy doesn't think of any-thing but sex, huh?
He doesn't think at all! He's just a useless adult!
Yes, yes. Stop your complaining.
!
Peeri! Peeri!
You... You are...
Ah... You're thinking of that dirty man...?

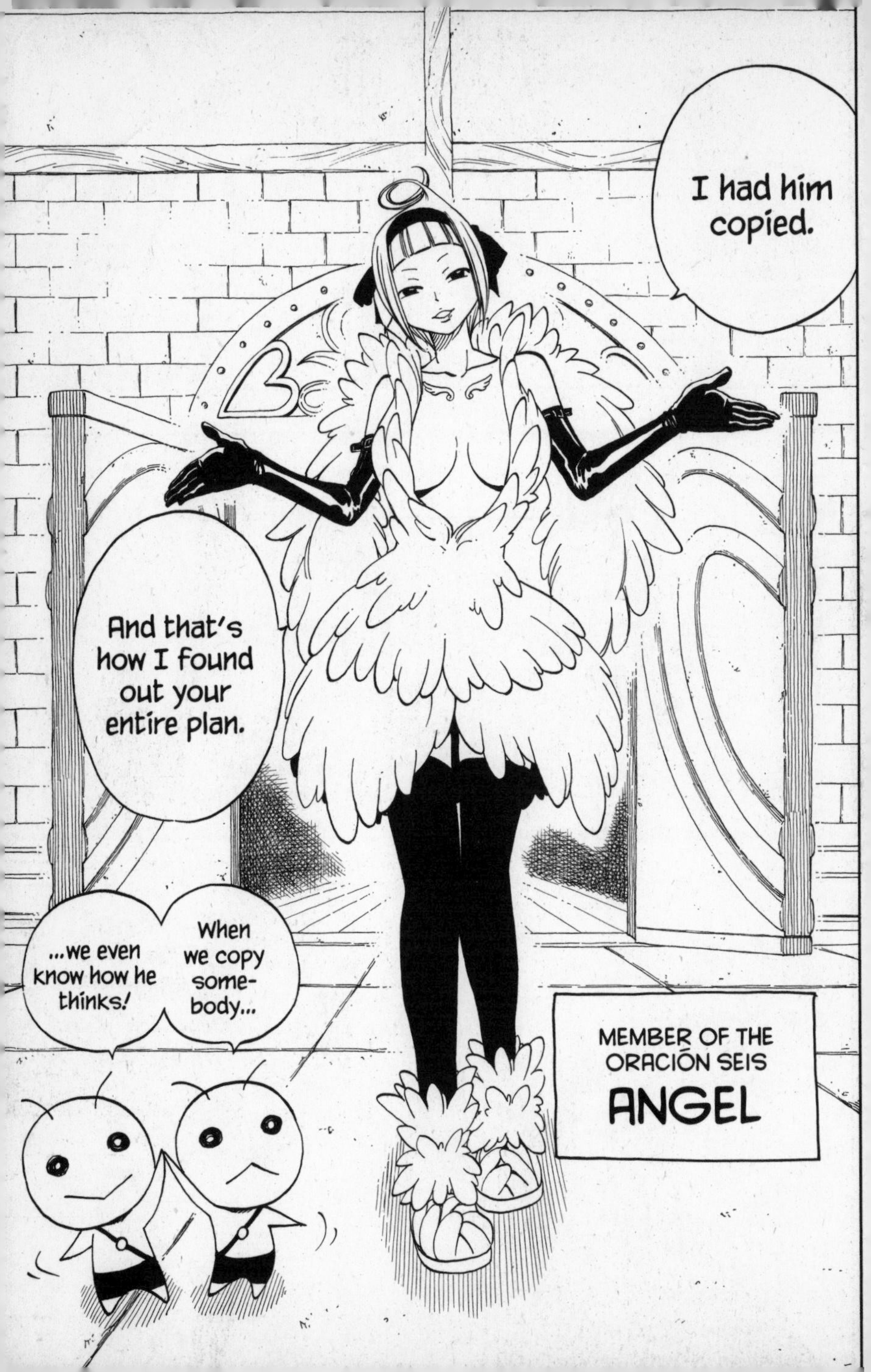
I had him copied.
And that's how I found out your entire plan.
When we copy somebody...
...we even know how he thinks!
MEMBER OF THE ORACIÓN SEIS
ANGEL

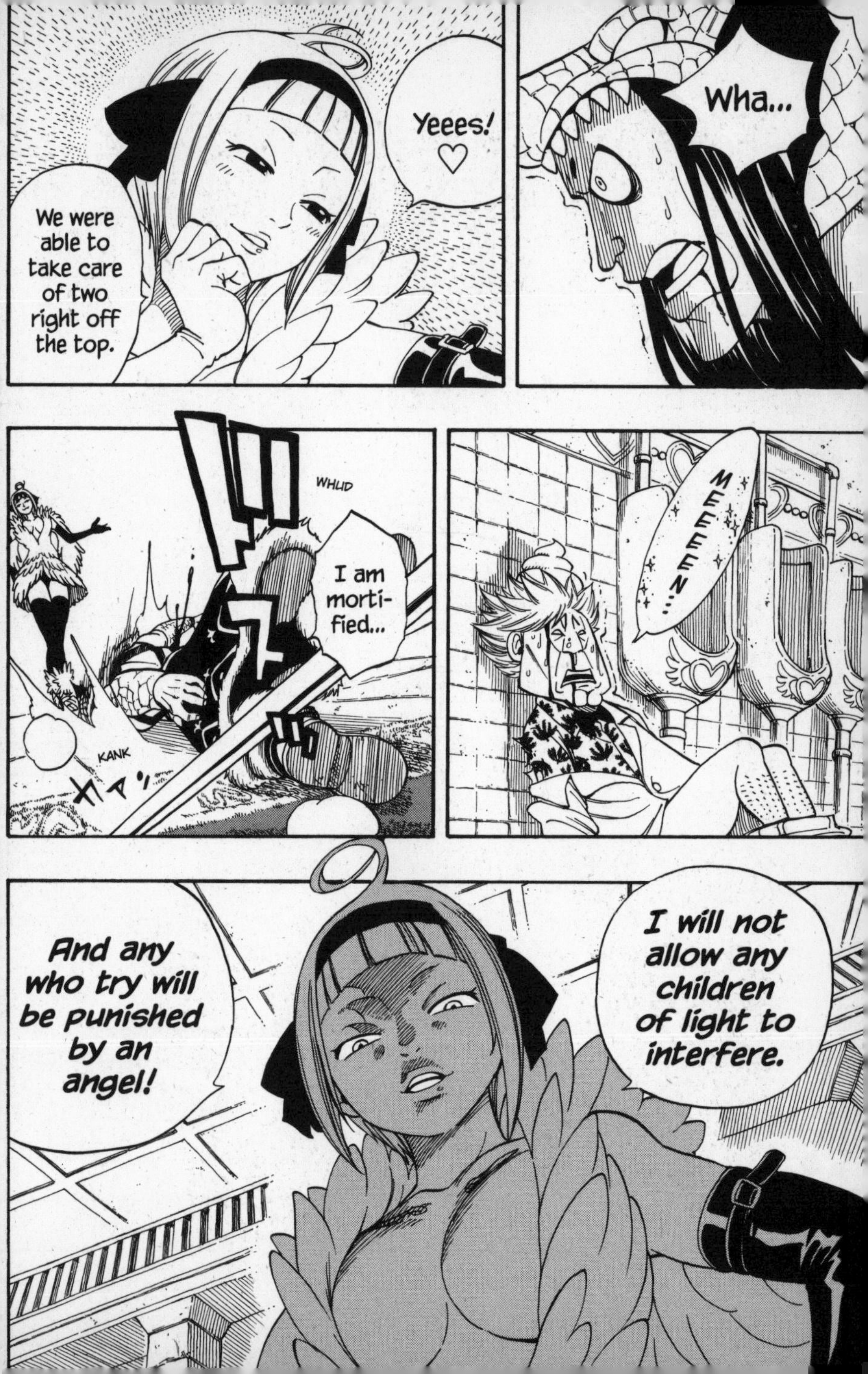
Wha...
Yeees! ♡
We were able to take care of two right off the top.
MEEEEN...!
WHUD
I am mortified...
KANK
I will not allow any children of light to interfere.
And any who try will be punished by an angel!

FAIRY TAIL

Chapter 134, Oración Seis Appears!

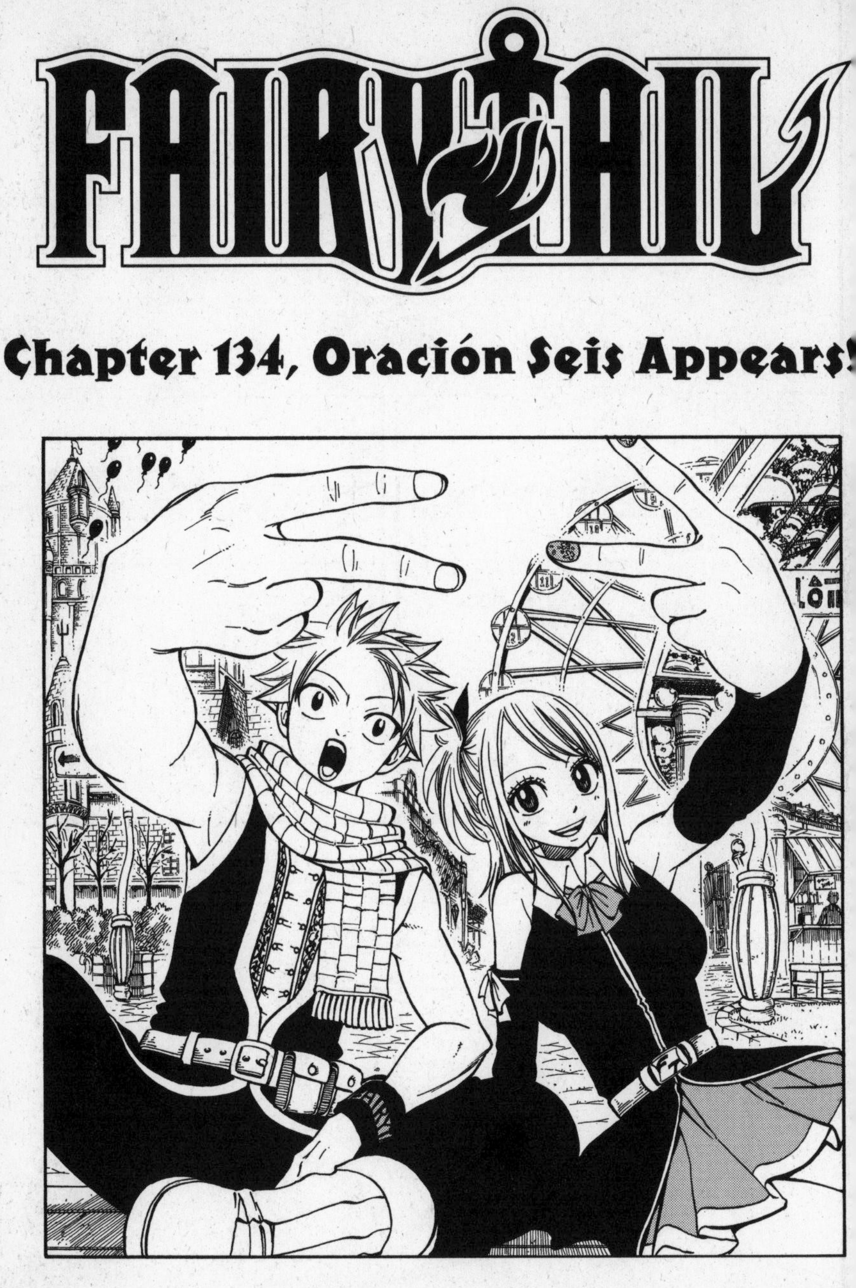

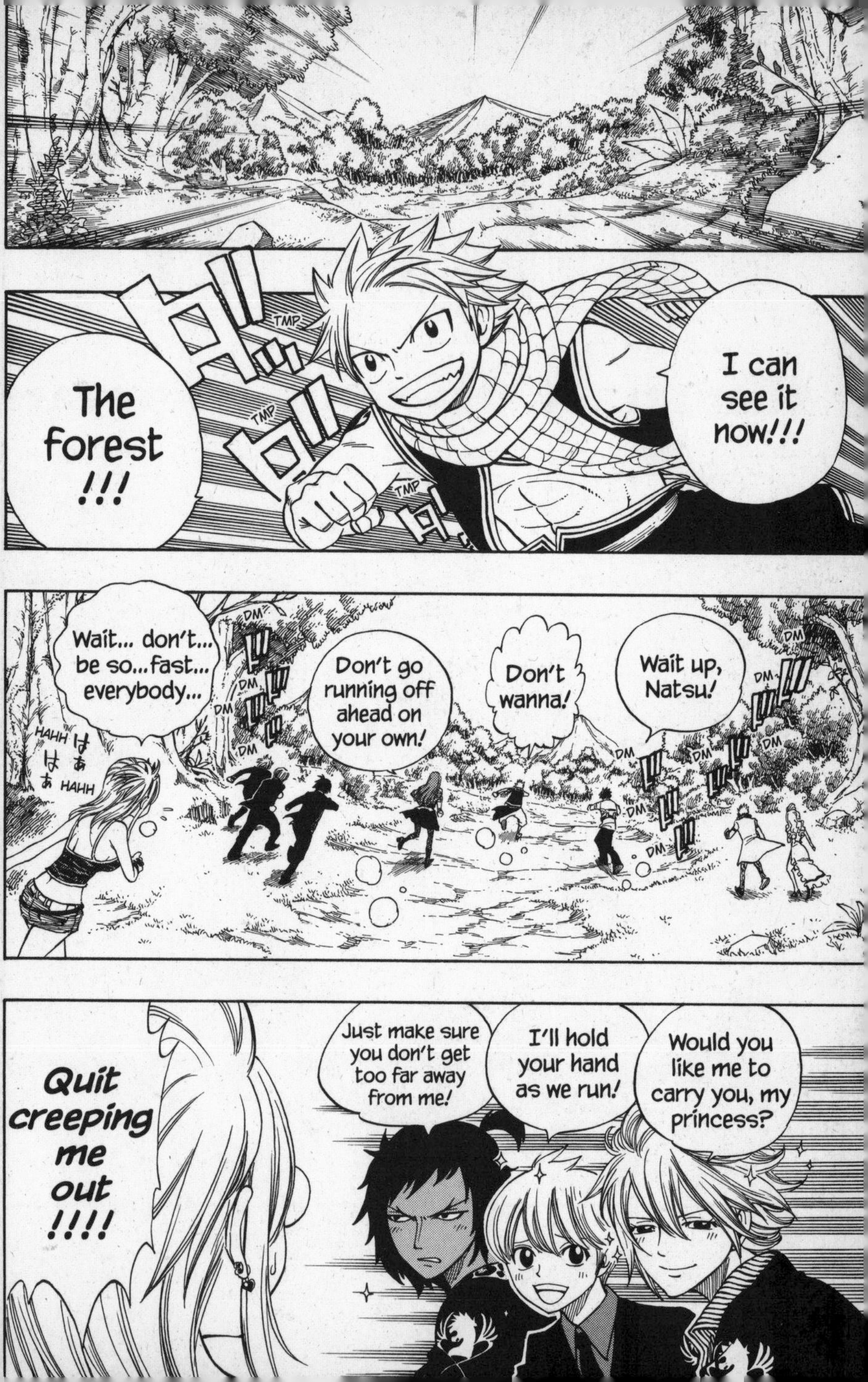
I can see it now!!!
TMP
TMP
TMP
The forest!!!
Wait up, Natsu!
DM
Don't wanna!
Don't go running off ahead on your own!
DM
Wait... don't... be so...fast... everybody...
HAHH はぁ はぁ HAHH
Would you like me to carry you, my princess?
I'll hold your hand as we run!
Just make sure you don't get too far away from me!
Quit creeping me out!!!!

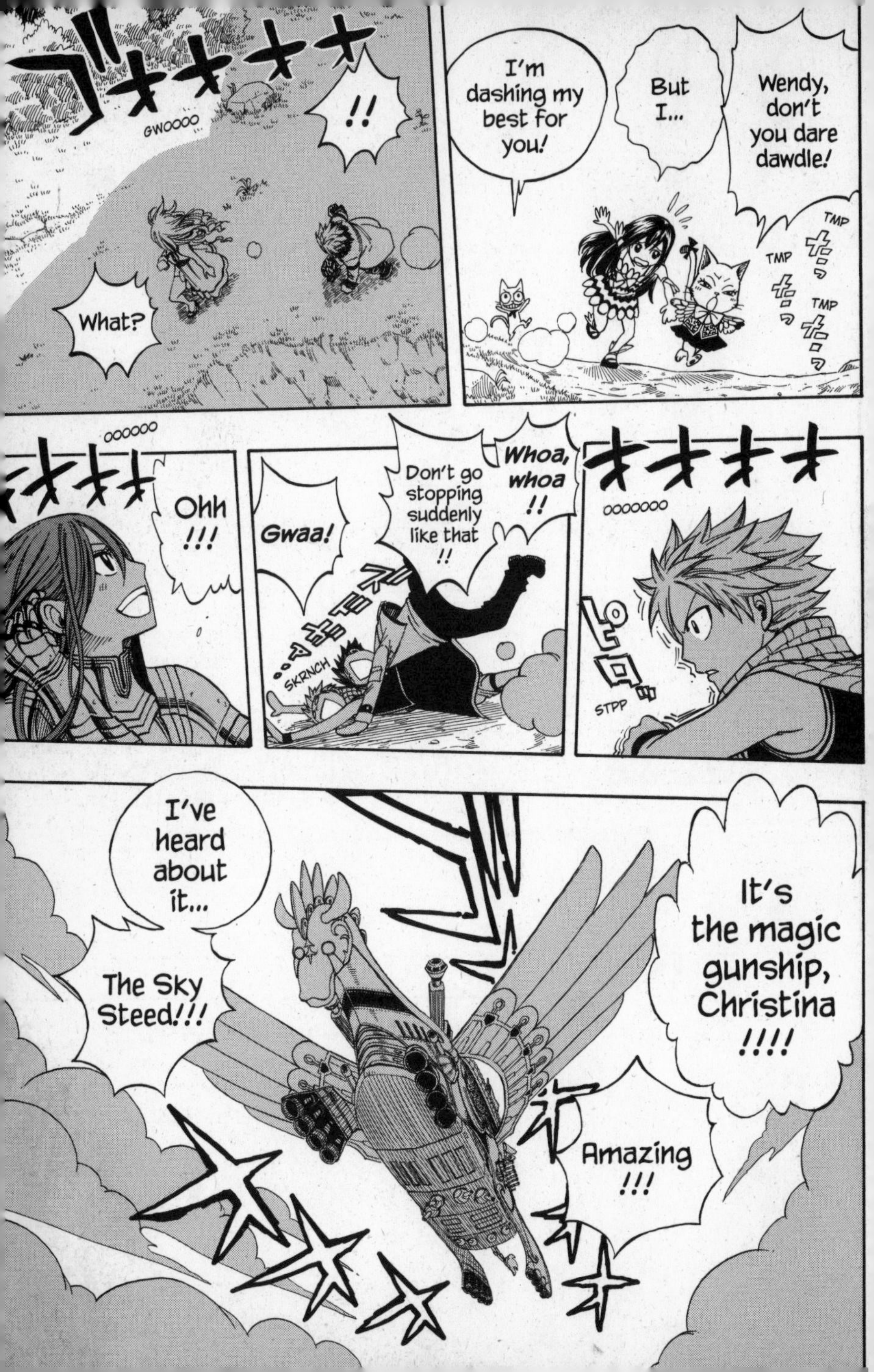
Wendy, don't you dare dawdle!
But I...
I'm dashing my best for you!
TMP
TMP
TMP
!!
GWOOOO
What?
OOOOOOO
STPP
Whoa, whoa !!
Don't go stopping suddenly like that !!
Gwaa!
SKRNCH
OOOOOO
Ohh !!!
It's the magic gunship, Christina !!!!
I've heard about it...
The Sky Steed!!!
Amazing !!!

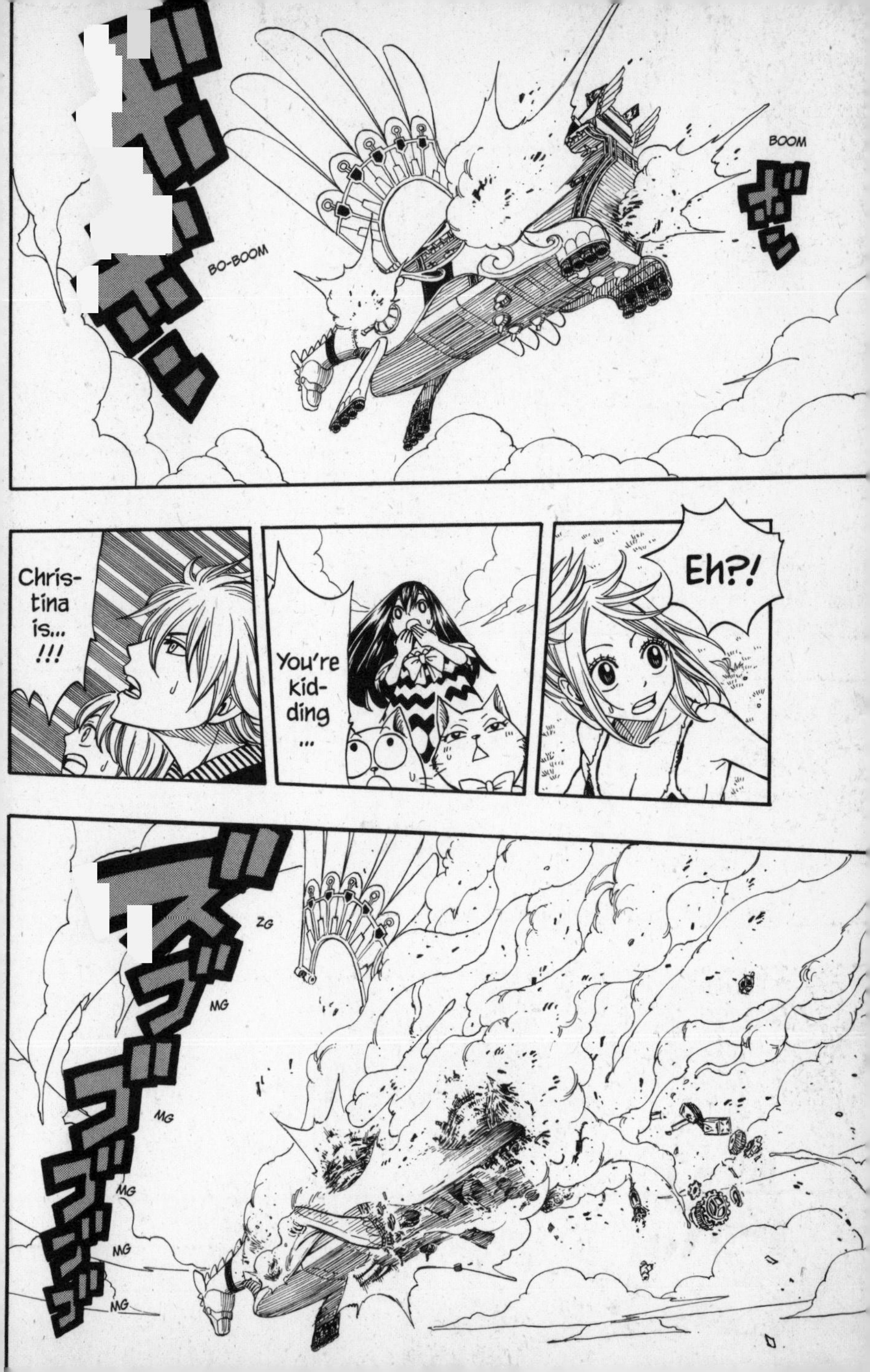
BOOM
BO-BOOM
Eh?!
You're kid-ding ...
Chris-tina is... !!!
ZG
MG
MG
MG
MG
MG

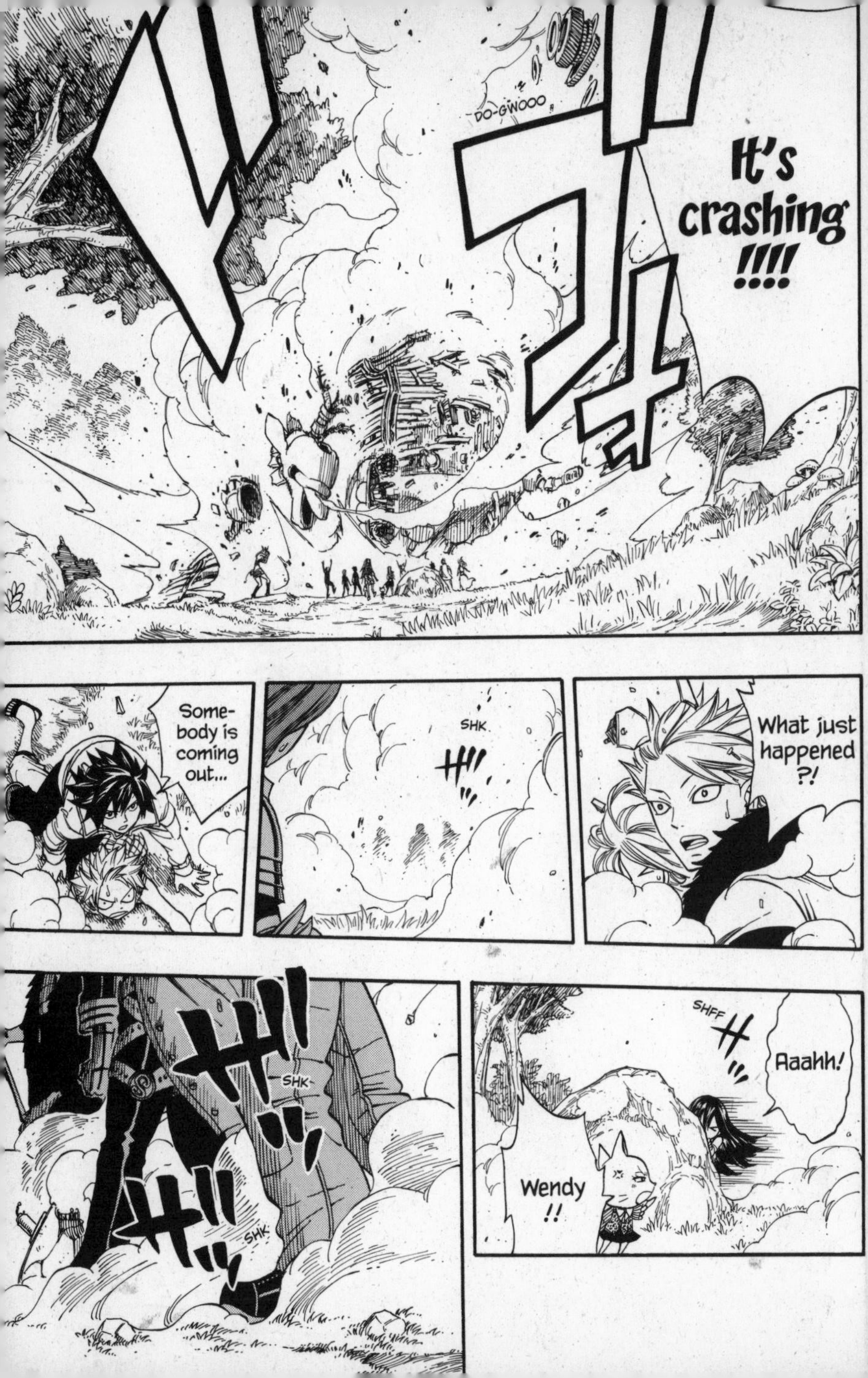
DO-GWOOO
It's crashing !!!!
What just happened ?!
SHK
Some-body is coming out...
SHFF
Aaahh!
Wendy !!
SHK
SHK

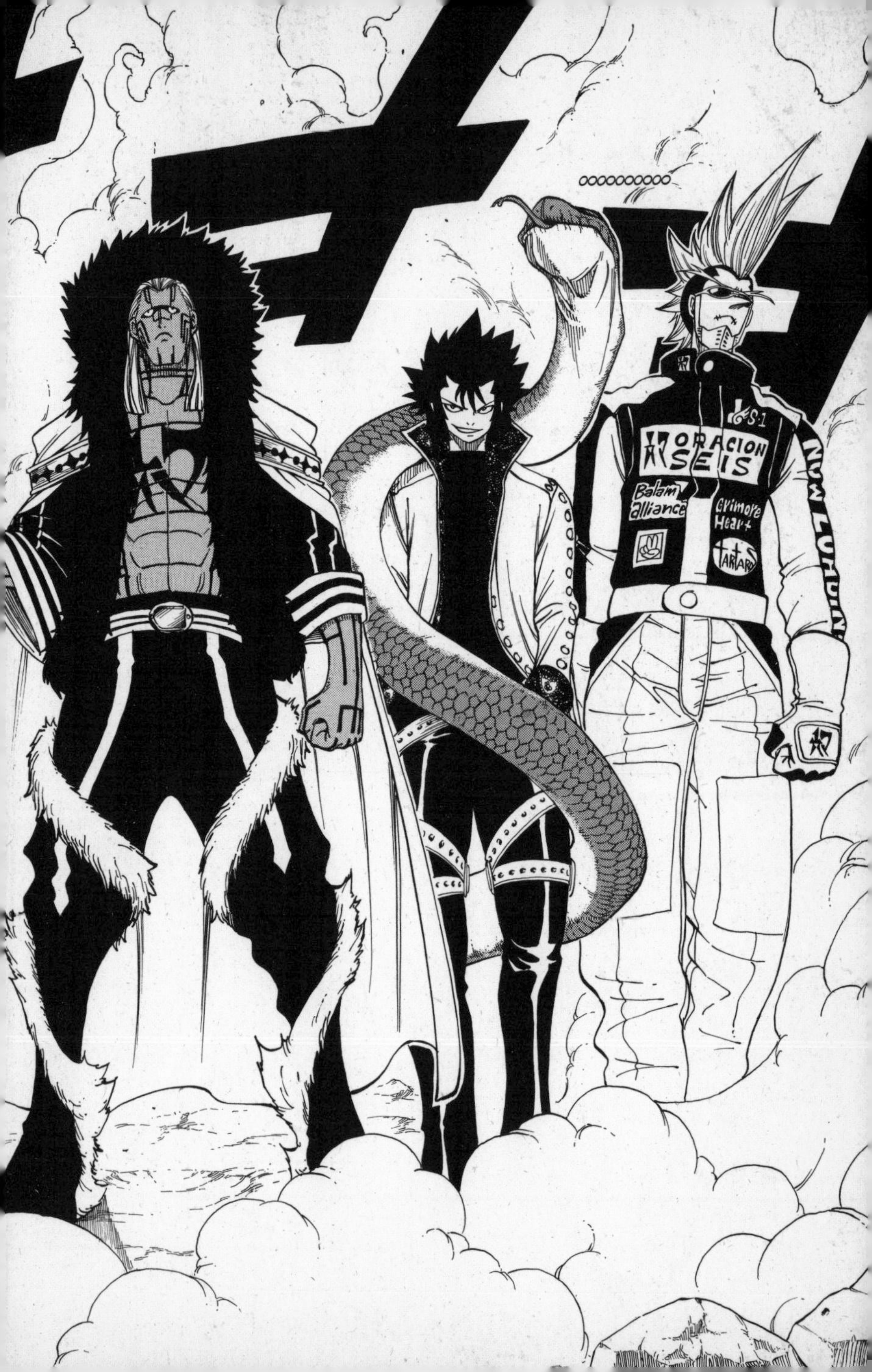

oooooooooo
ORACION SEIS
Balam alliance
Grimore Heart
TARTAROS

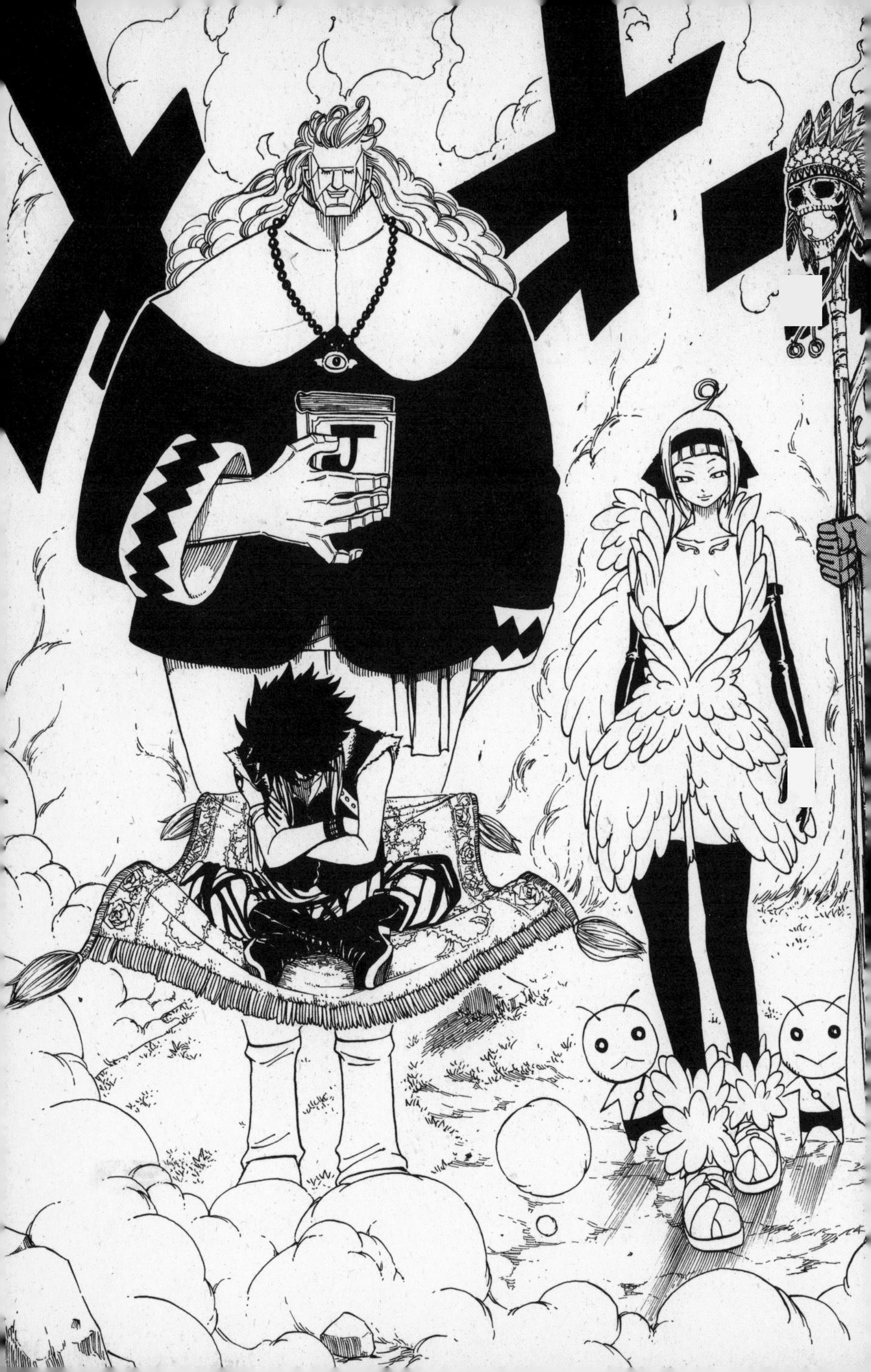

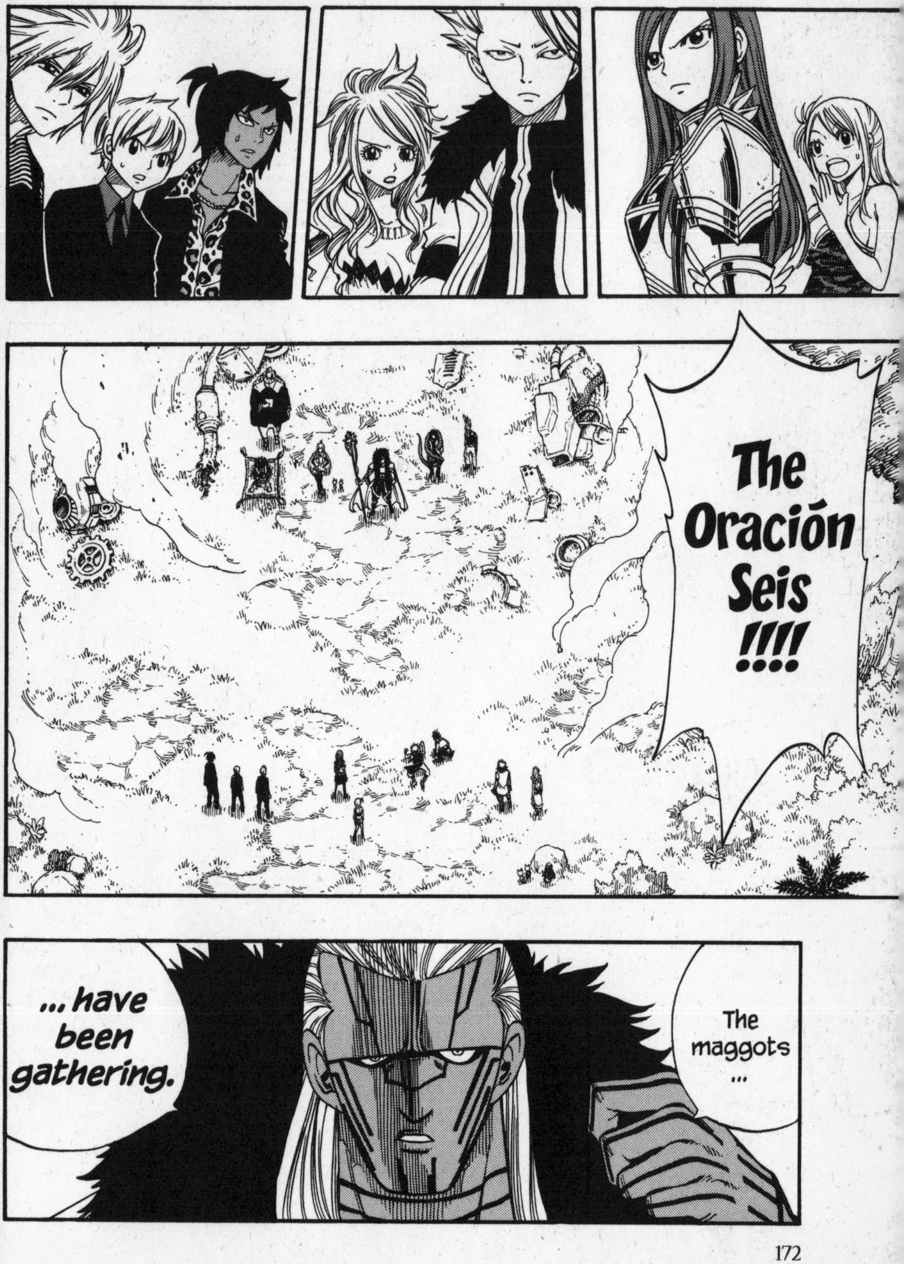
The Oración Seis !!!!
The maggots …
... have been gathering.

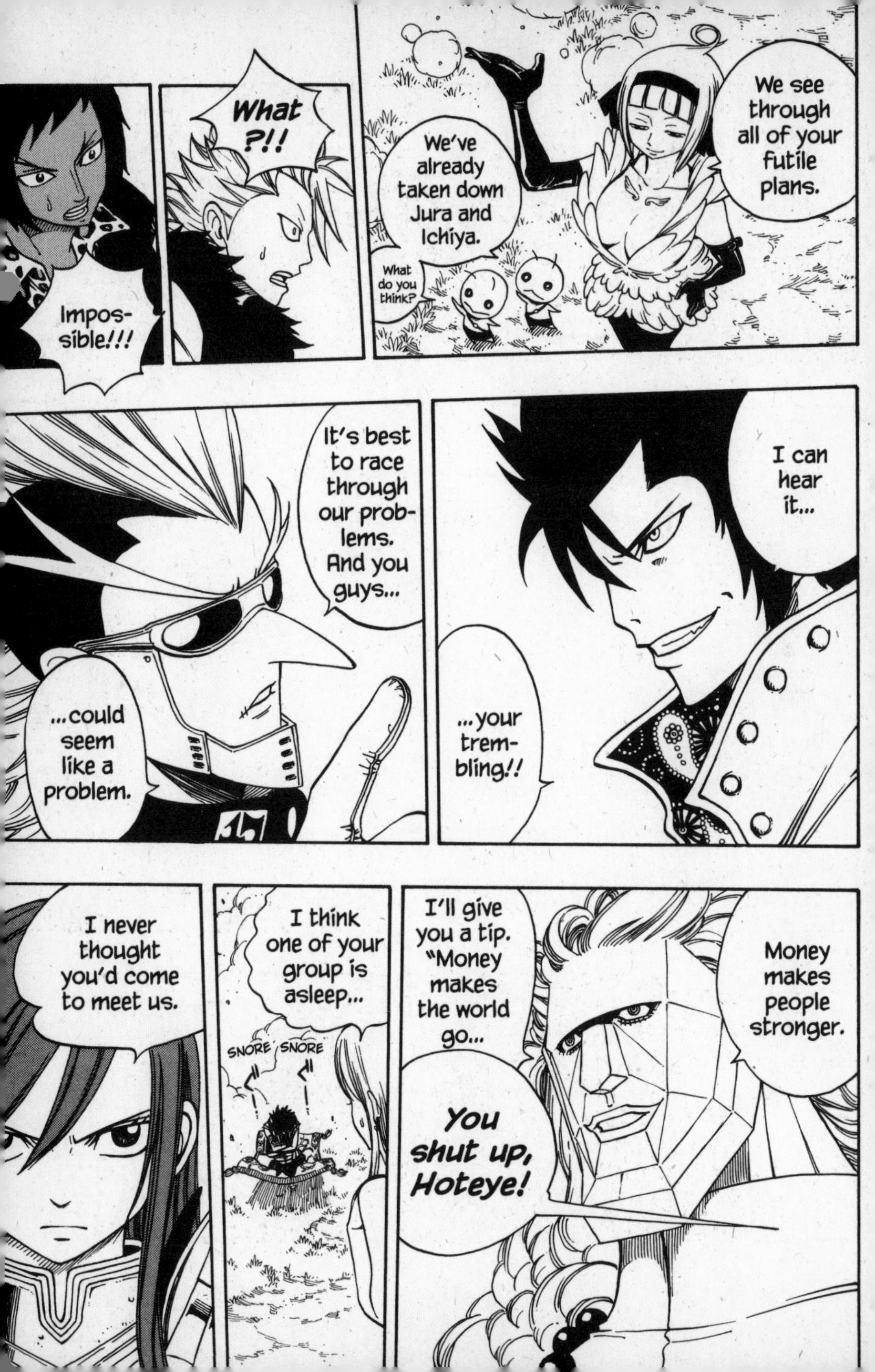
We see through all of your futile plans.
We've already taken down Jura and Ichiya.
What do you think?
What ?!!
Impos-sible!!!
I can hear it...
...your trem-bling!!
It's best to race through our prob-lems. And you guys...
...could seem like a problem.
Money makes people stronger.
I'll give you a tip. "Money makes the world go...
You shut up, Hoteye!
I think one of your group is asleep...
SNORE SNORE
I never thought you'd come to meet us.

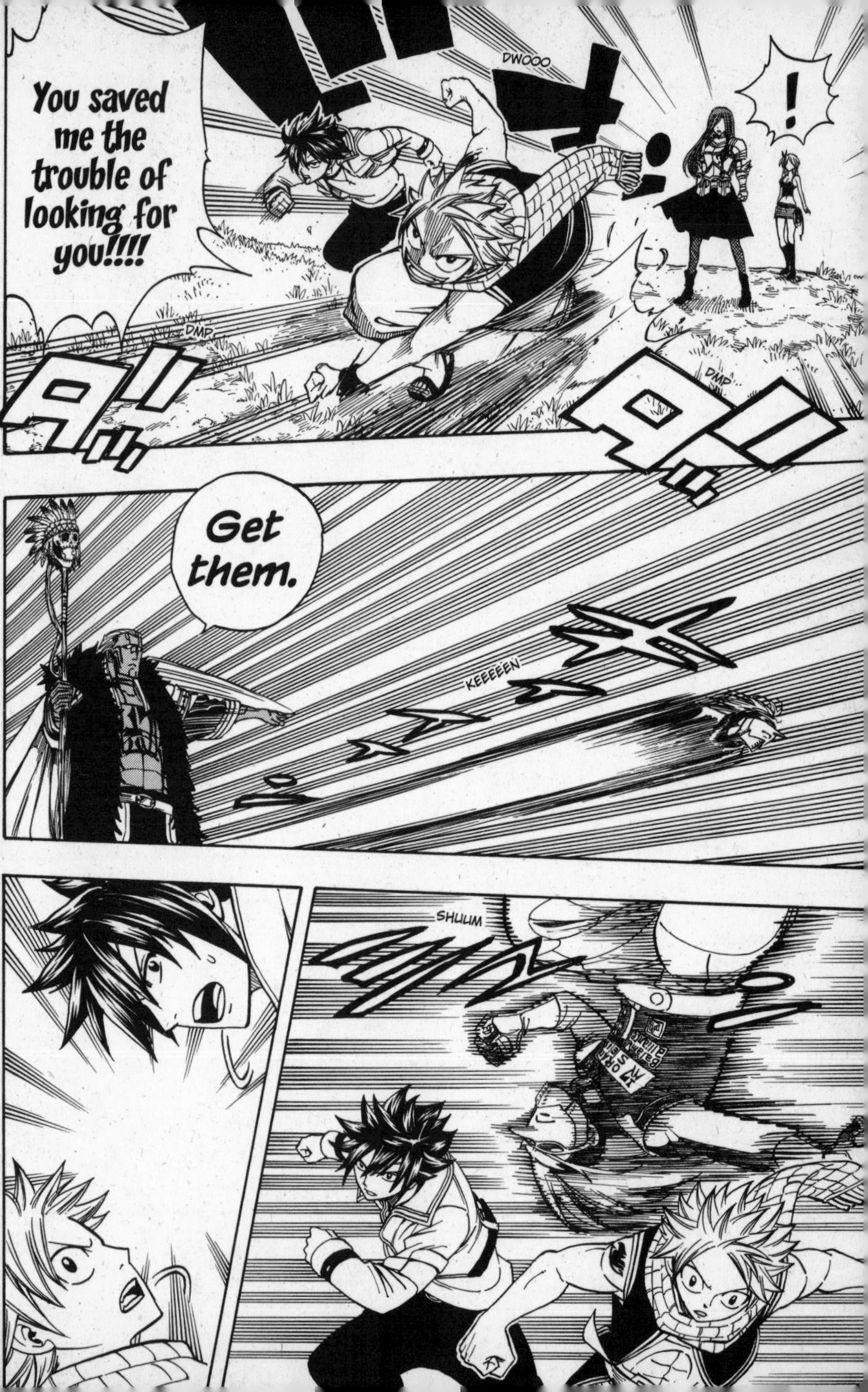
!
DWOOO
You saved me the trouble of looking for you!!!!
DMP
DMP
Get them.
KEEEEEN
SHUUM

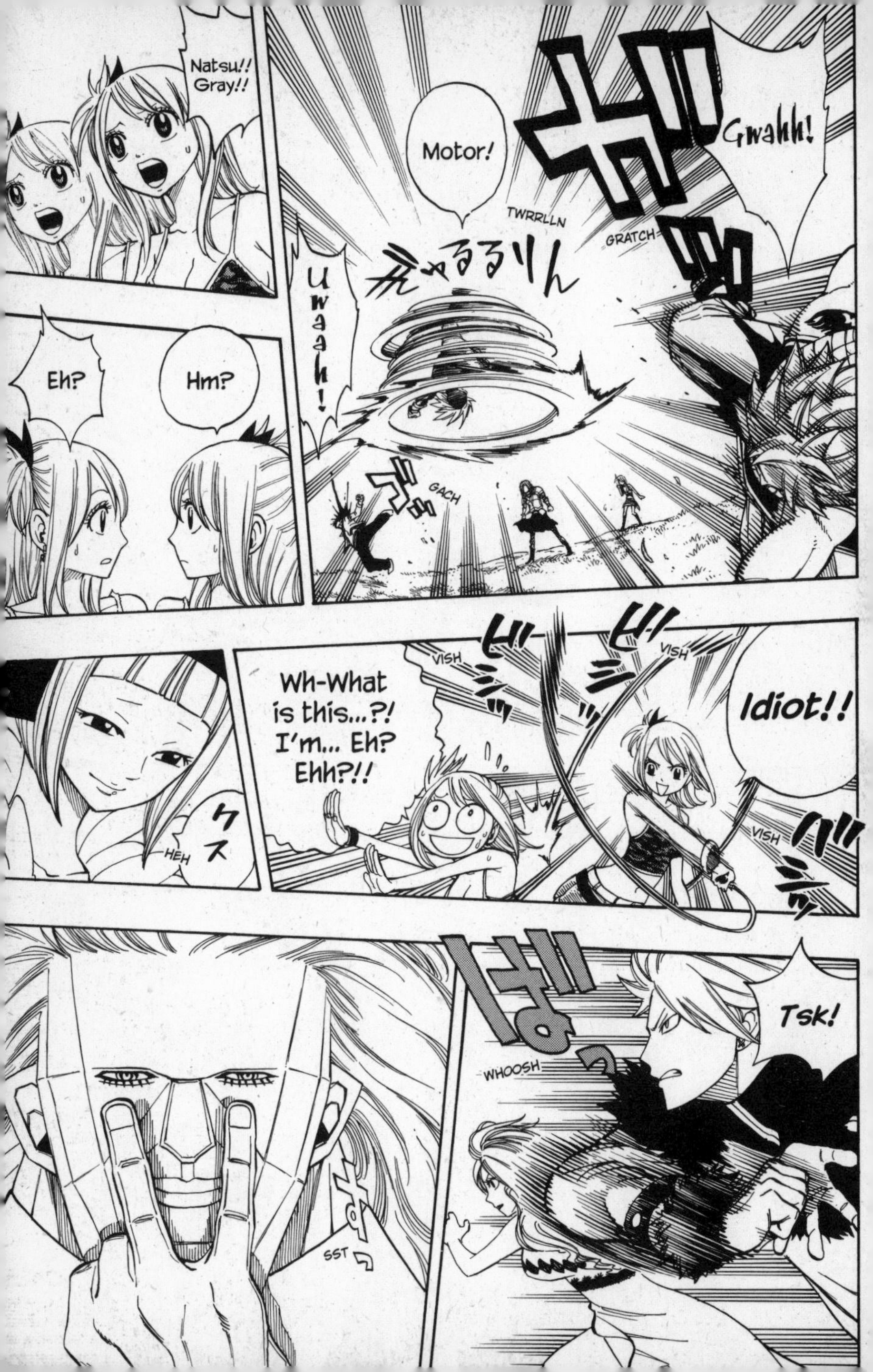
Gwahh!
GRATCH
TWRRLLN
Motor!
Uwaaah!
GACH
Natsu!! Gray!!
Hm?
Eh?
Idiot!!
VISH
VISH
VISH
Wh-What is this...?! I'm... Eh? Ehh?!!
HEH
Tsk!
WHOOSH
SST

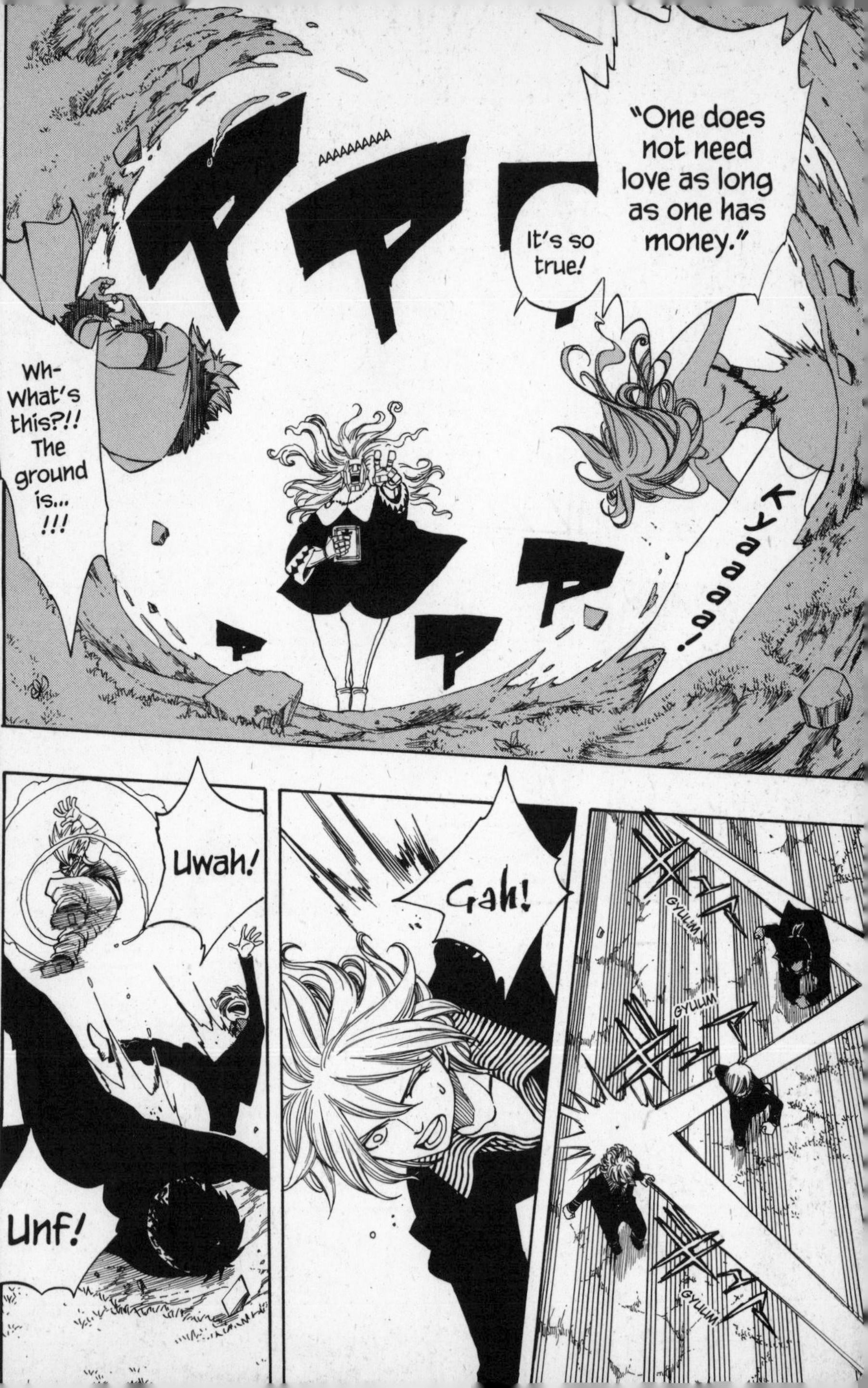
"One does not need love as long as one has money."
It's so true!
AAAAAAAAAA
Kyaaaaaa!
Wh-What's this?!! The ground is... !!!
GYULLM
GYULLM
GYULLM
Gah!
Uwah!
Unf!

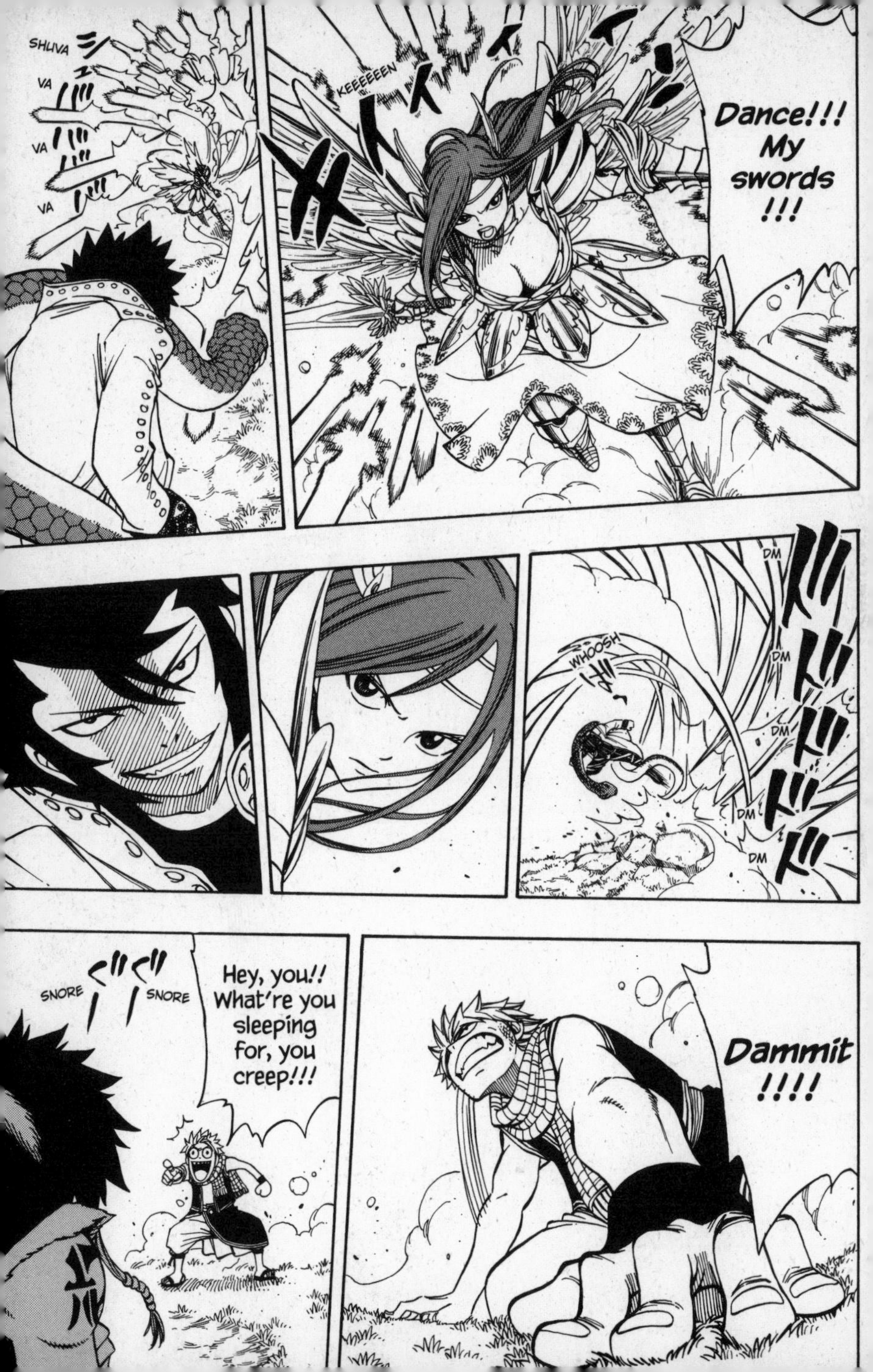
Dance!!! My swords !!!
KEEEEEEN
SHUVA
VA
VA
VA
DM
DM
DM
DM
DM
WHOOSH
Dammit !!!!
Hey, you!! What're you sleeping for, you creep!!!
SNORE
SNORE

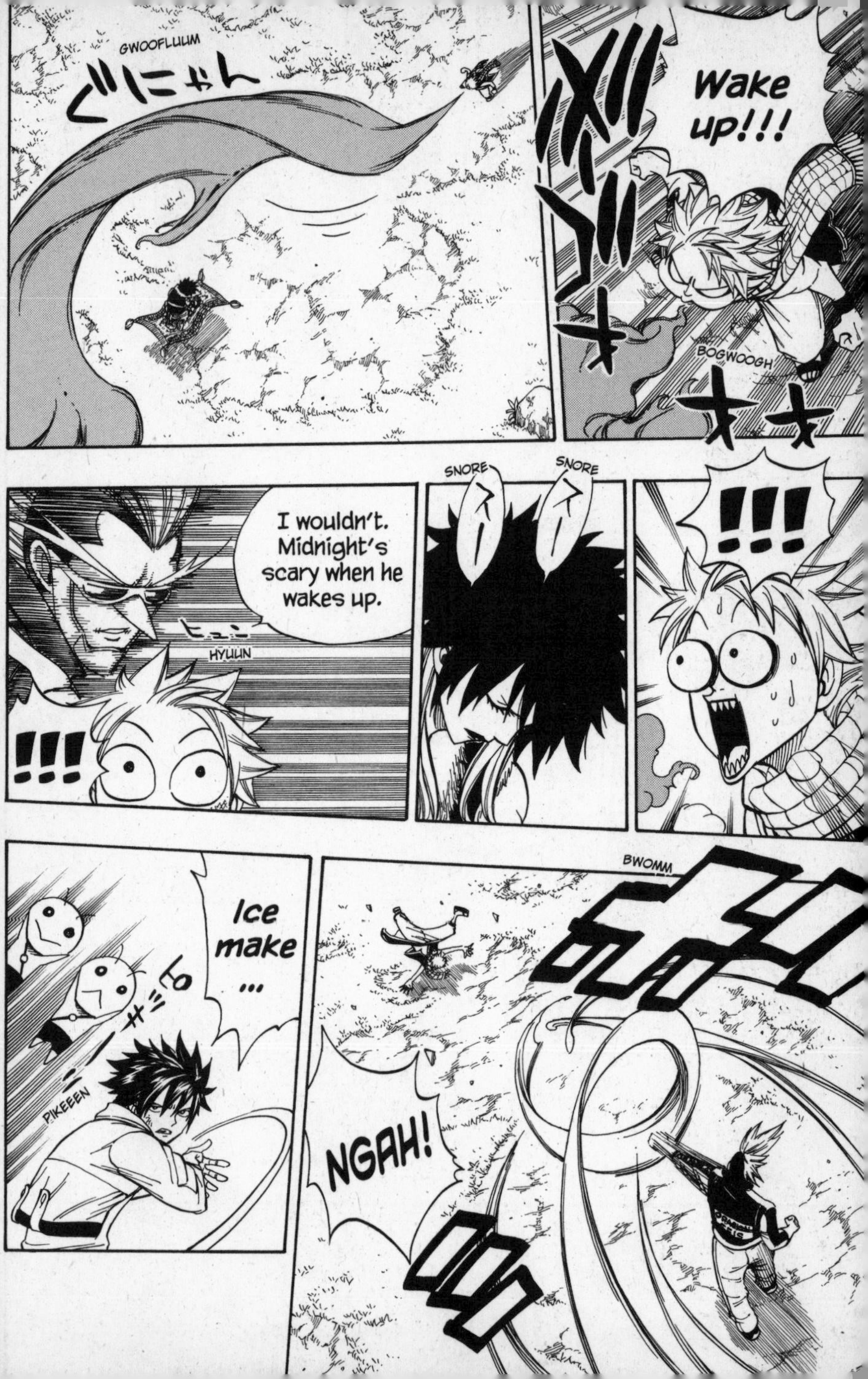

Wake up!!!
BOGWOOGH
GWOOFLUUM
ぐにゃん
!!!
SNORE
スー
SNORE
スー
I wouldn't. Midnight's scary when he wakes up.
HYUUN
!!!
BWOMM
NGAH!
Ice make ...
PIKEEEN

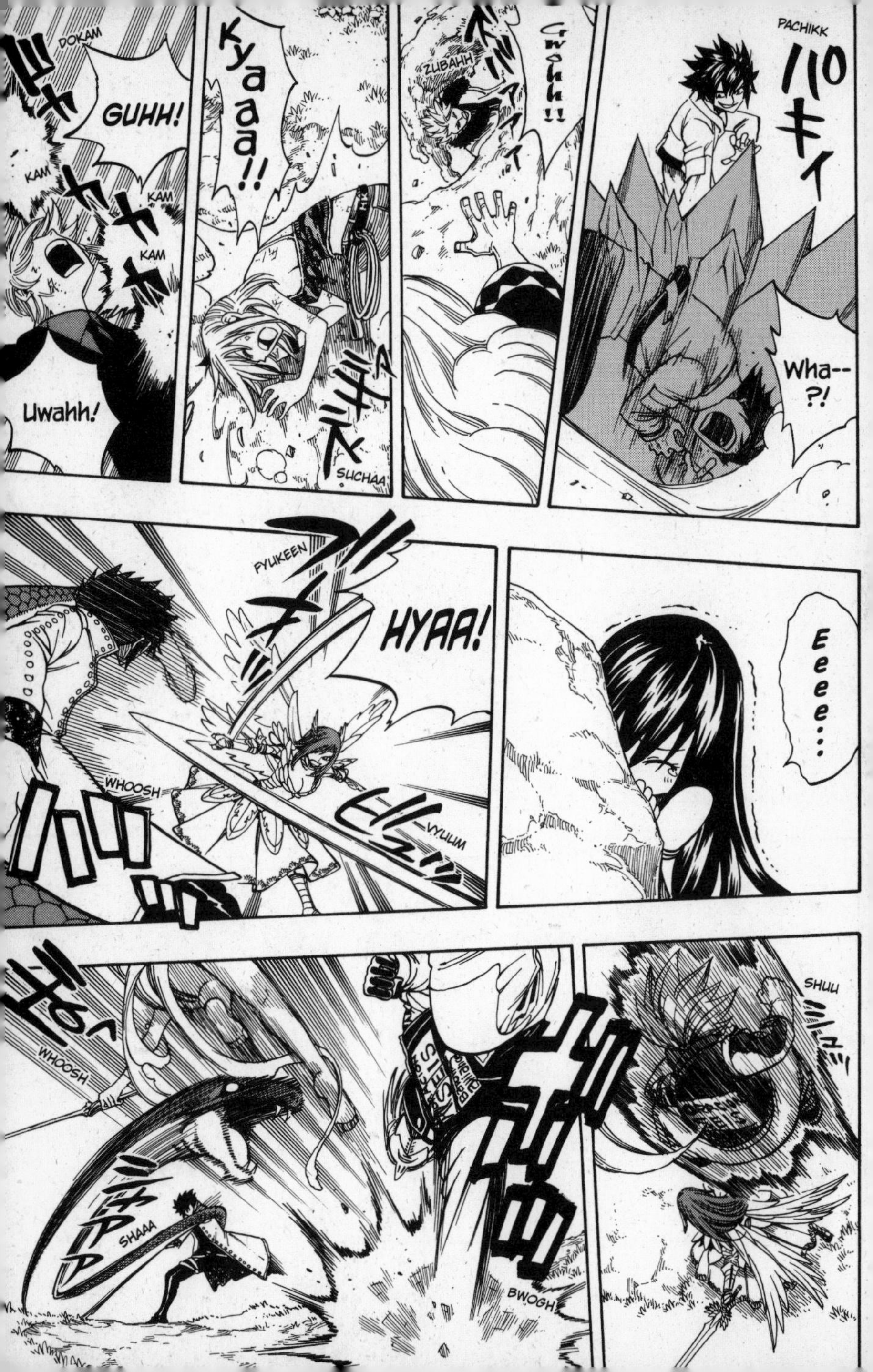
PACHIKK
Wha--?!
ZUBAHH
Gwohh!!
Kyaaa!!
SUCHAA
DOKAM
GUHH!
KAM
KAM
KAM
Uwahh!
Eeee...
FYUKEEN
HYAA!
WHOOSH
VYUUM
SHUU
WHOOSH
SHAAA
BWOGH

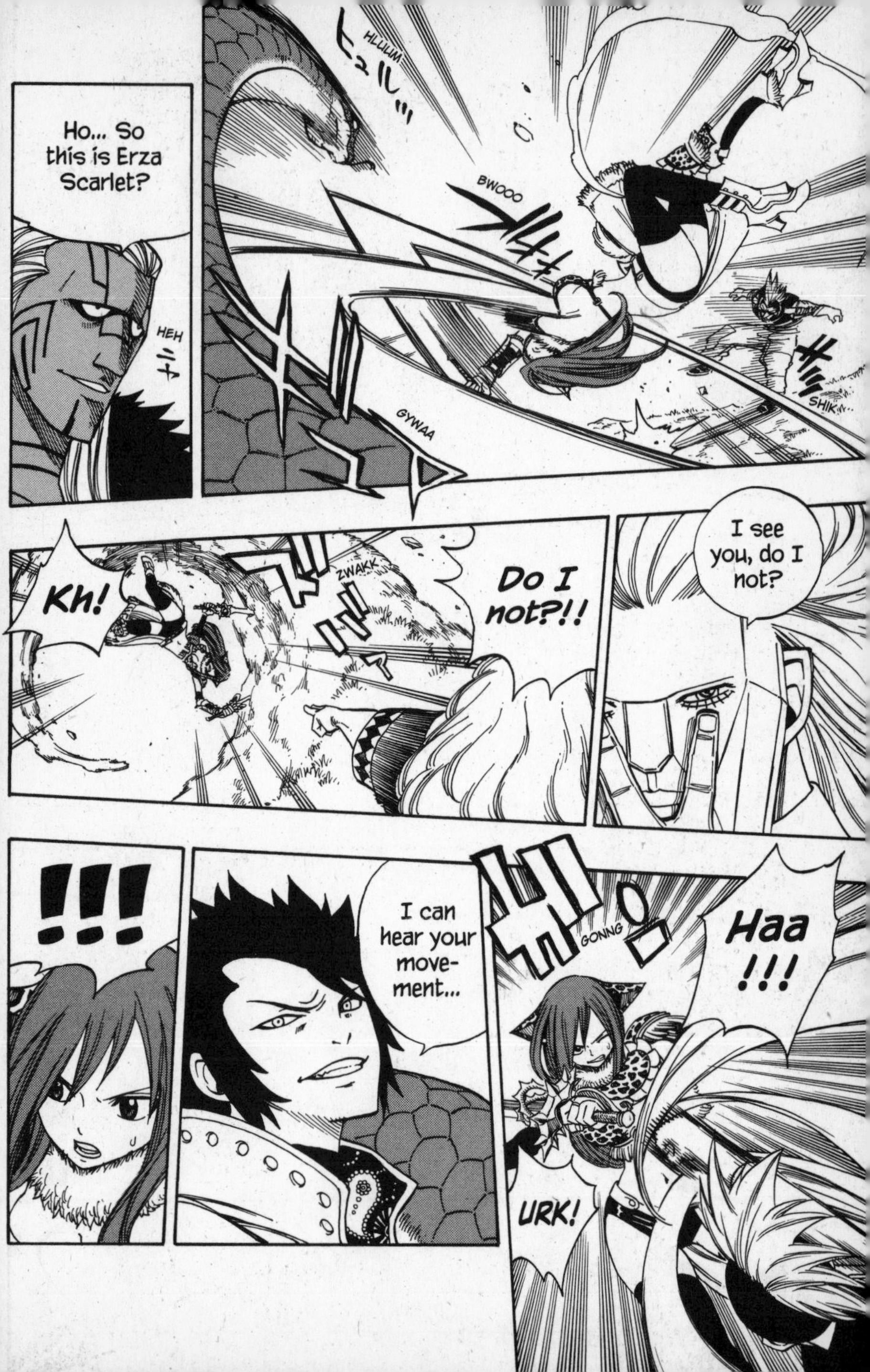

HLUUUM
ヒュル
BWOOO
SHIK...
GYWAA
Ho... So this is Erza Scarlet?
HEH
ニヤ
I see you, do I not?
Do I not?!!
ZWAKK
Kh!
Haa !!!
GONNG
URK!
I can hear your movement...
!!!

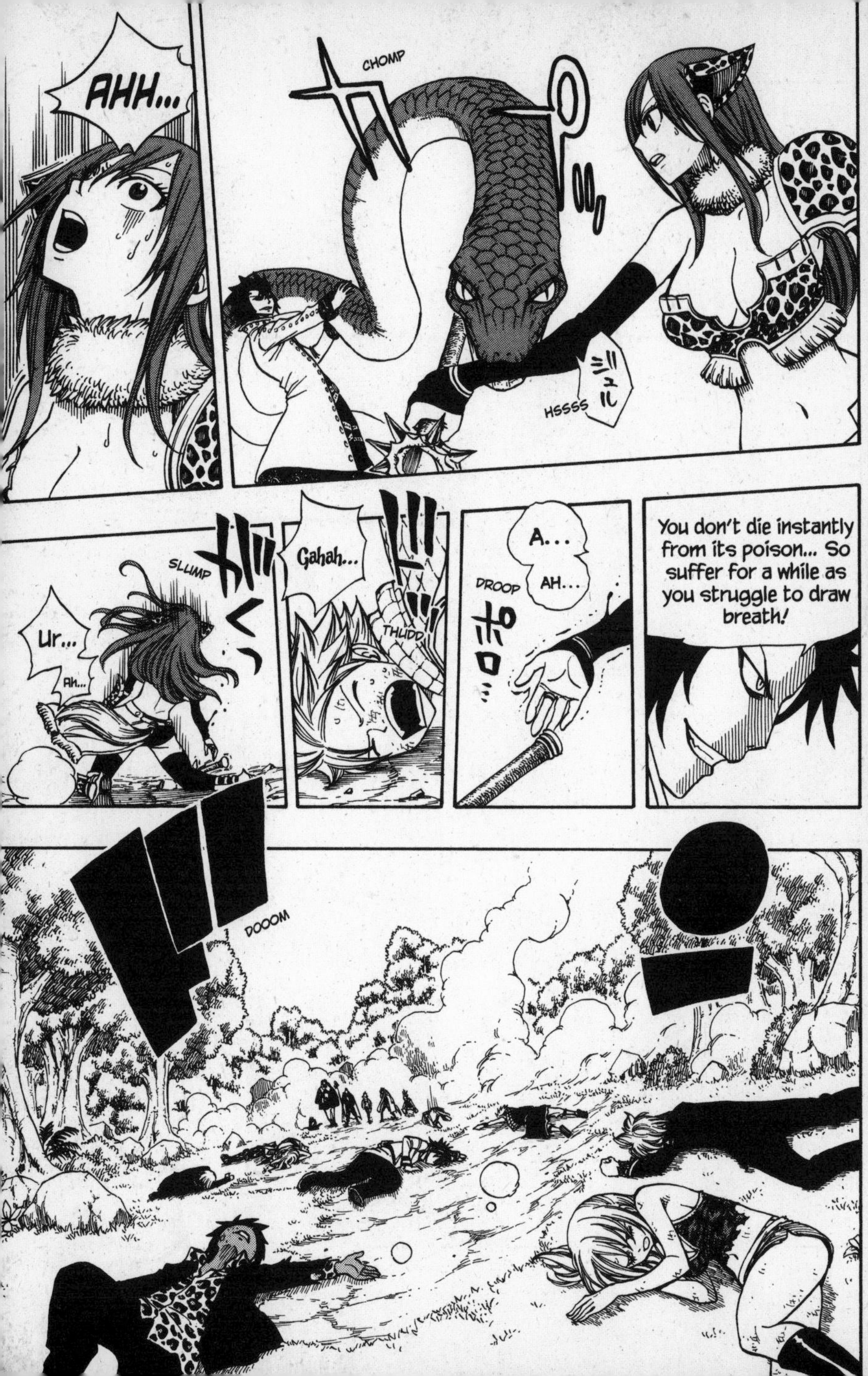
CHOMP
ジュル
HSSSS
AHH...
You don't die instantly from its poison... So suffer for a while as you struggle to draw breath!
A...
AH...
DROOP
ポロ
Gahah...
THUDD
SLUMP
Ur...
Ah...
DOOOM

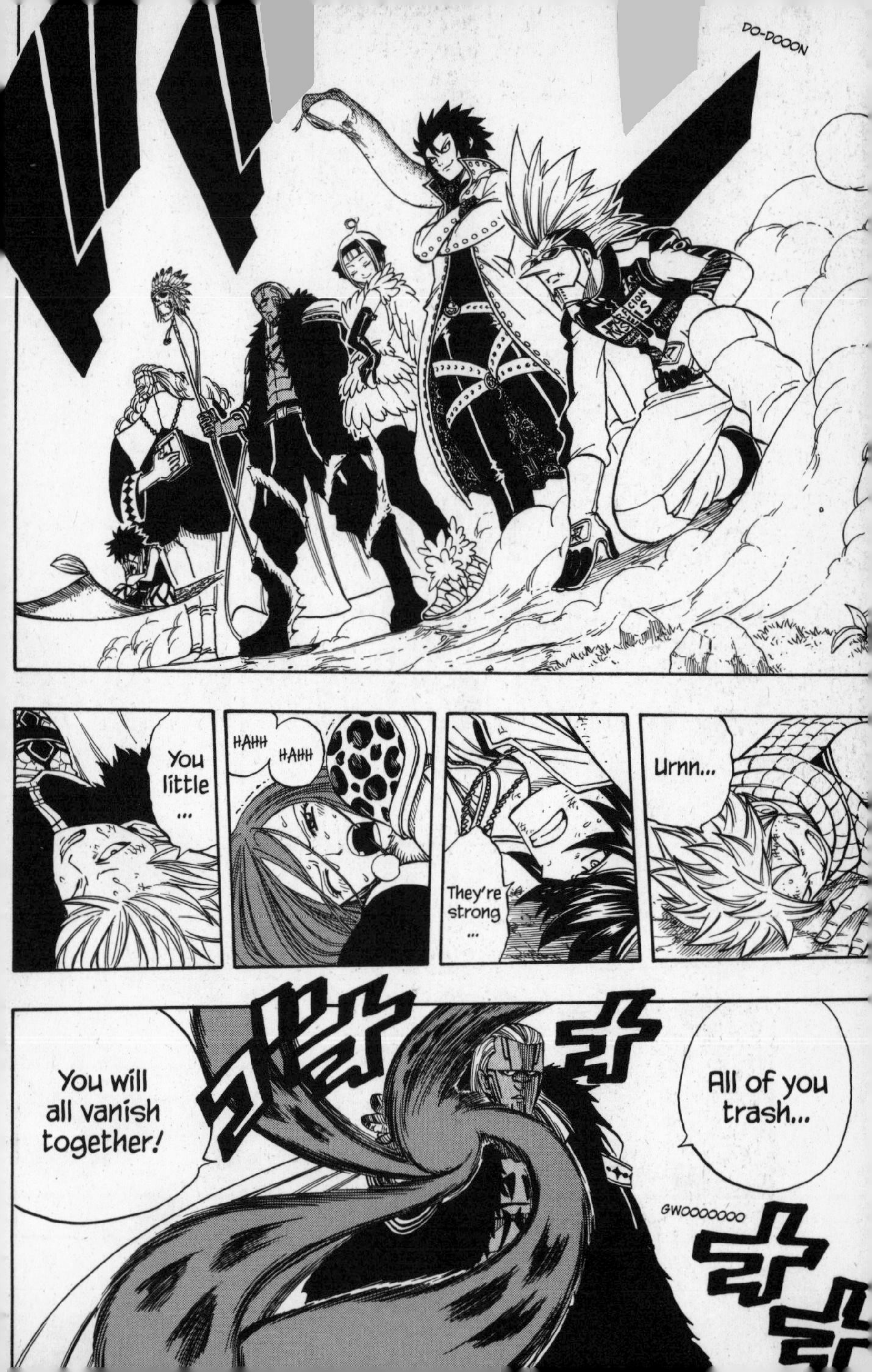
DO-DOOON
Urnn...
They're strong ...
HAHH HAHH
You little ...
All of you trash...
You will all vanish together!
GWOOOOOOO

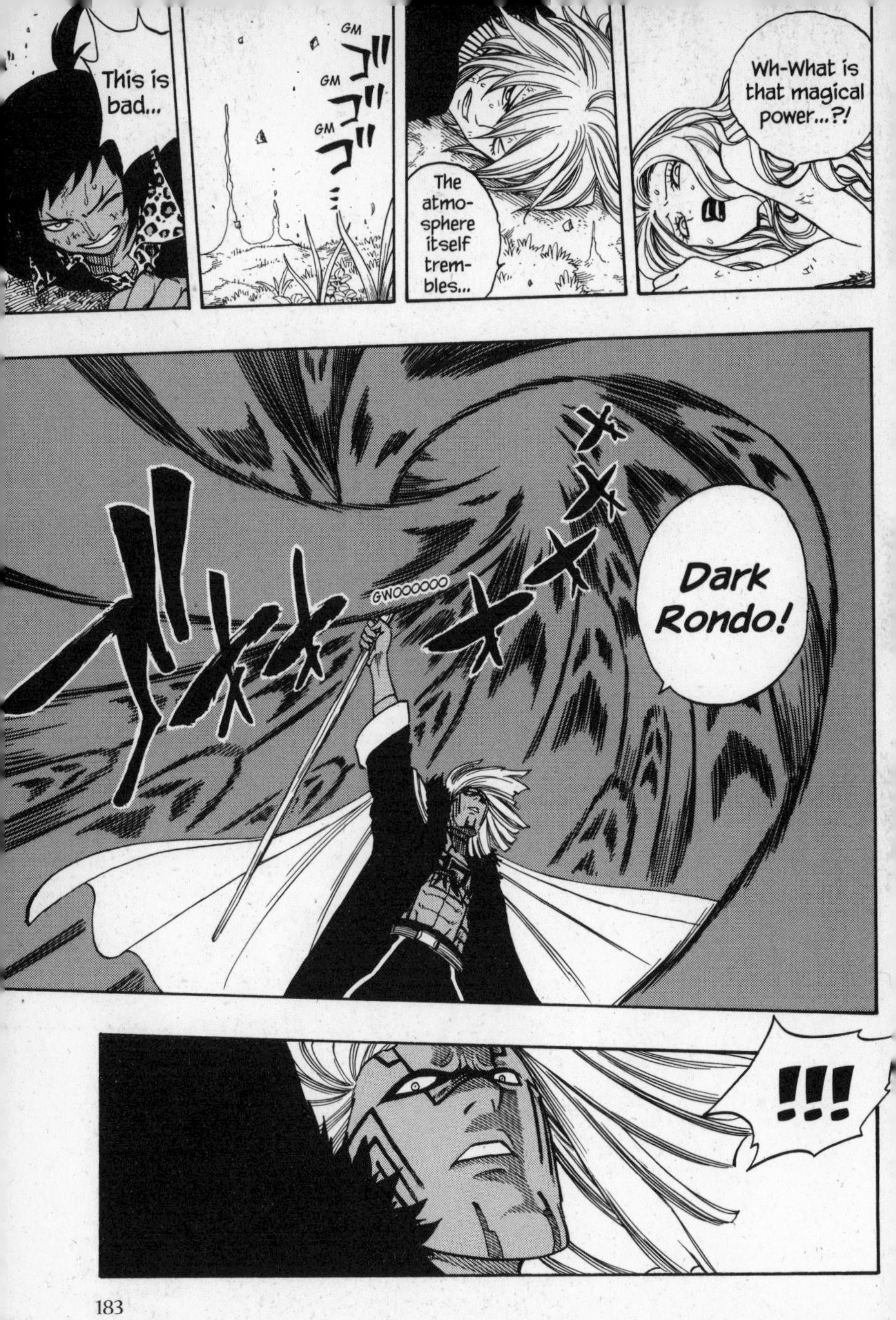
Wh-What is that magical power...?!
The atmosphere itself trembles...
GM
GM
GM
This is bad...
Dark Rondo!
GWOOOOOO
!!!

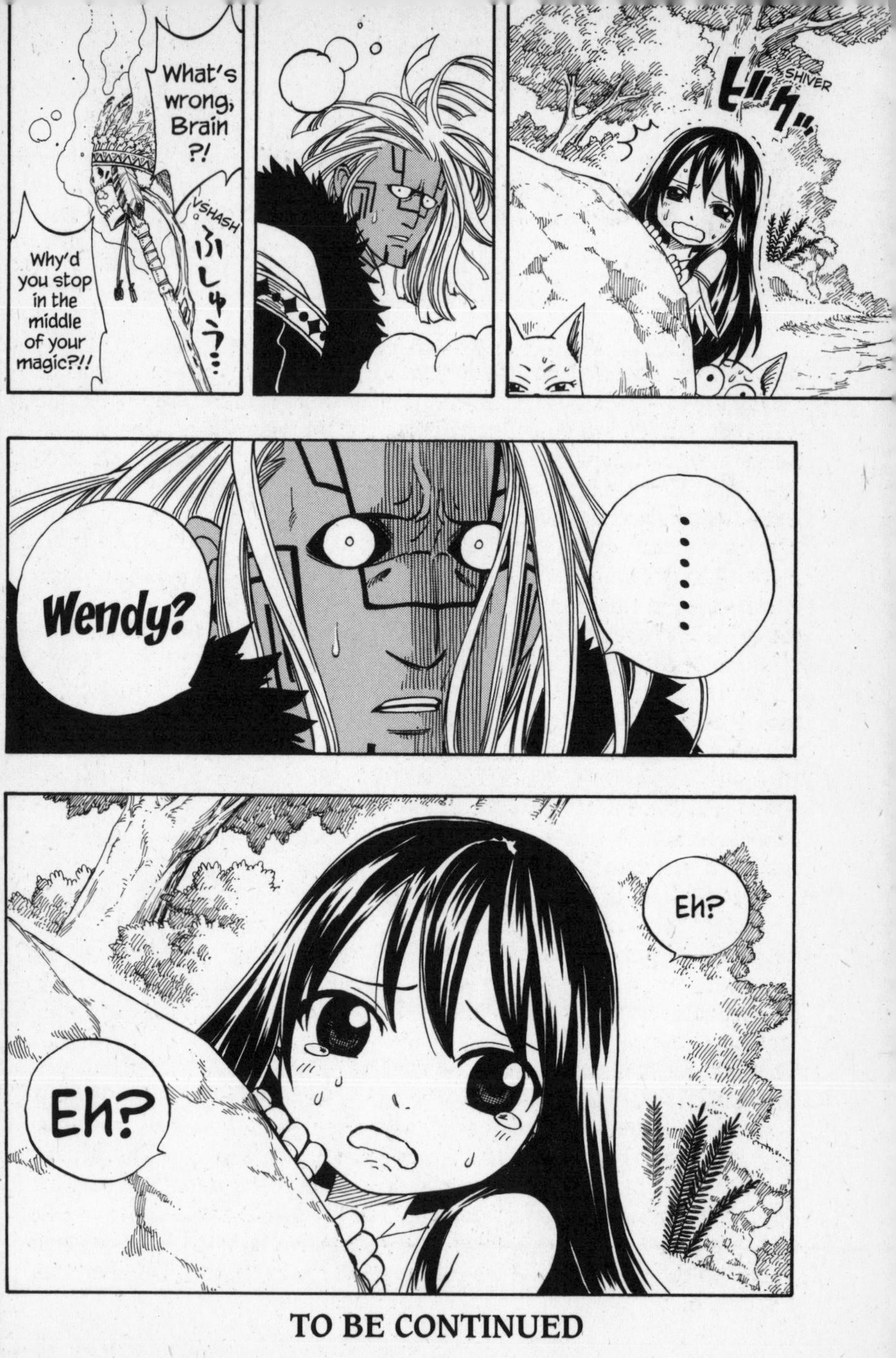
SHIVER
ビクッ
VSHASH
ふしゅう…
What's wrong, Brain?!
Why'd you stop in the middle of your magic?!!
......
Wendy?
Eh?
Eh?

TO BE CONTINUED

Afterword

How did you like the Director's Cut version of Fantasia? I'm sure anyone who doesn't read this manga in the magazine would be asking, "What's this all about?" It's about the fact that Fantasia appeared in a different version when it was serialized in the magazine. Here, it's expanded by ten full pages! Not only extra pages, but everything has been re-edited! If you ask why I went through the pain of all that additional work, my answer is, "Because I wanted to." (Yeah, I'm an idiot.) Actually, ever since I decided to do the Laxus story arc, I was really looking forward to drawing Fantasia, and as luck would have it, I was allowed extra pages in the very issue where it would occur. The magazine gave me a full 25 pages to draw the chapter! I was pretty giddy just thinking about it! But I had to cut a lot out, or the story just wouldn't work right. I'd be muttering, "Twenty-five pages just isn't enough," all the while I was drawing it. Well, I just couldn't live without showing a version that included the lively scenes I had envisioned, so I added the pages as a Director's Cut here in the graphic novel. Yeah, I know, the story is exactly the same, but I could only think that it was a good thing to give the readers an idea of how fun Fantasia is. The original version can only be read in a magazine long out of date now. Sorry.

And with all that, we bring the Laxus story arc to an end and start a new plot. There are a lot of characters here. It's really rough to draw it all. But it's a kick to draw Lyon after all this time, and Ichiya is a really fun character, if I do say so myself. (laughs) And then there's Wendy. One member of my staff mentioned that for some reason, little girls just don't appear in my manga. (Not that I'm against it or anything.) So I thought, "I'll show 'em!" and came up with up a character there on the spot. And somehow she just became strangely popular among the people I hang with. I have to admit that the more I draw her, I've come to like her more and more as well, and now I'm getting the feeling that she must might become a key player. On another interesting subject, I had been using the term "working title" with the name Oración Seis right up to the deadline. I never actually made a final decision on their name, so the working title wound up as their real name. But keep that a secret, okay?

Continued from the left-hand page.

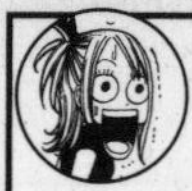
: Never!!

Mira: And here we have the next question.

Lucy's Father said his company was bought, but even so, he lost all of his personal possessions. That seems a little strange to me.

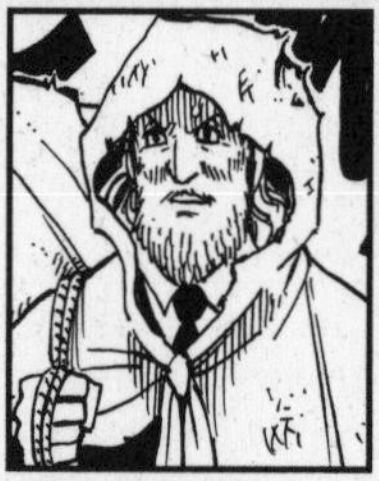

Lucy: Hey, that's one smart questioner...!

Mira: That's true. In present days, most companies use money out of the company's own budget, so even if the company should collapse, it wouldn't be something the president would lose his personal possessions over.

Lucy: So you're saying that in his case, he risked his own personal money to keep his company's budget going?

Mira: That's how it'd go. It's likely that his company wasn't in as good a financial condition as you would have thought, Lucy.

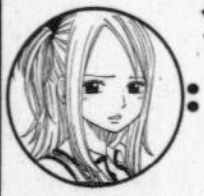
: Father...

Mira: Ah... I'm sorry. I'm sure he must have always worked hard at his job. Even if he named you on a whim.

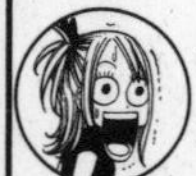
: Did you really need to say that?!!

Mira: And on to the final question.

Mystogan... Just who is he anyway?

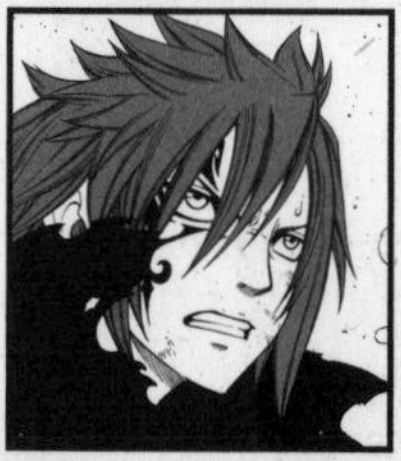

Lucy: You mean from that scene in Volume 15? You know, I'm burning with curiosity over that myself!!

Mira: Yes... I'm curious too.

Lucy: Tell me, Mira-san! What did he mean by, "Another..."?!

Mira: "Another" means one more of a certain subset of items. Aside from that, I haven't a clue.

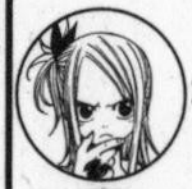
: And the one guy who did know, Laxus, isn't here anymore...

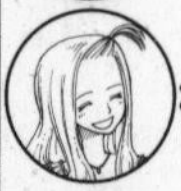
: So let's just look forward to the final reveal of the answer when it happens!♡

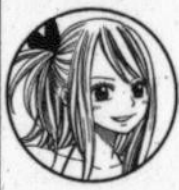
: I guess that's the answer!

Mira: ...So, Lucy... You're going to lend me Plue?

Lucy: What's that all about?! I don't want him used in some weird massage!

Mira: Nothing like that! *I'm doing research on what the voice of a mountain lion sounds like.*

Lucy: *But Plue is a dog!!!* And even so, his voice sounds nothing like a dog either...

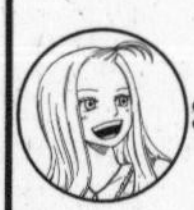
: And so, see you all next time! Moun•tain•li•on•poon, woof woof!!!

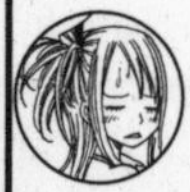
: Mountain ***LION***. It's one of the big cats! Wait, I said that last time...

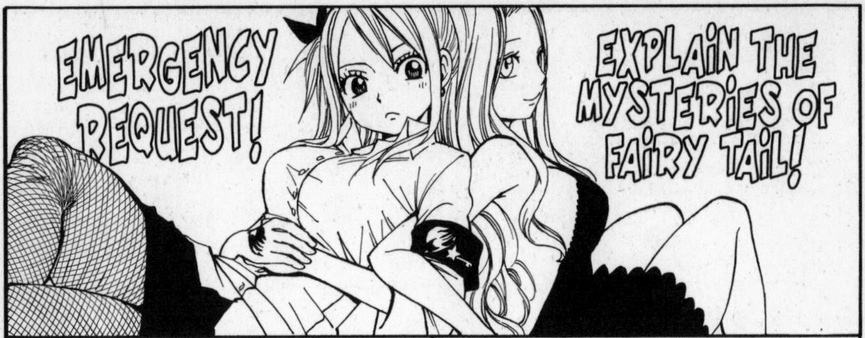
EMERGENCY REQUEST!
EXPLAIN THE MYSTERIES OF FAIRY TAIL!

: Moun•tain•li•on•poooon!!!

: Hi everybody! It's time for "Emergency Request! Explain the Mysteries of FT!" again!

Lucy: This time, we're going to give you the straight answers!

Mira: Here's the first question.

> ***I see these two all the time. Who are they?***
>
> 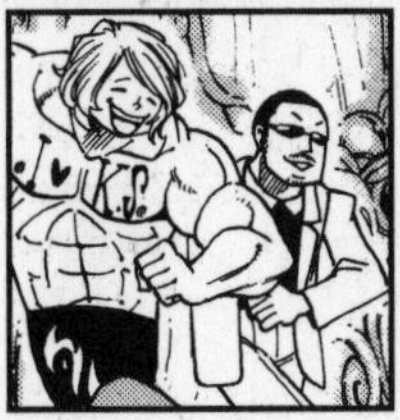

Lucy: You do see them every now and again in the guild scenes.

On the left is Joey Fullborn. And on the right is Wan Chanjii.

: That Joey guy... Don't you think he's a little overly macho?

: On top of that, he looses his teeth a lot. It's fun to try to find them.

Lucy: A guy who loses his teeth a lot...?

Mira: On to the next question.

> ***During the Tower of Heaven story, Lucy called Cancer (can only call on Tuesdays, Thursdays, Saturdays and Sundays) along with Aquarius (can only call on Wednesdays). They should never have been able to be called on the same day. What's the meaning of this?***
>
> 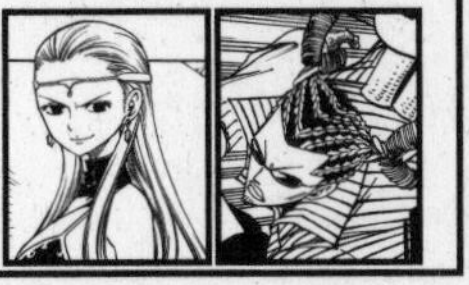

Lucy: Ohh... About that... Actually, the days of the week in the contracts can change. As the level of trust increases between myself and my celestial spirits, the number of days I can call them can increase as well.

Mira: Really? So since you can call Loke at any time of the day or night, your trust level with him is at maximum, huh?

: Yeah...maybe... If you say so. I can't really say myself.

Mira: What about Plue?

Lucy: Oh, Plue is a call-at-any-time spirit now. I can call Plue whewnever, and he'll come.

Mira: Good! Then let me borrow Plue, okay?

Lucy: Eh?

: I hear Plue is good for stiff shoulders.

Continued on the right-hand page.

TAIL de ART

The Fairy Tail Guild de Art is an explosion of fan art! Please send in your art drawn in black pen on large post-card stock!! Those chosen to be published will get a signed mini poster! ♪ Make sure you write your real name and address on the back of your postcard!

▼ This person claims to be rooting for Gajeel. Well this time he got a quiet-but-very-good role in the story!

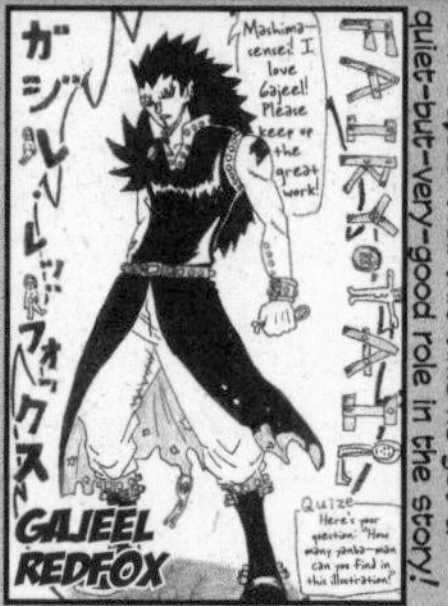

FAIRY TAIL
Mashima-sensei! I love Gajeel! Please keep up the great work!
GAJEEL REDFOX

Kanagawa Prefecture, Kenta Noro

▼ Oh, hey! That's cool... Although he was originally planned as a kind of dumb-guy character...

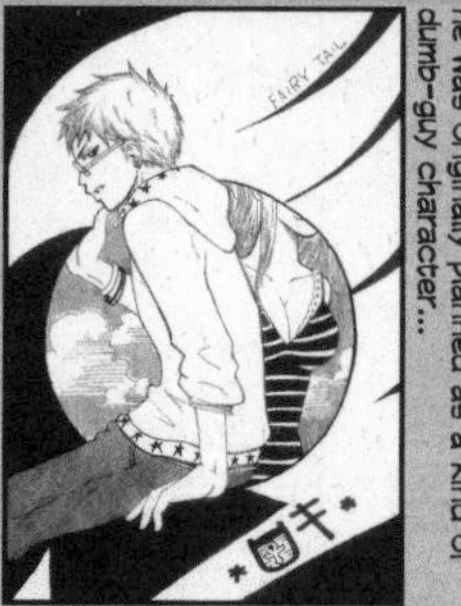

FAIRY TAIL

Ishikawa Prefecture, Mamorare-tai

▼ Everybody's got such great smiles! When I see a drawing like this, I just feel happy!

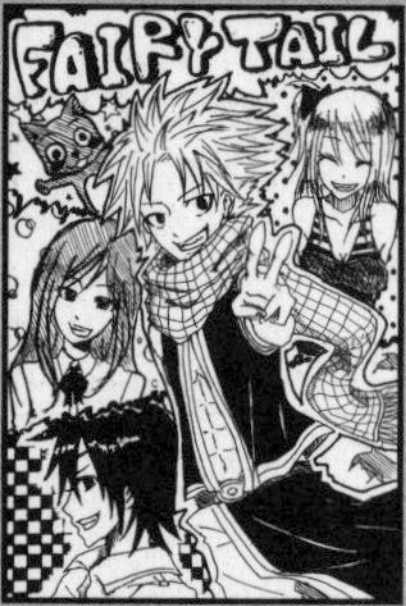

FAIRY TAIL

Kôchi Prefecture, Tomoki Takahashi

▼ Just recently a "sempai" of mine said, "Juvia's great! Put her in more often!"

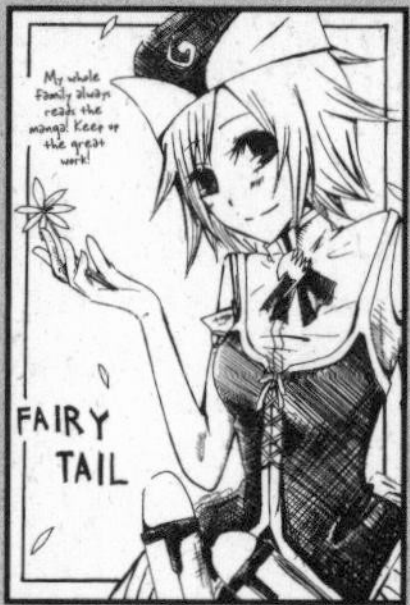

My whole family always reads the manga! Keep up the great work!
FAIRY TAIL

Nagano Prefecture, Kumousagi

▼ Scary! But it looks good on her, so I'm impressed!

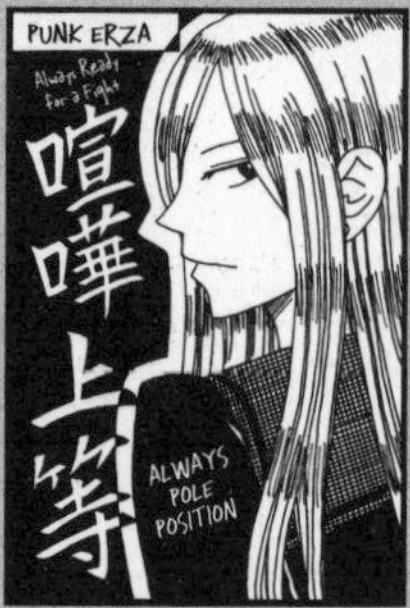

PUNK ERZA
Always Ready for a Fight
喧嘩上等
ALWAYS POLE POSITION

Saitama Prefecture, Yuko Fujimoto

▼ This Natsu is sort of cool, huh?

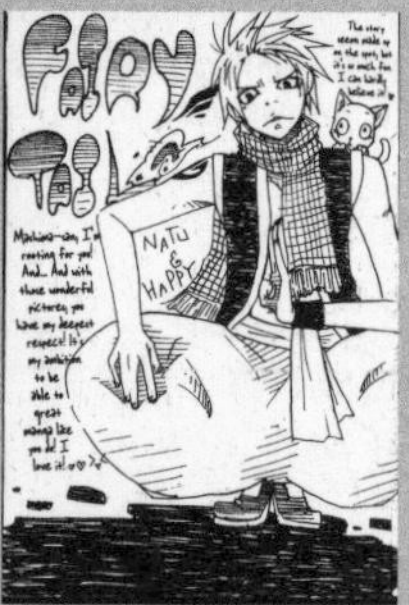

NATU & HAPPY

Aichi Prefecture, Yuzu-hime.

▼ Happy's full of energy! I wonder where he's going riding the wind like that!

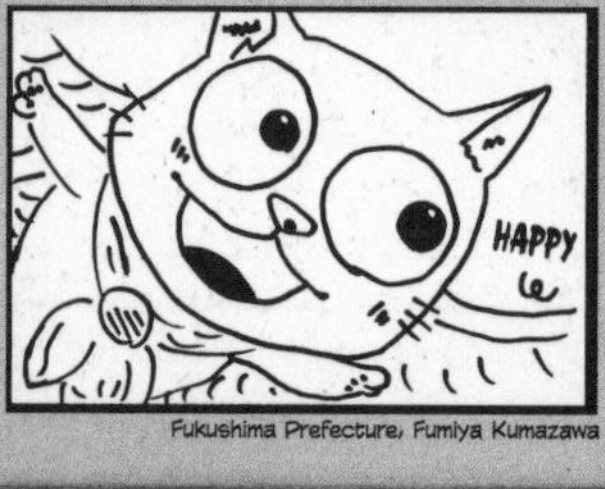

HAPPY

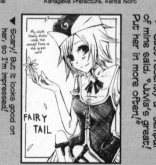

Fukushima Prefecture, Fumiya Kumazawa

▼ Oh, ho! Come to think of it, she was like that a long time ago, huh?

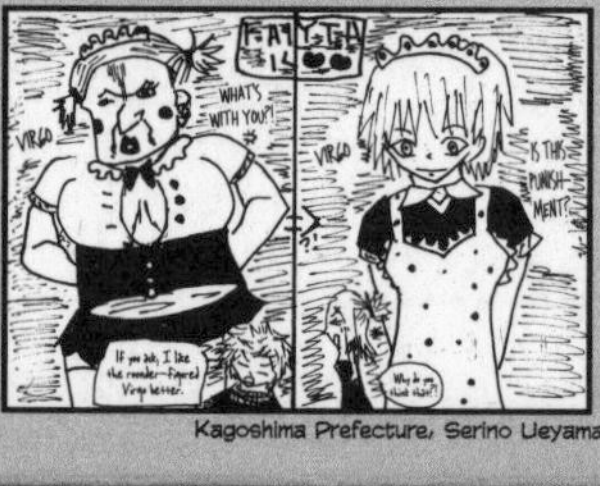

WHAT'S WITH YOU?!
VIRGO
IS THIS PUNISH-MENT?
VIRGO

Kagoshima Prefecture, Serino Ueyama

Send to Send to Hiro Mashima, Kodansha Comics
451 Park Ave. South, 7th Floor New York, NY 10016

FAIRY GUILD

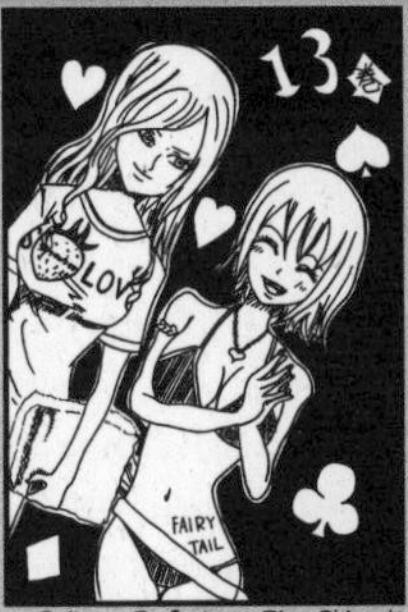

13
LOVE
FAIRY TAIL

Saitama Prefecture, Rina Shimada

▼ They were in the background in Volume 13. Now where have I seen them before...

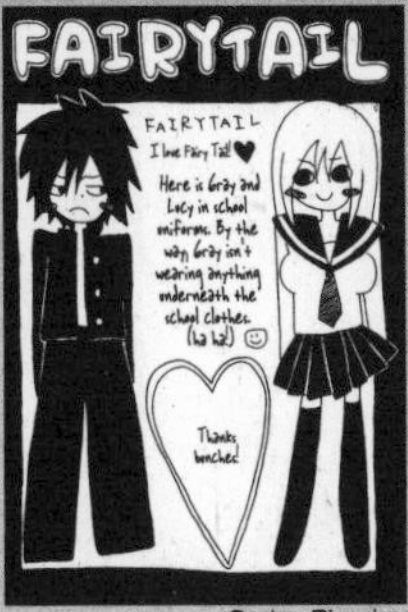

FAIRYTAIL
FAIRYTAIL
I love Fairy Tail!
Here is Gray and Lucy in school uniforms. By the way Gray isn't wearing anything underneath the school clothes. (ha ha)
Thanks bunches!

Osaka, Ri-cchan

▼ It's actually pretty rare to get a Gray/Lucy combo picture.

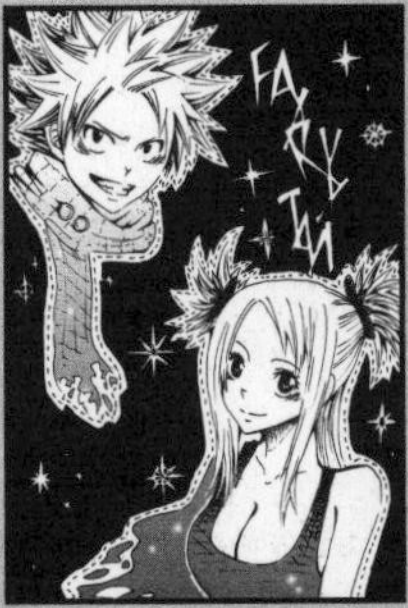
Niigata Prefecture, Rairi

▼ Well drawn! I really like Lucy's expression!

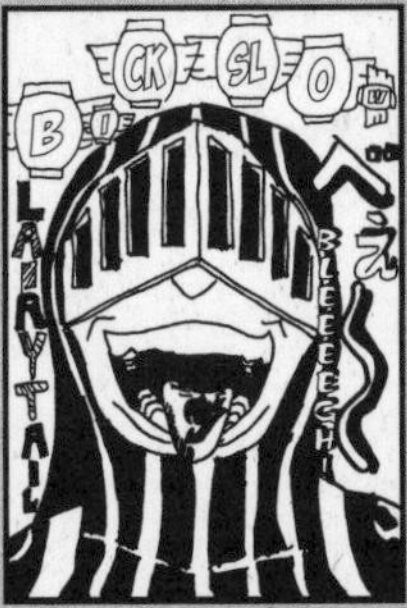
Saitama Prefecture, Moai

▼ For some reason I got a lot of postcards with Bickslow on it. I guess he just made people want to draw.

REJECTION CORNER

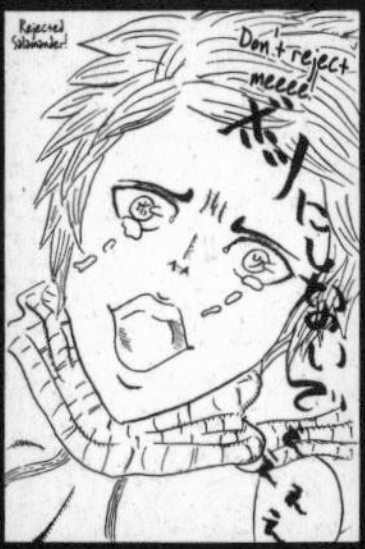

Rejected Salamander!
Don't reject meeee

Yuno Manaka

▲ But strangely, I like his expression a lot.

Any letters and post cards you send means that your personal information such as your name, address, postal code, and other information you include will be handed over, as is, to the author. When you send mail, please keep that in mind.

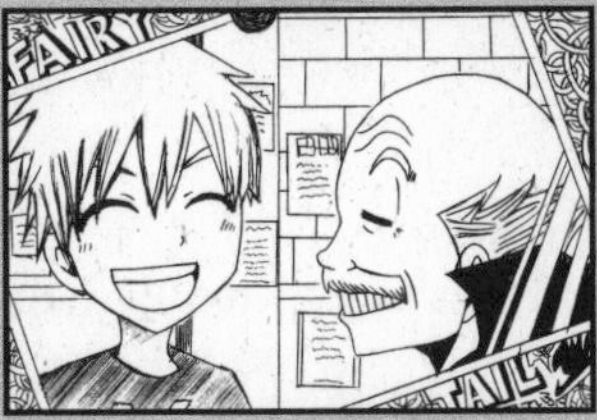

FAIRY
TAIL

Gifu Prefecture, Sun6

▼ What did you think of Fantasia? The bonds between the Master and Laxus.

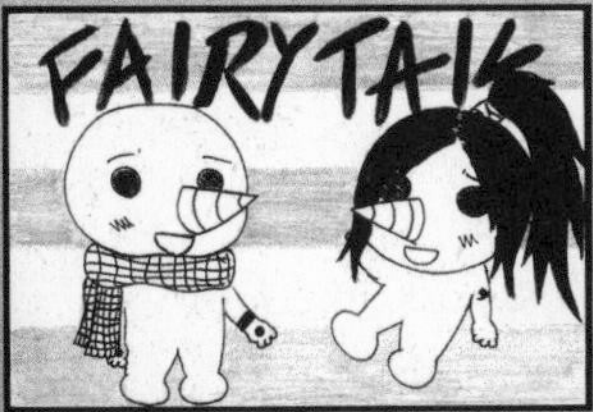

FAIRYTAIL

Hokaido, Mashima-sensei's Biggest Fan

▼ Natsu and Erza both turned into Plue!

Translation Notes:

Page 91, Ebi

As mentioned in Volume 2, *ebi* is Japanese for the sea life "shrimp." *Kani* is Japanese for "crab." In most children's books and manga, crab characters end their sentences with the sound, *kani*. This sounds fun and is easy for Japanese children to imitate. As Cancer is a crab, it would be expected for him to end his sentences with *kani* as well, but as a comic switch, he ends his sentences with the sound *ebi* instead.

Page 116, Oración Seis, Grimoire Heart and Tartaros

In the Japanese version, each of the three dark guilds in the Balam Alliance had names made up of *kanji* with the western names used as pronunciation guides. The kanji for Oración Seis means "Six Demon Generals," *kanji* for Grimoire Heart means "Devil's Heart," and for Tartaros means "Gates of Hell."

Page 132, Tsudere

Tsundere is a word coined within the past decade for characters who pretend to be annoyed and unfeeling toward another character whereas they are actually madly in love. The word comes from two onomatopoetic words, *tsun tsun*, the sound of poking someone, and *dere dere*, the sound of cuddling. Female *tsundere* characters have become very popular in anime.

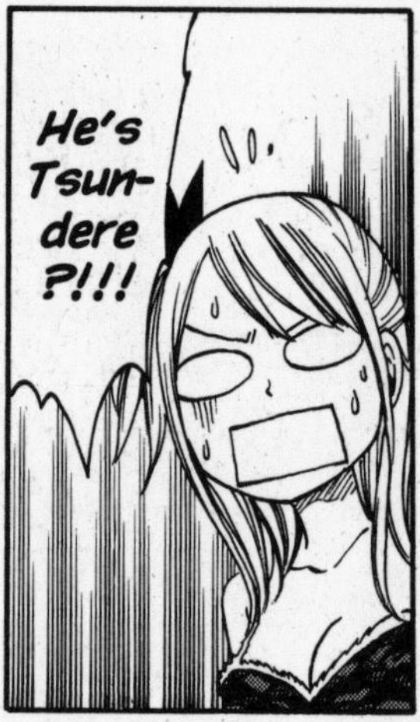
He's Tsun-dere ?!!!

Page 136, Meeeen

The Japanese seem to love the word men. Among it's primary meanings is as a borrowed word from English meaning males and a Japanese word meaning "face." One of the most popular uses of it is in the word, *ikemen* (the word for good looking men. In Japanese, the same word, men is used for singular and plural.

Page 139, Pretty!

In Japanese, he used the word ike which is the first part of "*ikemen*" (see above note). A translation for *ikemen* might be, "pretty boy."

Page 150, -dono

The suffix, *-dono,* is an archaic word that means approximately the same as the present use of *-sama.* It is a very respectful honorific taken from the Japanese word for Edo-period lords.

Page 150, Orange Juice

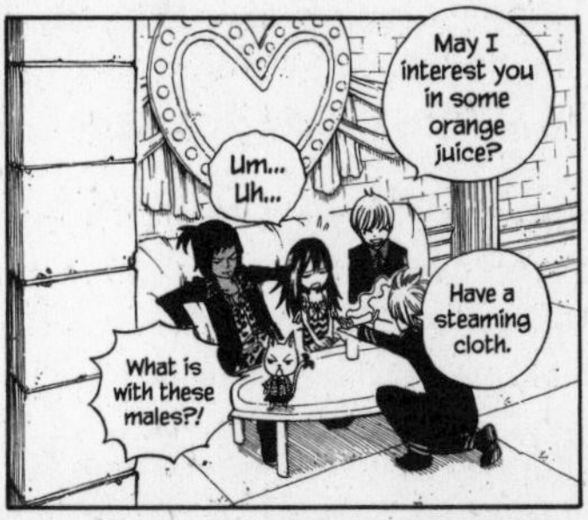
May I interest you in some orange juice?
Um... Uh...
Have a steaming cloth.
What is with these males?!

Whereas OJ is a great breakfast drink for people of any age in the US, in Japan orange juice (as well as any other sweet soft drink) is considered a children's drink. Even drinks like bottled sweetened ice café aulait and milk tea are given the generic term of "juice" (*jûsu* in Japanese) and are considered drinks for children.

Page 183, Dark Rondo

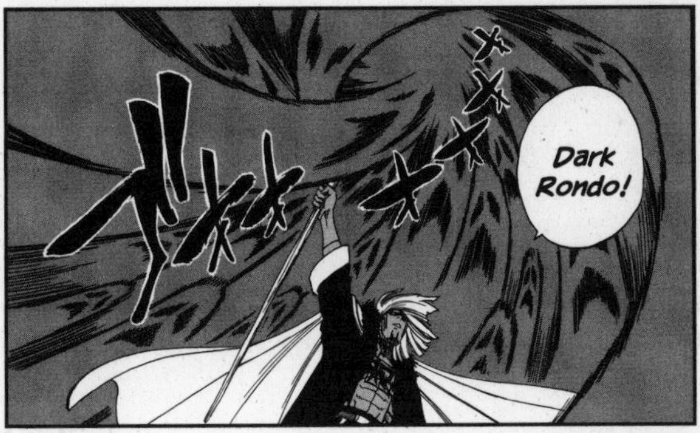
Dark Rondo!

In Italian, "rondo" means "round about." But in music, it refers to a musical theme that appears several times over the course of a musical composition.

Preview of Fairy Tail, volume 17

We're please to present you a preview from Fairy Tail, volume 17.
Please check our website (www.kodanshacomics.com) to see
when this volume will be available in English. For now you'll
have to make do with Japanese!

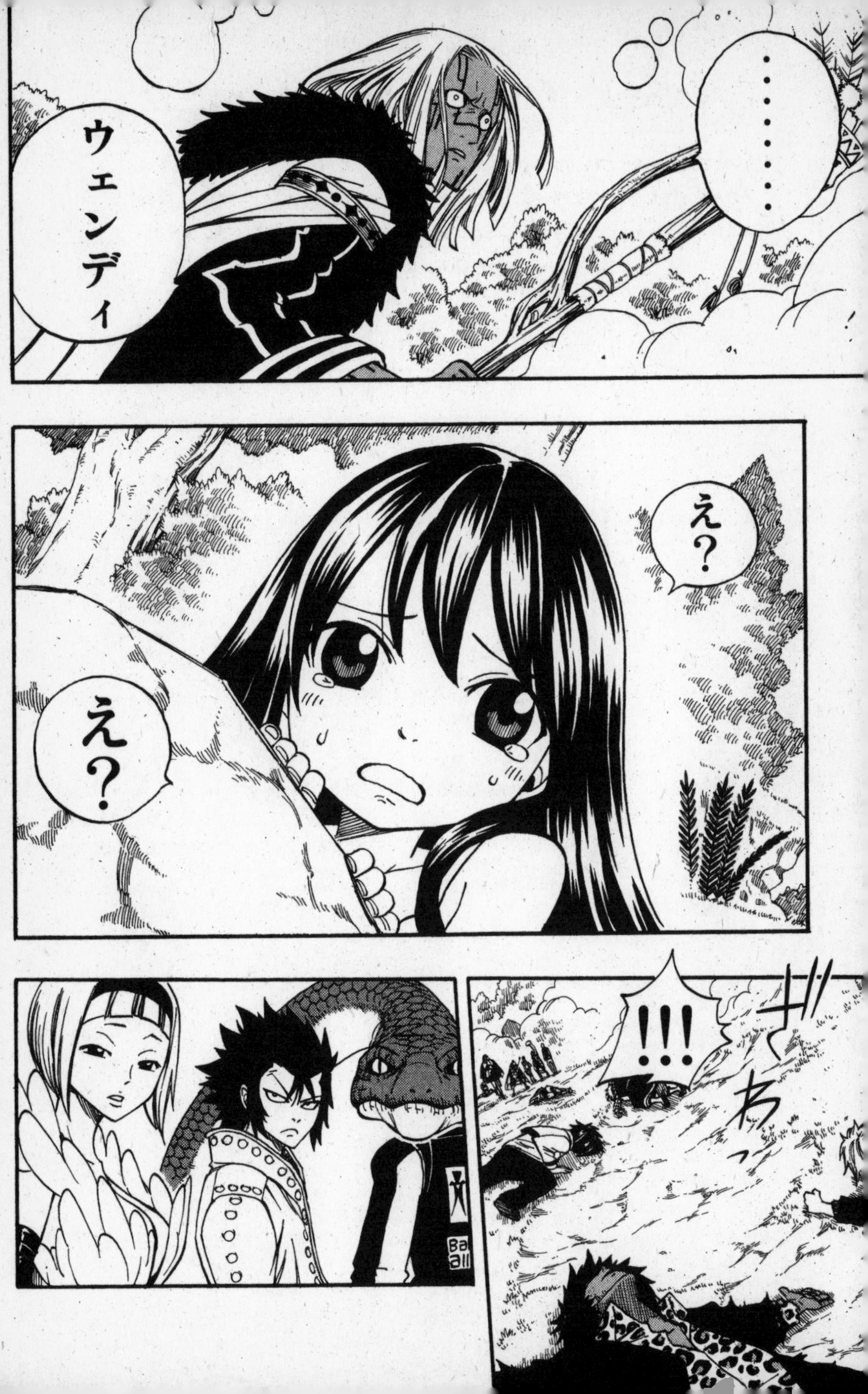
……
ウェンディ
え?
え?
!!!
ざわっ

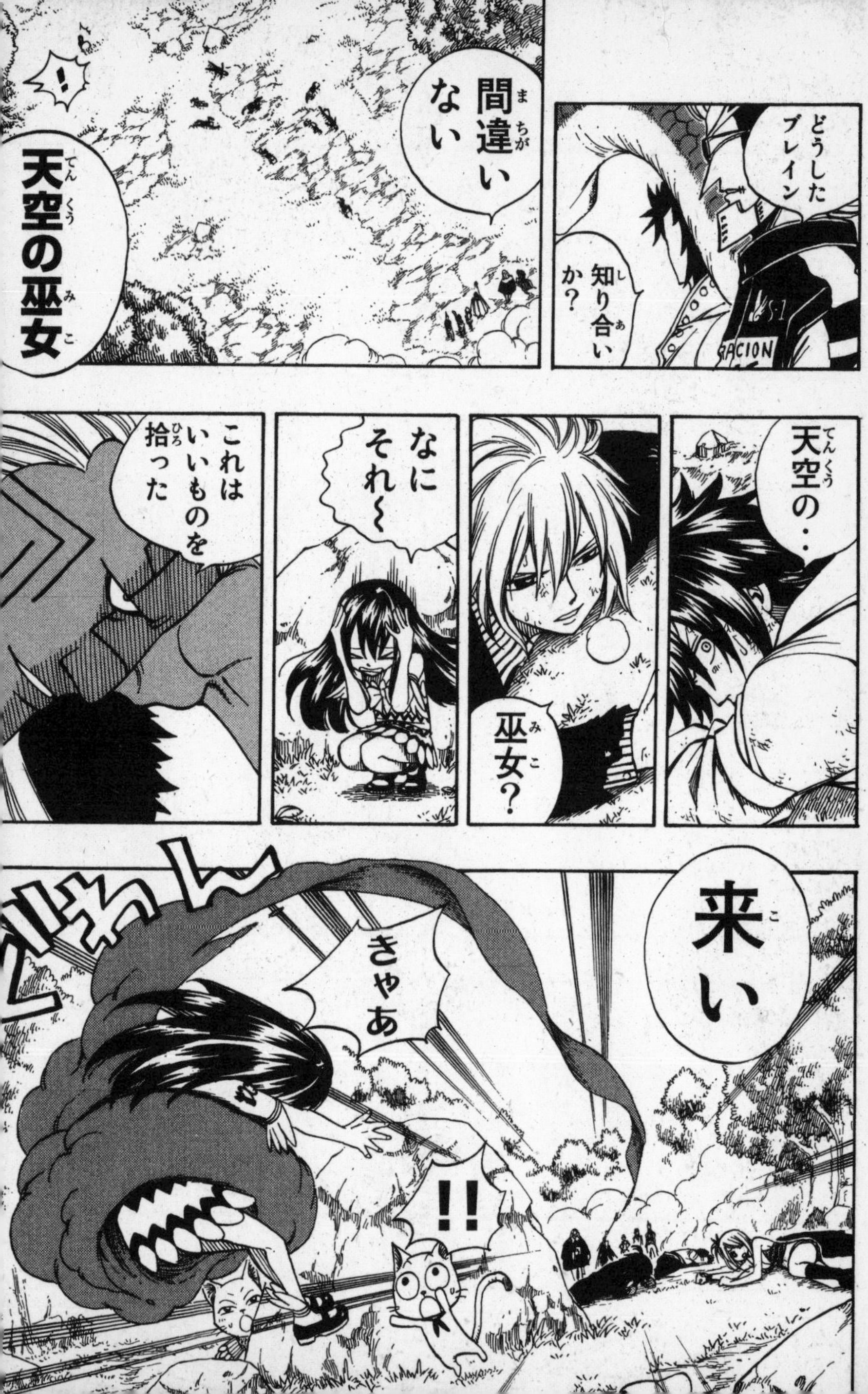
どうしたブレイン
知り合いか？
間違いない
!
天空の巫女
天空の・・
巫女？
なにそれ～
これはいいものを拾った
来い
きゃあ
!!

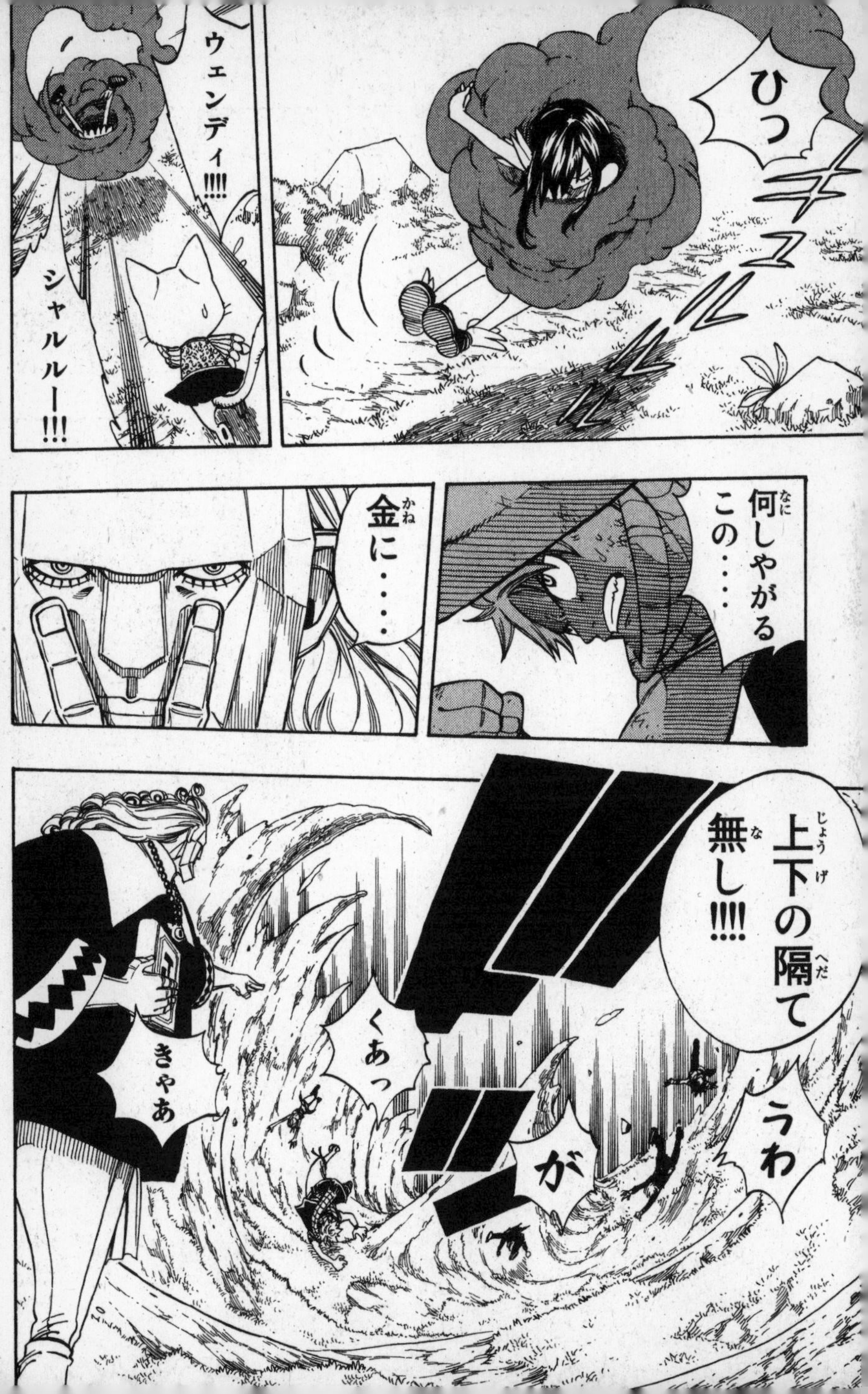
ひっ
キュルルル
ウェンディ!!!!
シャルルー!!!
何しやがるこの……
金に……
上下の隔て無し!!!!
うわ
が
くあっ
きゃあ

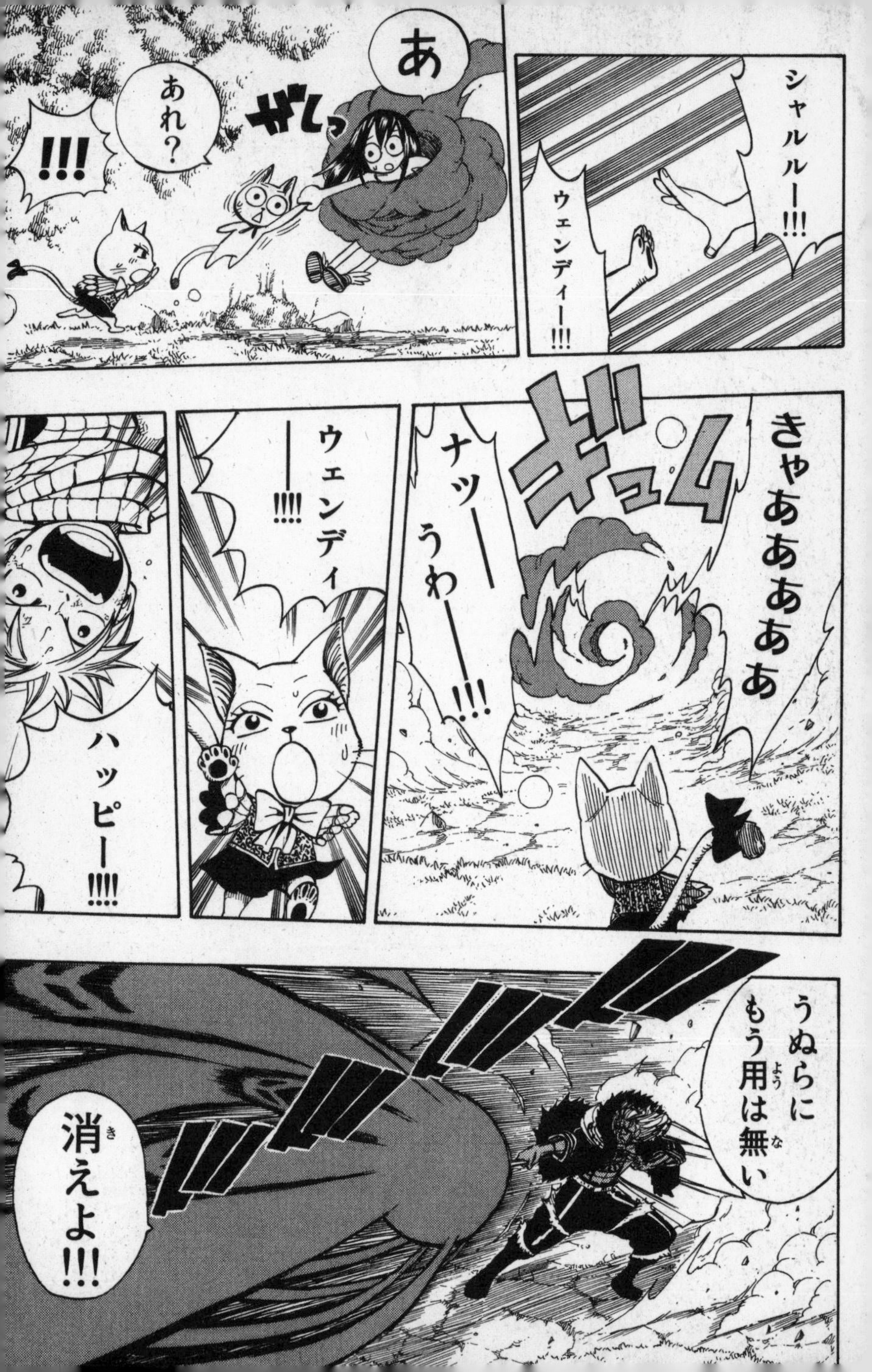
シャルルー!!!
ウェンディー!!!
あ
がしっ
あれ?
!!!
きゃあああああ
ギュム
ナツー
うわーー!!!
ウェンディーー!!!!
ハッピー!!!!
うぬらにもう用は無い
消えよ!!!

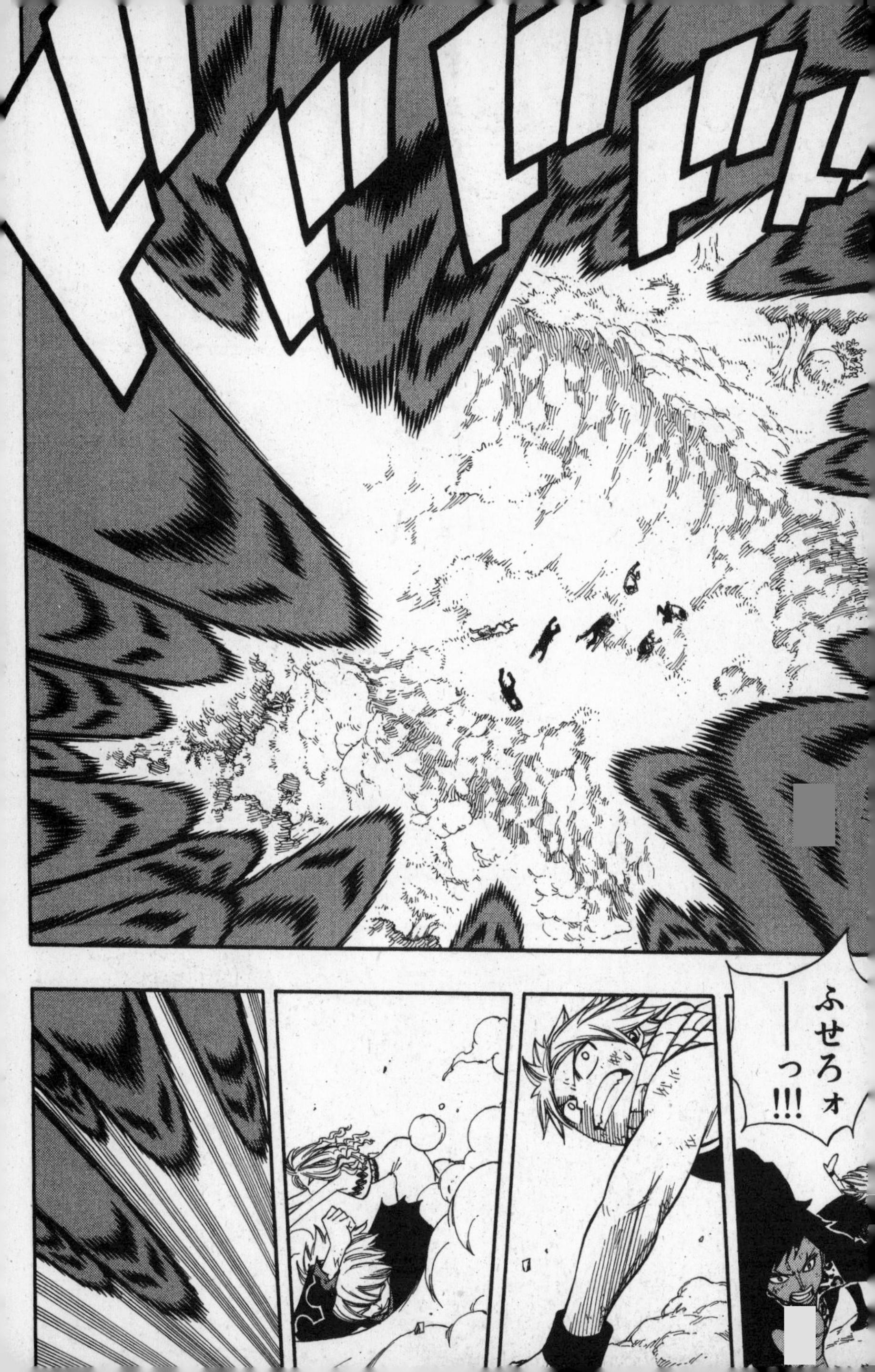
ふせろォ──っ!!!

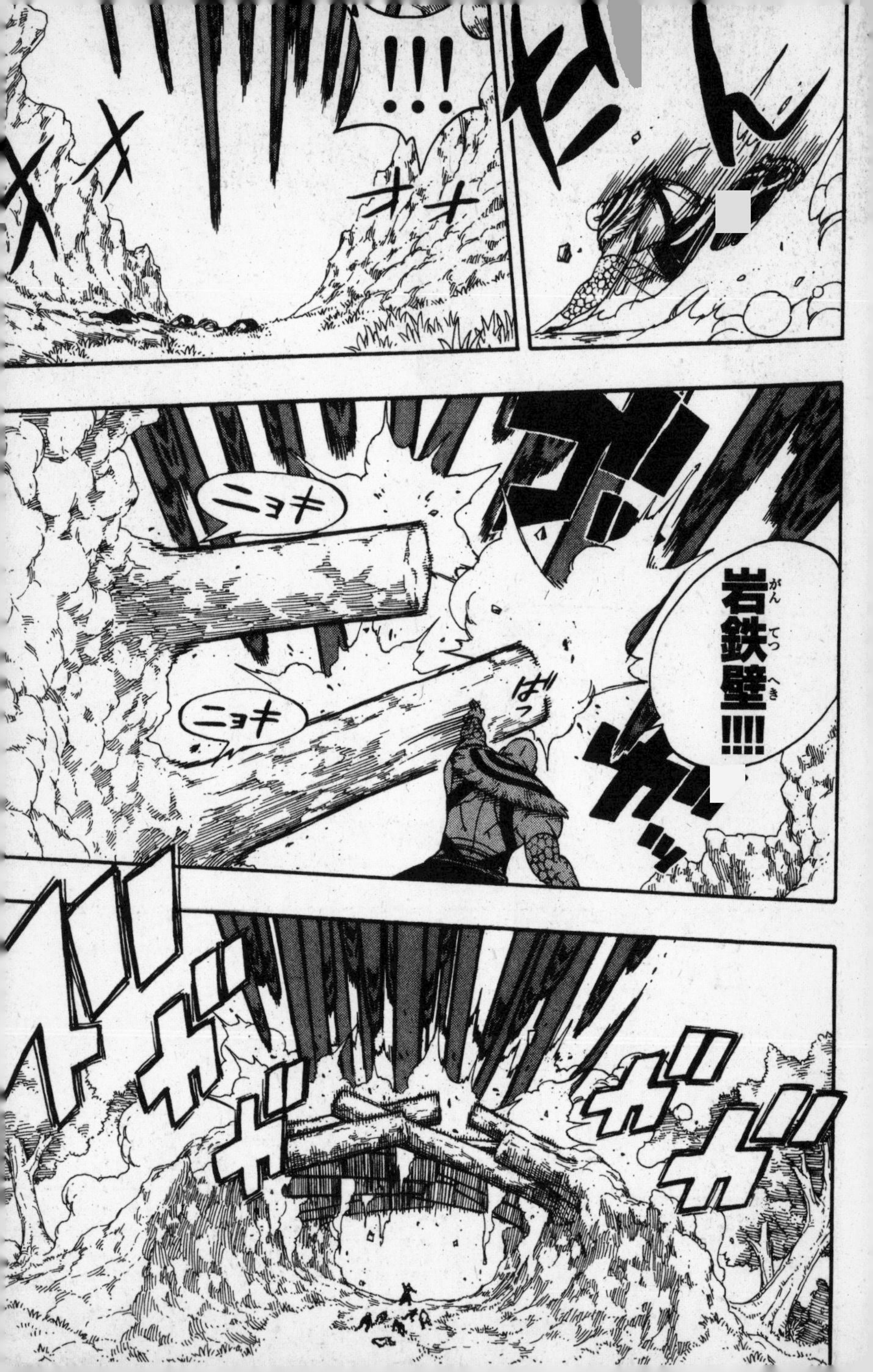
ズン
!!!
岩鉄壁!!!!
ばっ
ニョキ
ニョキ

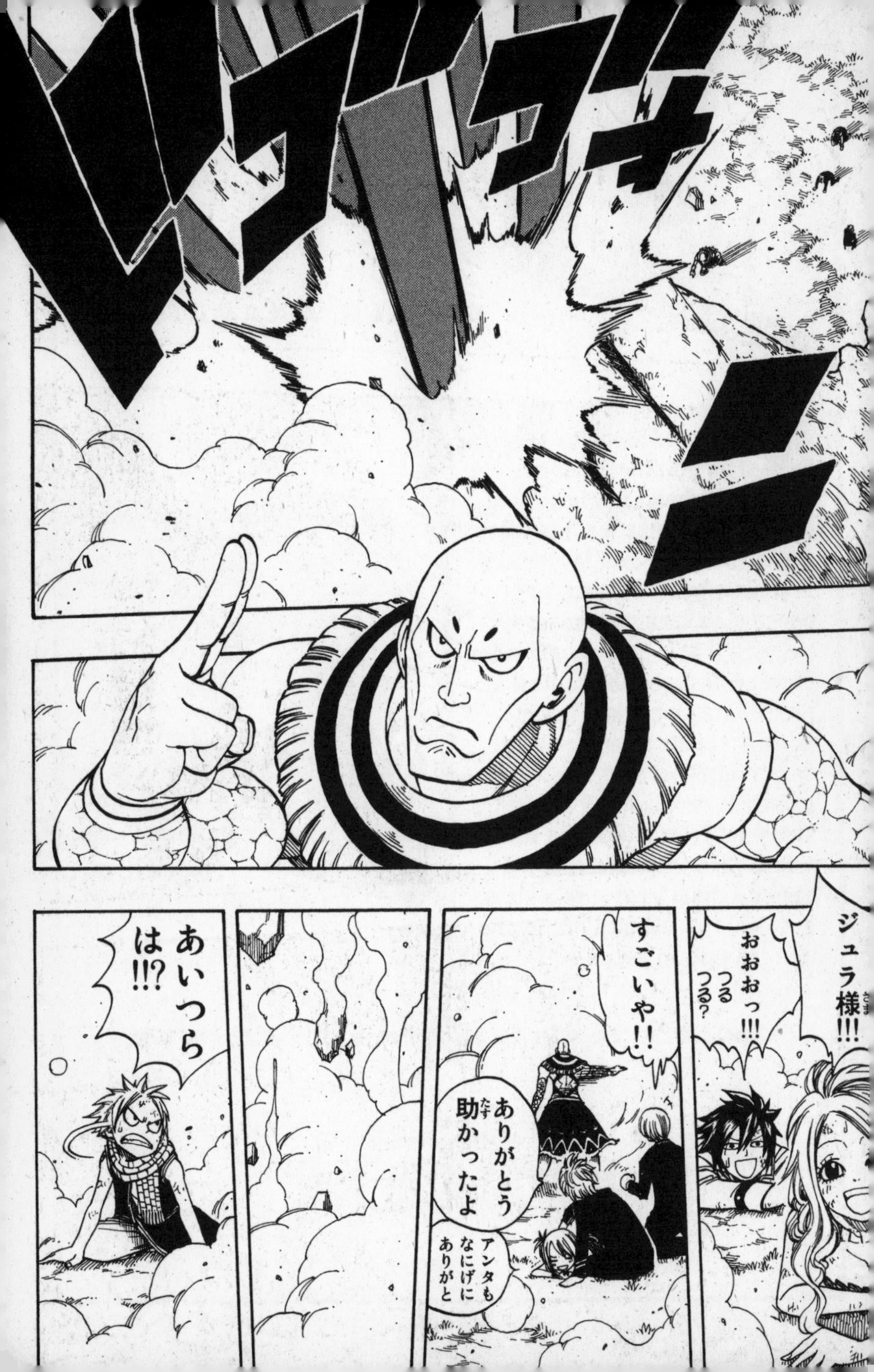
ジュラ様!!!
おおおっ!!!
つるつる?
すごいや!!
ありがとう助かったよ
アンタもなにげにありがと
あいつらは!!?

BY KEN AKAMATSU

Negi Springfield is a ten-year-old wizard teaching English at an all-girls Japanese school. He dreams of becoming a master wizard like his legendary father, the Thousand Master. At first his biggest concern was concealing his magic powers, because if he's ever caught using them publicly, he thinks he'll be turned into an ermine! But in a world that gets stranger every day, it turns out that the strangest people of all are Negi's students! From a librarian with a magic book to a centuries-old vampire, from a robot to a ninja, Negi will risk his own life to protect the girls in his care!

Ages: 16+

Special extras in each volume! Read them all!

VISIT WWW.KODANSHACOMICS.COM TO:
• View release date calendars for upcoming volumes
• Find out the latest about new Kodansha Comics series

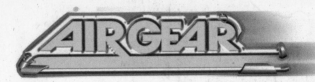

AIR GEAR

BY OH!GREAT

AIR GEAR
1
Oh!great

Itsuki Minami needs no introduction—everybody's heard of the "Babyface" of the Eastside. He's the strongest kid at Higashi Junior High School, easy on the eyes but dangerously tough when he needs to be. Plus, Itsuki lives with the mysterious and sexy Noyamano sisters. Life's never dull, but it becomes downright dangerous when Itsuki leads his school to victory over vindictive Westside punks with gangster connections. Now he stands to lose his school, his friends, and everything he cares about. But in his darkest hour, the Noyamano girls give him an amazing gift, one that just might help him save his school: a pair of Air Trecks. These high-tech skates are more than just supercool. They'll enable Itsuki to execute the wildest, most aggressive moves ever seen—and introduce him to a thrilling and terrifying new world.

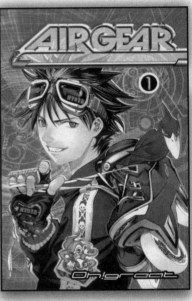

Ages: 16 +

Special extras in each volume! Read them all!

KC KODANSHA COMICS

VISIT WWW.KODANSHACOMICS.COM TO:

- View release date calendars for upcoming volumes
- Find out the latest about new Kodansha Comics series

TOMARE!

止まれ

[STOP!]

You're going the wrong way!

Manga is a completely different type of reading experience.

To start at the *beginning*,
go to the *end!*

That's right! Authentic manga is read the traditional Japanese way—from right to left, exactly the *opposite* of how American books are read. It's easy to follow: Just go to the other end of the book and read each page—and each panel—from right side to left side, starting at the top right. Now you're experiencing manga as it was meant to be!